Humankind and Humanity in the Philosophy of the Enlightenment

Also available from Bloomsbury:

Emotion, Reason, and Action in Kant, by Maria Borges
Finding Locke's God, by Nathan Guy
Skepticism: From Antiquity to the Present, edited by Diego E. Machuca and Baron Reed
The Human Vocation in German Philosophy, edited by Anne Pollok and Courtney D. Fugate

Humankind and Humanity in the Philosophy of the Enlightenment

From Locke to Kant

Edited by
Stefanie Buchenau and Ansgar Lyssy

BLOOMSBURY ACADEMIC
LONDON • NEW YORK • OXFORD • NEW DELHI • SYDNEY

BLOOMSBURY ACADEMIC
Bloomsbury Publishing Plc
50 Bedford Square, London, WC1B 3DP, UK
1385 Broadway, New York, NY 10018, USA
29 Earlsfort Terrace, Dublin 2, Ireland

BLOOMSBURY, BLOOMSBURY ACADEMIC and the Diana logo
are trademarks of Bloomsbury Publishing Plc

First published in Great Britain 2023
This paperback edition published 2025

Copyright © Stefanie Buchenau, Ansgar Lyssy and Contributors, 2023

Stefanie Buchenau and Ansgar Lyssy have asserted their right under the Copyright,
Designs and Patents Act, 1988, to be identified as Editors of this work.

Cover image: Nicolas Delaunay, (artist), French, 1739–1792, Jean-Michel Moreau the
Younger, (artist after), French, 1741–1814, Discours sur l'egalite des conditions: Il retourne
chez ses egaux. Sepia Times/Universal Images Group via Getty Images.

All rights reserved. No part of this publication may be reproduced or transmitted
in any form or by any means, electronic or mechanical, including photocopying,
recording, or any information storage or retrieval system, without
prior permission in writing from the publishers.

Bloomsbury Publishing Plc does not have any control over, or responsibility for,
any third-party websites referred to or in this book. All internet addresses given in
this book were correct at the time of going to press. The author and publisher regret
any inconvenience caused if addresses have changed or sites have ceased to exist,
but can accept no responsibility for any such changes.

A catalogue record for this book is available from the British Library.

A catalog record for this book is available from the Library of Congress.

ISBN: HB: 978-1-3501-4293-0
PB: 978-1-3503-8475-0
ePDF: 978-1-3501-4294-7
eBook: 978-1-3501-4295-4

Typeset by Integra Software Services Pvt. Ltd.

To find out more about our authors and books visit www.bloomsbury.com
and sign up for our newsletters.

Contents

Notes on contributors   vi

Introduction   *Stefanie Buchenau and Ansgar Lyssy*   1

1   The presumptive unity of humankind in Locke's *Essay*   *Philippe Hamou*   15
2   Human nature in Montesquieu   *Céline Spector*   29
3   The image of the human being in the Comte de Buffon   *Catherine Wilson*   43
4   Hume on humanity and the party of humankind   *Jacqueline Taylor*   59
5   Humankind and humanity in Diderot   *Ansgar Lyssy*   77
6   How do humans become human(e)? On Rousseau's *Second Discourse* and *Emile*   *Gabrielle Radica*   99
7   'In the human kind, the species has a progress as well as the individual': Adam Ferguson on the progress of 'mankind'   *Eveline Hauck and Norbert Waszek*   115
8   The association of science and civilization in the Enlightenment   *Stephen Gaukroger*   131
9   Philoctetes at the edge of humanity: The German Enlightenment debate on social exclusion and the education of feeling   *Stefanie Buchenau*   143
10   Enlightenment moral philosophy and moral psychology: Baumgarten, Kant and Herder on moral feeling(s) and obligation   *Nigel DeSouza*   163
11   Herder on humanity   *Michael N. Forster*   183
12   Blumenbach on the varieties of the human species   *François Duchesneau*   209
13   Can Kant's man be a woman?   *Charlotte Morel*   225
14   'Anthroponomy'. Kant on the natural and the rational human being   *Günter Zöller*   243

Index   259

Notes on contributors

Stefanie Buchenau is Professor of German and European History of Ideas at University Paris 8 Saint-Denis. She studied comparative literature and philosophy in Germany (Munich), France (Paris/Ecole Normale Supérieure Lyon) and the United States (Yale) and received a joint degree (co-tutelle) between the Ecole Normale Supérieure, Lyon and Yale University in 2004. She works mainly on German Enlightenment philosophy, aesthetics, anthropology and the relation between philosophy and medicine. In 2013, Buchenau published a monograph on *The Founding of Aesthetics in the German Enlightenment. The Art of Invention and the Invention of Art*, Cambridge University Press. She is currently co-editing the *Anthropologie in pragmatischer Hinsicht* in the new Kant Akademieausgabe and preparing a new book on *Menschenwürde. Kant und die Aufklärung*, to be published with Meiner in 2023.

Nigel DeSouza is Associate Professor in the Department of Philosophy of the University of Ottawa. He works on the philosophy of Herder, early modern philosophy and contemporary ethics. He has published articles on Herder's metaphysics, epistemology, philosophy of language, philosophy of history, and moral philosophy, and, in contemporary ethics, on the foundations of ethical agency. He co-edited *Herder: philosophy and anthropology* (2017) and is currently the lead editor of a five-volume edition of English translations of Herder's philosophical works for Cambridge University Press. He is also working on a monograph on the philosophy of the Herder.

François Duchesneau, Docteur ès Lettres et Sciences humaines (Paris I), is Professor Emeritus of History and Philosophy of Science at Université de Montréal. His present research explores the formation of theories in the modern life sciences. His publications include *Leibniz et la méthode de la science* (1993), *La Dynamique de Leibniz* (1994), *Philosophie de la biologie* (1997), *Les Modèles du vivant de Descartes à Leibniz* (Paris: Vrin, 1998), *Leibniz. Le vivant et l'organisme* (2010), *La Physiologie des Lumières*, 2nd edition (2012), with Justin Smith *The Leibniz-Stahl Controversy* (2016) and *Organisme et corps organique de Leibniz à Kant* (2018).

Michael N. Forster is currently Alexander von Humboldt Professor, holder of the Chair in Theoretical Philosophy and Co-director of the International Center for Philosophy at Bonn University in Germany. For twenty-eight years, he has taught at the University of Chicago, where he served as chairman of the Philosophy Department and was Glen A. Lloyd Distinguished Service Professor. His work combines historical and systematic aspects. His historical work is on ancient philosophy and especially German philosophy. His systematic work is mainly on epistemology and philosophy of language. He is the author of numerous articles and eight books, including *Hegel and Skepticism* (1989), *Hegel's Idea of a Phenomenology of Spirit* (1998), *Herder: Philosophical Writings* (2002), *Wittgenstein on the Arbitrariness of Grammar* (2004), *Kant and Skepticism* (2008), *After Herder: Philosophy of Language in the German Tradition* (2010), *German Philosophy of Language: From Schlegel to Hegel and Beyond* (2011) and *Herder's Philosophy* (2018).

Stephen Gaukroger is Emeritus Professor of History and Philosophy of Science at the University of Sydney. He is the author of a tetralogy on 'Science and the Shaping of Modernity': *The Emergence of a Scientific Culture* (2006), *The Collapse of Mechanism and the Rise of Sensibility* (2010), *The Natural and the Human* (2016), *Civilization and the Culture of Science* (2020).

Philippe Hamou is Professor of Philosophy at Sorbonne University. His research focuses on early modern philosophy and science. He is the author of *Dans la chambre obscure de l'esprit, John Locke et l'invention du mind*, Paris: Ithaque, 2018 and co-editor, with Martine Pecharman, of *Locke and Cartesian Philosophy*, Oxford University Press, 2018.

Eveline Hauck is a researcher at State University of Campinas, Brazil. Her research interests are the Scottish Enlightenment, political economy and political philosophy. She has published on Hume, Ferguson and Smith and translated some of their work into Portuguese. She is currently translating Smith's *Lectures on Jurisprudence*.

Ansgar Lyssy is currently a fixed-term professor of philosophy at the University of Leipzig. Before that, he was assistant professor ('Wissenschaftlicher Mitarbeiter') at the University of Heidelberg and LMU Munich. He received his PhD in 2011 from the Technische Universität Berlin with a thesis on Leibniz. Since 2019, he has been working on a research project on causality in Hegel, funded by the Thyssen Foundation. Some selected publications: *Kausalität und Teleologie bei G. W. Leibniz*, Stuttgart: Franz-Steiner (*Studia Leibnitiana* Sonderheft/Special Issue No. 48), 2016. With Giovanni Pietro Basile (eds): *System and Freedom in Kant and Fichte*, 2022.

Charlotte Morel is a researcher at Centre National de la Recherche Scientifique (CNRS), France. Her research focuses on eighteenth- and nineteenth-century German philosophy, with particular attention to textual hermeneutics and ideal-realist systems respectively. Her most recent book related to Enlightenment philosophy attempts to guide the reader through Lessing's *Education of the Human Race* (2021).

Gabrielle Radica is Professor in the Department of Philosophy of the University of Lille. As a specialist in moral and political philosophy and a historian of modern philosophy, she has published different works on Rousseau (including a monograph *L'histoire de la raison. Anthropologie, morale et politique chez Jean-Jacques Rousseau*

(2008); on law; on Locke, Hobbes and Montesquieu; and on the philosophy of family (*Textes-clés de Philosophie de la famille*, 2013).

Céline Spector is Professor of Philosophy at Sorbonne University. Her research interests include the French Enlightenment, Montesquieu, Rousseau and their contemporary legacy. Her publications include *Montesquieu. Pouvoirs, richesses et sociétés* (2004; republished Paris: Hermann, 2011); *Montesquieu et l'émergence de l'économie politique* (2006), which won the prix Léon Faucher of the Académie des Sciences morales et politiques; *Montesquieu. Liberté, droit et histoire* (2010) and *Au prisme de Rousseau. Usages politiques contemporains* (2011). Her most recent publications are *Eloges de l'injustice. La philosophie face à la déraison* (2016) and *Rousseau et la critique de l'économie politique* (2017).

Jacqueline Taylor is Professor of Philosophy at the University of San Francisco. She is the author of *Reflecting Subjects: Passion, Sympathy and Society in Hume's Philosophy* (2015; paperback 2017). She also co-edited, with David Fate Norton, the second edition of the *Cambridge Companion to Hume* (2009). She is editing a forthcoming collection, *Reading Hume on the Principles of Morals*. She has authored a number of articles on Hume's philosophy and articles that take up topics in contemporary moral psychology, including pride and hate. Her work has been supported by fellowships from the Center for Human Values at Princeton University, the Tanner Center for the Humanities at the University of Utah and the National Endowment for the Humanities.

Norbert Waszek is Distinguished Professor of German History of Ideas (Emeritus) at University Paris 8 (Vincennes-Saint-Denis). He works on eighteenth- and nineteenth-century thought, especially the Scottish Enlightenment and Hegel and his school. His publications include *The Scottish Enlightenment and Hegel's Account of 'Civil Society'* (1988; second edition, 1991), *L'Ecosse des Lumières: Hume, Smith, Ferguson* (2003) and his editions of Eduard Gans (1991, 1993, 1995) and of Hegel's philosophy of history (2009 and 2011).

Catherine Wilson was Anniversary Professor of Philosophy at York University from 2012 to 2018 and is currently Emeritus Professor of the Department. She writes on the history of modern philosophy and on early modern and Enlightenment science. Her major publications include *Kant and the Naturalistic Turn of 18th Century Philosophy* (2022), and *Leibniz's Metaphysics* (1989). *A Very Short Introduction to Epicureanism* (2015), *The Oxford Handbook of Philosophy in Early Modern Europe*, co-edited with D. Clarke (2011), *Epicureanism at the Origins of Modernity* (2008) and *The Invisible World: Philosophers and the Microscope 1640–1740* (1995).

Günter Zöller is Professor of Philosophy (Emeritus) at Ludwig Maximilian University Munich, Germany. His main research areas are Kant, German Idealism and political philosophy, on which he has published over 400 articles in journals, essay collections and reference works worldwide. Recent book publications include

Res Publica. Plato's 'Republic' in Classical German Philosophy (2015), *Reading Fichte* (2013; Japanese translation 2014, Spanish translation 2015, Italian translation 2018, Chinese translation 2019), *The Cambridge Companion to Philosophy* (co-edited with David James, 2016), *Philosophy of the Nineteenth Century. From Kant to Nietzsche* (2018), and *Hegel's Philosophy. An Introduction* (2020; Turkish and Spanish translations in preparation).

Introduction

Stefanie Buchenau and Ansgar Lyssy

Introduction

At the dawn of the eighteenth century, philosophers changed both their vocabulary and their focus. They not only began to ascribe a more central significance to concepts such as 'humankind'[1] and 'humanity', but they also spoke with a new solemnity about humanity, introducing the term into numerous book titles.

To some extent, the term 'humanity' and its European equivalents (*Menschheit*, in German, *humanité* in French, *umanità* in Italian) conserved its characteristic polysemy from antiquity, where it had expressed at least three different meanings. First, 'humanity', or *humanitas* in Latin, denoted a distinctive property of humans as compared to divinity or animality. Second, it expressed a civil, moral or 'humane' attitude equivalent to sociability, philanthropy, pity and compassion (*Menschlichkeit, Geselligkeit, Mitleid, civilization, pitié, compassione*). Third, it had a collective dimension, also expressed by the term 'humankind', which went beyond the mere description of the 'human species' to imply a moral and social ideal of humanity in its totality. Finally, the plural 'humanities' was still being used to refer to a certain course of study reminiscent of the medieval *humaniores litterae*, i.e. the propaedeutic curriculum of the faculties of arts.

Alongside this ancient heritage, new concepts were rising to prominence or being invented within the field of anthropology and a still fluctuating semantics.[2] The very interest in the notion of a humankind or species (*Menschengattung, espèce humaine, genere umano*) reflected new comparative approaches within natural history and its new classification schemes. The notion of a humankind expressed a biological interpretation of the ancient theory of natural kinds, which in the eighteenth century was often combined with the notion of a diachronic development of this kind and its adaptation to the environment.[3] Instead of postulating humans' singular position as extramundane or supernatural ('divine') beings, modern philosophers and natural historians tended to include the human animal within the animal kingdom as merely one animal among others. Starting from a comparison with the animal, they adopted an external, descriptive or empiricist[4] viewpoint regarding the human being's distinctive observable characteristics, such as particular behaviour and evolution, perfectibility or malleability or civilizational progress.

The term 'humankind' (or its correlated, but semantically slightly different, notions of 'genre humain', *Menschengeschlecht or Menschheit*) in turn stirred new interest, partly because of its collective or universalist dimension. This emphasis on the collective dimension and a universal human nature appeared to be the larger framework in which to reflect on an individual's moral and political duties.[5] Philosophers seemed to consider that human beings (ought to) constitute a kind of society that imposes particular social and civil standards and that these collective standards provide the foundations for morality and politics. They began to conceive of such notions as 'humanity' or 'humankind' and to view their corresponding political notions 'human(e) society' or 'world state' both as the ideal end points of a ceaseless 'progress', 'destination' or 'vocation' (*Bestimmung*) and as the larger collective framework within which to think about an individual's moral and political duties.[6] Such 'humankind' extended beyond the mere description of the human species. It generally denoted a moral and social ideal which in turn seemed only attainable within a collective framework and in the context of a broader development of human society. It supposed some mutual recognition, communication and reflection on collective rights and duties and even universal justice among humans. While still seeing a certain 'humanities' educational curriculum as the way to acquire such communicative and interpersonal skills, philosophers gave this education a new 'sentimental' and aesthetic dimension, as illustrated by the title of Schiller's famous *Briefe über die Ästhetische Erziehung des Menschen* (Letters on the Aesthetic Education of Man, 1794).

Parallel to the inflationary use of these anthropological notions, a traditional metaphysical vocabulary was gradually disappearing. This included terms from traditional metaphysics focused on 'God', 'soul' and 'substance', increasingly deemed old-fashioned or anachronistic. Obviously, these semantic changes in turn reflected deeper changes in philosophical views and *methodology*.

While Enlightenment philosophers did not simply turn away from metaphysics, they began to ascribe new meanings and functions to these older concepts. At least for a time, metaphysics stirred vivid debates, caught up in an intense dialogue between philosophy and its neighbouring empirical disciplines such as anthropology, medicine and natural history. In these debates, the ancient metaphysical concepts began to acquire a new philosophical and systematic function for empirical studies.[7] Sometimes, metaphysics was suspected of being too 'speculative' according to a novel and predominantly negative connotation of this word. This reflected an increased sensitivity to linguistic relativism and the way our thought is shaped by language. The suspicion that some words might simply be devoid of any content made them appear increasingly dubious to a number of Enlightenment metaphysicians. This led them to narrow down their earlier ambitions, question a set of earlier premises and take an epistemologically more modest view of the scope and limits of philosophy. A good example of this critical attitude is the way Locke deconstructed Cartesian dualism and contested the possibility of a metaphysical and real definition of human essence. The English empiricists (Locke, Hume, Reid, Smith, etc.) and the French materialists (Diderot, De La Mettrie, d'Holbach, etc.), as well as natural historians like Buffon, Rousseau or Herder, adopted different strategies, some of them ostensibly setting metaphysics aside.

Sometimes, the transformation of metaphysics also expressed new secular tendencies. Ancient traditions such as Epicureanism and/or Platonism and Stoicism could be used against Christian authorities to correct or reject their theological premises. For instance, the recourse to Epicureanism[8] helped to generate a new opposition to Cartesian dualism and the Christian doctrine of the soul, namely materialism, and also served as a correction to the Christian two-world view, which had downplayed mundane life in favour of eternal punishment and reward. The return to Stoic humanism, cosmopolitanism, natural law theory and ethical universalism gave philosophers food for a range of modern political theories, such as natural law theories, contractualism and republicanism. It enabled them either to dispense with a transcendent divine creator or at least to put the so-called duties to God into perspective; the latter were increasingly set aside or included within the duties to one's fellows and a set of collective moral and legal obligations.

While it would be wrong to assert that eighteenth-century philosophers gave up metaphysics altogether, it is certainly true that they attempted to radically rethink ancient Socratic self-knowledge (*gnothi seauton*) and they did set metaphysical assumptions aside whenever these appeared philosophically unfounded. In particular, they rejected the idea that metaphysical principles could be the sole starting points of any philosophical enquiry. They also approached what is nowadays called the mind – body problem in ways that radically departed from Cartesian dualism. Their efforts to 'recenter philosophy on anthropology' (Herder) signified their refusal to postulate two separate substances, body and mind and to presuppose human godlikeness and divine attributes. Instead, philosophers began to approach human nature via a new naturalism, from an external, descriptive and comparative angle, starting by comparing humans and animals (Buffon). They employed the methods of natural history, medicine, comparative anatomy and physiology and natural law as alternative paths towards establishing human attributes such as reason and freedom from external attributes, using classifications which were often not sharply drawn – as exemplified by Linnaeus's inclusion of the mermaid in his classification of human races.

One major claim here, which was to be discussed throughout the Enlightenment, was that anatomical and physiological structures *condition* and *express* mental faculties and development, so that understanding the biological differences between humans and other animals enables us to better understand humans' mental faculties, drives and desires.[9] This was an important idea that furthered the rise of anthropology, and it also influenced a number of protagonists of what has been called the Radical Enlightenment.[10]

Philosophers, furthermore, showed a growing interest in the differences not only between humans and other animals but also between varieties or races within humankind, engaging with issues of humankind's unity and diversity. In a century characterized by the birth of anthropology and ethnology, scholars debated over the dividing lines between 'civilized' people and 'barbarians' and the presumed hierarchies among races, genders and religions. The fluctuations and expansions of biological vocabulary to include terms like 'races', 'stems', 'stocks', 'variants', etc., show that Enlightenment thinkers paid a great deal of attention to issues of race; they could even be said to have invented the modern concept, often using it to justify colonial exploitation and oppression. And yet, within this fluctuating semantics, employing words such as 'race' did not necessarily amount to racism. Nor was polygeneism (as opposed to monogeneism) tantamount to a defence of human inequality, hierarchy and ethnocentrism. Paradoxically, the inquiry into human diversity could at times even serve the cause of humanity and human unity.[11] In such a global unity of humankind, the 'barbarian', 'savage' or 'heathen' was no longer seen as the opposite of 'Roman' or 'Christian'. A new philosophical tendency emerged, according to which humanity was grounded in humane sentiment and compassion towards the whole of humankind. This proved to be fertile ground for the development of modern forms of moral universalism, and it also allowed for a conception of alienation as loss of natural humanity. Humanity became increasingly associated with humane sentiments and thus was increasingly considered a question of education and civilization.[12]

Both empirical and philosophical anthropology were therefore closely linked to emerging moral, political and educational projects. This nexus often left room for dynamic and philosophically open views on human 'hominization' and 'humanization': on the biological evolution and on the collective or individual progress, education and history of human beings or humankind. Here, philosophers and other scholars and researchers introduced new genealogical and historical viewpoints, focusing on the education and shaping of the individual or the vocation, the progress of humankind (*Bestimmung des Menschen, der Menschheit*). The notion of universal history gained new significance, as scholars debated over the diverging historical trajectories and velocities of civilizational development, the 'simultaneity of the unsimultaneous'.[13] The emerging historical narratives, often produced as contributions to Enlightenment philosophies of history, in turn demonstrated their emancipation from theology, biblical narratives, Christian eschatologies and universal histories. Instead of building on notions of (lost) human unity and divine providence, they increasingly approached humanity as an expression of human action and as a philosophical, moral and political topic. Distant human origins also moved into focus, as the biblical narrative of paradise and the creation was increasingly questioned.[14]

Furthermore, the Enlightenment witnessed the birth of novel aesthetic approaches to the education of humankind or the 'humanities', shifting the emphasis from the cultivation of civil virtues to humane feeling, compassion and sympathy. Most often, the arts or what now began to emerge as the 'Fine arts' were seen as the school for this education of feeling. The emphasis on feeling, sympathy and compassion seemed to reflect deeper structural changes in society, with new economic practices creating new hierarchies and new distances between humans.

The aim of this collective volume is to develop a panoramic view of this Enlightenment humanism through its selection and presentation of a series of singular but crucial and influential authors, topics and questions. It also aims to show the mutual entanglement of the different dimensions of humanity. This humanism defies any easy compartmentalization that seeks to contrast theoretical and practical philosophy with an overly abstract conception of Enlightenment universalism. Whatever humanism's variants, descriptive and normative approaches to it are intrinsically related. Moreover, this multifaceted Enlightenment humanism still has particular relevance for us today, in our debates on racism, feminism and the current planetary challenges. They invite us to return to the Enlightenment, disentangle the complicated relationship between human unity and variety and reflect on shared duties and universal rights, as well as on our common humanity.[15]

Book structure and summaries

The book comprises fourteen contributions, following a broadly chronological order.

In the first chapter, entitled 'The presumptive unity of humankind in Locke's *Essay*', Philippe Hamou reflects on the surprising *absence* of a clear-cut and unequivocal definition of a human being in Locke's *Essay on the Human Understanding*. As Locke himself points out, 'none of the definitions of the word man which we yet have, nor descriptions of that sort of animal, are so perfect and exact as to satisfy a considerate inquisitive person; much less to obtain a general consent' (III, 6, 27). Although Locke has a fixed definition of the 'moral man' (a mixed mode, an ideal entity used in moral and political discourse), the nominal essence of the 'physical man' (the substance), or mankind (the species), is typically indeterminate. It is unclear whether it is the external figure of men that should be considered as the unique distinctive feature or whether it is rationality, or rationality plus figure. To further complicate things, these features are not clear-cut but seem to admit degrees and variations. While this instability should come as no surprise, it seems to conflict with an implicit postulate of the *Essay*, namely the postulate of a unity of the constitution of human understandings. It is because Locke and his readers have the same simple ideas and the same acquisitive faculties that they can understand the pathways of reflection described in the *Essay*. Without this unity, not only philosophical communication but language and communication in general would be impossible. As Hamou points out, the argument of the *Essay* relies in many ways on this presumptive unity of mankind. For example, while the *Essay* acknowledges the possibility that men may have entirely different simple ideas about the same things, 'successful' human communication makes this hypothesis highly unlikely. Locke's conviction is also illustrated by his anti-nativist use of 'ethnographic' arguments, based on the observation of cultural diversity: if the fact that some peoples are entirely devoid of moral principles or an idea of divinity argues against the innateness of principles, it may only be because human diversity, however great, does not imply a diversity of mental constitutions. What is true for these uncultured and barbaric peoples must, in a sense, also be true for us. Hamou thus concludes that there is a tension in Locke's work between a strong nominalist view allowing for different individual constitutions among 'men' and the necessary presumption of a constitutive unity of humankind that allows for the universalization of the results of Locke's enquiry into the human mind.

The second contribution by Céline Spector on 'Human Nature in Montesquieu'. raises the question whether Montesquieu's political science is built on the denial of the science of man. Spector shows that despite his account of human nature in the state of nature, Montesquieu shifts his emphasis to peoples as subjects of history. *The Spirit of the Laws* indeed offers two competing theories: on the one hand, Montesquieu's political science focuses on 'principles' (virtue, honour and fear) as the dominant political passions specific to each distinctive form of government; on the other, his culturalistic approach attempts to explain social diversity between peoples. Mankind is influenced by various causes: by climate, religion, laws, the maxims of government, precedents, morals and customs. This makes Montesquieu a key figure in the prehistory of cultural anthropology.

The third chapter, 'The image of the human being in the Comte de Buffon' by Catherine Wilson, engages with the concept of human nature as it was developed by the Comte de Buffon, who was the author/compiler of the thirty-six volumes of the *Histoire Naturelle* (1749–1788) and one of the most influential figures of the eighteenth century. Wilson's chapter describes Buffon's deeply thought-out views on the place of human beings in 'living nature', the relationship of human beings to apes, 'thinking matter', the life cycle and extinction. It explores the connections between these views and Buffon's concern for the subjection of women and his anti-war stance. Wilson suggests that Buffon's anthropology has been largely ignored by Anglophone scholars because of his reputation as a popularizer and rhetorician. In fact, he was a radical and often fierce critic of contemporary orthodoxies.

In 'Hume on humanity and the party of humankind', Jacqueline Taylor explores Hume's views on humanity as a distinctive form of sympathy and on the historical and cultural variability in our ways of life in the *Enquiry Concerning the Principles of Morals* and the *Treatise of Human Nature*. A first aim is to detail how Hume's experimental method works in his *Enquiry* and to show how it advances Hume's main goal of establishing humanity as the foundation of morality. Hume's use of an experimental method in his *Enquiry* is focused on moral discourse as part of common life. We use a variety of linguistic conventions, and observation and experience reveal our commitment to a shared language of virtue and vice, merit and demerit and to a vocabulary of praise and blame. Hume systematically shows that *utility* is the common circumstance in the terms we use for meritorious or virtuous mental qualities. He also appeals, more experimentally, to the notion of *force*, drawing our attention, first, to the force with which utility commands our esteem and, second, to the forces of our nature that interest us in utility. We have several person-directed concerns that elicit character evaluations: self-love, partiality and a more general concern for the happiness or misery of others that is rooted in our humanity. Against those who take self-interest to be our overwhelming concern, Hume shows that several circumstances combine to allow humanity to *acquire* a force sufficient to impart authority to the moral sentiments grounded in it. This leads Taylor to formulate a second aim, that of showing how Hume's particular use of an experimental method reveals several normative dimensions of his sentiment-based ethics. First, Hume's naturalistic approach does not merely describe psychological tendencies but shows us to be embedded in common life, using a moral language because humanity gives us a shared commitment to value some human traits over others. Second, the circumstances in which humanity acquires force may not hold in all historical or cultural contexts; Hume makes it clear that we can evaluate social arrangements with respect to how well they allow for the cultivation of humanity. Finally, Hume's references to 'the party of humankind' suggest an Enlightenment ideal of inclusion in our moral practices.

Contribution number five, Ansgar Lyssy's 'Humankind and humanity in Diderot', explores the systematic connection between Diderot's materialist account of human nature and its normative implications. Diderot's materialism contains traces of normative elements that arise from the notion of an economy of nature, i.e. the 'appropriateness' of natural entities within the whole of nature. Herein, Diderot adopts the idea of a system of nature from Shaftesbury, centred on the claim that in the economy of the world, no thing, no species is in the wrong place or does not fulfil its function. Human beings have, qua members of the same species, an inherent tendency towards good and evil. But observation shows us that human beings will act for their own good, motivated only by self-love. They need to be constrained by politically established, efficient and just laws, not by morality or religion. Diderot proposes a naturalized conception of normativity – the agreement of the particular will with the general will of the species – that becomes indistinguishable from the moral psychology of ideal, reasonable beings in ideal, reasonable societies. This serves as an evaluative criterion against which societies can be measured and judged. The 'ought' of the general will follows from the 'is' of the human species insofar as it is neither desirable nor justifiable to act against nature. Despite Diderot's radical materialism, the human 'ought' derives from this general concept of an economy of nature in which 'is' and 'ought' have never been fully separated.

In her '"How do humans become human(e)?" On Rousseau's *Second Discourse* and *Émile*', Gabrielle Radica turns to Rousseau's views on hominization and humanization. When discussing the variety of human beings, Rousseau rejects theological, philosophical and purely zoological explanations. These explanations, he argues, tend to reduce humans to an eternal essence or to physiological properties, neglecting the way they are conditioned and developed through social factors. In this sense, Rousseau transforms the question 'What is the human being?' into a new question: 'How do human beings become human(e)?' This allows him to approach the question via what was, for his epoch, a highly original method. Human existence should not be explained from a presumably atemporal perspective, but rather through the medium of a narrative since this allows us to include in our account of human existence the transformation of human beings through time as irreducibly significant in an understanding of what we are. This also allows Rousseau to deal with a fundamental contradiction in human nature: since the human being is an animal, we are always on the verge of becoming human. Radica's chapter presents and compares both issues, 'hominization' and 'humanization' – the bodily and the moral process of becoming (a) human – in the second *Discourse* and in *Émile*, briefly reflecting on their reception in France (Lévi-Strauss, Goldschmidt, Duchet, Labussière, Binoche).

The seventh chapter by Eveline Hauck and Norbert Waszek bears the title '"In the human kind, the species has a progress as well as the individual": Adam Ferguson on the progress of "mankind"'. Here, the two authors explore the notion of progress in Ferguson. Regarding notions of 'humankind' and 'humanity' in the European Enlightenment, Adam Ferguson (1723–1816), a pivotal figure in the Scottish Enlightenment, is important both in his own right and because of his wide impact on thinkers and currents of thought far beyond his native Scotland, in Germany in particular (for instance on Garve, the early pre-critical Kant, Schiller, Jacobi, Hamann and Hegel). The chapter begins with a reconstruction of Ferguson's *Essay on the History of Civil Society* (1767), spelling out the exact place and significance of his reflections on humankind. In what sense is his book a 'natural history' of humankind? The question is related to the universal characteristics of human nature that Ferguson identifies, two of which need to be explained in some detail: what he describes as its 'active power' and sociability. The crucial task is then to analyse the way in which Ferguson links these reflections with his conception of the 'progress' of humankind and in what ways he differs from his eminent colleagues and friends (Hume and Adam Smith). An overview of the influence of his ideas on German thought concludes the chapter.

Stephen Gaukroger's contribution is entitled 'The association of science and civilization in the Enlightenment'. He here discusses a question routinely posed regarding the idea of civilization in eighteenth- and nineteenth-century explorations of human nature: both morality and culture were measured against the template of the values of civilization, a core concept in modern universal history, which were often understood as a history of humanity. Prior to the eighteenth century, civilization was associated with features like successful political institutions, a cultural and religious life, literacy levels, social cohesion, prosperity and a system of laws. But by the beginning of the nineteenth century, Western thinkers had begun to consider civilization impossible without science. How did this shift to science come about? Condorcet provides the key: as the embodiment of reason, science stands above the events that history describes, providing a prescriptive guidance that enables us to secure not just freedom from barbarism and superstition but something unlimited in its potential. Civilization is thereby given a rationale as dynamic in contrast to 'static' societies. Correspondingly, the view of human nature as fixed – as opposed to something to be realized in future human development – becomes associated with primitive or backward societies.

In the chapter entitled 'Philoctetes at the edge of humanity. The German Enlightenment on social exclusion and the education of feeling', Stefanie Buchenau explores the eighteenth-century aesthetic debate around Sophocles's *Philoctetes*. The tragedy's hero, Philoctetes, is an anti-hero: a non-person, a being 'without a friend', 'a dead man among the living'. Abandoned on a desert island by his fellow Greeks, he has been excluded from human society and he has even lost almost all the features that characterize him as human: language, appearance, habitat and even upright posture. His situation changes when encountering two visitors, Odysseus and Neoptolemos, whose initial plan is to attempt to gain Philoctetes's trust and steal his weapons by trickery. But progressively, Neoptolemos is led to recognize the humanity in Philoctetes, being moved by Philoctetes's pain. Severely condemned by Cicero, this tragedy was later the object of a double rehabilitation, aesthetic and moral, in eighteenth-century Scotland

and Germany. The debate concerns the psychological mechanisms of social exclusion and the formation of affective bonds: why do we have humane feelings towards others, and why do we form affective links with them, considering them to be human *like us* and placing ourselves in a relationship of equality? Or conversely, why do we fail to establish such a relationship? Why do we find them repulsive, too different to elicit a desire to identify or at least compassion? These questions are discussed by authors such as Adam Smith in Scotland and Winckelmann, Mendelssohn, Lessing and Herder in the German-speaking world, who all ascribe a central significance to this tragedy in their aesthetics.

In Chapter 10 on 'Enlightenment moral philosophy and moral psychology: Baumgarten, Kant and Herder on moral feeling(s) and obligation', Nigel DeSouza turns to Herder. The overarching theme of his chapter is the relationship between the natural and the normative in the moral philosophies of Baumgarten, Kant and Herder. It begins with an overview of how Baumgarten makes the concept of obligation the focal point of his practical philosophy: obligations are rationally grasped and derive from our own nature, the motive behind their performance being to contribute to one's own or another's perfection. The second section addresses the pre-critical Kant's criticisms of Baumgarten on obligation, which centre on the distinction between physical and moral perfection, the former merely concerning the effects of actions, the latter concerning their intentions and motives, such as the disinterested feeling of concern for others. Kant is suggesting here that our perception of and motivation to achieve moral perfection are grounded in moral feeling. The third section explores how Herder, rejecting Baumgarten's conception of ethics as the science of our obligations, takes up the concept of moral feeling (to which he was likely first introduced in Kant's lectures) and conceptualizes it within the framework of a philosophy of life where moral feelings are psycho-physiological in nature and the inescapable basis of all normative principles.

Michael N. Forster's contribution is entitled 'Herder on humanity'. According to Forster, 'humanity' is one of Herder's most central and most influential concepts. It played an increasingly salient role in his work as his career developed, in particular coming to be one of the main concepts behind his *Ideas for a Philosophy of History of Humankind* (1784–91) and *Letters for the Advancement of Humanity* (1793–7). However, as the distinguished German scholar Hans Dietrich Irmscher has pointed out, the concept is also notoriously difficult to pin down exactly. Forster's chapter starts with an analysis of the concept offered by Irmscher himself. It argues that while some of the components of the concept are properly identified, others do not really belong to the concept and yet others are omitted. The chapter therefore proceeds to offer a more satisfactory and complete analysis. Having done that, Forster then turns to an evaluation of the concept's components in terms of defensibility. Certain important components are found to be justifiable, including a commitment to the unity of the human species, a moral sentimentalism and a moral cosmopolitanism, but others are found to be more questionable, including moral universalism and the concept's theological underpinning. Besides its interpretive lessons, therefore, the main message of the chapter is that the former components should be retained but the latter rejected.

Chapter 12, by François Duchesneau, is entitled 'Blumenbach on the varieties of the human species'. Johann Friedrich Blumenbach (1752–1840) was one of the protagonists in the vivid debate on race that shook up the eighteenth century. Siding with the so-called monogeneists against the polygeneists, he addressed two questions concerning the varieties of the human species. On the one hand, how did heritable anatomical and physiological differences among representatives of the human species come about? On the other hand, did these differences flow from a single-stem species or race or, alternatively, from different stock species? It was, for Blumenbach, essential to pursue these questions as a matter of natural history, that is, using the methods of experimental philosophy. This is not to say that speculative considerations were absent from his arguments and conclusions. Actually, he considered that the empirical data he started from and worked on – including his pioneering observations of human skulls – should be consistent with his systematic conception of the living organism, animal as well as human. He held that all varieties of organisms flow from adjustments of the formative drive (*Bildungstrieb*) to external conditions, whereby it builds the individuals of the species whose form it embodies. Some of these adjustments can be stable enough to generate genetically transmissible patterns that yield the complex sets of morphological and physiological traits occurring in the five main varieties of humankind. But these sets of characteristics only represent abstract averages, and consequently the properties of those varieties are present in manifold degrees. There are therefore no fixed boundaries separating the varieties because of the common endowment in biological and cognitive powers that characterizes the species. Though Blumenbach posits that humankind possesses a species-specific nature significantly different from that of the higher animal species, especially in terms of cognitive powers, he does not rule out the possibility that natural-historical processes may have entailed mutations of the stock's formative drive. His appraisal of the human condition remains confined within the limits of a natural-historical approach whose most significant theoretical premise is that formative drives provide sufficient reasons for the observable features which lead us to differentiate human populations. Such an empirical discrimination of varieties is doubly relative. On the one hand, it is historically contingent, depending upon adaptations of the original human formative drive to changing biogeographical circumstances. On the other hand, the core species-specific properties that the formative drive yields, notwithstanding those variations, cannot be derived from a metaphysical view of what human nature consists in. The sets of these properties can only be empirically assessed from the consequent behaviour of humans in their diverse living environments. And it could even reasonably be presumed that the formative drive thereby revealed has itself resulted from previous mutations of organic forces in nature. Blumenbach the naturalist remains reluctant to accept metaphysical presuppositions that would involve extrapolating from natural-historical data to a transcendent system of final causes. He prefers to pragmatically endorse the limited and essentially heuristic teleological interpretation of the specific harmony of traits and actions that appears to be needed account for the historical development of humans as similarly endowed organic beings across their varieties.

In the thirteenth chapter, Charlotte Morel raises the question: 'Can Kant's "man" be a woman?' The play on words in the title of this chapter directly points to the gender bias that can unconsciously affect the concept of 'humanity' in its effective scope – a bias heightened and made especially acute by the fact that Kant shapes this concept as an ideal of the Enlightenment. Indeed, there is evidence from far more than one text – or perhaps subtext – in Kant's work that his normative approach towards what humans can and should be (i.e. the approach of a *pragmatic* anthropology in Kant's sense of what humans 'have to make of themselves') fits women as adequately as it does men. In other words, the concept of humanity *should* apply to every human being. However, its application turns out to be problematic when it comes to such a generic feature as gender. The pre-critical *Observations on the Feeling of the Beautiful and Sublime* (1764) offers an answer: presenting us with a *binary conception of virtue* in terms of the difference between the sexes, this text appears to threaten Kant's later view of humanity as the universal community of humans converging towards a unique ideal. But that duty is perhaps not Kant's last word, given that ideals have to be realized by concrete individuals. The chapter provides evidence of how prevalent the issue of desire between the sexes is in Kant's anthropology, thereby supporting the following thesis: this issue of desire is responsible for the highly contrasting ways Kant constructs male and female gender, and as such it is responsible for a theoretical clash between his construction of gender and his concept of humanity.

The fourteenth and final chapter by Günter Zöller is titled '"Anthroponomy". Kant on the natural and the rational human being'. It aims to assess the alleged anthropological dimension of Kant's practical philosophy in four sections on (1) the recent anthropological slant in work on Kant, (2) the manifestly marginal status of anthropology in Kant's overall œuvre, (3) the special split status of the human being in Kant and (4) the normative nature of Kant's practical philosophy. The focus is on the historic and systematic relationship between Kant's various writings on physical and cultural anthropology ('human nature') and his entirely differently based and differently oriented work on moral philosophy, including law and ethics, which draws on an account of reason-informed freedom ('rational nature'). Particular attention is paid to the intricate interplay between the natural and the normative in Kant's assessment of the forms and norms of human individual and social existence. The chapter argues for the primacy of principles over facts and of obligation over inclination in Kant's praeter-anthropological account of rationally free will and action.

Notes

1. Note that the eighteenth century often employed the older word 'mankind' rather than 'humankind'.
2. See the contemporary dictionary entries such as 'Humanité' in the *Encyclopédie*, where Jean-François de Saint-Lambert and Edmé-François Mallet define it as 'feeling of benevolence for all men, which is hardly inflamed except in a great and sensitive soul'.
3. See Smith (2017) and Duchet (1995).

4   The term 'empiricist' sometimes causes confusion, suggesting a Kantian perspective and opposition between empiricism and rationalism which was not necessarily shared by his contemporaries.
5   On these changes, see also the excellent chapter by Bödeker (1982).
6   For a comprehensive interpretation of the notion of a vocation of humanity, see Macor (2013). For the cosmopolitical notion, see for example Cheneval (2002); for the historical dimension of humankind, see Palmieri (2016).
7   An example would be the application of older metaphysical dogmata, such as 'Nature does nothing in vain' to principles of physics, such as the Principle of Least Action. Hence, there was more of a transformation than a rejection of traditional metaphysical notions in line with the emergence of multiple sub-genres of philosophy and the sciences as well.
8   For the resurgence of Epicureanism at the dawn of the Enlightenment, see Wilson (2008).
9   Concerning the naturalization of the soul, see, for example, Martin & Barresi (2004) and Taylor (1989).
10 See Israel (2002) and (2008).
11 For a more nuanced take on how polygenism and monogenism were used to serve both racist and egalitarian theories, see Doron (2016).
12 See, for example, Gaukroger (2016).
13 See Koselleck (1979).
14 See, for example, Stoczkowski (1996) or Petri (1990).
15 This volume grew out of a workshop organized by the editors at LMU Munich in 2017. We are grateful for the generous funding by the Fritz Thyssen Foundation, without which the workshop would not have been possible. We would also like to thank the Alexander von Humboldt foundation and the German Research Foundation for providing financial support for our respective research projects on human dignity and on the relationship between humankind and humanity in the Enlightenment. Finally, we would also like to extend our thanks to Michael Preyer for his help with establishing the index.

References

Bödeker, E. (1982), 'Menschheit, Humanität, Humanismus', in *Geschichtliche Grundbegriffe. Historisches Lexikon zur politisch-sozialen Sprache in Deutschland*, Stuttgart: Klett-Cotta, 1063–128.

Cheneval, F. (2002), *Philosophie in weltbürgerlicher Bedeutung: über die Entstehung und die philosophischen Grundlagen des Supranationalen und kosmopolitischen Denkens*, Basel: Schwabe.

Doron, C. O. (2016), *L'homme altéré: races et dégénérescence (XVIIe-XIXe siècles)*, Ceyzérieu: Champ Vallon.

Duchet, M. (1995), *Anthropologie et histoire au siècle des lumières*, Paris: Michel (reprint).

Gaukroger, S. (2016), *The Natural and the Human: Science and the Shaping of Modernity, 1739–1841*, Oxford: Oxford University Press.

Israel, J. (2002), *Radical Enlightenment: Philosophy and the Making of Modernity 1650–1750*, Oxford: Oxford University Press.

Israel, J. (2008), *Enlightenment Contested: Philosophy, Modernity, and the Emancipation of Man, 1670–1752*, Oxford: Oxford University Press.

Koselleck, R. (1979), *Vergangene Zukunft: zur Semantik geschichtlicher Zeiten*, Frankfurt A. M.: Suhrkamp.

Macor, L. A. (2013), *Die Bestimmung des Menschen (1748–1800): eine Begriffsgeschichte*, Stuttgart-Bad Cannstatt: Frommann-Holzboog.

Martin, R. & Barresi, J. (2004), *Naturalization of the Soul: Self and Personal Identity in the Eighteenth Century*, London: Routledge.

Palmieri, F. (2016), *State of Nature, Stages of Society: Enlightenment Conjectural History and Modern Social Discourse*, New York: Columbia University Press.

Petri, M. (1990), *Die Urvolkhypothese: ein Beitrag zum Geschichtsdenken der Spätaufklärung und des deutschen Idealismus*, Berlin: Duncker & Humblot.

Smith, J. E. (2017), *Nature, Human Nature, & Human Difference: Race in Early Modern Philosophy*, Princeton: Princeton University Press.

Stoczkowski, V. (1996), *Aux origines de l'humanité*, Paris: Pocket.

Taylor, C. (1989), *Sources of the Self: The Making of the Modern Identity*, Cambridge: Harvard University Press.

Wilson, C. (2008), *Epicureanism at the Origins of Modernity*, Oxford: Oxford University Press.

1

The presumptive unity of humankind in Locke's *Essay*

Philippe Hamou

The question I wish to raise in this chapter concerns what seems to be an important tension in Locke between epistemology and moral philosophy. On the one hand, Locke's *Essay Concerning Human Understanding*[1] pleads for a notion of the human species that is just as unstable and arbitrary as the notion of any other species or natural kind. The definition of 'man'[2] indeed is the illustration par excellence of the conventional nature and instability of our abstract ideas of substances, what Locke calls 'nominal essences'. This, in turn, is clearly related to Locke's nominalism. Each individual human being is necessarily what it is, but nothing is essential to it. As Locke explains, reason itself is not essential to the being that I am, 'a fever or fall may take [it] away'.[3] As a consequence, there are no perfections of a human being that could be considered intrinsic. All are somehow accidental, detachable. On the other hand, Locke's moral and political philosophy is grounded on the idea that a moral norm (a 'law of nature') is binding on all men universally, thus tacitly assuming an understanding of which entity counts as a human being. In the *Second Treatise on Government*, Locke makes it clear that the common subjection of all men to the law of nature presupposes that they are equal in natural rights, duties and faculties, 'sharing all in one community of nature', and all of the same 'rank':

> The state of nature has a law of nature to govern it, which obliges every one: and reason, which is that law, teaches all mankind, who will but consult it, that being all equal and independent, no one ought to harm another in his life, health, liberty, or possessions: for men being all the workmanship of one omnipotent, and infinitely wise maker; all the servants of one sovereign master, sent into the world by his order, and about his business; they are his property, whose workmanship they are, made to last during his, not one another's pleasure: and being furnished with like faculties, sharing all in one community of nature, there cannot be supposed any such subordination among us, that may authorize us to destroy one another, as if we were made for one another's uses, as the inferior ranks of creatures are for our's.[4]

'Mankind' receives here a rigid definition: it is the class of finite rational individuals, all being the workmanship of one omnipotent and all wise maker and subject to His law. As it appears, this fits closely the definition that Locke gives in the *Essay* of 'the moral man' – a phrase that occurs only once in the whole book, in a passage where Locke 'boldly' suggests that morality could be made demonstrative.[5] On this occasion he suggests that the issue of the definition of man is markedly different, depending on whether one considers man from the naturalist's or from the moral philosopher's point of view:

> And, therefore, whether a Child or Changeling be a *Man*, in a physical sense, may amongst the Naturalists be as disputable as it will, it concerns not at all the *moral Man*, as I may call him, which is this immoveable, unchangeable *Idea, a corporeal rational Being*. For, were there a Monkey, or any other Creature, to be found that had the use of Reason to such a degree, as to be able to understand general Signs, and to deduce Consequences about general ideas, he would no doubt be subject to Law, and in that sense be a Man, how much soever he differ'd in Shape from others of that Name.
>
> (III, xi, 16; 516–7)

The 'physical man', object for the natural philosopher, is an abstract idea for a particular type of substances and general ideas of substances, though they are, as Locke insists, the 'making of the understanding', must still 'follow nature' (III, ix, 11; 481) – as they only unite those ideas that have been seen regularly joined in natural beings. This is why assignation of humanity may be an object of dispute, and its definition highly uncertain. The definition of 'moral man' as a *corporeal rational creature, submitted to law* is not constrained in such a way. The terms 'immoveable and unchangeable' suggest that 'moral man' is an *Idea* in an almost Platonic sense, although it should be clear that Locke does not mean that the idea could exist independently of the minds that framed it. The Platonic element resides rather in the fact, that the definition of the moral man, just like that of a mathematical notion, is almost axiomatic. It is submitted neither to a criterion of empirical adequacy nor to the conformity to the ordinary use of language. To know what 'moral man' means, no tribute is to be paid to the changing and uncertain nature of the concrete individuals that we ordinarily call men. For all we know, the term could very well designate a category of beings of which there are no known empirical examples or beings that may not be 'human' in the physical sense of the term. In other terms, moral man is not a descriptive notion; it is a stipulative and normative term, whose definition indicates what is expected of an individual in order to be subject of moral or political discourse.[6]

There is some debate in the literature whether Locke's 'moral man' should be construed as a 'mixed mode', on account of the stipulative character of its definition. According to Locke, *modes* are complex ideas, composed of several simple ones, either of the same kind (simple modes) or of several kinds (mixed modes), and containing not in them 'the supposition of subsisting by themselves' (II, xii, 4; 165). In this last respect, they differ from another category of complex ideas, ideas of substances. Typically, moral ideas such as *parricide* or *theft* are mixed modes, mathematical ideas such as numbers and shapes, simple modes. Although *moral man* is clearly a substance name, this should not imply that its primary reference in moral discourse is an actual, existing substance. 'Moral man' may still be construed as a mixed mode in so far as it refers to an ideality that could be exemplified in a substance (such as a physical man) but not modelled on it, just like the immutable idea of a sphere can be (imperfectly) exemplified in substantial globes.[7] As Locke explains,

> The Names of Substances, if they be used in them, as they should, can no more disturb Moral than they do Mathematical Discourses: Where, if the mathematician speaks of a *Cube or Globe of Gold*, or of any other body, he has his clear, settled idea, which varies not, though it may by mistake be applied to a particular body to which it belongs not.
>
> (III, xi, 16; 517)[8]

It seems thus that Locke's moral and political philosophy requires the very univocity and ideality of *mankind* that Locke's epistemology strongly undermines. How are we to deal with this duality? Are we to resort to the usual (but unsatisfying) idea that there is a deep, impassable theoretical gap between the two sides of Locke's philosophy? I shall rather take another path and suggest that the moral view of man plays an important, albeit implicit, role in the epistemological enquiry in so far as it helps to define, presumptively, the unity of mankind – a unity that we have to postulate if we want to make sense of an enquiry into the '*human* understanding'. Unity of mankind is presumptive, in the sense that it is not given; it has to be postulated. It can't be an intrinsic perfection, an essence, a rational or moral *telos* that would be inscribed in the hearts of men.[9] As we shall see, the unifying factor is extrinsic; it is a law, the law of reason, that is up to each man individually to recognize or to ignore. In this sense, human identity is never dissociated from the very opinion that everyone has of their own humanity, the 'mixed mode' that they may decide to frame in order to define what it means for them to be human.[10]

The subject matter of the *Essay* is, as its title makes clear, not universal reason as such but rather the 'human' understanding – a faculty, Locke explains in the very first sentence of the book, 'that sets Man above the rest of sensible Beings, and gives him all the Advantage and Dominion which he has over them' (I, i, 1; 43). This opening statement clearly indicates that in pursuing research on human understanding, Locke was primarily interested in what constitutes, if not the specificity, at least the excellence of the human kind. Paradoxically, however, Locke remained rather elusive on what the word 'man' means precisely. No doubt the issue of the definitions of *man* is frequently mentioned. It is used as a privileged illustration on various themes such as the paradoxes of identity (II, xxvii, 8, 21, 29), the establishment of our nominal concepts of substances (III, iii, 7; III, vi, 21–2, 26–7), the abuse of words (III, xi, 20), the reality of knowledge (IV, iv,13–16) and the abuse of universal maxims (III, vii, 16–17). On these various occasions, Locke considers different possible definitions that may have gained some currency among his contemporaries, but he does not seem to want to commit himself to one or the other. In the end, the *Essay* does not appear to have reached a stabilized definition, as Locke himself acknowledges: 'None of the Definitions of the word *Man*, which we yet have, nor

Descriptions of that sort of Animal, are so perfect and exact as to satisfy a considerate inquisitive Person; much less to obtain a general Consent' (III, vi, 27; 455).

The difficulty here is not only related to the general issue of the inscrutability of the 'real essences' of substances, although of course it would not have arisen if the real essence of the human being, his or her inner constitution, were known to us, as it is to God and perhaps to certain higher intelligences.[11] The issue is also linked to an inherent instability of the 'nominal essence' or abstract idea of man, the relevant set of qualities and powers that would delimit the species in a sufficiently consensual manner. To understand this, let us consider the various definitions of the human species that are competing in Locke's *Essay*. In an interesting concluding passage of chapter II. xxvii on 'Identity and Diversity', Locke, in order to show that the criteria of identity are always relative to a general abstract idea of some kind, takes the example of three different possible definitions of man:

> For, supposing a rational Spirit be the *Idea* of a *Man*, it is easy to know what is *the same Man*, viz. the *same Spirit* – whether separate or in a Body – will be *the same Man*. Supposing a rational Spirit vitally united to a Body of a certain conformation of Parts to make a *Man*, whilst that rational Spirit, with that vital conformation of parts, though continued in a fleeting successive Body, remains, it will be the *same Man*. But if to any one the *Idea of a Man* be but the vital union of Parts in a certain shape; as long as that vital union and shape remain in a concrete, no otherwise the same but by a continued succession of fleeting Particles, it will be *the same Man*. For, whatever be the composition whereof the complex *Idea* is made, whenever existence makes it one particular thing under any denomination the same Existence continued preserves it the same individual under the same denomination.
>
> (II, xxvii, 29; 348)

This is a telling passage, for the three definitions proposed here for the idea of man – 'rational spirit', 'rational spirit vitally united to a body of a certain shape', 'vital union of parts in a certain shape' – certainly correspond to the three main philosophical representations of man, that Locke recognizes around him, and between which it seems that one would have to decide.

According to the first, man is essentially a spiritual being, a 'rational spirit' whose existence is somehow indifferent to the body in which it dwells and which it moves like a pilot. This may be dubbed the Platonic view, but to Locke who sees Descartes as a Platonist, it also has strong Cartesian overtones. The second definition insists on the union of body and mind and insists that the identity criterion is neither the one nor the other but the vital principle unifying both in their fleeting existence. The third definition is the one which, as we shall see, is most in line with linguistic usage and is likely to satisfy a materialist philosopher: man is a living corporeal substance maintaining a certain common shape or outward appearance through continuous change of 'fleeting particles'.

Considering the merits and shortcomings of these three definitions, we may better understand why none is fully satisfying. Indeed, Locke may have serious concerns with each one of them.

The first one, the Platonic definition, separates human beings from the condition of corporeality, construing them as pure disincarnated rational souls. This definition allows men to be ranked among the superior spirits, but it is certainly the one that is the less conformable to the ordinary use of language. As Locke says in *Essay* II, xxvii, 6, if it were the soul – understood as an immaterial principle distinct from the body – that made up the identity of man, it could make the same man of Socrates and Pilate, just as well as it would make *the same man* of the embryo and the adult. But even an adept of metempsychosis would not say that Socrates and Pilate are *the same man*. He would rather say that they are two men inhabited by the same soul. So the intellectualist definition of man may allow us to accept as possible situations where a conscious soul would be so to speak separated from the body it inhabits – situations illustrated in some of the 'puzzle cases' that Locke is pleased to devise in chapters II, i and II, xxvii. By affirming the real distinction between body and mind, as some Cartesians do, we make at least epistemically possible cases of separation or transmigration, where the soul is considered as having its life, memory and consciousness apart from the body. Locke has no qualms considering these unlikely situations, insofar as they help him to construct *ad hominem* arguments against doctrines that would allow the human being (body and soul) to be a different 'person' from his or her (separated) soul. In chapter II, i, Locke questions the supposed intellectual superiority of a pure soul, detached from the commerce of the body, and thinking apart, just as we do in our dreams:

> This I would willingly be satisfied in, Whether the Soul, when it thinks thus apart, and as it were separate from the Body, acts less rationally than when conjointly with it, or no: If its separate Thoughts be less rational, then these men must say, that the Soul owes the perfection of rational thinking to the body: if it does not, it is a wonder that our Dreams should be, for the most part, so frivolous and irrational; and that the soul should retain none of its more rational Soliloquies and Meditations.
>
> (II, i, 16; 113)

The suggestion here is that embodiment is essential to the condition of a rational creature. Perception as well as memory and language, without which rationality would be impossible, all require a living corporeal creature, endowed with external organs of sensation, brain traces and a voice or corporeal motions to express her thoughts. It is very dubious that these faculties could fulfil their functions without a body in a pure disincarnated soul. I argued elsewhere[12] that this idea of an embodied rationality was a strongly entrenched conviction of Locke's, motivating his head on opposition to the Cartesian view of the soul.

Let us turn now directly to the third definition (a living body with a certain shape). This definition, that may be favoured by materialist philosophers, is also certainly the one that is closest to the ordinary acceptation of the term 'man'. Locke points out that, on the one hand, we would be reluctant to call Balaam's donkey a 'man', however loquacious and rational it is (III, vi, 29), or to consider as a 'man' the seemingly rational parrot in the story of William Temple reported in II, xxvii, 8. On the other hand, we commonly call *men* (we baptize them) beings who do not manifest any signs of reason but are of human descent and have the common physical appearance of human beings (the 'changelings'). These two reciprocal linguistic facts suggest that common physical appearance together with shared descent is more decisive trait in establishing the reference of the term in ordinary usage than possession of reason or language:

> whatever is talked of other definitions, ingenious observation puts it past doubt, that the *Idea* in our Minds, of which the Sound *Man* in our Mouths is the Sign, is nothing else but of an Animal of such a certain Form. Since I think I may be confident, that, whoever should see a Creature of his own shape or make, though it had no more reason all its Life than a *Cat* or a *Parrot*, would call him still a *Man*; or whoever should hear a *Cat* or a *Parrot* discourse, reason, and philosophize, would call or think it nothing but a *Cat* or a *Parrot*; and say, the one was a dull irrational *Man*, and the other a very intelligent rational *Parrot*.
>
> (II, xxvii, 8; 333)

Locke's 'historical' or genetic account of the formation of our complex idea of man may help understand why ordinary usage tends to specify the human being more by figure than by reason. In III, iii, 7 Locke offers an account of the formation of our abstract idea of '*man*'. He evokes the child who, from the mental picture of her mother and her nurse (the first human beings she came through), and by successive comparisons and exclusions established on the occasion of new encounters, comes to form a general abstract idea of man, leaving out of her particular idea aspects that are peculiar to such or such individual, and including into the general idea 'certain common relationships of figures and several other qualities'. In the progressive formation of this abstract idea, two guiding forces are at play: resemblances on the one hand allow the child to group particular ideas under some common standard or type; social constraint of the child's linguistic community, on the other hand, confirms and corrects the acts of designation carried out by her. The general idea of *man* is formed and adjusted at the somewhat hazardous confluence of these two forces. Prejudices, misunderstandings and abuse of language may arise on this occasion. This is why, before being eventually corrected by his parents or masters, 'the Child can demonstrate to you that *a Negro is not a Man*, because White colour was one of the constant simple *Ideas* of the complex *Idea* he calls Man' (IV, xvi, 7; 607).[13]

This genetic approach to the constitution of our general idea of man illustrates Locke's thesis about classes and nominal essences: they are the 'workmanship of the understanding' (III, iii, 12–13), and their formation is accordingly fraught with inherent arbitrariness, depending on the particular history of the individuals, on the peculiar demands of their linguistic community and finally, on the most considerable appearances, those that stand out in perception, and are most clearly distinctive of species, such as figure (the external shape) or colour.[14] It should be clear that Locke in this respect is neither a descriptive metaphysician nor an ordinary language philosopher. The arbitrariness of meaning formation that prevails in ordinary language forbids considering that the ordinary language definition (man is an animal of a certain shape) should have any philosophical or normative privilege over any other. Besides, the emphasis the ordinary language definition places on the external figure alone is intrinsically problematic. Even though it is true that shapes are easily classified in types, shapes are nevertheless eminently labile, deformable, and so by itself a mere shape cannot offer a stabilized criterion for a nominal essence, as it does not carry with it an indication of when the figure obtained through continuous deformations ceases to *resemble* its original. Locke makes this point quite clear in this stunning *morceau de bravoure*:

> The well-shaped *Changeling* is a Man, has a rational Soul, though it appear not: this is past doubt, say you: Make the Ears a little longer, and more pointed, and the Nose a little flatter than ordinary, and then you begin to boggle: Make the face yet narrower, flatter, and longer, and then you are at a stand: Add still more and more of the likeness of a Brute to it, and let the Head be perfectly that of some other Animal, then presently 'tis a *Monster*; and 'tis demonstration with you, that it hath no rational Soul, and must be destroy'd.
>
> (IV, iv, 16; 572)

Finally, the third possible definition of the human species, the middle term definition mentioned in the concluding passage of II, xxvii, insists on the idea of a 'vital union' between body and soul and maintains both the usual philosophical criterion of reason (for the soul) and that of a specific conformation of parts (for the body). Such definition has clearly an Aristotelian overtone: the soul, described here as the principle that 'vitally' unites the parts of the body, is supposed to be endowed with rationality and thought.

Locke himself often seems to recognize that there are specific Aristotelian-type traits for humankind. In particular in the eleventh chapter of book II, devoted to the 'operations of the mind', he considers a number of faculties which, taken together, tend to specify men among other animals: perception, memory, the ability to distinguish ideas, to compare them and to abstract them. In these passages, Locke systematically confronts men and brutes. Acknowledging that sense, memory and even some sort of reasoning could be attributed to certain species of non-human animals, he finally considers that it is the ability to form general ideas, a condition for language, that makes the true difference.

> If it may be doubted, Whether *Beasts* compound and enlarge their *Ideas* that way to any degree; this, I think, I may be positive in, That the power of *Abstracting* is not at all in them; and that the having of general *Ideas* is that which puts a perfect distinction betwixt Man and Brutes, and is an Excellency which the Faculties of Brutes do by no means attain to.
>
> (II, xi, 10; 159)

Man would thus be a rational animal of a certain shape capable of abstracting and communicating his thoughts in language. Although this middle term definition is probably the one that was most congenial to Locke's views, it is important to see that it has its own shortcomings. It shares the same sort of arbitrariness that befalls definition of nominal essences in general. The very fact that other 'rational corporeal beings' of non-human shape (such as rational parrots) are easily conceivable shows that the conjunction of the two criteria (human shape and rationality) may be a purely contingent one. There is no ways of assessing its necessity (as we do not see into real essences), and this realization may threaten the middle-term definition of being reduced either to the first one or to the third.

Besides, Locke's (pseudo-)Aristotelian definition of man must be considered in the context of his head-on opposition to the Aristotelian ontology and the Porphyrian doctrine of predicables that has been derived from it.[15] According to this old view, the objects of science are substances, endowed with an essential nature – a 'form' – that is a set of properties such that if the object lacked one or the other it would no longer be what it is. According to Porphyry's table of predicables, the substantial form, say of man, is determined by the genus (*animal*), the difference (*reason*), the species that results from the application of the difference to the genus (*man*), the properties that are directly deductible from the difference (from the possession of reason one can derive that of *laughter, possession of hands, possession of language*).[16] Genus itself can be defined by higher genus and difference, up to the ultimate category of substance. We are therefore faced with a rigidly ordered scheme of discrete natural classes. In this scheme, individuals belong to one species and one only, one genus and one only, and so on. For each natural substance there is a real definition, by genus and specific difference, a definition that both determines its essence and assigns it its place in the natural order. While it is always possible to define a kind of being 'nominally' by singling out an accident or a bundle of accidents that it alone would possess, this is not the right kind of definition. True definition espouses the true order of nature. For Aristotle, there is indeed a fundamental difference between a nominal definition of man (for example, the one attributed to Plato, 'featherless biped, with large nails') and the real definition of man by genus and specific difference, such as 'rational animal'.

In Locke, on the other hand, no definition can be held to be better than another on the grounds that it would touch on something more interior or essential (cf. III, iii, 10). Even the definition attributed to Plato, which has traditionally been scoffed at, would have rights to be asserted.[17] Flat fingernails or upright posture may be relevant symptoms of an inner constitution common to the species, as well as reason or language. But since this constitution is not known, it remains unclear whether this or that trait, or all traits together, specifies a set of beings with the same inner constitution. Similarly, an Aristotelian definition of man remains a possible and even a legitimate one, provided that we renounce seeing it as a definition constructed from an a priori categorization of natural beings. Locke clearly stated his principled position on what our definitions of substances in general should be: they are not meant to show the real essence of the thing defined but only to make others see what ideas are meant by the word, the *definiendum* (for the speaker or for the linguistic community he represents). In other words, the definition can only circumscribe a 'nominal essence'. Aristotle's definition, reduced to a simple nominal definition of the Lockean type, amounts to saying that man is a living, sensory, self-moving, thinking person, capable of reason and language. The genus 'animal' simply becomes an abbreviating term, encapsulating the first three ideas.

Thus, there is no doubt that the definition of *man* is markedly instable in the *Essay*. No definition can be deemed better than another on the grounds that it would touch on something more interior or more essential (cf. III, iii, 10) or agree with a natural hierarchical order. The specifying or defining character of a trait or a bundle of traits is not grounded in the nature of the thing but in the state of the surrounding world and in the fact that, in the present circumstances, a certain bundle of similarities makes it possible to single out a group of individuals in a relatively clear-cut manner. The categories that the language selects correspond to certain populations of individuals resembling each other by several traits and thus forming relatively isolated islands in the archipelago of particular things opened up by our sensitive horizon. In a universe where there would be a large number of featherless bipeds with broad nails, all different from each other in all other respects, some rational and some irrational, some bird-faced and some monkey-faced: by immersing our world in this larger universe, Plato's definition would however certainly lose some of its value. The same would hold true for Aristotle's definition: in a larger universe with a diversity of rational animals, wise horses (such as Swift's Houyhnhnms), speaking donkeys and intelligent parrots, 'rational animal' would not be a suitable definition of man. The success of Aristotle's definition is therefore contingent, being dependent on our limited perspective on this created world. In the little canton of the universe opened up to our view (and, as we should also say nowadays, in this particular period of evolutionary times), it happens that, as a general rule, the rational animal category and the biological category 'homo' coincide. But in the infinite spaces, it is unlikely that God gave himself up to only one reasonable creature (cf. II, i, 3 and IV, iii, 23), that there are no other beings with other constitutions capable of language and knowledge.

All this is quite well known, and it would not be necessary to insist on this strong relativistic dimension of Lockean anthropology, if only the instability of the definition of man was not threatening the very project of Locke's enquiry into human understanding and the universality of its results. Nothing forbids that men, considered as belonging to a nominal kind, have radically diverse constitutions, and whatever Locke says on the 'human understanding' could be contested on this very ground. In principle, other 'men' may have other types of cognitive access to the world and therefore other faculties. Locke, a consistent nominalist, often concedes that point. Some men may have innate ideas (many pretend they have), some may be always thinking (II, i, 10), some may have positive ideas of the infinite (II, xvii, 21) or a direct communication with God (IV, xix), etc. Locke is keen on considering these possible cases of radical human diversity, although this is clearly part of a rhetorical strategy, that allows him to offer for consideration his own private and modest experience, his own 'dull soul' (II, i, 10; 108), in a non-dogmatic way. This is nominalism in practice: whatever could be said about the kind comes from our experience of the individuals. The enquiry on human understanding has to be, for methodological reasons, carried out in first-person perspective. What is discovered, therefore, concerns not primarily *man* as a species but rather this particular man, John Locke – an author claiming to have written only for his own instruction and that of his close friends (*Essay*, Epistle to the Reader; 7).

As a result, the universalization of Locke's discoveries about the nature and genesis of ideas and the extension of their validity to the whole humankind is, as Locke himself concedes, a matter of conjecture. In other words, the implicit postulate governing the communicability of the discoveries made in first-person inquiry is *the presumption of a common constitution of human understandings* and the possibility of building this unity from the consideration of one's own mind. Locke's readers should have the same simple ideas and the same acquisitive faculties as Locke himself, otherwise they won't be able to understand the reflexive paths described in the *Essay*. Without this sameness of constitution, not only philosophical communication but language and communication in general would be impossible.

Of his belief in the presumptive unity of the humankind, Locke gives many clues. Thus, while the *Essay* leaves open the possibility that human beings may have entirely different simple ideas about the same things, the fact of successful human communication makes this hypothesis highly unlikely: 'if it should happen that any two thinking Men should really have different *Ideas*, I do not see how they could discourse or argue with another' (II, xiii, 27). Another clue lies in Locke's anti-innatist use of 'ethnographic' arguments, based on the observation of cultural diversity: if the fact that some peoples are entirely devoid of moral principles or of any idea of divinity argues against the innate nature of principles,[18] it can only be because human diversity, however great, does not coincide with a diversity of mental constitutions. What is true for those uncultured and barbaric peoples must in a sense also be true for us. A third important sign can be found in the chapter on enthusiasm (IV, xix). There, Locke condemns the kind of religious particularism that consists in arrogating to oneself or attributing to certain men a supra-rational mode of knowledge or communication with God. This would make them constitutionally different from the rest of the humankind. Here again the argument rests on the presupposition of a constitutive unity of the human species that shares reason but not any sort of supra-rational knowledge.

In short, if Locke refuses to define *man* by stating the distinctive features of a class of individuals, it is clear that his *Essay* does indeed appeal to *men*, or *humankind*, understood as the category open to all those who are likely to recognize themselves in the results of his reflexive enterprise, to discover themselves as similarly constituted rational thinking beings. If there is to be a unity of the humankind, it is the condition of the rational creature described in the *Essay* that shall give it: the beings who participate in this unity should be endowed with more or less the same set of simple ideas, the same limited faculties of knowledge, the same five senses, the same embodied rationality and the same limitations. This unity, however, can only remain a presumptive one: not only because we do not know from what internal constitution this set of attributes and faculties derives – and whether all those whom we presume to be men on some apparent signs are endowed with it (some men are almost like beasts, others close to the higher intelligences) – but also because the ideas that men have of themselves, the ideas of their own *humanity*, are often different.

This reflexive aspect of the definitional issue is very important to Locke and its consideration may help disentangle the seemingly conflicting accounts of man that we get from the moral and from the epistemic perspectives. Although the difference of opinions that men have about themselves, about what makes them human, cannot be arbitrated in epistemic terms, it may be evaluated in moral ones. This may be seen particularly clearly in an important exchange of letters between Locke and Damaris Cudworth, written in 1682. Asked to give an assessment of Cambridge Platonist John Smith's fourfold division of 'men',[19] Locke suggested to Damaris that the right way of distinguishing men should not be based on what Smith supposed to be a constitutional difference of men's faculties and virtues. What makes human beings different, what allows to classify them in types, is only the opinion they have of their own 'humanity', of what it takes to be a 'human being':

> Therefor I cannot quit my former[20] division of men – who either thinke as if they were only body and minde, not soule and spirit at all, or those who in some cases at least think of them selves as all soule separate from the commerce of the body and in those instances have only visions or more properly imaginations, and a third sort who considering them selves as made up of body and soule here and in a state of mediocrity make use and follow their reason until you tell me what sort of persons those are who are not included in any part of it.[21]

This threefold division is of course reminiscent of Locke's three definitions of man presented in II, xxvii 29. But here Locke makes it quite clear that the two first options, the Platonic/enthusiast and the materialist/Epicurian, are, if not epistemically, at least morally inadequate. Both could be considered as expressing a condemnable disregard for the rational norm, symmetrical in character, as one exceeds the right measure of rational thought (considering it useless) and the other comes short of it (considering it inexistent). A passage from the draft of a later letter even better exhibits this dual criticism:

> Enthusiasme is a fault in the minde opposite to bruitish sensuality as far as in the other extreme exceeding the just measures of reason as thoughts groveling only in matter and things of sense come short of it.[22]

Thus, the understanding that each individual has of himself or herself as human, the idea everyone has of their own humanity, is morally constrained by how each one is ready to answer the divine command of rationality. Human beings are (probably) animals endowed with reason, but what really counts for assessing their humanity is how they are ready to use reason and acknowledge its virtue. Some men do not make much of their faculties (as Locke insists in the *Conduct of the Understanding*);[23] some act as if they were pure beasts, reduced to base instincts, and some on the contrary consider themselves as pure intelligences, angels, capable of entering in direct communication with God, without the help of sense and reason – an attitude that Locke is sternly denouncing as enthusiasm.[24] What makes an individual being *human* in a moral sense is his or her aptitude to answer the injunction to be rational, and responsible, without forgetting his or her corporeal condition. This is how, I think, the 'unmovable and unchangeable' idea of the 'moral man', this *corporeal, finite and rational creature, subjected to the law of reason*, re-enters the picture of Lockean epistemology, ensuring the presumptive unity of humankind that Locke's epistemology needs but cannot guarantee.

Notes

1. References to Locke's *Essay Concerning Human Understanding* (henceforth, *Essay*) are given through the triplet 'book, chapter, paragraph', followed with the page number in the Nidditch edition: Locke ([1689] 1975).
2. For the sake of historical accuracy and because of the implicitly quotational nature of this passage and others, I will occasionally use the forms 'man'/'mankind' instead of 'human being'/'humankind', tacitly including women, as Locke would have intended.
3. See *Essay* (III, vi, 4; 440): ''Tis necessary for me to be as I am; GOD and Nature has made me so: But there is nothing I have, is essential to me. An Accident, or Disease may very much alter my Colour or Shape; a Fever or Fall may take away my Reason or Memory, or both; and an apoplexy leave neither Sense, nor Understanding, no, nor Life. Other Creatures of my Shape may be made with more and better, or fewer and worse Faculties than I have: and others may have Reason and Sense, in a shape and body very different from mine.'
4. Locke ([1689] 1993, §6, 117). This statement flies in the face of Locke's supposed advocacy of slavery. As do the numerous passages of the first and second *Treatise on Civil Government* where Locke argues against natural or inherited inequality between men. The thorny issue of Locke's involvement with slave policies has been the matter of vivid debates for more than fifty years. For a contextualized account of Locke's part in the administration of slave-owning colonies, and his effort to reform it in the later decade of his life, see Brewer (2017).
5. *Essay* (III, xi, 16; 516): 'I am bold to think that *Morality is capable of Demonstration*, as well as Mathematicks: since the precise real Essence of the Things moral Words stand for may be perfectly known, and so the Congruity and Incongruity of the Things themselves be certainly discovered; in which consists perfect Knowledge.'
6. For another 'normative' definition of humankind, grounded on the sense of humanity rather than moral law, see the chapter by Jacqueline Taylor on Hume in the present volume.
7. Here I take side with Lolordo (2010) against Winkler (1991).
8. Another interpretive issue concerning Locke's *moral man* is whether the term may be intended as a synonymous for *person* – that is a rational being, subject to law, and for that reason accountable for his or her deeds. In II, xxvii, 25, Locke considers that 'person' is a term that only belongs to 'intelligent agents, capable of a law, and happiness, and misery'. It seems clear thus that all moral men are persons, although it may be disputed whether all persons are moral men, depending on whether corporeality (a necessary feature of moral men) is required or not for being subject to the divine law.
9. This point has been persuasively made, from a slightly different perspective, in Forde (2011).
10. For a larger view of the question of man in Locke, and how its concept relates to those of self, person, agent and spirits, see Yolton (2001) and Yolton (2004). In his important book on the 'Early Modern Subject', Udo Thiel (2011, 108–9) suggests a distinction between the human subject (the particular substance that we call *man*) and the various abstract ideas under which we may consider it, ideas such as 'spirit or soul, man and person(ality)'.
11. Cf. *Essay*, III, vi, 3; 440: '[H]ad we such a Knowledge of that Constitution of *Man*, from which his Faculties of Moving, Sensation, and Reasoning, and other Powers

flow, and on which his so regular shape depends, as it is possible angels have, and it is certain his Maker has, we should have a quite other *Idea* of his *Essence* than what now is contained in our definition of that species, be it what it will.'

12 See Hamou (2008) and Hamou (2018).
13 This passage should also be considered as a piece of evidence in the debate over Locke's attitude towards slavery (see supra note 4). At the very least, it shows that Locke was alive to the issue of racialist prejudices, and keen on denouncing them.
14 Locke indicates that shape is singled out when it comes to recognizing the belonging of an individual to a species occurring by generation, such as the human species, whereas with regard to bodies that are not produced by seeds (e.g. metals or minerals) it is rather colour that is most strongly indicative of species membership. In support of this, he points to our remarkable ability to recognize almost immediately on painting the type of animal substance represented by a simple outline or the type of stuff represented by a mere spot of colour (III, vi, 29; 456–7).
15 On this opposition, see Ayers (1981).
16 By contrast, possession of accidental attributes is contingent: it cannot be inferred from knowledge of the essence. 'Accident' is thus a predicable of a different kind, encompassing the non-essential attributes of a substance, whether separable (the coldness of water) or inseparable (the darkness of the crow).
17 This is implicit in III, x, 17; 500: 'Thus, when we say that *Animal rationale* is, and *Animal implume bipes latis unguibus* is not a good definition of a man; it is plain we suppose the name *Man* in this case to stand for the real essence of a species, and would signify that a *rational Animal* better described that real Essence than a two-leg'd Animal with broad Nails, and without Feathers. For else, why might not *Plato* as properly make the word ἄνθρωπος, or man, stand for his complex *Idea*, made up of the *Idea* of a Body, distinguished from others by a certain shape and other outward appearances, as *Aristotle* make the complex *Idea* to which he gave the name ἄνθρωπος, or man, of Body and the faculty of reasoning join'd together; unless the name ἄνθρωπος, or *Man*, were supposed to stand for something else, than what it signifies; and to be put in the place of some other thing than the *Idea* a Man professes he would express by it ?'
18 See for instance *Essay*, I, ii, 9.
19 Locke and Damaris are commenting the first of Smith's *Selected Discourse*, 'On the true way or method of attaining divine knowledge'. There Smith proposed to distinguish four hierarchical degrees of knowledge: the senses combined with reason; reason associated with innate notions; reason disembodied in its act of reflection on itself; finally 'divine love'. To these four types of knowledge were to correspond four types of individuals, virtue being presented as the means or the way which allows men to rise towards the supreme type of knowledge and being (the 'anthropos theoreticos'), by gradually transcending all the terrestrial passions. See Smith ([1660] 1901, 96).
20 Locke had probably (in a lost letter) already explained to Damaris this tripartite division.
21 Circa 21 February 1682, in Locke (2002, 87). For an assessment of this exchange between Locke and Damaris, see Hamou (2008).
22 Locke (1976–1989, vol. II, 500, Letter 696, note b).
23 See for example *Conduct*, §71 ('Presumption') in Locke (2000, 224): 'This man presumes upon his parts that they will not faile him at time of need and soe thinks it superfluous labour to make any provision beforehand. His understanding is to him

like Fortunatus's purse which is always to furnish him without ever puteing any thing into it before hand. And soe he sits still satisfied, without endeavouring to store his understanding with knowledg. 'Tis the Spontaneous product of the country and what need of labour in tillage?'

24 In IV, xix, 3, Locke equates *enthusiasm* with a sinful disregard for reason: enthusiasm, '[w]hich, laying by reason, would set up revelation without it. Whereby in effect it takes away both reason and revelation, and substitutes in the room of them the ungrounded fancies of a man's own brain, and assumes them for a foundation both of opinion and conduct' (IV, xix, 3; 698).

References

Ayers, M. R. (1981), 'Locke versus Aristotle on Natural Kinds', *Journal of Philosophy*, 78 (5): 247–72.

Brewer, H. (2017), 'Slavery, Sovereignty, and "Inheritable Blood": Reconsidering John Locke and the Origins of American Slavery', *The American Historical Review*, 122 (4): 1038–78.

Forde, S. (2011), '"Mixed Modes" in John Locke's Moral and Political Philosophy', *The Review of Politics*, 73 (4): 581–608.

Hamou, P. (2008), 'Enthousiasme et nature humaine, à propos d'une lettre de Locke à Damaris Cudworth', *Revue de Métaphysique et de Morale*, 59 (3): 337–50.

Hamou, P. (2018), 'Locke and Descartes on Selves and Thinking Substances', in P. Hamou & M. Pécharman (eds), *Locke and Cartesian Philosophy*, Oxford: Oxford University Press, 120–43.

Locke, J. ([1689] 1975), *An Essay Concerning Human Understanding*, ed. P. H. Nidditch, Oxford: Clarendon Press.

Locke, J. ([1689] 1993), *Two Treatises of Government*, ed. M. Goldie, 3rd ed., London: Everyman.

Locke, J. (1976–1989), *The Correspondence of John Locke*, ed. E. S. de Beer, 8 vol., Oxford: Clarendon Press.

Locke, J. (2000), *Of the Conduct of the Understanding*, in P. Schuurman, Dissertation, University of Keele (text online at https://repub.eur.nl/pub/11839/)

Locke, J. (2002), *Selected Correspondence*, ed. M. Goldie, Oxford: Oxford University Press.

Lolordo, A. (2010), 'Person, Substance, Mode and "the Moral Man" in Locke's Philosophy', *Canadian Journal of Philosophy*, 40 (4): 643–67.

Smith, J. ([1660] 1901), 'Select Discourses', in E. T. Campagnac (ed.), *The Cambridge Platonists*, Oxford: Clarendon Press, 77–210.

Thiel, U. (2011), *The Early Modern Subject*, Oxford: Oxford University Press.

Winkler, K. (1991), 'Locke on Personal Identity', *Journal of the History of Philosophy*, 29 (2): 201–26.

Yolton, J. (2001), 'Locke's Man', *Journal of the History of Ideas*, 62 (4): 665–83.

Yolton, J. (2004), *The Two Intellectual Worlds of John Locke*, Ithaca, NY: Cornell University Press.

2

Human nature in Montesquieu

Céline Spector

For many Enlightenment philosophers, Newton inspired the method of establishing the laws of human nature.[1] At the time when Montesquieu was writing *L'Esprit des Lois* (The Spirit of the Laws, 1748), 'anthropology' was defined as such a study and embraced both anatomy and psychology.[2] It included the study of mind and culture, as well as of bodily form and structure. Under the influence of the empiricist method introduced by Locke and Condillac, metaphysical dualism had been replaced by an inquiry into the interactions between body and mind. Simultaneously, philosophy came to terms with humankind's particular place within the animal realm and raised the issue of the varieties of human. It was aiming for a general theory of human nature that would embrace the history of civilization. In France, these issues would merge at the end of the century, with the founding of the *Société des Observateurs de l'homme* and under the impulse of the *Idéologues*.[3]

As a speculation on mankind's nature and development, anthropology was first conceived in the Enlightenment: 'no age of European intellectual history was more fascinated by ideas of human nature – by its biological and moral dimensions, and its physical and spiritual attributes.'[4] Yet surprisingly enough, Montesquieu, unlike Buffon or Rousseau, is never mentioned among the founders of this new science. Despite being considered the father of sociology by Auguste Comte and Émile Durkheim, Montesquieu is not cited as one of the pioneers of cultural or social anthropology.[5] When Jean-Baptiste-René Robinet mentioned his predecessors, he cited Buffon's *Histoire Naturelle de l'Homme* (Natural History of Man), Charles Bonnet's *Essai de psychologie* (Essay of Psychology), Condillac's *Traité des sensations* (Treatise on Sensations), Helvetius' *De l'homme* (Treatise on Man) and even the Marquis de Gorini Corio's *Anthropologie*, but not *The Spirit of the Laws*:

> Anthropology is properly that important branch of philosophical science which makes us know Man in his different physical and moral relationships. It teaches us the origin of man, the various states through which he passes, his qualities or affections, his faculties or actions, in order to deduce the knowledge of his nature, his relations, his destination and the rules to which it must comply in order to respond appropriately. Anthropology is thus related to all the sciences; it borrows

from them or provides their principles, and provides all the consequences for man's utility, that is to say for his conservation, his perfection and his happiness.⁶

Montesquieu's attempt to introduce the experimental method of reasoning into human affairs must therefore be analysed from scratch: attending to historical evidence, he traces his observational experiments back to general principles by explaining political effects through physical and moral causes. Adopting the Newtonian method and relating phenomena to principles, *The Spirit of the Laws* uses the comparative method to obtain social knowledge. Before the Scottish Enlightenment, also inspired by Hume,⁷ Montesquieu is thus a landmark in the history of social sciences. Social institutions (government, law, family, religion, culture) are to be explained by natural and social causes. Historical cases exemplify the more generic references to national character. More often than not, the role of historical figures can be minimized, considering the general pattern of social institutions. In this respect, the use of history and ethnography are key. Travellers' accounts are crucial to the understanding of mankind in all its diversity.

This contribution will examine how to interpret Montesquieu's ambition of inventing a new political science able to match the success of the natural sciences.⁸ I will distinguish between his general understanding of mankind and his contribution to this new scientific discipline, with its particular objet and its own method of inquiry. First, I will summarize Montesquieu's theory of human nature, in response to Hobbes; second, I will show how *The Spirit of the Laws* shifts from the individual to society and culture. Montesquieu's focus is on *collective* sensibility. His study of our common ways of thinking, feeling and acting presents a new political science, stressing the importance of the 'general spirit' (*esprit général*). Before Cabanis, De Gérando and Destutt de Tracy, Montesquieu is thus deeply interested in ethnography and in the different *varieties* – not *races* – of human. Decrying colonialism and slavery, he is of much more than antiquarian interest to the history of anthropology; his assumptions illustrate how difficult it is to separate the descriptive and normative aspects of the science of man.

I. Human nature

In the Preface to *The Spirit of the Laws,* Montesquieu defines mankind by its plasticity: 'Man, that flexible being who adapts himself in society to the thoughts and impressions of others, is equally capable of knowing his own nature when it is shown to him, and of losing even the feeling of it when it is concealed from him.'⁹ What, then, is this hidden 'nature' that *The Spirit of the Laws* claims to bring to self-awareness? Book I answers this question by considering the human being within the realm of natural law. Mankind stands between the physical world and the moral world. While bodies are governed by the necessary laws of motion, intelligences are governed by invariable laws of justice. According to Montesquieu, 'the intelligent world also has laws that are invariable by their nature'.¹⁰

In this disputed section of the work, Montesquieu engages with ancient and modern natural law theorists. His *Traité des Devoirs* (Treatise on Duties), which dates from 1725, was inspired by Pufendorf's *De Officio Hominis et Civis Juxta Legem Naturalem* (On the Duty of Men and Citizens according to Natural Law), first published in 1673. According to Cecil Courtney, Montesquieu had then become 'an unequivoqual supporter of natural law, both in its early form as elaborated by the Stoics and by Cicero, as well as in its more modern form as presented by Grotius, Pufendorf and Barbeyrac'.[11] Yet the picture is more complex. In Book I of *The Spirit of the Laws,* Montesquieu provides a definition of laws in general. This definition was to come as a shock to his ecclesiastic readers, who accused its author of following Spinoza and endorsing determinism:

> Laws, taken in the broadest meaning, are the necessary relations deriving from the nature of things; and in this sense, all beings have their laws: the divinity has its laws, the intelligences superior to man have their laws, the beasts have their laws, man has his laws.[12]

Montesquieu thus contends that men have their own laws. As *embodied minds*, they have passions and prejudices, and they can even ignore their own nature. As bodies, they follow the same rules as any material body, yet as minds, they also follow another kind of rule, namely moral relations of equity or fairness whose truth is analogous to mathematical truths. For instance, men are supposed to be grateful when they receive something useful, they deserve harm when they have done harm, etc. Moral psychology is grounded on reciprocity.

But the key issue here is that humankind, at once intelligent and sensitive, does not consistently follow these moral rules. Intelligent creatures do not follow their laws as consistently as bodies follow their own laws. Montesquieu debunks Hobbes as well as Spinoza. Chapter 1 of Book I offers proof: mankind's place lies in the middle of the universe, between God and the material world, between intelligent beings and purely sentient beings (beasts). This framework accounts for the deeply ambiguous condition of mankind. Montesquieu isolates the 'moral' or cultural world, which has to deal with human freedom: 'The intelligent world is far from being as well governed as the physical world.'[13] Mankind is inherently unstable: particular intelligent beings are of a finite nature, and consequently liable to error, and their nature requires them to be free agents. Hence they do not steadily conform to their primitive laws. In order for man to follow his laws, someone must 'remind' him of these moral duties. This is the role of the lawgiver.

However, Montesquieu introduces an additional prerequisite: that of the state of nature. While the state of nature may not have existed historically, it exhibits human nature in its essential form. Laws of nature are rooted in 'the constitution of our being', and to know them well, one must consider the situation of the individual 'before the establishment of societies. The laws he would receive in such a state will be the laws of nature'.[14] The basic laws of human nature can be deduced from the definition of what we were before civil society was instituted.

Montesquieu's main target is Hobbes. What Hobbes allegedly 'observed' could not be the original, primitive, 'savage'. Men are not naturally eager for war: Hobbes gives men first the desire to subjugate one another, but this is not reasonable. The idea of empire and domination is so complex and depends on so many other ideas, that it would not be the one they would first have. Hobbes asks, '*if men are not naturally in a state of war, why do they always carry arms and why do they have keys to lock their doors?* But one feels that what can happen to men only after the establishment of societies, which induced them to find motives for attacking each other and for defending themselves, is attributed to them before that establishment'.[15]

Before Rousseau, Montesquieu sees humanity as naturally peaceful until civilization comes along. Hobbes was wrong to believe that what is valid in the civil state is already true in the state of nature. Man, in the state of nature, would not be moved by a desire for power. In the beginning, he would not be sufficiently knowledgeable to even imagine establishing his own dominion. Instead, he would be acutely sensitive to his own weakness, timid, and instinctively inclined to keep peace and seek means of subsistence. Montesquieu even thinks that natural men would be sociable, drawn to their own kind by an awareness of reciprocal fear and also by 'the pleasure that an animal feels at the approach of an animal of its own kind'. Consequently, the third law of nature is related to the 'natural appeal' that human beings have for one another. The fourth law – the desire to live in society – is rooted in the knowledge attained in the course of human interactions, which constitutes a further social bond.

Nevertheless, Montesquieu does not deny that the human condition does at some point degenerate into a state of war. He also objects to Pufendorf, who had previously rejected the Hobbesian picture of the state of nature as a state of war. In *De jure naturae et gentium* (On the Law of Nature and of Nations), man seeks peace because his reason enables him to follow his duties and obligations.[16] This is precisely what Montesquieu challenges, while rejecting the command theory of law which predominated at the time. Certainly, man in the state of nature seeks peace, not war. But this drive is neither a rational imperative nor a moral obligation; it is a mere desire for preservation which leads to peace in a situation of individual vulnerability. At the same time, natural law is shared by men and animals. As we learn from a passage from the manuscript that was not finally incorporated in the printed version of the book, the laws of nature apply to both humans and animals.[17] Before Rousseau's *Discours sur les origines et le fondement de l'inégalité parmi les hommes* (Discourse on the Origin and the Foundation of Inequality among Men), *The Spirit of the Laws* classifies the wild savage as a mere animal, beneath good and evil, unable to understand natural law. Natural man cannot grasp the relations of equity which concern purely rational creatures; he can only be ruled by the laws of nature which derive from his sentient being. The laws discovered in the state of nature – the desire for peace, for nourishment, for sexual and social partners – are first born out of his desire for preservation, prior to the development of reason.

Natural laws are desires, instincts or needs, rather than rational standards. They are descriptive rather than normative laws and describe a natural tendency rather than a duty or an obligation. Just as in Hobbes, the state of nature is an ethical vacuum. Yet if pre-social man is governed by instinct, the development of reason is a turning point in human history: men become aware of natural laws and realize what they owe to each other.[18] In civil society, natural laws will still be felt: *défense naturelle* (self-preservation) and *pudeur naturelle* (natural modesty) are universal standards: 'Who can fail to see that natural defense is of a higher order than all precepts?'[19] 'The laws of modesty are a part of natural right and should be *felt* by all the nations in the world.'[20]

However, Montesquieu introduces a historical evolution within the state of nature itself. Men depart from their animality as soon as they acquire more complex ideas. They educate their sensibility. Thanks to sexual attraction, socialization is refined; sensitivity to pleasure is cultivated. While Montesquieu does not use the concept of 'perfectibility' that Rousseau would later invent, he argues that originally, man only possesses a faculty for knowledge without any innate ideas or any moral dispositions. Only the simple notions of subsistence are within his reach before an educational process leads to the acquisition of more complex and abstract ideas. Human nature is understood as a capacity to change: in the state of nature, man is certainly provided with laws that 'derive uniquely from the constitution of [his] being',[21] but his first feelings are modified as soon as he acquires more subtle ideas. The development of his passions follows that of his ideas. Mankind does not really keep its natural 'constitution': its desires multiply depending on the nature of societies and political systems.

On this account, human nature is doomed to change according to its natural and social environment. Book I of the *Spirit of the Laws* depicts such a social dynamic: entering into society, for mankind, means acquiring new beliefs and new social passions. In the state of nature, the feeling of weakness associated with individuals' reciprocal fear causes flight rather than fight (equal weaknesses repel each other) and then union (they attract each other). But from this union between weak individuals arises a feeling of *strength* which in turn provokes disunity and even a state of war:

> As soon as men are in society, they lose the feeling of their weakness; the equality, which was between them, ceases, and the state of war begins. Every particular society comes to feel its strength; which produces a state of war from nation to nation. Individuals in every society are beginning to feel their strength; they seek to turn in their favor the principal advantages of this society; what makes between them a state of war.[22]

The institution of the state is a remedy for this unfortunate condition and stems from the union of the individuals' 'forces' and 'wills'. What occurs then is a transformation of their former desires: natural desires become social passions differentiated according to societies and political regimes.

II. The principles of political science

Yet Montesquieu offers two competing theories: on the one hand, his political science is focused on 'principles' (virtue, honour and fear), namely the dominant political passions specific to each distinctive form of government; on the other, his culturalistic approach attempts to explain the social diversity of peoples. Mankind is influenced by various causes: by climate, religion, laws, the maxims of government, precedents, morals and customs.[23]

First, Montesquieu outlines a theory of the dominant passions of men. These 'principles' (*principes*) are 'springs' (*ressorts*) that move men within each political regime: 'the force of the principle pulls everything along'.[24] *Greed* and *ambition* appear with society itself. These passions aim at power, prestige and riches:

> As soon as men are in society, they lose their feeling of weakness; the equality that was among them ceases, and the state of war begins. Each particular society comes to feel its strength, producing a state of war among nations. The individuals within each society begin to feel their strength; they seek to turn in their favour the principal advantages of this society, which brings about a state of war among them.[25]

But just like any other kind of force, pending on how they are steered, greed and ambition can lead to different results: when they are reoriented from the private to the public, they give rise to political *virtue*; when expressed as a desire for recognition and regulated by a precise social code, they give rise to *honour*; when inhibited, they give rise to *fear*.

Self-sacrifice and moral strength are required for democratic citizenship. In Sparta, and even in Athens or Republican Rome, civic virtue is considered as a *force*: 'The political men of Greece who lived under popular government recognised no other force to sustain it than virtue. Those of today speak to us only of manufacturing, commerce, finance, wealth and even luxury.'[26] In decadent Rome already, the people 'lost the strength of liberty and fell in the weakness of license'.[27] Yet this vocabulary of force also applies to honour. Montesquieu uses a Newtonian metaphor to depict the relationship between conflicting ambitions: 'You could say that it is like the system of the universe, where there is a force constantly repelling all bodies from the center and a force of gravitation attracting them to it.'[28] In monarchies, individuals are thus mobilized for the benefit of the state: 'And is it not impressive that one can oblige men to do all the difficult actions *and which require force,* with no other reward other than the renown of these actions ?'[29] Finally, despotism can only be maintained if it inhibits all available moral forces.[30] Since despotism is ruled by a mechanical law of conservation of motion, human nature is here denied and reduced to animality: in these regimes, the lot of men is instinct, blind obedience and punishment. Despotism is the most unnatural regime: the despots mock human nature (*se jouent de la nature humaine*) and insult it. Montesquieu talks about human nature when he considers despotic cruelty: 'When we read, in the stories, the examples of the atrocious justice of the sultans, we feel with a kind of pain the evils of human nature.'[31] Political liberty depends precisely on feeling that we enjoy security. Judith Shklar thus calls Montesquieu's theory a *liberalism of fear*, 'an effort to avoid oppression rather than directly to promote rights to political action or self-development'.[32]

Human history is best explained as the interplay between the 'principle' and the 'nature' of governments. Consequently, Montesquieu transposes Aristotle's politics into the field of Newtonian physics. The theory of 'principles' is based on a mechanics of forces. In a given regime, the relation between nature and principle is understood as action and reaction: 'This relation between the laws and the principle tightens all the springs of the government, and the principle in turn receives a new force from the laws. Thus, in physical motion, an action is always followed by a reaction.'[33] Correspondingly, moderation is knowledge of the balance of power because the passion for power is a restless desire. The force of ambition is the fuel of political life:

> By a misfortune attached to the human condition, great men who are moderate are rare; and, as it is always easier to *follow one's strength* than to restrain it, perhaps, in the class of superior people, it is easier to find extremely virtuous people than extremely wise men.[34]

Montesquieu's famous expression 'power must check power by the arrangement of things'[35] here finds its true rationale: civil man needs institutional checks. *The Spirit of the Laws* fleshes out the conditions of political liberty within a particular natural, cultural and social context.

III. Fibres and forces: The rise of cultural anthropology

In the third part of the book, the identification of physical and moral causation lies at the heart of Montesquieu's account of human science (book XIV to XXV). Whereas Hume, in his essay *Of National Characters* (1748), argues that he overestimated the climate factor, Montesquieu insists that mankind is embedded in its natural environment. Climate dominates our physical and emotional development; it dictates the degree of freedom and wealth we may enjoy. Yet lawmakers may counter the effect of natural causes; their task is precisely to resist the vices of climate, not to yield to them. Montesquieu stresses that moral causes (laws, customs, religious beliefs) actually contribute more than do physical causes to the general character of a nation. In the end, the 'general spirit' results from the joint influence of geography and religion, economics and politics.[36] In this peculiar kind of determinism, the manners of individuals are determined by physical and moral causes, yet to a different extent in each society: 'Many things govern men: climate, religion, laws, the maxims of the government, examples of past things, mores and manners; a general spirit is formed as a result.'[37] Montesquieu examines the functional connection of different factors to address cultural diversity. This is what stands out as the origin of cultural anthropology.

In the wake of Baglivi, Boerhaave, Glisson or Arbuthnot, Montesquieu first focuses on the *fibre* that composes the human being, whether it be muscular or nervous. The main characteristic of the fibre is its *contractility*: the narrower the fibre, the more strength and 'spring' (*ressort*) it has. In an *Essai sur les Causes qui peuvent affecter les Esprits et les Caractères* (An Essay on the Causes That May Affect Men's Minds and Characters), drafted between 1736 and 1743, Montesquieu follows the greatest physicians of his time (Borelli, Willis, Glisson, Boerhaave and Winslow).[38] The *Essay* shows that all the operations of the human mind derive from the faculty of feeling, which is more or less sensitive depending upon the flexibility of the brain's fibres.[39] Depending on its natural environment, the human machine is devoted to agency (*strength*, vigour, courage) or to passivity (*weakness*, laziness, cowardice). The soul is the nervous centre; it is situated 'in our body, like a spider in its web'. What matters, therefore, is the ease of 'communication' of movements at the heart of the nervous system: 'the sentiment of the mind is almost always a result of all the different movements that are produced in the various organs of our body.'[40] Montesquieu uses this famous metaphor: 'The soul is in our body like a spider in its web.'[41] *The Spirit of the Laws* endorses this controversial view: when the heat of the climate becomes excessive, the laziness of the body becomes dejection of the mind and discouragement of the will, leading to civil and political servitude. While in the North people are ready to fight for their freedom, in the South nations are too lazy to govern themselves:

> The heat of the climate can be so excessive that the body there will be absolutely *without strength*. So, prostration will pass even to the spirit; no curiosity, no noble entreprise, no generous sentiment; inclinations will all be passive there; laziness there will be happiness; most chastisements there will be less difficult to bear than the action of the soul, and servitude will be less intolerable than the *strength* of spirit necessary to guide one's conduct.[42]

Moral and physical strength, prevailing in the North, give rise to courage, confidence, ability to conquer or to defend one's freedom. Conversely, in the torrid regions, the feeling of weakness goes from body to mind: laziness, sexual drive and passive tendencies give rise to political, civil and domestic slavery. In this Newtonian framework, the concept of force is key: on Montesquieu's account, the natural spring of fibres and the moral spring of governments are related.

Finally, before the Scottish Enlightenment (Adam Ferguson, Adam Smith, John Millar), Montesquieu drafted a conjectural history of the human race, from 'savage' and 'barbarian' societies to more 'polished' or 'refined' ones. In Book XVIII of *The Spirit of the Laws*, the particular social, cultural and political features of nomadic societies are identified.[43] The stadial history of mankind gives an account of the passage from communities of hunters or shepherds to agricultural and trading societies; it explains how civil law and government arose.

IV. From Montesquieu to Bonnet

Yet Montesquieu does not give an account of physical anthropology nor of brain physiology. Contrary to Buffon, who published the first volume of his *Histoire naturelle* one year after *The Spirit of the Laws* (1749), he does not address the developmental and degenerative characteristics of human nature. Auguste Comte regretted that Montesquieu did not have the opportunity to become acquainted with the biological physiology of Haller, Jussieu, Linné, Buffon and Vicq d'Azyr.[44] This becomes clear when we compare Montesquieu with Charles Bonnet, who credited Montesquieu with being the 'Newton of the intellectual world'.[45] Frequently mentioned among the founding works of anthropology, Charles Bonnet's *Essai de Psychologie* (Essay on Psychology) further explores the fabric of the brain:

> The seat of the soul is a wonderfully composed little Machine, yet very simple in its composition. This is a very comprehensive compendium of the whole nervous system. We can imagine an admirable instrument of the operations of our soul, under the image of a harpsichord, of an organ, or of a clock ... The soul is the musician who performs different tunes on this machine, or who judges which are performed, and who repeats them. Each fiber is a kind of touch, or hammer intended to give a certain tone.[46]

Bonnet's *Essai analytique sur les facultés de l'âme* (Analytical Essay on the Faculties of the Soul) extends the method of natural history to the individual psychology of men. It is in vain that we seek the nature of things. On the other hand, we must observe the mechanics of our faculties and substitute physics (the study of fibres) for metaphysics.[47] Ignorance of the 'secret' of the union of substances and of their 'real essence' does not hinder any knowledge of man nor any 'science of the mind', according to the experimental method: within the Newtonian framework, ignorance of causes does not prevent the study of effects nor the discovery of psychological laws.[48]

Bonnet thus provides the laws of the mind and body as constant relationships between variable phenomena. Nerve fibres relate the physical and the moral world. The brain is the keystone of the science of man:

> Anatomy reveals that our nerves are one of the main instruments of the Union. This science, now so perfected, shows us that the soul feels and can only feel with the help of the nerves. It proves that the nerves take their origin from the brain, and that beyond that they spread into all the recesses of the body. Discovery of the origin of nerves led to placing the soul in the brain.[49]

Should we conclude that Bonnet completed what Montesquieu had set out to do and that his work contained, so to speak, the neurophysiology underlying *The Spirit of the Laws*? At the end of his book, a chapter titled *Observations on a few Places in the Spirit of the Laws* provides an outline of an answer. After affirming Montesquieu's genius,[50] Bonnet rejected the difference he had introduced between the government of the intelligent world and that of the physical world:

> Every intelligent being has invariable laws: these laws are those of his particular nature. His nature is his ideas, his inclinations, his affections, in a word everything that constitutes his individual character. Its character is its moral or intellectual essence; for it is not the mere ability to know that forms this essence. A being is not intelligent, simply because he has the capacity to be: he is intelligent because he has notions, and he can only act as a consequence of what he knows.
>
> The collection of laws which move particular intelligent beings, therefore, forms the General System of Laws which govern the intelligent world.

> The intelligent world is therefore governed by invariable laws; for he is not intelligent who does not act in a manner consistent with his intellectual essence, or with the ideas he has of things.
>
> The intelligent world is therefore as well governed as the physical world, since particular intelligent beings are as faithful in following the laws of their individual nature as bodies are in following the laws of theirs.[51]

According to Charles Bonnet, Montesquieu was wrong to distinguish the fate of men from that of animals or plants. Everything that belongs to nature follows its laws *in the same way*: men follow the laws of their intelligent nature. It is principally here that he parts ways with Montesquieu, who sticks to a collective psychology because physical and moral causes appear less arbitrary where large numbers are involved.[52]

Montesquieu is thus a key figure in the prehistory of cultural anthropology. His political science relies on an account of the varieties of human. Rousseau was right in placing him among the philosophers who could contribute to the empirical knowledge of mankind.[53] Before the Scots, Montesquieu provides an analysis of both social statics and social dynamics which shifts the focus away from the individual, characteristic of the early modern theory of natural law, giving considerable impetus to the emergence of the human sciences. Yet in *The Spirit of the Laws*, anthropological issues are not addressed as such. They are valid only to the extent that they can constitute useful knowledge for legislators: studying the general spirit of nations reveals the provisions of the laws. The diversity of the 'characters of the mind' and of the 'passions of the heart' provides the bedrock on which statecraft and soul craft can be built. In this respect, Montesquieu's role in the rise of cultural anthropology should be reconsidered.

Notes

1. See Smith (1995), 92. This chapter is a revised version of my previous article Spector (2013). I thank Christophe Litwin for his careful reading of this chapter.
2. See Gusdorf (1974); Moravia (1970); Andrault, Buchenau, Crignon & Rey (2014), chap. 1.
3. Gusdorf (1972), 356; Stocking (1964).
4. Wokler (1995), 32.
5. See Duchet (1995).
6. Robinet (1778), 333, our translation.
7. Berry (2011); Sebastiani (2013), 23–32.
8. Montesquieu (1992), nr. 1940, 581. See Binoche (1998).
9. Montesquieu (1989) (henceforth *SL*), Preface, xliv-xlv.
10. *SL*, I, 1, 4.
11. Cf. Courtney (2001), 48; Shackleton (1961), 253–61; Waddicor (1970).
12. *SL*, I, 1, 3. See *Défense de l'Esprit des lois*, in Montesquieu (2010), 71–5.
13. *SL*, I, 1, 4.
14. *SL*, I, 2, 6.
15. Ibid.
16. Pufendorf (1734), II, I, §9.

17 *Dossier de L'Esprit des lois*, in Montesquieu (1951), 996. See Justinian, *Institutes*, Book I, title 2.
18 See Krause (2003).
19 *SL*, XXVI, 7, 501.
20 *SL*, XV, 12, 255.
21 *SL*, I, 2, 6.
22 *SL*, I, 3, 7.
23 *SL*, XIX, 4. See Aron (1998), chap. 1.
24 *SL*, VIII, 11, 119.
25 *SL*, I, 2, 7.
26 *SL*, III, 3, 22–3.
27 *SL*, VIII, 12, 122.
28 *SL*, III, 7, 27. See Spector (2011), chap. 1.
29 Ibid., 27, my emphasis.
30 *SL*, III, 8–10; IV, 3.
31 *SL*, VIII, 11, II, 4; VII, 9; VIII, 8; VI, 9.
32 Shklar (1987), 89.
33 *SL*, V, 1, 43.
34 *SL*, XXVIII, 41, 595, our emphasis.
35 *SL*, XI, 4, 155.
36 See Spector (2008a).
37 *SL*, XIX, 4, 310.
38 Casabianca (2008); Barrera (2006). Barrera points out, among Montesquieu's most important sources, Boerhaave, Eustache, Vieussens, Senac, Malpighi and Stahl. A collection of excerpts from Montesquieu entitled *Anatomica* is now lost.
39 Richter (1976).
40 *Essai sur les causes*, 240. See Spector (2008b).
41 Ibid., 240.
42 *SL*, XIV, 2, 234, our emphasis.
43 Meek (1976).
44 Comte (1975), 89.
45 'Newton a découvert les lois du monde matériel, vous avez découvert, Monsieur, les lois du monde intellectuel' (Charles Bonnet, letter to Montesquieu, 14 November 1753).
46 Bonnet (1978), 13.
47 Bonnet (1973), XIII.
48 Ibid., XIV, XVI–XVII.
49 Ibid., 18.
50 Ibid., 541.
51 Bonnet (1978), 544–5.
52 *Essai sur les Causes*, 219.
53 Rousseau (1964), 213–14; cf. Rousseau (1969), 836.

References

Andrault, R., Buchenau, S., Crignon, C. & Rey, A. L., eds (2014), *La Refonte de l'homme: médecine et philosophie de la nature humaine en Europe de l'Âge classique aux Lumières*, Paris: Classiques Garnier.

Aron, R. (1998), *Main Currents in Sociological Thought*, London: Routledge.

Barrera, G. (2006), notes from the *Essai sur les causes*, in Montesquieu, *Œuvres et écrits divers* II, P. Rétat (ed.), *Œuvres complètes*, vol. IX, Oxford: Voltaire Foundation, 205–70.

Barrera, G. (2009), *Les Lois du monde. Enquête sur le dessein politique de Montesquieu*, Paris: Gallimard.

Berry, C. J. (2011), 'The Science of Man and Society in the Scottish Enlightenment', *The Kyoto Economic Review*, 80 (1): 2–19.

Binoche, B. (1998), *Introduction à 'De l'esprit des lois' de Montesquieu*, Paris: P.U.F.

Bonnet, C. ([1760] 1973), *Essai analytique sur les facultés de l'âme*, Hildesheim, New York: Georg Olms Verlag.

Bonnet, C. ([1755] 1978), *Essai de psychologie, ou considérations sur les opérations de l'âme, sur l'habitude et sur l'éducation*, Hildesheim, New York: Georg Olms Verlag.

Bourdieu, P. (1982), 'La rhétorique de la scientificité: contribution à une analyse de l'effet Montesquieu', in *Ce que parler veut dire*, Paris: Fayard, 227–39.

Casabianca, D. de (2008), *Montesquieu. De l'étude des sciences à l'esprit des lois*, Paris: Honoré Champion.

Comte, A. (1975), *Cours de philosophie positive*, Paris: Hermann.

Courtney, C. P. (2001), 'Montesquieu and Natural Law', in D. Carrithers, M. Mosher & P. Rahe (eds), *Montesquieu's Science of Politics*, Lanham, Boulder, New York, Oxford: Rowman & Littlefield, 41–67.

Duchet, M. (1995), *Anthropologie et Histoire au siècle des Lumières*, Paris: Albin Michel.

Esquirou de Parieu, P. F. (1870), *Principes de politique*, Paris: Sauton.

Gusdorf, G. (1972), *Dieu, la nature, l'homme au siècle des Lumières*, Paris: Payot.

Gusdorf, G. (1974), *Introduction aux sciences humaines. Essai critique sur leurs origines et leur développement*, Paris: Ophrys.

Karsenti, B. (2002), 'Politique de la science sociale. La lecture durkheimienne de Montesquieu', *Revue Montesquieu*, 6: 33–55.

Krause, S. (2003), 'History and the Human Soul in Montesquieu', *History of Political Thought*, 24 (2): 235–61.

Larrère, C. (1999), *Actualité de Montesquieu*, Paris: Presses de la Fondation nationale des Sciences politiques.

Manent, P. (2000), *The City of Man*, Princeton: Princeton University Press.

Meek, R. L. (1976), *Social Science and the Ignoble Savage*, Cambridge: Cambridge University Press.

Montesquieu, C. L. (1949–1951), *Œuvres complètes*, 2 vol., ed. R. Caillois, Paris: Gallimard.

Montesquieu, C. L. (1989), *The Spirit of the Laws*, trans. A. Cohler, B. C. Miller & H. S. Stone, Cambridge: Cambridge University Press.

Montesquieu, C. L. (1992), *My Thoughts*, trans. H. Clark, Indianapolis: Liberty Fund.

Montesquieu, C. L. (2003), *Œuvres et écrits divers*, I, *Œuvres complètes*, vol. VIII, ed. P. Rétat, Oxford: Voltaire Foundation.

Montesquieu, C. L. (2006), '*Œuvres et écrits divers* II', in P. Rétat (ed.), *Œuvres complètes*, vol. IX, Oxford: Voltaire Foundation.

Montesquieu, C. L. (2010), '*Défense de l'Esprit des lois*', in P. Rétat (ed.), *Œuvres complètes de Montesquieu*, vol. VII, Lyon-Paris: ENS Editions-Classiques Garnier.

Moravia, S. (1970), *La scienza dell'uomo nel Settecento*, Bari: Laterza.

Pufendorf, S. (1734), *Le Droit de la nature et des gens*, trans. J. Barbeyrac, Amsterdam: Pierre de Coup.

Richter, M. (1976), 'An Introduction to Montesquieu's *An Essay on the Causes That May Affect Men's Minds and Characters*', *Political Theory*, 4 (2): 132–8.

Robinet, J. B. (1778), 'Anthropologie, ou traité de l'homme', in *Dictionnaire universel des sciences morale, économique, politique et diplomatique*, vol. V, Londres: Libraires Associés, 333–35.
Rousseau, J. J. (1964), *Discours sur les origines et les fondements de l'inégalité parmi les hommes*, in *Œuvres complètes*, vol. III, Paris: Gallimard.
Rousseau, J. J. (1969), *Émile*, in *Œuvres complètes*, vol. IV, Paris: Gallimard.
Sebastiani, S. (2013), *The Scottish Enlightenment Race, Gender, and the Limits of Progress*, trans. J. Carden, London: Palgrave Macmillan.
Shackleton, R. (1961), *Montesquieu: A Critical Biography*, Oxford: Oxford University Press.
Shklar, J. N. (1987), *Montesquieu*, Oxford: Oxford University Press.
Smith, R. (1995), 'The Language of Human Nature', in C. Fox, R. Porter and R. Wolker (eds), *Inventing Human Science. Eighteenth Century Domains*, Berkeley: University of California Press, 88–111.
Spector, C. (2008a), 'General Spirit', in C. Volpilhac-Auger (ed.), *Dictionnaire Montesquieu*, http://dictionnaire-montesquieu.ens-lyon.fr/fr/article/1376474276/en/, accessed 19 January 2022.
Spector, C. (2008b), 'Soul', in C. Volpilhac-Auger (ed.), *Dictionnaire Montesquieu*, http://dictionnaire-montesquieu.ens-lyon.fr/fr/article/1376473664/en/, accessed 19 January 2022.
Spector, C. (2011), *Montesquieu. Pouvoirs, richesses et sociétés*, Paris: Hermann.
Spector, C. (2013), 'De l'union de l'âme et du corps à l'unité de la sensibilité: l'anthropologie méconnue de *L'Esprit des lois*', *Les Etudes philosophiques*, 106 (3): 383–96.
Spector, C. (2014), 'Civilisation et empire: la dialectique négative de l'Europe au siècle des Lumières', in A. Lilti and C. Spector (eds), *Penser l'Europe au XVIIIe siècle. Commerce, civilisation, empire*, Oxford: Oxford University Press Studies in the Enlightenment, 93–115.
Stocking, G. W. (1964), 'French Anthropology in 1800', *Isis*, 55 (2): 134–50.
Waddicor, M. H. (1970), *Montesquieu and the Philosophy of Natural Law*, La Haye: Martinus Nijhoff.
Wokler, R. (1995), 'Anthropology and Conjectural History in the Enlightenment', in C. Fox, R. Porter & R. Wolker (eds), *Inventing Human Science. Eighteenth Century Domains*, Berkeley: University of California Press, 31–51.

3

The image of the human being in the Comte de Buffon

Catherine Wilson

In his multi-volume *Histoire Naturelle*, George-Louis Leclerc, Comte de Buffon (1707–1788) combined the detached perspective of the observer of the anatomy, moral and physical qualities and customs and habits of human beings with an enthusiastic view of the extent, diversity and magnificence of physical nature. His writings were further embellished by; with anguished moralizing over warfare and oppression and by sharp criticism of religious superstition and the subjection of women. The image of the human being that emerges from these writings is naturalized and desacralized but never debased. The epithet 'crude materialism' cannot by any means be applied to his philosophical stance.

Although Buffon is as significant for philosophy and the history of science as his better-known eighteenth-century contemporaries, he currently has only a small footprint in the Anglophone critical and interpretive literature.[1] There are several reasons for this neglect. First, Buffon was no firebrand, at least most of his contemporaries thought not, and contemporary students of the Enlightenment in large measure concur.[2] Where the books of Hume, Voltaire, Rousseau, Montesquieu, Diderot, Helvétius and Holbach were banned in France and caused displacement and sometimes imprisonment for their authors,[3] Buffon – after a short skirmish with the Sorbonne over the 'Premier Discours' of the first volume of his *Histoire Naturelle* – sailed through difficulties with his *privilège du roi*. Second, Buffon is typically considered a compilator and expositor, admired for his excellent sales record and his elevated and gracious style.[4] Third, thanks to this popularity, there exist many editions and abridgements of the originally thirty-six-volume *Histoire Naturelle*. These were edited and partially reassembled into six, eight and later ten volumes in English, beginning in the late eighteenth century.[5] As many of Buffon's most provocative thoughts are buried in individual articles on the ass, the ox, the sloth, etc., referencing and cross-checking can be a discouraging task for the scholar or student, who may be drawn to a less-troublesome author and corpus.[6]

Adding to the difficulties, as Samuel Butler noted, Buffon's writing is 'twofold, serious and ironical'. His formula – presenting his own unorthodox opinion, raising objections to it and then concluding the orthodox opinion must be correct – needs to be appreciated to understand him.[7] He repeatedly invoked the magnificence of the

Creator. He assured the Sorbonne in his preface to Volume IV of the *Histoire* that he accepted it that the Church was right about everything and that his mechanistic account of the formation of the earth and the planets was to be taken as 'a purely philosophical supposition' (IV: xii), but this retraction was purely pro forma.[8] In his sensational *Époques de la Nature* (Epochs of Nature) of 1778, he shattered Scriptural chronology with his 90,000-year-old earth (privately he thought of its age in the millions) without apologies.[9] He insisted that the presence of a soul elevated humans above all other animals, but, despite his extensive treatment of death, references to immortality appeared only four times – two of them strictly literary – in the entire *Histoire*.[10]

The human being as enquirer and object of enquiry in the *Premier Discours*

In the *Premier Discours* of Volume I (1749), Buffon celebrated the variety to be found in nature, attacked the systems of botanical classification of his contemporaries, praised the observational and compilation efforts of Aristotle and Pliny and questioned whether the notion of truth is really understood and is univocal across the disciplines of mathematics, physics and morality.

The exposition of a science, Buffon states, should begin with the actual situation of the observer, his needs and interests. Here he displays the 'mixture of sensuality and intellectualism' that Jacques Roger finds throughout his work.[11] An adult human suddenly brought to life would awaken first to a sense of self; then to an awareness of light, the heavens, foliage and the transparency of water; and then to the sun, birdsong, harmony, pleasure, colours and perfumes. He would be surprised by his ability to move; the existence of external objects would be indicated by collision with them; he would discover appetite, its satisfaction and sleep, and he would eventually come to the idea of mortality (I: 35). His first scientific interest would pertain to domestic animals, as the most useful and familiar; only later would his curiosity extend to animals, plants and minerals of other climates and of no evident utility (I: 37). This anthropocentric sequence is to be followed for the study of the animal realm.

After commending the study of nature and especially living nature to young people, Buffon observes that the first result that emerges is 'possibly humiliating for the human being; namely that he must place himself in the class of animals whom he resembles in every material way. Further, their instinct may appear to him more reliable than his reason and their industry more admirable than his arts' (I: 12).

In the 'Discours sur la nature des Animaux' (Discourse on the Nature of Animals, 1753) at the start of Volume IV, these points were amplified. The interior of the human and every quadruped is essentially the same; only the envelope is different (IV: 9–10). The heart is in the centre of the 'machine animale', and the other internal organs are present in them as they are in us. The skeletal bones of different animals are only more or less elongated or shortened; the extremities are more or less elevated or sunken; the number of vertebrae varies (IV: 10).

In the non-human animal, as well as in man, sensation arouses intention and action according to its needs (IV: 17–21). 'I ascribe them everything, except thought and reflection' (IV: 41). However, the animal is purely material, a composite of organic molecules of 'matière vivante', which Buffon regarded as primitive and irreducible units of living matter as opposed to dead 'matière brute' (II: 6). Its organization – anatomy and physiology – is sufficient to explain even the most complex behaviour, which follows mechanically from the laws of nature (IV: 101–10).[12]

The anatomical similarity between apes and humans is possibly humiliating. But the psychological difference is equally striking. 'The Creator', Buffon observes in his chapter disarmingly titled *On the Nomenclature of Apes* (1766), 'did not wish to use an entirely different model for the body of the human being from that of the animal ... but at the same time he endowed him with a physical form similar to that of the ape; he infused this animal body with his divine breath' (XIV: 32).

> If we consider only the external form of the orang-utan, we might regard this animal as the highest rank of the ape species or the lowest of the human species, for except as regards the soul, it lacks nothing that we possess ... soul, thought, and speech therefore do not depend on the form or organization of the body. Nothing proves more forcefully that those are gifts bestowed on man alone.
>
> (XIV: 30)[13]

The actions of the ape resemble those of a maniac. He is 'indocile ..., difficult to teach, indifferent to being petted, responsive only to punishment ... possible to capture but impossible to domesticate, always sullen or, petulant'. He is unlike the dog or the elephant who when well treated 'form faithful attachments, willing obedience, good service, and unreserved devotion' to man (XIV: 40–1).

Matter and thought

Accordingly, only humans have souls, in virtue of which they think and reflect (IV: 22). 'The soul of man, in its essence and action, is entirely different from the external and internal senses' (IV: 33). As Buffon tirelessly emphasizes, humans differ from other animals in their psychological complexity and competencies. Although their individual senses may be sharper and more trustworthy than ours and their particular skills remarkable, animals do not invent or perfect anything; 'they never do anything except the same thing in the same manner' (IV: 39). The ability to compare ideas, language, the accumulation and transmission of knowledge and inventiveness and ingenuity are either ours alone or at least developed differently and to a remarkable degree. The special competence of the human being is revealed in their arts – for example the arts of the painter or the musician (IV: 32).

Non-human animals are repeatedly described as automatic machines. But it did not strictly follow from the assumptions of animal automatism and human achievement that the soul must be a simple and therefore indestructible substance. Buffon's own references to the 'spiritual substance' within us, like Locke's 'something within us that thinks' – a spiritual being[14] – are not backed by explicit arguments for the existence of incorporeal substance of the Cartesian or Leibnizian variety.[15]

The question whether matter 'suitably organised' might have the power of thought had been raised explicitly by Locke,[16] and this possibility engaged nearly every eighteenth-century philosopher.[17] Locke's answer to his own question was that organized matter could think, as organized matter could vegetate, but only if that power too was 'superadded' to matter by a divinity. After Newton's success in introducing attraction, and later repulsion, as mathematically demonstrated, invisible powers, such as chemical affinity, electricity, etc., acquired new respect. They could be admitted into science as superadded or just as inherent in matter itself.

In his discussion of the powers of nutrition and reproduction, in the first part of his second volume, entitled the 'Histoire Générale des Animaux' (General History of Animals), Buffon asserts that mere mechanism operating on inanimate matter cannot account for feeling, consciousness of existence or thought and agency. There is more in the animal – and even the plant – body than the mechanism that governs the mineral realm (II: 3). 'It appears … that there exist forces in Nature, like those of gravity, which belong to the interior of matter and which have no relationship to the exterior qualities of bodies, but which agitate in their innermost regions and penetrate them at every point' (II: 17; cf. 486–7). The human power to alter nature by applying external force to the surfaces of bodies, he declares later, bears no comparison to the power of nature to work invisibly from within (XIV: 23–4).

Buffon admits that '[i]t is very difficult to distinguish the effects of the action of that spiritual substance [our souls] from those that are produced by the forces alone of our material being' (IV: 22) and that the actions of the soul depend on 'the state of the material organs'. The defect differentiating an 'imbecile' from another person 'is certainly in the material organs, for the imbecile has a soul like any other'. Moreover, because 'from one person to another, a difference so slight as to be imperceptible is sufficient to destroy thought or prevent its occurrence, we must not be astonished that thought never appears in the ape, which has not the necessary principle' (XIV: 32). In a Letter to Du Tour of 1739, Buffon observes that all researches into the incorporeality of the soul have been obscure and inconclusive and that 'many people agree with you that the soul is material, that thought, like hearing, results from a particular organisation. … One tries in vain,' he adds, 'to comprehend how thought is made. [I]n the same way that the fingertip cannot touch itself, or the eye see itself, thought cannot understand itself (which is in itself a forceful proof of materialism because, in this regard, it is analogous to the nature of body which cannot by itself act upon its neighbours)'.[18]

Animal and human experience

The animal's consciousness of its own existence, Buffon decided, is less clear and extensive than ours. Like us, in our moments of being 'hors de soi', the other animals do not know that they exist, but they feel it (IV: 54). The animal has no idea of time, or past and future, only the interior sentiment that its sensations produce. It has no memory (IV: 54), only a form of 'reminiscence matérielle' (IV: 64), and although it dreams, it cannot distinguish its dreams from reality (IV: 67). In us, the sense of self, as Locke had suggested, is constituted by the feeling of present existence together with the memory of our past, which can affect us as strongly as the present. 'Each conserves in himself a certain number of sensations relative to different existences … their succession forms a train of ideas … which give us the idea of time' (IV: 51). In infancy, old age and imbecility, the faculty of comparing ideas is absent or diminished: Buffon does not offer to explain why the soul becomes incompetent if it is distinct from the body.

The other animals live in the present moment without comparing past, present and future and as unconflicted, unified beings. 'The animal whose nature is simple and purely material experiences neither internal combat, nor opposition, nor vexation; it has no regrets and remorse, neither our hope nor our fears' (IV: 77). The young child is like an animal and is happy, but, beginning in adolescence, the spiritual principle begins to develop, and conflict ensues (IV: 74). The adult human is double – there is a continuous opposition between the spiritual principle and the material animal principle (IV: 70). The first is 'a pure light accompanied by calm and serenity, the beneficial source of knowledge, reason, and wisdom'. The other is a 'false torch … burning in the dark and the tempest, an impetuous torrent which rolls over us and brings passions and errors' (IV: 70).

Most human beings 'live a timid and contentious life and die in misery' (IV: 48). Nevertheless, we are happy in one or the other of two states: in the one in which we give way to tastes and passions without reflection; and in the one in which we pursue tranquil, rational occupations. The wise person is 'master of himself';

> [h]e is always occupied in the exercise of the faculties of his soul; he perfects his understanding, cultivates his intelligence, he acquires new knowledge, and satisfies himself in each instant without regrets, without disgust and enjoys the entire universe in enjoying himself … [H]e joins the pleasures of the body which he has in common with the animals, to those of the mind, which are his alone.
>
> (IV: 47)

The human being has a special sensitivity to pastel colours, sweet sounds, light touches, subtle perfumes and flavours and is pained by loud, violent or exaggerated stimuli (IV: 42). Unlike the other animals, he suffers more psychological than physical pain and pleasure (IV: 44). But even in states of severe physical suffering, the human being is sustained by his reason and the forces of his soul and can even take satisfaction in his consciousness of his endurance of his suffering (IV: 47).

In adulthood, one experiences opposition, setbacks, the effects of chance, discouragement and injustice. Glory from brilliant actions and useful work proves hollow. 'The heart hardened by its scars and blows becomes insensible, and one arrives easily at that state of indifference, and indolent quietude, no longer moved by vain phantoms' (IV: 76). When both animal appetite and intellectual motivation are absent, the lack of affect and loss of the sense of selfhood and agency can produce suicidal depression. The worst condition to be in is inertia: 'the state of the most horrible self-disgust which leaves us with no other desire than that of ceasing to be and permits no actions except to coldly turn our weapons against ourselves' (IV: 73).

The life cycle and reproduction

Buffon regarded the sexual maturation and emotional awakening of the adolescent with a reverence that underwrote his considered view: that inscribed in every organism is the imperative to produce a lineage, to be part of and to continue the 'succession of beings' that constitutes living nature. Up to that point, the young human being simply vegetates, taking in nutrition like, one might suppose, the caterpillar. Criticized by Friedrich Melchior Grimm for his apparent cynicism about love,[19] Buffon was enthusiastic about sex. Adolescence is the 'springtime of life, the season of pleasures' (II: 478). In the supplement to the original chapter, added more than twenty-five years later in 1777, he amplified: 'The wish of nature is not to enclose our existence in ourselves; by the same law with which she submits all beings to death she has consoled them by the faculty of reproduction' (XXXIII: 385). Puberty 'is the moment when all the faculties, bodily as much as intellectual come to their full exercise, in which, the organs having reached their full development, sentiment unfolds like a beautiful flower which will soon produce the precious fruit of rationality' (XXXIII: 384).

The original text was immediately followed by lengthy descriptions of male and female circumcision, infibulation and castration, the inventions of 'dark and fanatical minds that have dictated cruel and terrible laws, where privation is virtue and mutilation is meritorious' (II: 481). Young women especially are the victims of barbaric practices, and the source of these cruelties is a 'jalousie brutale et criminelle' (II: 500). The cult of virginity is irrational, Buffon declares. Virginity is 'a moral entity, a virtue that consists in the purity of heart' (II: 492), mistakenly treated as an anatomical condition tied to false opinions, customs, ceremonies and superstitions. Sexual repression causes disease, and deprivation turns people into animals (II: 503). Monogamous marriage is natural, as is shown by the equal numbers of men and women.[20] Reason, humanity and justice argue against the harem (II: 502).

Having reached the peak of its physical perfection – here Buffon spends a long time discussing the facial features and figure of full grown, attractive persons of both sexes – and the peak of emotional and intellectual intensity, the human organism begins to decline, as does every other living being. Wrinkles, stiffness, white hair, lost teeth and hunched posture are the indications of this downward course (II: 558). The power of generation is lost to all women and only somewhat later to most though not all men. However, women who marry much older men risk bearing disabled children (II: 577). Death is not an interruption, merely the end point of a lengthy process. 'All the causes of deterioration we have just indicated act continually on our material being and lead it little by little to its dissolution; death, that ever so marked, ever so dreaded change of state is thus in Nature nothing but the final nuance of a preceding state' (II: 578).

Old age is not an entirely unpleasant condition, as it brings back sweet memories without the anxieties and sorrows with which they were experienced in youth. And death, Buffon claims, is no more to be feared than sleep, for, as Epicurus and Lucretius had memorably observed, there is nothing it is like to be dead:

> Each night we cease to be, and accordingly we cannot regard life as an uninterrupted suite of sensed existence; life is not a continuous train, but a thread divided by knots or rather by cuts which are similar to death. Why bother oneself about the greater or lesser length of a chain that is cut every day?
>
> (XXXIII: 414)

Conjectural history

The eighteenth-century travel literature brought to attention the variety of human cultures, languages, modes of dress and means of subsistence. A literary tradition of the 'Golden Age' represented life before urbanization and political consolidation as a period of peace and equality, and it was accordingly debated whether the life of the *homme sauvage* was happier and more virtuous than the life of man in civilized societies (*sociétés policées*). The historical origin of ranks and social classes, the fictionality of kingship and aristocracy, or its origins in slaughter and appropriation, and concerns over colonization and enslavement were prominent themes. The Abbe Raynal's *Histoire des Deux Indes* (History of the Two Indies), with its fiery anti-colonial passages written by Diderot, and Herder's outspoken denunciation of European brutality are moral landmarks in this regard.[21]

One of the great reference texts was Rousseau's *Discours sur les origines de l'inégalité* (Discourse on the Origins of Inequality, 1755), itself an embellished retelling of Lucretius's history of humanity in Book V of the *De rerum natura* (Nature of Things). Rousseau described the invention of language by human beings and their conversion from hardscrabble solitary foraging to happy familial sociability, and then the downward arc to hierarchy, oppression and misery, resulting from the discovery of metallurgy and agriculture. Although Rousseau's condemnation of the arts and sciences and civilized society in general were widely condemned as paradoxical and absurd and as expressions of misanthropy by a famously unsociable human being, it had to be admitted in pre-revolutionary France that civilization had not worked to everyone's advantage.

A few years before Rousseau, Buffon came to the defence of the *homme sauvage* in his chapter on the 'Varietés dans l'espèce humaine' of 1749. 'Perhaps', he comments, the observer may 'recognise more gentleness, tranquillity and calm in him than in himself; perhaps he will see clearly that more virtue belongs to the savage than to the civilized man, and that vice arises only within society' (III: 297). However, this remark is strongly qualified. Buffon rejects primitivism and dismisses what he takes to be the motives behind it. 'Throughout history certain austere philosophers, savages by temperament, have reproached social man; enhancing their personal pride through the debasement of the entire species' (III: 297).

Buffon understood the species nature of human beings as inherently social. 'This state of pure nature, wherein we suppose man to be without thought and speech, is', he argues, 'imaginary'. Thought and speech are species-specific characteristics. Humans were never vegetarians. They have always lived in families and small groups (XIV: 36). And in nations without laws and without a master, human society is 'a chaotic collection of independent and barbarous people who heed only their individual passions' in the absence of any 'common interest' (III: 296).

Human varieties are the subject of a long essay in Volume III describing the typical appearance of skin, figure, facial features, hair, beards, cosmetic practices, superstitions and character traits of mainly tribal peoples all over the globe. The details are taken at second hand and, though frequently judgemental – the beauty of women is frequently commented upon, but also the laziness, credulousness, etc., of entire ethnic groups – they are for the most part of little philosophical significance. It is nevertheless worth remarking that Buffon states clearly that there is only one species of human being 'which has multiplied and spread itself over the whole surface of the earth and has been subject to variations on account of the influence of climate, differences in nourishment, manner of life, and epidemic illnesses' (III: 530). Small differences have become magnified through the reproduction of similar individuals and thereby entrenched, so that they persist over many generations, even if environmental conditions change.

Buffon was an enthusiastic believer in social, technological and intellectual progress and in the values of the fully policed society – though not an admirer of aggressive, unstable attempts at colonization, which he roundly condemned (EN, 187–9). A sort of prehistoric yet civilized Golden Age situated in Siberia is sketched in the *Époques de la Nature* of 1788. These early Asians were not only happy and peaceful but also had the leisure to develop the sciences (EN, 174).[22] Their civilization was allegedly destroyed by barbarian invasions leading to thirty centuries of ignorance. Thereafter, civilization was gradually recovered, as India and China reconstructed some of the mathematical and astronomical knowledge left by the extinct savants, and as the Europeans perfected agriculture and architecture, drained swamps, cleared forests and traversed the seas bringing the world to 'the state of perfection and magnificence we see today' (EN, 186). Humanity has substantially modified the climates of the various regions of human habitation; 'every movement, every action produces heat' raising the temperature of densely populated regions (EN, 194–5).

At the same time, Buffon agrees with the civilization critics that evil 'proceeds more from ourselves than from Nature'. In his chapter on the sloth, he reflects that

> for a single person who is unhappy, because he was born feeble or deformed, there are millions rendered miserable by the oppression of their superiors. The animals, in general are happier because the species have nothing to fear from individuals … Moral evil, of which [man] himself is the fountain, has accumulated into an immense ocean, which covers and afflicts the whole surface of the earth.
>
> (XIII: 40)[23]

The urge and ability of the stronger to dominate and exploit the weaker are evident not only in the practices of sexual mutilation and restriction but in political, religious and domestic institutions and practices.

The worst use of the greater physical strength of men versus women, Buffon declares, is the abuse made of that advantage, whereby 'that half of the population, though made to share the pains and pleasures of life, is treated tyrannically' (II: 553). Yet like most of his contemporaries, Buffon regards civilization as improving or potentially improving the condition of women. Women in the 'savage' condition do most of the work of cultivation while men hunt or fish and rest in their hammocks. In 'civilized' societies, men dictate laws to women injurious to them, but in the most advanced and polished societies, where beauty is valued over force, women have obtained 'that equality of condition, so natural and conducive to the sweetness of living' (II: 554).

The enslavement of Africans is briefly discussed in Volume III under the topic of 'Varieties'. Buffon remarks that the enslaved are sensitive, highly resentful of maltreatment and appreciative of kindness. 'They have excellent hearts, the seeds of all the virtues' (III: 469). I cannot write about them, he adds,

> without commenting on their condition, how miserable they are to be reduced to servitude, to be obliged always to work for others without ever being able to accumulate anything! Is it necessary to go beyond this, to beat them, and to treat them like animals? Humanity is repelled by such hateful treatment which the greed for profit has made acceptable and which will perhaps persist forever unless our laws can apply restraint to the brutality of masters and limit the misery of the slaves.
>
> (III: 469)

Enlightenment optimism and Enlightenment pessimism

In an optimistic mood, Buffon described the human being as the 'vassal of Heaven, and king of the Earth'. In the essay *De la Nature: Première Vue* (1764), he praised the power of humanity to beautify the world and to render its resources useful. Mankind 'ennobles it, populates it, and enriches it. He establishes order, subordination, and harmony amongst living beings. He embellishes Nature; he cultivates it, extends and polishes it; he prunes away thistle and bramble to multiply the grape and the rose' (XII: xi).

Humanity turns the insect-infested swamps, terrains covered with rotting fruits, and vine-choked trees, and the wild, thorny desolate regions of a 'hideous and perishing brute Nature' (XII: xiii) into a new, living and pleasing nature. The human being perfects flowers, fruits and grains through selective breeding; multiplies the number of useful animals and reduces the harmful ones; and digs gold and iron from the earth. Rich pastures and fields, roads and communication, and thousands of other 'monuments of power and glory' follow from these efforts (XII: xiv). Yet these achievements are precarious because once effort is suspended nature reclaims her rights, effaces all the works of man, destroys all his constructions and covers them in dust. Barbary and depopulation, the effects of warfare, succeed civilization (XII: xv). Though humans are individually weak, powerful only in co-operation and although they thrive in peace, they have 'an urge to arm themselves for misery and to fight for their ruin':

> Excited by an insatiable greed, blinded by an even more insatiable ambition, [the human being] renounces all sentiments of humanity, turns all his powers against himself, seeks to defend himself, destroys himself anyway, and when the days of blood and carnage have passed, when the smoke of glory has dissipated, he regards with a mournful eye a devastated earth, the arts buried, the nations dispersed, people weakened, his entire happiness ruined and his real power destroyed.
>
> (XII: xv)

Buffon implores God to help humanity to unite, to drop its weapons and to restore the fecundity of the abandoned and sterile scorched earth (XII: xv–xvi).

Purposiveness and the individual

As Philip Sloan remarks: 'To his contemporaries and successors, particularly those in the German tradition, no feature of Buffon's thought was more in need of philosophical repair than his historical pessimism which seemed to be a consequence of his scientific cosmology.'[24] The Lucretian theme of impermanence and futility is marked in Buffon's appeals to the mutability of every aspect of the visible world and the wider cosmos. The universe offers perpetual scenes of creation and destruction: 'Suns … appear and disappear as if they were alternately kindled and extinguished. They can expire and annihilate a world or a system of worlds' (XII: vi).[25] The 'torrent of time carries off and absorbs all individuals' (XIII: iv–v). Enormous animals, now extinct, once roamed in Europe (IX: 126).[26] The entire earth, though now about 93,000 years old (EN 149), will cool down to a block of ice that spells the end of living nature in only an estimated 75,000 years. In this perspective, expressed in 'De la Nature: Deuxième Vue' (On Nature: Second View):

> An individual, of any species whatsoever, is nothing in the Universe. A hundred individuals, a thousand are still nothing. The species are the only true beings in Nature; as perpetual, as old, as permanent as she is; in order to reason properly, we will no longer consider them as a collection or series of similar individuals, but as a whole independent of number, independent of time; an always living whole, always the same; a whole, which counts as a single thing in the works of creation, and which consequently makes only one unit in Nature.
>
> (XIII: i)

Within the lives of individuals, physical and psychological sufferings are inevitable, persecution and oppression ubiquitous, and the downward slide into decrepitude and death subject only to the most minor variation from the pattern. Piled onto natural suffering are the works of man and moral evil.[27] Buffon's gloomiest thoughts occur in his entry on 'The Sloth' whose life he considers miserable. 'Why', he asks, 'should not some animals be created for misery, since, in the human species, the greatest number of individuals are devoted to pain from the moment of their existence?' (XIII: 40).

Conclusions

Once his subterfuges are taken into account, Buffon is properly seen as a figure of radical enlightenment.[28] The self-formation of the earth through the forces of nature; the foreseeable extinction of our species and the annihilation of all of living nature; the disregard for Genesis[29] as well as for the Christian theory of immortality belong to the intellectual history of the desacralization of nature. The purpose of life is not to prepare for death and the next world but simply 'to have lived'. Death is irreversible and could not be the effect of a supernatural punishment meted out on our disobedient but formerly immortal ancestors, as Christian theology teaches. The role of the individual is not to pass spiritual and moral tests, to find the way to heaven or to be elected to the Kingdom of Grace but simply to serve as a link in the series of living beings that constitutes a lineage.

In the *Époques*, Buffon invoked the old trope of fear as the cause of religion, depicting primitive humanity as terrified by the meteorological violence of an earth still in its early stages of geological formation and as helpless against the forces of nature (EN, 164–8). In an attempt to find security and assuage their fears, early people turned to the placation of imaginary malign divinities; remnants of this cowering superstition persist in the form of belief in a universal deluge or conflagration (EN, 167).[30]

The theory of organic and brute molecules as the original and enduring constituents of nature and the suspicion that some not easily detectable feature of their brains might explain the vast difference between the experiences and behaviour of humans and those of other mammals belong to the history of materialism, while Buffon's phenomenalism, the suggestion that matter may be only an appearance, anticipates that of Kant.

From the Abbé de St. Pierre's '*Projet pour rendre la Paix perpétuelle en Europe*' (Project for Perpetual Peace in Europe, 1713) to Voltaire's ridicule and condemnation of kings and their pursuit of glory through bloodshed, in his *Candide* (1759), to the decisively critical stance of the *Encyclopedia* article 'Guerre' (War) by Louis de Jaucourt,[31] warfare was ridiculed and condemned in French social thought. It was understood as an atavism left over from the savage state, unbefitting civilized persons, and at the same time as the inevitable product of pointless aristocratic rivalries and greed. Buffon's contrast between 'individual passions' and the 'common interest'; his revulsion against glory and the greed for gold that inspires the prejudices and rationalizations of slaveholders (III: 470); his evident realization that, as Mary Wollstonecraft so bluntly put it, 'brutal force has hitherto governed the world, and ... the science of politics is in its infancy'[32] belongs among the compelling achievements in moral philosophy of the eighteenth century.

An even greater departure from orthodoxy and conventional philosophy lies in Buffon's presentation of the emergence of erotic sentiment and sexual prowess in adolescence as the high point of human existence and as having cosmological significance. While these themes are related to the general interest in human customs, and the sexual frankness of Rousseau and Diderot, Buffon's presentation does not reflect any of the taste for the prurient in French clandestine literature. The extensive discussion of both women and men as physiological beings whose sole purpose is to generate other living beings upends the background assumption that the purpose of women is to use their bodies to generate, while the purpose of men is to use their strength and their intellect to achieve dominion and contribute to culture. Women, Roger comments, citing a remark of Raynal who did not, tended to like the *Histoire* very much.[33]

In Germany, the theme of human existential significance emerges in connection with the neo-Epicureanism and so-called Spinozism of the eighteenth century.[34] If, as Buffon claimed, the so-called truths of morality are partly real and partly arbitrary and concern in the end 'only conventions and probabilities' (I: 55), if the individual is 'nothing', and if all of nature will come to an end, not by way of the preparation of a new heaven, a new earth and the reign of justice but simply as a further step in the cosmic process of recycling matter, what is the point of obedience to priests and self-denial? As Immanuel Kant asked, what must we believe, do and hope for?

Kant, best considered a representative of 'moderate enlightenment', addressed the questions of extinction, warfare, the transformation of species, living matter, the building forces of nature, and thinking matter directly in his *Critique of Judgement* (1790), and in his anthropological essays, indirectly in his *Critique of Pure Reason* (1781/86). He drew explicitly on Buffon's first volumes in his early lectures on physical geography and in his essay on cosmology, the *Universal Natural History* of 1755. Although direct references to Buffon in his later writings are scarce, the comparison between the two throws into sharp relief Kant's efforts to re-sacralize history, nature and morality without affirming experience-transcendent principles. The individual matters, in Kant's view, and we must – he purports to show – think with, though not assign ontological reality to the transcendental ideas of God, the soul and life after death, the topics of Buffonian intentional ambiguity and obfuscation. Kant was troubled by the apparent clash between the dignity of man, his grave moral obligations, and the hope of progress by future generations, and the animalistic quality of the human mode of generation.[35] Buffon admitted that he could arrive at no reasonable explanation for the need for sexual congress either, but his valuation was clearly different to Kant's.

From a contemporary point of view, Buffon can be considered the originator of the concept of the 'Anthropocene'. In his seventh 'Époque', the world of plants, animals and minerals is dramatically transformed by the human urge to improve upon nature by digging, chopping, draining, exterminating, pruning, heating and breeding. We now regard the social compulsion to exploit all possible natural resources and to improve on nature wherever possible with scepticism and even alarm, but Buffon's conviction, expressed so eloquently in his 'First View of Nature', that humanity is as capable of constructive practices as of the destructive practices to which it is also driven, offers a stable point of departure for critical reflection.

Notes

1. A number of symposia and collections have appeared in French, especially on Buffon's moral, political and psychological thought. See Caponi (2017), Lyon/Sloan (1981) and Jacques Roger's superb biography. *Buffon: A Life in Science* (1997). In French, see esp. Hoquet (2005), Roger (1963) and Gayon (1992) including articles by Blaenkaert and Mengal.
2. Buffon receives no sustained attention in Jonathan Israel's major study of Enlightenment thought, *Radical Enlightenment: Philosophy and the Making of Modernity* (2001). This reflects Buffon's lack of interest in Spinozism, which Israel sees as central to Enlightenment psychology and political thought, and his greater affinity to a hedonistic, finitistic, molecule-based Epicureanism; see Note 25.
3. For details, Darnton (1996).
4. See the *Éloge* of 1788 reported by Grimm (1829), 14: 209–15.
5. The current standard edition, including illustrations and material added after Buffon's death, is George-Louis Leclerc Buffon, *Histoire Naturelle, Generale et particuliere*, 44 vols (1749–1804). References in the text are to this edition by volume and page. The English editions include a six-volume edition, *The Natural History of Animals, Vegetables and Minerals: With the Theory of the Earth in General* (1775–6), trans. W. Kenrick and J. Murdoch, London: T. Bell; the *Natural History, General and Particular, by the Count de Buffon*, 9 vols, trans. by William Smellie (1780–5) and *Barr's Buffon*, 10 vols, London: J. S. Barr (1792–7). References to the *Époques de la nature* (originally Suppléments V, volume XXXIV) from the Swiss 1792 edition are marked as EN.
6. The website *Gallica* of the *Bibliothèque Nationale* has made the first edition available online. *Barr's Buffon* is accessible through eighteenth-century collections online.
7. Butler, S. (1882), chap. 9.
8. See Descartes's description of the imaginary formation of 'another world, a wholly new one', in *Le Monde*, chap. 6, *Œuvres* (1964–74); XI: 31.
9. The *Époques*, according to Jean-Felix Nourrisson in his 1887 *Philosophies de la Nature*, was 'of all the works of the eighteenth century ... the one that elevated people's imaginations to the greatest extent'. Smellie, however, declined to translate the work he considered 'too fanciful for the cool and deliberate Briton' (IX: 258).
10. Buffon referred to the nightingale's immortal love and to immortal prose styles. The Sorbonne had marked his statement in his *Premier Discours* that 'our soul will see in a far different manner after our death and all that that causes our sensations now, matter in general, may no longer exist then, no more than our own bodies which will no longer do anything for us' (IV: x) as objectionable. (The 'true resurrection of the flesh' is essential Christian dogma.) Buffon cheerfully conceded that the theologians must be correct and that we will certainly have bodies that perceive external objects after death (IV: xiv).
11. Roger (1997), Preface, xv.
12. Nevertheless, Buffon had explicitly rejected Cartesianism in vol. II: 50–1 and 61. The properties we must ascribe to matter are not only those of which we have clear and distinct ideas.
13. Buffon notoriously compares the form of the orangutan to that of the Hottentot. On the issue of Buffon on 'racial' difference and the theory of 'degeneration' (which is

for the most part intended neutrally by Buffon as 'variation'), see Hudson (1996), Doron (2012) and Smith (2015).
14 *Essay* IV: vi.6.
15 Buffon cannot be recruited to the cause of 'materialism'. 'Matter', he declares, 'is not a principle but an accessory. It is a foreign covering, united to us in a manner unknown; and its presence is noxious. Thought is the constituent principle of our being and is perhaps totally independent of matter' (II: 2). But see the discussions of Roger (1997), 236 and Thomson (2008), 175–216.
16 Locke (1975), IV.iii.6.
17 Yolton (1984); See also Springborg and Wunderlich (2016).
18 Lettre a M. Du Tour, 6 January 1739, in Bertin/Bourdier (1952), 189.
19 Letter to Diderot 1 October 1753, in Grimm (1829), I: 69.
20 Buffon's libertine private life did not reflect a commitment to sexual fidelity.
21 Diderot ([1783] 1992), 209. See Muthu (2003).
22 Buffon's views on lost civilizations were influenced by the historian of astronomy J. S. Bailly, *Discourse on the Origin of the Sciences and the Peoples of Asia* (1777), *Discourse on Plato's 'Atlantide'* (1779) and *A Treatise on Indian and Oriental Astronomy* (1787) and by Peter Simon Pallas, a traveller who purported to find the ruins of buried cities in Siberia. These views were widely influential according to Perty ([1859] 2010).
23 Buffon, trans. Smellie, *Natural History* (VII: 155).
24 Lyon and Sloan (1981), 132.
25 See Lucretius (2001), II, 1143–50. In time, 'the ramparts that surround the mighty world will be taken by storm and will collapse and crumble into ruins ... all things gradually decay and head for the reef of destruction'.
26 See Stalnaker (2011).
27 See Vyverberg (1958).
28 'How', one critic asked, 'did one of the most brilliant minds of the Christian world come in the eighteenth century to revive the extravagant opinions of the pagan philosophers, who, ignorant of the great creator of heaven and earth, confabulated with empty words to explain the formation of created beings?' Royou (1780), 60.
29 The reported age of the patriarchs interested Buffon, who collected tables of mortality and noted the fixity of the modern human lifespan at a generous 90–100 years.
30 Buffon draws here on Boulanger (1766), who makes this point forcefully, 215–17.
31 *Encyclopédie, ou Dictionnaire raisonné des sciences, des arts, et des métiers*, II: 157. See Delia (2010), 93.
32 Wollstonecraft (1792), 74.
33 Roger (1997), 184.
34 See Brandt (2007); Wilson (2016). The English translator of Hermann Samuel Reimarus's *Vornehmste Wahrheiten der natürlichen Religion* translated and embellished the title as: *The Principal Truths of Natural Religion Defended and Illustrated, in Nine Dissertations; Wherein the Objections of Lucretius, Buffon, Maupertuis, Rousseau, La Mettrie, and Other Ancient and Modern Followers of Epicurus are Considered, and their Doctrines Refuted*. Trans. R. Wynne, London 1766.
35 'The contingency of conception, which in humans as well as in irrational creatures depends on opportunity, but besides this also on nourishment, on government, on its moods and caprices, even on vices, presents a great difficulty for the opinion of the eternal duration of a creature whose life has first begun under circumstances so trivial and so entirely dependent on our liberty' Kant [1781] 1999, A 779/B 807.

References

Bailly, J. S. (1787), *Histoire de l'astronomie indienne et orientale, ouvrage qui peut servir de suite à l'Histoire de l'astronomie ancienne*, Paris: Debure.

Bailly, J. S. (1779), *Lettres sur l'Atlantide de Platon et sur l'ancienne histoire de l'Asie*, Paris: Debure.

Boulanger, N. A. (1766), *L'Antiquité dévoilée par ses usages, ou Examen critique des principales opinions, cérémonies et institutions religieuses et politiques des différens peuples de la terre*, Amsterdam: Rey.

Brandt, R. (2007), *Die Bestimmung des Menschen bei Kant*, Hamburg: Felix Meiner.

Bertin, L. & Bourdier, Fr. et al., eds (1952), *Buffon. 30 Lettres Inédites*, Paris: Museum Nationale d'Histoire Naturelle.

Blanckaert, Cl. (1992), 'La Valeur de l'homme: L'idee de nature humaine chez Buffon', in J. Gayon (ed.), *Buffon 88: Actes du Colloque International Paris-Montbard-Dijon*, Paris: Vrin, 583–600.

Buffon, G. L. L. (1749-1804), *Histoire Naturelle, Générale et particulière*, 44 vols, Paris: Imprimerie Royale.

Buffon, G. L. L. (1775-6), *The Natural History of Animals, Vegetables and Minerals: With the Theory of the Earth in General*, London: Kenrick and Murdoch.

Buffon, G. L. L. (1780), *Natural History, General and Particular, by the Count de Buffon*, 9 vols, trans. W. Smellie, vols 1-8, Edinburgh: W. Creech, vol. 9, London: Strahan and T. Cadell.

Buffon, G. L. L. (1792-7), *Barr's Buffon*, 10 vols, London: J. S. Barr.

Buffon, G. L. L. (1792), *Époques de la nature* (originally Suppléments V, volume XXXIV), Berne: Société Typographique.

Butler, S. (1882), *Evolution, Old and New; or, the Theories of Buffon, Dr. Erasmus Darwin, and Lamarck, as Compared with That of Mr. Charles Darwin*, 2nd ed. London: D. Bogue.

Caponi, G. (2017), 'The Discontinuity between Humans and Animals in Buffon's Natural History', *História, Ciências, Saúde-Manguinhos*, 24 (1): 59–74.

Darnton, R. (1996), *The Forbidden Best-Sellers of Pre-Revolutionary France*, New York: W. W. Norton.

Delia, L. (2010), 'Guerre juste et droit de la guerre dans l'Encyclopédie', *Montesquieu.it*, 2 (1): 93–108.

D'Alembert, J. l. R. and Diderot, D. ([1751–1772] 1986), *Encyclopédie, ou Dictionnaire raisonné des sciences, des arts, et des métiers* (articles choisis), 2 vols, ed. A. Pons, Paris: Flammarion.

Descartes, R. (1964–74), *Œuvres*, 13 vols, ed. Ch. Adam & P. Tannery, Paris: Vrin.

Diderot, D. (1783), *Histoire philosophique et politique des établisssments et du commerce des euoropéens dans les deux indes*, ed. G. T. Raynal, 3rd ed., 10 vols, Genève: Libraires Associées.

Diderot, D. (1992), *Political Writings*, ed. J. H. Mason and R. Wokler, Cambridge: Cambridge University Press.

Doron, C. D. (2012), 'Race and Genealogy. Buffon and the Formation of the Concept of "Race"', *Humana. Mente Journal of Philosophical Studies*, 5 (22): 75–109.

Gayon, J., ed. (1992), *Buffon 88. Actes du Colloque international pour le bicentenaire de la mort de Buffon (Paris-Montbard-Dijon, 14-22 juin 1988)*, Paris: Vrin.

Grimm, F. M. (1829), *Correspondance littéraire, philosophique et critique de Grimm et de Diderot*, Paris: Frune.

Hoquet, T. (2005), *Buffon: histoire naturelle et philosophie*, Paris: Champion.
Hudson, N. (1996), 'From "Nation" to "Race": The Origin of Racial Classification in Eighteenth-Century Thought', *Eighteenth-Century Studies*, 29 (3): 247–64.
Kant, I. ([1781] 1999), *Critique of Pure Reason*, trans. and ed. P. Guyer and A. Wood, Cambridge: Cambridge University Press.
Locke, J. ([1689] 1975), *Essay Concerning Human Understanding*, ed. P. H. Nidditch, Oxford: Clarendon.
Lucretius ([c. 55 BCE] 2001), *De Rerum Natura*, trans. M. F. Smith, Indianapolis: Hackett.
Lyon, J. and Sloan, Ph. (1981), *From Natural History to the History of Nature*, South Bend: University of Notre Dame Press.
Mengal, P. (1992), 'La Psychologie de Buffon à travers le Traité de l'Homme', in J. Gayon (ed.), *Buffon 88: Actes du Colloque International Paris-Montbard-Dijon*, Paris: Vrin, 601–12.
Nourrisson, J. F. (1887), *Philosophies de la Nature. Bacon – Boyle – Toland – Buffon*, Paris: Didier.
Perty, M. ([1859] 2010), *Grundzüge der Ethnographie*, Leipzig and Heidelberg: C. F. Winter, 1859, reprint Charleston, SC: Nabu.
Reimarus, H. S. (1754), *Die vornehmsten Wahrheiten der natürlichen Religion in zehn Abhandlungen auf eine begreifliche Art erkläret und gerettet*, Hamburg: Bohn.
Reimarus, H. S. (1766), *The Principal Truths of Natural Religion Defended and Illustrated, in Nine Dissertations; Wherein the Objections of Lucretius, Buffon, Maupertuis, Rousseau, La Mettrie, and Other Ancient and Modern Followers of Epicurus are Considered, and Their Doctrines Refuted*, trans. R. Wynne, London: B. Law.
Roger, J. (1963), 'Diderot et Buffon en 1749', *Diderot Studies*, 4: 221–36.
Roger, J. (1997), *Buffon: A Life in Science*, trans. S. Bonnefoi, Ithaca NY: Cornell University Press.
Royou, T.-M. (1780), *Le Monde de Verre Reduit En Poudre Ou Analyse Et Refutation Des Époques de La Nature de M. Le Comte de Buffon*, Paris: Mérigot.
Sankar, M. (2003), *Enlightenment against Empire*, Princeton: Princeton University Press.
Smith, J. E. H. (2015), *Nature, Human Nature, and Human Difference: Race in Early Modern Philosophy*, Princeton: Princeton University Press.
Springborg, P. & Wunderlich, F., eds (2016), 'Varieties of Early Modern Materialism', *British Journal for the History of Philosophy*, 24 (5): 797–813.
Stalnaker, J. (2011), 'Buffon on Death and Fossils', *Representations*, 115 (1): 20–41.
Thomson, A. (2008), *Bodies of Thought: Science, Religion, and the Soul in the Early Enlightenment*, Oxford: Oxford University Press.
Vyverberg, H. (1958), *Historical Pessimism in the French Enlightenment*, Cambridge, MA: Harvard University Press.
Wilson, C. (2016), 'The Presence of Lucretius in Eighteenth-Century French and German Philosophy', in L. Blake and J. Lezra (ed.), *Lucretius and Modernity*, New York: Palgrave Macmillan, 107–32.
Wollstonecraft, M. (1792), *Rights of Women*, London: J. Johnson.
Yolton, J. (1984), *Thinking Matter: Materialism in Eighteenth-Century Britain*, Minneapolis: University of Minnesota Press.

4

Hume on humanity and the party of humankind

Jacqueline Taylor

The main aim of the overarching argument of Hume's *Enquiry Concerning the Principles of Morals* is to establish that the principle of humanity (a form of sympathy) is the foundation of morality.[1] In the concluding section of the work, Hume explicitly connects the principle of humanity with an apparently ideal or normative notion of humankind. Regarding the origin of the moral sentiments, he observes that they spring 'from principles, which may appear, at first sight, somewhat small and delicate ... But these principles ... are social and universal: They form, in a manner, the *party* of human kind against vice or disorder, its common enemy' (EPM, 9.9). The paragraph in which Hume introduces the party of humankind begins by discussing another form of social sympathy that can outweigh self-interest by communicating (often by way of contagion) the kind of partial sentiments that sustains political or religious zeal or factions. Hume introduces *this* instance of the force of social sympathy because it supports the case for the force of humanity: sympathy-based or humanity-informed sentiments can outweigh those arising from self-interest. But humanity is, in a technical sense discussed below, different from a broader social sympathy, especially in the light of the latter's tendency to create or sustain partiality. Does Hume intend 'the *party* of humankind' as a metaphor that reflects how we in fact create a common moral ground that mitigates harmful social partialities that lead to divisiveness and moral discord? Or does the party of humankind represent a moral *ideal* given the circumstances, often resulting from what Hume refers to as *moral causes*, that militate against individuals or communities cultivating a sense of humanity?

In this chapter, I follow the suggestion of the editors of this volume that in Enlightenment moral thought, particular empirical approaches to human nature and humankind can yield a normative dimension that speaks to a shareable understanding and valuation of humanity. Hume presents himself as a scientist of human nature who deploys an experimental method of reasoning to settle the matter of the foundation of morals: does it lie in reason or sentiment? Hume shows how his use of this method establishes sympathy and humanity as the foundation of a sentiment-based ethics. Any normative dimensions of Hume's system of ethics must arise out of his use of empirical methods and findings. How might a kind of ethical naturalism that depicts the facts about human nature and 'common life' provide reasons for embracing morality, and what kind of reasons would or could these be? To understand better any normative aspirations in his *Enquiry*, I will take as my main task the reconstruction of Hume's central argument, namely to establish the principle of humanity as the foundation of morality. His objective is twofold: first, to show that the principle of humanity is the source of our most authoritative moral sentiments, and second, to argue that our sense of humanity can *acquire* the force to counter other sentiments or motives grounded in either self-love or partiality. *Force* is Hume's term, and I shall show that it is a crucial explanatory concept in his use of an experimental method in EPM.

In Section 1, I briefly sketch Hume's experimental approach in his *Treatise of Human Nature*, after which I show that Hume uses an experimental method differently in the *Enquiry* with a clearer focus on 'common life'. I then turn to examine how Hume builds the case for the utility of mental qualities as a species of moral merit. I begin in Section 2 with the utility of benevolence and turn in Section 3 to the utility of justice. We can then consider, in Section 4, the case made for the distinction between self-love and humanity. That positions us to look more closely, in Section 5, at Hume's argument that humanity, as the principle of human nature that gives us a concern for the happiness of our fellow persons, has sufficient force to be the foundation of morals. After reconstructing Hume's central argument, I identify three normative dimensions in the system of ethics set out. First, attention to common life, and especially our use of a moral discourse, shows that the moral sentiments are an inherent part of human nature and central to our life in society. Second, Hume shows how the principle of humanity can acquire force precisely because of our sociability; our moral sentiments thus gain an authority for us. Finally, in comparing shareable general views grounded in humanity with the partiality of partisanship, Hume points to the *party of humankind* as an important Enlightenment ideal.

1. As is well known, Hume regarded his earlier work, *A Treatise of Human Nature*, as 'an attempt to introduce the experimental method of reasoning into moral subjects' (T, title page).[2] Moral subjects comprise 'the science of man', the foundation of which must be established on 'experience and observation' (T, Intro. 7). Hume has a sophisticated understanding of how an experimental method of reasoning can accomplish for the science of human nature what everyday observation cannot; for example, explaining the origin and nature of complex perceptions such as belief, indirect passions or the moral sentiments; or establishing the foundational principles that explain how we establish a standard of virtue.[3] To give an example: one of the most experimental parts of the *Treatise*, concerning the origin or causes, nature and effects of the complex indirect passions (such as pride or love and esteem) begins, as a proper experiment should, with the observable phenomena; in the case of the passion of pride, this includes our evident experience of pride both in ourselves and as we observe its signs and effects in others.[4] Hume moves from this readily observable evidence to introduce more theoretical entities. For example, he distinguishes two aspects of the cause of pride: an idea of its subject (what we take pride in) and its (independently) pleasurable impression, and the comparable aspects of its effect: an idea of its object (the self) and pleasurable impression (or an idea of oneself as advantaged by possession of the pride producing quality and a feeling of pride).

These more theoretically refined observations provide the grounds for a hypothesis regarding the double association of ideas and impressions as the efficacious circumstances that produce pride. Examining each of the particular kinds of cause of pride (e.g. virtue or wealth) tests the hypothesis, resulting in a more *general* causal explanation of the production of pride. As with the natural experimenter, Hume seeks not simply to set out facts as they are disclosed to us in everyday experience but to establish facts, e.g. about general causes and effects or general principles, that are constituted and made meaningful through the use of an experimental method of reasoning.

Now in EPM, Hume remains committed to 'following the experimental method' (EPM, 1.10). In one important sense, his use of this method remains the same, to reason from particulars to general causes or principles. But in EPM the objects to which the method applies differ from those of the *Treatise* and attending to this reveals the extent of the revision of his project in ethics and what it accomplishes. In the *Treatise*, Hume's investigations are guided (as shown by the brief account in the previous paragraph) by what he took to be the significance of his discovery of mental principles of association; much of the focus was thus on the ways in which various perceptions (and aspects of them) combine to produce other perceptions, in particular belief, the indirect passion of pride and the moral sentiments. In EPM, Hume begins more explicitly with 'common life' (EPM, 2.17). His starting point, for example, focuses on our use of moral discourse and the terms we use when praising or blaming elements of human character. The aim is to show that the particular terms ascribed to individual 'mental qualities' within the several categories of virtues can be brought together under a more general description, e.g. either *useful* or *immediately agreeable*, that comprises the common circumstance that elicits certain evaluative responses from us.[5] A second and quite neglected aspect of the experimental method in EPM is the introduction of two distinct senses of *force*. The first sense is the force that utility and its opposite (*pernicious* in the case of character traits) have to elicit a response from us. Those mental qualities are useful, either for ourselves or others, *commands* our esteem, as Hume puts it, while pernicious mental qualities elicit our disapprobation. The second sense of force pertains to principles of human nature that have or acquire energy or force with respect to affections, attitudes or actions. These principles are threefold: self-love, a partial affection for (or commitment to) some particular persons, and the sense or principle of humanity; the latter two have their source in sympathy. These three forces of our nature give us three distinct perspectives from which we can regard something as useful or advantageous. Our recognition of something as having or not having utility, and thus the force to elicit a particular evaluative response, is relative to the particular perspective from which we assess something as useful or harmful. We examine this in more detail below (Sections 4 and 5) with respect to both our selfishness and our sympathetic sociability. In establishing humanity as the foundation of morals, Hume aims to show that humanity can *acquire* the force to outweigh the claims of self-love or partiality with respect to our evaluation of character.

2. I now turn to examine how the experimental method of reasoning applies to the roles of utility and the principles of human nature relevant for moral considerations.

I follow Hume's strategy, which is to introduce the usefulness of mental qualities before asking *why* we approve of it. EPM, Section 1 introduces the controversy over the foundation of morals; at issue is whether reason or sentiment determines us to make moral distinctions such as *virtuous* or *vicious*.[6] Rather than focusing explicitly at the outset on the roles of reason and sentiment (e.g. the operations or 'office' of each), Hume instead charts a more neutral course, using the experimental method, 'and deducing general maxims from a comparison of particular instances' (EPM, 1.10). He begins with the catalogue of those particular mental qualities that make up 'personal merit' and to a lesser extent the catalogue comprising vices. The terms we use for these various mental qualities typically have a descriptive meaning regarding the passion or trait and the action it tends to produce (courage, for example, is a trait that requires surmounting fear to face danger), and an evaluative meaning (our use of the term 'courageous' typically implies praise). To call someone courageous is thus to describe the kind of person she is when she encounters danger and to evaluate her as praiseworthy in this respect. Hume writes that 'the very nature of language guides us almost infallibly in forming a judgment of this nature, and … in collecting and arranging the estimable and blamable qualities of men' (EPM, 1.10).[7] Collecting and arranging estimable qualities that vary in terms of their objects and ends assigns a crucial role to reasoning in order to engage in a systematic comparison to find out whether these various mental qualities possess some 'common circumstance' that contributes to their praiseworthiness (EPM, 1.10).

Hume primarily surveys those mental qualities that comprise personal merit (rather than vices), which leads him to identify two different 'species of merit' or what I will refer to as the *general* good-making features of these qualities: utility and immediate agreeableness. The method allows us to distinguish three classes of useful qualities: the social virtues of benevolence, the social virtues comprising justice and a set of self-regarding qualities that are useful for their possessor. The other species of merit, immediate agreeableness, also allows for a division of those qualities according to whether they are agreeable to the person possessing the quality or to others. Hume proceeds by treating each class of qualities separately, allowing him to make distinct points about the importance of utility and to draw a significant contrast between utility and immediate agreeableness, especially in terms of the moral sentiments each elicits.

Let us follow Hume in beginning with the virtues of benevolence. The term 'benevolence' refers to a set of virtues, the exercise of which aims at benefiting in various ways some particular person or persons. *Benevolence* thus includes a number of different traits or motives, including friendliness, compassion, beneficence, gratitude, mercy, charity and generosity. While the terms we use for these qualities 'express the highest merit' of those motivated by them and earn our approbation, the particular traits typically each have a distinct object and aim: for example, charity focuses on offering relief to the unfortunate who may be strangers, while a good friend provides affection and companionship to some particular person to whom she is close (EPM, 2.1). Yet these traits or motives taken together can also be described more generally as *useful* insofar as they all directly tend to the good or well-being of others. Just as the utility of, for example, medicinal plants, the well-built house or the accurate history makes them commendable, the utility of the benevolent affections renders them praiseworthy. Hume furthers the case that utility comprises (at least in part)[8] the merit of benevolent motives by arguing that when, under certain circumstances, a formerly benevolent action stops being useful, or even becomes harmful, we revise our judgement 'and adjust anew the boundaries of moral good and evil' (EPM, 2.17). For example, in certain circumstances, we might regard a too lavish princely liberality as wastefulness or look askance at charitable actions that enable idleness. In such cases, we draw on experience to reason about how best the benevolent virtues might serve 'the true interests of mankind' and thus adjust as needed 'the bounds of duty'. That we adjust in these ways the boundaries of benevolence, both in changing our more specific conception of the conduct to which we apply the terms of benevolence and changing our own conduct to conform to that revised conception, underscores the importance to us of utility as the praiseworthy feature common to the various benevolent motives (EPM, 2.17). Hume concludes that this *general circumstance of utility*, common to all the *particular* benevolent virtues, has 'a command over our esteem and approbation' (EPM, 2.23).

Moving from consideration of the particular traits that fall under benevolence to establishing that utility is the general circumstance common to all of them supports the conclusion that utility and the approval elicited by it renders meritorious all benevolent traits. Hume began by focusing on our common moral idiom, the terms we use to describe and praise the various traits that are part of the class of benevolent motives. In our common moral discourse when we refer to or praise someone as generous, for example, we likely do not describe the person as useful. Our description and our praise typically focus on the particular trait or action that it motivates: we may speak of someone's disposition to generosity or charity, or of the specific generous or charitable action that benefits another, or we may point to the grateful response of the recipient, or to her improved situation, as evidence of the agent's generosity and praiseworthiness. Hume has identified the utility not only of generosity, but of friendliness, mercy and all of the benevolent motives, through a systematic comparison to find what this set of motives has in common. The term 'useful' thus functions to describe more generally the meritorious aspect, aiming to benefit another or to diminish her misfortune, common to all benevolent motives. Ordinarily, while we *may* use the term 'useful' to describe another's character, we more typically use the term (such as 'generous') that describes and implies praise of a particular motive or action. Utility, as an instance of the general feature arrived at through a comparison of particular instances, is thus an *experimental* finding in Hume's system of ethics.

3. With this first move from particular traits to a general shared circumstance in place, Hume turns to show that the general descriptor of 'useful' applies to other classes of meritorious qualities and the particular traits that fall under them; these useful qualities also command our esteem or approval. Justice forms a second class of social virtues. While we can identify particular virtues of justice, such as honesty or loyalty to government, as we did with the virtues of benevolence, Hume does not repeat the comparative experiment to show that the virtues of justice also fall under the general descriptor of useful. Because justice is so evidently useful for society, Hume advances his argument about the importance of utility by arguing that justice, beginning as a set

of conventions, has its origin *entirely* in its utility and that the merit of justice likewise lies *solely* in its utility. Hume thus shifts his strategy to examine the circumstances of human nature that make justice possible and necessary for us.[9] The strategy envisions different material conditions for humankind: an abundance of goods would make justice *unnecessary*, as would enlarged affections and an extensive benevolence that prompts us to put others' interests on a par with our own. In contrast, extreme scarcity would make self-preservation our foremost concern, rendering justice (secure property or equitable dealings) impossible. Justice would be likewise impossible if human beings were entirely ruthless, focused on short-term gain and followed no laws.

Self-interest and partiality for particular others motivate us most often, but we can also appreciate the advantages of cooperating with others for mutual gain, convenience or security. Our condition is one of interdependence, beginning, Hume suggests, with family life. If we were completely self-sufficient and able to meet all our own needs, we would be incapable of justice. If, instead of interdependence, some were inferior and dependent on other superior beings, justice would not apply to the former. But we do recognize an equality between ourselves and our fellow persons, even if that equality is not always respected. The capacity we have to make expressed resentment at inequity or mistreatment felt by others can function as a form of demand or an assertion of human agency. Human society is a 'medium amidst' the various hypothetical extremes Hume has set out, and the rules of justice 'depend entirely on the particular state and condition' in which we are placed and have their origin in the utility to society of their observance (EPM, 3.13). Our actual circumstances find us capable of reflecting on our mutual needs, cooperating to satisfy those needs through art and industry, and then reflecting on and approving of the advantages of cooperation enforced by rules (or laws). Indeed, given our fundamental interdependence and the need to live together in society, we must cooperate and restrain natural partiality and avidity through rules of justice. As society increases, and we enlarge our views to take into account the larger and more complex collective through new rules or the extended or more fine-grained scope of existing laws, 'the boundaries of justice grow still larger'. Thus, 'history, experience, reason sufficiently instruct us in this natural progress of human sentiments, and in the gradual enlargement of our regards to justice, in proportion as we become acquainted with the extensive utility of that virtue' (EPM, 3.21).

As Hume shows in Section 4, 'Of Political Society', we approve of conformity to a variety of conventions that are useful and make life more convenient. Rules of good manners, for example, are 'a kind of lesser morality, calculated for the ease of company and conversation' (EPM, 4.13); likewise, the rules of various games and sports, as well as the rules of the road, which, while not as 'absolutely requisite' as the rules of justice, nevertheless show us 'the necessity of rules, wherever men have any intercourse with each other' (EPM, 4.18–19). Our abiding by the rules of various conventions, whether those of justice, etiquette, sexual morality or sports, gives rise to forms of conduct that we understand as, for example, just or unjust, elegant or oafish manners, modest or immodest or that of the good or bad sport. We are, then, the kind of creatures who establish rules to regulate conduct in various arenas where we come together, not necessarily as family or acquaintances but as participants cooperating with one another in a broader social context.

Justice has its *origin* in its utility: justice is necessary for preserving 'human society, or even human nature' (EPM, 3.39). The *merit* of justice also lies in its utility as we find when we reflect on the advantages of justice (or the disadvantages of rampant injustice) and on our capacity to form a habitual regard for it. In the concluding paragraph of Section 2, Hume indicated that turning to the merit of the virtues of justice would show us 'how considerable a part' of the merit of the social virtues 'we ought to ascribe to their utility' (EPM, 2.22). In the concluding paragraph of Section 3, Hume proceeds by analogy and with reference to Newton's 'chief rule of philosophizing'. Regarding the force of the principle of utility, we can now 'determine what degree of esteem of moral approbation may result from reflections on public interest and utility':

> The necessity of justice to the support of society is the sole foundation of that virtue; and since no moral excellence is more highly esteemed, we may conclude, that this circumstance of usefulness has, in general, the strongest energy, and most entire command over our sentiments.
>
> (EPM, 3.48)

Usefulness explains part of the merit of the virtues of benevolence and 'is the sole source of the moral approbation' paid to the virtues of justice.

> It is entirely agreeable to the rules of philosophy, and even of common reason; where any principle has been found to have a great force and energy in one instance, to ascribe to it a like energy in all similar instances. This indeed is Newton's chief rule of philosophizing.
>
> (EPM, 3.48)[10]

Hume's fundamental aim is to point to the importance of utility *for us*. If nothing other than utility serves to render justice meritorious, or to render injustice morally pernicious, and utility has 'the *strongest energy*, and *most entire command* over our sentiments', utility takes on even more significance as the general circumstance that unites different classes of virtues. It is thus not inconsequential and deserves further examination, that justice, as a set of virtues ('fidelity, justice, veracity, integrity') and especially as a set of conventions, has the most utility for us (emphasis added).[11] The appeal to Newton on analogies signals the significance of the experimental method in establishing utility as not just *a* source but the *most* considerable source of the merit that commands our esteem.[12]

4. As the point about the rules of philosophy indicates, Hume proceeds systematically, in keeping with the method of the experimental investigator, to establish the foundation of morality. While he had initially put the matter in terms of whether moral distinctions are grounded in reason or sentiment, it is worth emphasizing that he has in Sections 2 and 3 already framed our response to utility in terms of *sentiment* (see e.g. EPM, 2.5, 3.21, 3.39, 3.48).[13] In Section 5 Hume turns to inquire whether the pleasure of or esteem for utility has its grounding in our self-love or a more social or public affection. The first part of §5 concerns the source of the esteem or approbation

commanded by useful mental qualities and arguments against self-interest as that source. Although in common life we readily allow that we approve of whatever is useful, moral philosophers, unable to connect the *utile* with the *honestum*, have sought 'any other principle' than the useful and the pernicious to explain moral good and evil (EPM, 5.2).[14] Indeed, the partisans of utility have been primarily the sceptics, both ancient and modern, who argue that political leaders invent moral distinctions and use education to teach virtue and honour, which proves useful to society overall. Hume responds that terms such as 'shameful' or 'honorable' could not influence our conduct unless our nature already inclines us to make such distinctions. We find that the social virtues have a 'natural beauty' such that we readily respond with approbation prior to 'all precept and education' (EPM, 5.4). If our approval and blame are genuine, rather than artificially inculcated, sentiments, they must have their source in some principle of human nature. We do not praise and value the useful simply for its own sake. While the public utility of benevolence and justice commands our esteem, that *utility is itself a tendency to promote an end*, namely the good of particular others and of society. Our valuing of utility entails that we must value that end, finding it 'agreeable to us' and taking 'hold of some natural affection'. Given the facts about our natural affections, the good of society must please us, 'either from considerations of self-interest, or from more generous motives or regards' (EPM, 5.4). The more sophisticated versions of the selfish theory, recognizing our interdependence, argue that self-interest prompts our approval of whatever habits or conduct helps to maintain the social confederacy that we rely on to survive or flourish.[15] But Hume suggests that a number of arguments militate against the plausibility of this theory, including our felt approval or blame for what has occurred in the historical past or in places too remote from us to have any effect on our own interest. He also offers an *experimentum crucis* that undermines the selfish theory: we do sometimes morally approve an action that redounds to public interest even when it opposes our own private interest (EPM, 5.17).

Despite his criticism of the selfish *theory*, Hume allows that self-love is a principle of human nature, one with 'extensive energy' (EPM, 5.16). But our own interest or well-being is not our only concern, for we also have a general concern for the good of society or the well-being of others and generally resent whatever harms or injures others. We thus possess 'a more public affection' that naturally engages our interest in others. That more public affection arises from sympathy and what Hume terms our *sense* or the *principle* of humanity. When some useful quality tends to the good of others rather than solely our own good, sympathy engages our affection, giving us a pleasure in what promotes the happiness of others. Hume suggests that the sympathy that grounds our moral approbation of the useful 'accounts, in great part, for the origin of morality' (EPM, 5.17). While self-love has extensive force and energy, sympathy and humanity likewise have their own force. Much of what occupies us in our life 'presents us with the view of human happiness or misery', so that sympathy exerts its 'active energy' (EPM, 5.23). Sympathy makes possible our interest in and sharing of others' emotional experiences, whether from 'the very aspect' of another's joy or grief; our witnessing of someone's comfort or distress; and the 'careless amusements' of the theatre, poetry or literature (EPM, 5.18, 5.23). Similarly, news from either local or distant parts, as well as histories of the fates of past peoples, can arouse our interest, our pleasures and pains, as we sympathize with both acquaintances and strangers. After highlighting various ways that sympathy interests us in others, and in particular whatever affects their happiness or misery, Hume sets out to show that moral approval and blame have our sense of humanity as their source. That the principle or sense of humanity can *acquire* additional force is central to undermining the case for the selfish theory and establishing humanity as the foundation of morality.

Hume had introduced sympathy as a form of benevolence in what had originally been part of Section 2, 'Of Benevolence', but which became in the 1777 edition and after Appendix 2, 'Of Self-Love'. In a note in that Appendix, we find, 'Benevolence naturally divides into two kinds, the *general* and the *particular*'. Particular benevolence is a more active principle issuing in actions and attitudes on the basis of the relationship or esteem we have for the person. With respect to general benevolence, 'we feel only a general sympathy' with someone, responding with compassion to her pains, and congratulations to her pleasures (EPM, App. 2, n. 60). General benevolence may also be termed 'humanity' or 'sympathy', and Hume says he assumes it as a real sentiment 'from general experience, and without any other proof' (EPM, App. 2.5, n. 60).[16]

As with the case of justice, hypothetical sketches of a nature other than that of the human person help to make the case for sympathy and humanity as inherent features of our nature. Although some people may be more focused on their own interests, none remain entirely indifferent to the happiness or misery of others. Particularly, when someone's own interest is not at stake, there is at least a cool preference for the happiness rather than misery of others. If we were entirely indifferent to others, then we would be 'equally indifferent to the images of vice and virtue' since the useful virtues aim at promoting that happiness while the vices do the opposite (EPM, 5.39).[17] In a similar vein, if it were in our nature to be 'absolutely malicious and spiteful', we would be worse than indifferent, approving evil and desiring that it befall others, while disapproving what tends to the good of others and society (EPM, 5.40). In human beings, other emotions such as revenge or envy may provoke malice and spite, but we find no purely disinterested desire to see harm befall others. The hypothetical cases allow Hume to establish basic and universal facts about human nature: our recognition of others as fellow human persons and our sympathy with their pains and pleasures (allowing that our sympathy may fail when we are influenced by other human motives such as envy). We can thus conclude that humanity inclines us to prefer the happiness of others and so to approve the useful mental qualities or virtues that promote it.

Sympathy and humanity thus have sufficient force to engage our affections and prefer the happiness of others to their misery. Although humanity might not have the strength to prevail against self-interested (vicious or indifferent) *motives*, humanity always has '*some* authority over our sentiments' and gives us 'a general approbation of what is useful to society and blame of what is dangerous or pernicious' (EPM, 5.39). Hume's point, I think, is that the way in which sympathy and humanity contribute to our sociability gives these principles an authority insofar as we acknowledge the *real existence* of the moral sentiments they ground. The public affection of humanity entails that moral sentiments do not reduce to considerations of self-interest.

5. We can now begin to see how these sentiments of approval and blame are moral sentiments with their source in the principle of humanity. Recall that Hume's experimental strategy has been twofold: to move from the beneficial tendencies of particular social virtues to the general conclusion that we value all social virtues either partly or entirely for their usefulness and to focus on the facts of human nature as revealed through a comparison between hypothetical cases of differently constituted beings and the actual needs, affections, preferences and sentiments of human beings. That we all possess some capacity for sympathizing with others and some degree of humanity makes it possible for us to aim for a shared outlook on which mental qualities or character traits tend to human happiness. While sympathy naturally varies depending on how close to or distant from the person, or how vividly her situation is presented to us, Hume appeals to 'the judgment' as that which 'corrects the inequalities of our internal emotions and perceptions' analogously to the natural correction of visual perception (EPM, 5.41).[18] Such corrections reflect the importance for us of being able to think consistently, as well as to converse together, and to make ourselves 'intelligible' to one another, with respect to moral distinctions and preferences.

From this 'common point of view' we form more general views on useful or harmful character traits, the praiseworthy and the blameworthy. The point of view that we share with others provides us with an opportunity for 'an intercourse of sentiments'; we converse with one another so that we form 'more general views' that are distinct from the particular views based on self-interest or partiality. Our shared sense of the praiseworthiness or blameworthiness of various qualities gets reflected in a general moral language (our 'common life' use of which was Hume's initial starting point in his inquiry), rather than the language of self-love, and signals our participation in a shared or common point of view. The conversations or debates through which we establish 'the general interests of the community' in turn 'makes us form some general unalterable standard, by which we may approve or disapprove of characters and manners'. While disagreement may arise, the use of a shared moral language helps us to make ourselves 'intelligible' to one another. Although we may naturally tend to focus mainly on ourselves and those to whom we are close, and although our sympathetic concern varies according to our connection with, closeness to or distance from those with whom we sympathize, our sense of humanity and the general differences between virtue and vice that we collectively sustain still exert an influence on our sentiments (EPM, 5.42).

Hume concludes Section 5 with an a priori and an a posteriori argument; these arguments keep our focus on the facts of human nature and the nature of morality. Observation and experience show us that in addition to self-interest, sympathy and humanity are fundamental principles of human nature. We can thus conclude a priori that we cannot be indifferent to the condition of our fellow persons. If we prefer their happiness to their misery and consider how mental qualities or character traits affect that, we get 'the faint rudiments, at least, or outlines, of a *general* distinction between actions' (EPM, 5.43). And if our sympathy is further enlivened by our connection to others or an 'eloquent recital', a 'cool approbation' gets 'converted into the warmest sentiments of friendship and regard. These seem necessary infallible consequences of the general principles of human nature, as discovered in common life and practice'

(EPM, 5.43). Now consider the a posteriori case; we see as a matter of fact that the merit of the social virtues derives from their effect on our 'feelings of humanity'; it is a further fact that utility is a source of our approbation and that it is inseparable from the merit of social virtues (EPM, 5.44). Moreover, the tendency of the social virtues to the public good and the maintaining of security and order in society engages our humanity, exciting 'the strongest censure and applause'. Hume concludes that 'the present theory' he has set out 'is the simple result of all these inferences, each of which seems founded on uniform experience and observation' (EPM, 5.45).

6. Hume continues with a 'progress of this argument' that 'will bring a farther confirmation of the present theory' (EPM, 5.47). We will discover 'other sentiments of esteem and regard from the same or like principles' (EPM, 5.47). The *same* principle, that of humanity, explains our approbation of a final set of useful qualities, namely those that are useful for the person possessed of them. *Like* or similar principles account for our more immediate sympathetic response to those mental qualities (or aspects of them) that are *immediately agreeable* (without our reflecting on their tendencies) to the person possessed of them or to others. I look briefly at the argument for our approval of the self-regarding useful qualities with the aim of highlighting how the use of the experimental method establishes the principle of humanity as the foundation of morals.

Considerations of utility fix the 'due medium' of self-regarding qualities, such as discretion, industriousness or frugality. Hume thinks it is evident we disapprove of others for qualities that harm their own interests; we hold negligence or credulity, for example, to be faults in the person's character. The principle of humanity accounts for our approval of the due medium and disapproval of the excessive or defective states. The selfish theory is here undermined: we simply do approve of qualities that tend to the well-being of their possessor, even when they have no effect on our own lives. There is, once again, 'a plain foundation of preference, where every thing else is equal' (EPM, 6.5). The preference may be 'cool', but we still distinguish between the agent's qualities that are useful for her and those that are pernicious. In this regard, Hume writes:

> Now this distinction is the same in all its parts, with the *moral distinction*, whose foundation has been so often, and so much in vain, enquired after. The same endowments of the mind, in every circumstance, are agreeable to the sentiment of morals and to that of humanity ... By all the rules of philosophy, therefore, we must conclude that these sentiments are originally the same; since, in each particular, even the most minute, they are governed by the same laws, and are moved by the same objects.
>
> (EPM, 6.5)

Although the self-regarding meritorious qualities have a different direction, as we might put it, than the social virtues, towards an agent's own good rather than that of others, both kinds of qualities share the same circumstance of usefulness and tend to promote the same end of well-being. The foundation for the moral distinctions we make lies in the principle of humanity. Hume furthers his case by drawing an analogy here with gravity:

> Why do philosophers infer, with the greatest certainty, that the moon is kept in its orbit by the same force of gravity, that makes bodies fall near the surface of the earth, but because these effects are, upon computation, found similar and equal? And must not this argument bring as strong conviction in moral as in natural disquisitions?
>
> (EPM, 6.6)

The principle of gravity explains the different movements of both local and heavenly bodies. The principle of humanity explains the approbation of virtues with different directions: the social towards public good and the self-regarding towards private good. The sentiment of morals by means of which we distinguish between virtue and vice (or merit and demerit) is the same as the sentiment or principle of humanity. That principle is thus the foundation of (the chief part of) morals.

I turn even more briefly to the immediately agreeable qualities (the other part of morals) with the aim of emphasizing that both the aspect of the mental quality eliciting an immediate pleasurable response and the character of our sentimental response differ from the qualities with beneficial tendencies preferred by the principle of humanity and the source of our moral approbation of the latter. We value the former because of the immediate pleasure they communicate either to the person possessed of them (e.g. the lustre of courage, the contentment afforded by mental tranquillity or the tenderness of benevolence) or to others (e.g. by someone's good manners, decency or genteelness). With the immediately agreeable (aspects of) qualities, we are *seized* or *struck* with admiration; the immediate pleasures of them are *contagious* and *catch* our affections powerfully without our reflecting on the tendencies of the traits. In contrast, our principle of humanity actuates our preference for the beneficial *tendencies* of social and self-regarding virtues. We must thus use reason and reflection to assess those tendencies as well as to form accurate views of what happiness or misery consists in. Hume does assign an importance to the immediately agreeable qualities: they add a different kind of pleasure that contributes to happiness and form part of a system of ethics that represents 'virtue in all her genuine and most engaging charms' (EPM, 9.15).[19] Moreover, different kinds of social arrangements, and in particular, political arrangements such as the form of government, might favour the agreeable qualities over the useful. For example, an absolute monarchy places more importance on good manners and eloquence than industry and other useful qualities (EPM, 6.35). Yet Hume also indicates that our sentiment of humanity can correct an unreflective immediate admiration, for example, of heroic courage and the hero's sublime sense of himself, since humanity, informed by reason and reflection, can assess both the useful and the destructive tendencies of this form of courage. I say a bit more about this in the final section below.

Hume's inquiry, relying on an observation of our moral language and our common life, has revealed that, taking the whole of morals, 'personal merit consists altogether in the possession of mental qualities, *useful* or *agreeable* to the *person himself* or to *others*' (EPM, 9.1). The principle of humanity forms the foundation of 'the chief part' of morals and is the source of our preference for and approbation of useful mental qualities, and our disapprobation of pernicious ones. Our felt preference and approbation here nonetheless require reason 'to instruct us in the tendency of qualities and actions, and point out their beneficial consequences to society and their possessor' (EPM, App. 1.2). As participants conversing from the common point of view we have both an epistemic and an evaluative responsibility to accurately assess characters and conduct, circumstances and consequences, and the interests of those involved. Moral judgement of the useful or pernicious thus has us thinking, feeling and conversing together: while '*reason* instructs us in the several tendencies of actions, and *humanity* makes a distinction in favor of those, which are useful and beneficial' (EPM, App. 1.3).

7. We can now turn to consider the ways in which Hume's investigation and findings, explicitly set out as part of an experimental approach to establish the foundation of morality, might also contribute to our understanding of the normativity of a sentiment-based ethics. As I said in the introduction to this chapter, any normative dimension to Hume's system of ethics must arise from his use of empirical methods. I now identify three aspects of normativity in Hume's moral philosophy: a sentiment-based morality as an inherent part of human nature itself; the fact that humanity can acquire force and also provide us with a stance from which we can criticize inhumanity; and the party of humankind as an Enlightenment ideal.

As discussed earlier, while both the *Treatise* and the *Enquiry* engage in 'a cautious observation of common life' (T, Intro. 10), EPM differs from the *Treatise* in the way that Hume puts common life at centre stage in the later work. The focus is on human beings already immersed in robust social contexts, using a moral discourse that reflects how sympathy and humanity interest us in one another's happiness and misery. Hume gives evidence to show that we will find a sentiment-based approval of the useful across history (see the comparison of ancient and modern societies in 'A Dialogue') and across cultures. The universality of approval of the useful holds despite significant variability in who decides what counts as useful (e.g. in societies characterized by extreme inequality), and what in fact counts as useful (e.g. courage, where benevolence and justice are not firmly established), as well as in the descriptive content of trait concepts (see, e.g. EPM, 7.15 on the contrast between the ancient and modern conceptions of courage). We nevertheless all use moral language, and we learn how to use it as we do other linguistic conventions. We are all inculcated into various aspects of morality, such as appropriate sentiments, language and conduct, so that we understand, even if we do not conform to, the expectations of our community. Our moral sentiments of praise and blame, along with other attitudes such as resentment, compassion, gratitude and esteem, signal the ways in which we hold one another accountable. Hume has shown that our natural sociability and sympathy give us reasons to engage with and take an interest in one another. Our humanity in particular gives us some concern for the happiness or misery of others, influencing our sentiments at least, if not our actions. And the moral sentiments arising from our humanity show that we care about whether an agent has mental qualities that move her to act in ways that show good will or ill will towards others or a proper self-love instead of self-destructiveness. Hume's hypothetical situations, imagining us with a nature other than that of the human, both in his account of the origin and merit of justice, and in his account of the naturalness of our moral sentiments, emphasize that we are neither angels nor monsters, nor are we entirely self-sufficient or without the ability to make the effects of our resentment felt by our oppressors. The examination of common life reveals that we are interdependent, embodied and passionate persons, with the capacities for reasoning and reflection, and using an organic moral discourse as we affirm or negotiate the interests of our community.

A second aspect of normativity concerns the way in which humanity acquires force. Given the ease with which we communicate our emotions and sentiments to one another, Hume notes the natural 'force of humanity' and the 'active energy' of sympathy (EPM, 5.18, 5.23). In addition, 'the intercourse of sentiments' in our moral conversations leads us to form, affirm or negotiate 'a general standard of vice and virtue', and the moral distinctions embodied by that standard have 'a considerable influence' on the sentiments of the individual; morality as something we maintain collectively imparts greater force to humanity (EPM, 5.42; 5.42, n. 25). From our enlarged or general views, the principle of humanity has a 'powerful' influence on our moral sentiments (EPM, 5.45). As Hume notes in §9, the existence of collectively acknowledged moral distinctions 'implies some sentiment common to all mankind, which recommends the same object to general approbation'. This sentiment is 'so universal and comprehensive as to extend to all mankind', so that we praise or blame even persons remote in time or place (EPM, 9.5). 'These two requisite circumstances belong alone to the sentiment of humanity', and since 'the humanity of one man is the humanity of every one', then 'it alone can be the foundation of morals, or of any general system of blame or praise' (EPM, 9.5, 9.6). Moreover, the force humanity acquires, given the common point of view we participate in, serves also to put shared and social interests above more selfish ones. Humanity is the same in all of us, while for each of us ambition or avarice differs; either we are ambitious for different things, or if we are ambitious for the same thing then we stand in competition with one another. Hume writes, 'Whatever conduct gains my approbation, by touching my humanity, procures also the applause of all mankind, by affecting the same principles in them'; these 'universal principles', leading to a shared moral outlook can thus often control or limit 'the particular sentiments of self-love' (EPM, 9.8). Hume notes explicitly that, '[o]ther passions, though perhaps originally stronger, yet being selfish and private, are often overpowered' by the force of humanity so that the 'social and public principles' gain 'dominion' over us (EPM, 9.9). Love of fame, a passion we might regard as part of self-love, requires the esteem of others and earning that esteem can help to strengthen an agent's humanity and the moral sentiments. Love of fame moves us to consider our character and reputation. We *earn* a reputation and good character, so that it is important to us to consider how others regard us. We thus survey ourselves 'in reflection', which 'keeps alive all the sentiments of right and wrong' in us (EPM, 9.10). We find displayed here 'the force of many sympathies', as others' sentiments directed towards us mingle with and inform our own self-approbation (EPM, 9.11). While humanity may sometimes produce only a 'cool preference' for the happiness of others, we acknowledge the 'superiority' of those possessed of 'a warm concern for the interests of our species'; they have a greater delicacy, in the sense of discernment, in identifying and responding to salient moral particulars and thus serve as a model of humanity in practice (EPM, 5.39).

Finally, we turn to consider the role of the party of humankind. As a metaphor for a potential cosmopolitan stance, the party of humankind contrasts with the notion of political parties. In Section 5, in observing the force or energy of sympathy, Hume had given as an example the 'powerful concern' we might feel, one that outweighs 'the narrow attachments of self-love and private interest', when the 'less laudable effects of this social sympathy in human nature' help to produce 'party zeal' or devotion to a faction or cause (EPM, 5.35). He repeats this point in the paragraph invoking the party of humankind: 'From instances of popular tumults, seditions, factions ... passions, which are shared with a multitude, we may learn the influence of society, in exciting and supporting any emotion'; 'no selfishness' can prevail in the face of the 'common blaze' (EPM, 9.9). The point is that if the common cause engendered by a contagious social sympathy can outweigh selfish concerns, then so too can the moral sentiments arising from the reason-informed principle of humanity. While some may think sympathy and humanity too 'delicate' to found a system of morality, these principles are in fact 'social and universal: They form, in a manner, the *party* of human kind against vice or disorder, its common enemy' (EPM, 9.9).

If we go back to the point about how, from a common point of view, we form more general views and make general moral distinctions founded on the general preferences we might arrive at in moral conversation and debate, we find an implicit tension in Hume's stance here. Partiality seems as much a part of our nature as self-love and humanity. Hume observes that 'the first rude, unpracticed enquirers concerning morals', would have agreed with his own definition of personal merit, identifying mental qualities that are useful or agreeable to oneself or others (EPM, 9.1). But these enquirers, lacking the general views and enlarged reflections of those in more well-established societies, would have regulated their love or hatred, praise or blame, 'by the ideas of private utility and injury' (EPM, 9.8, n. 57). Those of us accustomed to society take a wider view and know that human society fares best when we can recognize that the courage of an enemy, as a quality of character, may be identical to the courage of a local heroine. We thus correct 'our ruder and narrower passions' and pronounce both to be persons of merit (although our felt sentiments may be unequal) (EPM, 9.8, n. 57). But the partiality characterizing the first enquirers is not extinguished in us once we are in a more robust social setting with a complex system of justice. Even while we pay 'homage to general rules, which we are accustomed to respect', we find that people commonly distort the conduct of an adversary and use the language of morality to ascribe vice, injustice or inhumanity, for example, to him; by this means the passions 'arising from self-love and private interest' gain a hearing (and the expectation of the concurrence of others) that is really not their due (EPM, 9.8, n. 57).

Moral language, Hume had noted at the outset of this inquiry, 'guides us almost infallibly', but this particular kind of discourse is not without abuse by its practitioners. Of course, moral language might not guide us infallibly, not because of abuse by the self-interested, but because of differences arising from ideology or contested conceptions of terms due to struggles for recognition on the part of those oppressed by a social elite that regard them as not quite equal.[20] Hume notes these differences in the descriptive content of our moral terms, from the general terms 'virtue' or 'vice' to the more particular trait terms such as 'courage' in his essay, 'Of the Standard of Taste'. While we should pay attention to these differences in our language, it is the cultivation of humanity both within the individual and across a society, where this motivates us to assess the true interests of all members of a moral community that can guide us in the better assessment and ascription of the terms of moral merit and demerit: 'That people, who invented the word *charity*, and used it in a good sense, inculcated more clearly and much more efficaciously, the precept, *be charitable*, than any pretended legislator or prophet.'[21] In that essay, Hume contrasted a modern sense of humanity with the greater inhumanity practiced by the ancients and concluded that the cultivation of humanity provides 'the rectitude of that moral standard' by which we judge and of which we should be 'justly jealous'.[22] As Hume knew and as readers of this volume know fully well, moral progress is not inevitable but is an achievement by those who strive to recognize and value our shared human nature. Hume has set out the possibility of and reasons for cultivating our sense of humanity, but the party of humankind remains as his Enlightenment ideal.[23]

Notes

1 Hume ([1776] 1998; henceforth abbreviated as EPM, followed by section and paragraph number).
2 Hume ([1739/40] 2007; henceforth abbreviated as T followed by book, part, section and paragraph number).
3 I develop the case in more depth for Hume's experimentalism in the *Treatise* in Taylor (2015a); see especially Chapter One, 'Experimenting with the Passions'. See also Demeter (2016) and Wood (2006).
4 Passmore (1952) declares Book 2 as 'that most Newtonian section of the *Treatise*'.
5 Hume gives a truncated version of the argument concerning the useful and immediately agreeable in the *Treatise*; see T, 3.3.4.5–12; T, 3.3.5.1.
6 Although he purports here to set aside selfish theorists and sceptics who deny the reality of moral distinctions, he does advance arguments against the selfish view. As we shall see below, Hume takes seriously the strength of self-love as a motivational principle of our nature.
7 The qualification that language guides us 'almost infallibly' is important, as I discuss later.
8 The benevolent motives are also 'softer affections', that softness is itself a pleasure that is immediately agreeable to the benevolent person herself; see EPM, §7.
9 Part of the reason for Hume's shift in strategy here would have been more perspicuous to those reading editions of EPM published prior to the 1777 edition. In 1776, the year of his death, Hume created what we now know as Appendix 2, 'Of Self-Love', taking what had originally been Part 1, of three parts total, in Section 2. Readers would thus have read that for this class of social virtues the terms we use such as 'benevolence', 'generosity' or 'friendship', refer to real affections directed towards others and the very meaning of which distinguishes them from self-interest. Justice as a set of motives is not natural to us in the same way that the various benevolent motives are. We *acquire* a 'regard' for justice, and the evident

success of rules and conventions of justice in providing security and social stability can sustain and render habitual the regard that issues in our approval of justice and disapproval of injustice, and motivate our conformity to the requirements of justice.

10 Hume references *Principia*, lib. 3 of Isaac Newton's *Philosophiae naturalis principia mathematica*.
11 See Taylor (2015b).
12 Hume draws a contrast between the useful and the immediately agreeable as the two sources of merit. Humanity, as the principle that gives rise to our moral approval of the useful, accounts 'in great part, for the origin of morality', while a more immediate or contagious sympathy accounts for the response to immediately agreeable qualities (EPM, 5.17).
13 He most fully addresses the essential yet limited role of reason in Appendix 1.
14 See Moore (2002), Garrett (2021) and Harris (2020).
15 See Maurer (2019).
16 In a note in Section 5, Hume writes: 'It is needless to push our researches so far as to ask, why we have humanity or a fellow feeling with others. It is sufficient, that this is experienced to be a principle in human nature' (EPM, 5.41 n. 19). This contrasts with the *Treatise*'s associative explanation of sympathy based on the resemblance of others to ourselves.
17 Hume uses a similar hypothetical example at EPM 6.4 with respect to self-regarding qualities that are useful or harmful to oneself.
18 Hume's view here appears similar to that of Locke, who describes how we form habits of judgement that naturally correct sense perception. See Locke, J. ([1690] 1975), Book II, Chap. IX, §§8–10. On Locke on judgement, see Hamou (in this volume).
19 For more on the importance of the immediately agreeable virtues, see Feiser (2021), and Watkins (2021).
20 On this, see Gallie (1955–56).
21 Hume (1985), 229.
22 Hume (1985), 247.
23 I am grateful to Ansgar Lyssy and Stefanie Buchenau for organizing and inviting me to the conference, Humankind and Humanity in the Philosophy of the Enlightenment, held in Munich in 2017. I appreciate their patience and encouragement. I also benefited from comments provided by Rachel Cohon on a draft of this chapter presented at the NYU Conference on Modern Philosophy in 2019.

References

Demeter, T. (2016), *David Hume and the Culture of Scottish Newtonianism: Methodology and Ideology in Enlightenment Enquiry*, Leiden: Brill.

Feiser, J. (2021), 'Hume on Talents and Moral Virtues', in E. Engels Kroeker and W. Lemmens (eds), *Hume's* An Enquiry Concerning the Principles of Morals: *A Critical Guide*, Cambridge: Cambridge University Press, 112–33.

Gallie, W. B. (1955–56), 'Essentially Contested Concepts', *Proceedings of the Aristotelian Society*, 56: 167–98.

Garrett, A. (2021), 'Hume, Cicero, and the Ancients', in E. Engels Kroeker and W. Lemmens (eds), *Hume's* An Enquiry Concerning the Principles of Morals: *A Critical Guide*, Cambridge: Cambridge University Press, 192–218.

Hamou, P. (forthcoming), 'Locke on the Presumptive Unity of Humankind', in S. Buchenau and A. Lyssy (eds), *Humankind and Humanity in the Philosophy of the Enlightenment*, London: Bloomsbury.

Harris, J. A. (2020), 'Justice in *An Enquiry Concerning the Principles of Morals*', in J. Taylor (ed.), *Reading Hume on the Principles of Morals*, Oxford: Oxford University Press, 77–94.

Hume, D. ([1739/40] 2007), *A Treatise of Human Nature*, ed. D. F. Norton and M. J. Norton, Oxford: Oxford University Press.

Hume, D. ([1776] 1998), *An Enquiry Concerning the Principles of Morals*, ed. T. L. Beauchamp, Oxford: Oxford University Press.

Hume, D. (1985), 'Of the Standard of Taste', in E. F. Miller (ed.), *Essays, Moral, Political, and Literary*, 226–49, Indianapolis: Liberty Fund.

Locke, J. ([1690] 1975), *An Essay Concerning Human Understanding*, ed. P. H. Nidditch, Oxford: Clarendon Press.

Maurer, C. (2019), *Self-Love, Egoism and the Selfish Hypothesis: Key Debates from Eighteenth Century British Moral Philosophy*, Edinburgh: Edinburgh University Press.

Moore, J. (2002), 'Utility and Humanity: The Quest for the Honestum in Cicero, Hutcheson, and Hume', *Utilitas*, 14 (3): 365–86.

Passmore, J. (1952), *Hume's Intentions*, London: Duckworth.

Taylor, J. A. (2015a), *Reflecting Subjects: Passion, Sympathy, and Society in Hume's Philosophy*, Oxford: Oxford University Press.

Taylor, J. A. (2015b), 'Justice, Sympathy and the Command of Our Esteem', *Diametros*, 44: 173–88.

Watkins, M. (2021), 'Virtues Suspect and Sublime', in E. Engels Kroeker and W. Lemmens (eds), *Hume's An Enquiry Concerning the Principles of Morals: A Critical Guide*, Cambridge: Cambridge University Press, 134–53.

Wood, P. (2006), 'Science, Philosophy and the Mind', in K. Park and L. Daston (eds), *The Cambridge History of Science*, vol. 4, Cambridge: Cambridge University Press, 800–24.

5

Humankind and humanity in Diderot

Ansgar Lyssy

1. Introduction

How is humanity as a moral norm connected to our given human nature? This is part of a broader question, namely which conceptual resources are available to a materialist like Diderot to reject traditional sources of practical normativity, such as revelation and providence? As I cannot tackle this problem in its entirety here, I will use the relationship between humankind as a species and humanity as a practical norm to discuss some crucial aspects of Diderot's answer to the problem of practical normativity within a materialist framework. Before I start to develop my argument, I will briefly set out some landmarks to help us navigate the landscape of Diderot's writings.

Speaking broadly, materialism is a field of theories that often entail two claims, one negative and one positive. Many materialists reject the idea that we can have objective knowledge of supernatural entities, and they claim that nature can be reduced to matter and its properties. Materialism entails both epistemological and ontological claims, albeit there is disagreement about the type of reductionism that is considered viable and about the determinacy of matter.[1] Ontological claims are often reflected through an epistemic lens. Like Locke and Hume, Diderot affirms that all cognition starts with and is shaped by experience and language. Words and concepts are given meaning through experience, though they cannot fully capture the complexity of reality. Hence we should be sceptical regarding all claims of universal knowledge or metaphysical speculation, as both conflict with the contingencies of individual experience. Notions that refer to something that cannot be an object of experience or immediate cognition, such as 'soul', 'God', 'final cause' or 'realm of ideas', should be regarded with scepticism. Not only are these notions unclear, with objects that cannot be known with certainty, but they are also often used as tools to manipulate people and gain political power.

This rejection of certain claims of traditional metaphysics goes hand in hand with social criticism directed against religious authority, unchecked political power, institutionalized religion and the justification of morals through traditions. Diderot frequently engages with ethical, meta-ethical and political questions that challenge older standards of morality and promote personal liberty. His scathing criticism of eighteenth-century France makes it clear that he envisions a comprehensive overhaul of society, tradition and the general way of life.

However, the rejection of traditional metaphysics and epistemology renders the established ways of justifying normative claims problematic. Without the concepts of a causally efficacious free will and a supernatural source of normativity, ethics may appear arbitrary or impossible. There seems to be no reason to follow any norms other than hedonism, habit or social incentives. Different versions of this picture of Enlightenment materialism as struggling to reconcile ethics and politics with metaphysics are presented by authors such as Cassirer (1968), Gay (1996), Kondylis (1981) and many others. One concise example:

> The philosophy of materialism leads, then – at least, if we follow its logic strictly – to an ethics deprived of moral responsibility. Good will is replaced by social pressure, and the moral experience by habit and habituation. Crocker (1959, 174).

Materialism cannot be used as a source for normativity – philosophy is led into the 'dead end of moralistic materialism'.[2] Within the materialist framework, it seems that agency has only two sources: either it is guided and motivated by an innate striving towards happiness and leads to hedonism, or it is guided and constrained by social norms and legal coercion and leads to cultural relativism or nihilism. Such ethical theory is suspended between anthropology and politics; on its own, it seems to have no philosophical merit or scope. The moral question 'what should I do?' expresses nothing but utilitarian self-interest. But there may be more to this story. In this paper, I will construct an argument concerning Diderot's take on materialism and morality that deviates to a significant degree from this bleak picture.[3]

Since the seminal studies of Duchet ([1971] 1995) and Proust ([1962] 1995), the tension between ethics and materialism in Diderot has been subject to discussion. Some researchers suggest that ethics and materialism are juxtaposed in Diderot (e.g. Proust (1995, 304–10); Winter (1972, 219–22)), while others view Diderot as successful at integrating materialism and ethics (e.g. Duchet (1995, 407–73); Mensching (1971, 94–7)). With some reservations I will argue in favour of the latter position. My claim is this: Diderot conceives of a normativity inherent in nature which serves as the grounds for his ethical and political positions. To support this claim, I will first sketch the notion of an economy of nature that introduces a very basic notion of normative relation. Then I discuss what it means to be part of a species in a more general sense and how the economy of the world conveys its normativity to the species. Finally I turn to discuss the more particular notions of humankind and humanity.[4]

2. The economy of the world

In 1745, Diderot published a translation of Shaftesbury's *An Inquiry Concerning Virtue or Merit* (in French: *Essai sur le Mérite et la Vertu*). He provides a commentary to the text in the footnotes, usually agreeing with Shaftesbury.[5] Diderot took up several of these ideas in his own works, such as the *Pensées Philosophiques* (Philosophical Thoughts, 1746) and the *Pensées sur l'Interprétation de la Nature* (Thoughts about the Interpretation of Nature, 1754).[6] Several claims made therein provide the grounds for what I will call Diderot's relational theory of values, such as the claim is that the world is an ordered whole in which all parts are *functionally* aligned. The core idea is this. Nature, especially living nature, contains dichotomies and relations, such as organ – organism, prey – predator, male – female, etc., and each side of these dichotomies would be incomprehensible without the other. Natural entities are not merely understood through themselves but through their relations which each other. They complement each other, ontologically and epistemically, by virtue of their relational nature: the whole of nature determines the identity of its parts. For example, the existence of the fly is a necessity to the spider and the functional arrangement of organic properties can be understood through the relations within a species or between the species: the spider has fangs and can build a net to trap for flies, etc. Every being has its place which is determined holistically, by the relations to other beings. Diderot writes: 'The absolute independence of a single fact is incompatible with the idea of a whole; and without the idea of a whole, philosophy is impossible.'[7] Many researchers have read this as ontological monism,[8] but here I want to ignore the ontological reasoning that is involved and focus on the corresponding epistemic holism.

From the vantage point of epistemic holism, according to which everything relates to the whole, we need to conceive the order of nature by assuming a benevolent 'watchmaker', but we gain no further insight into their morality, intentions or behaviour. This is a philosophically thin notion of God that does away with the metaphysical speculation which Diderot derides as baseless, especially in his later writings. The functional arrangement of parts can be observed and understood without speculative metaphysical thought, even though it might be a never-ending empirical enterprise[9] – for now, it is nothing but a 'reasonable presumption'.[10] Diderot strives to qualify his epistemic claims as conjecture but not as speculative metaphysics. For the finite embodied mind, our understanding of nature will always be provisional. We can speculate about a divine plan, as the observable order of the world may at first glance appear to testify to creation by a divine intelligence,[11] but he also points out that this divine intelligence can never be known.[12] For human minds, only a more naturalistic understanding of the origins of forms is possible, as only this can be based on observation; everything else is speculation and faith.

Nature is an ordered whole in which everything is 'in its place', namely 'a machine which has its wheels, its ropes, its pulleys, its springs, and its weights'.[13] This was a frequently used metaphor in the seventeenth century.[14] All entities and their properties are situated in an order wherein everything has its function. Furthermore, the relations between parts have *value* that they derive from being appropriate to the context, the whole. The order of nature can hence be understood as an *economy*, as relations arranged in accordance with principles or as goods arranged in accordance with their functionality. The economy of the whole confers natural ends on its parts: being in one's natural arrangement is beneficial, harmonious and desirable. Diderot's materialism is infused with a distinct view of relational values inherent in nature. The existence of flies is *good for* spiders, the dichotomy of men and women is *good for* the entire species, etc. The whole is ontologically and epistemologically prior to the parts. If one could conceive of the whole of nature, one would see how all parts are good for nature as a totality. Adopting such a holistic perspective is impossible for finite minds, but it can be used as a guiding principle to investigate the efficacy of nature. We can observe deviations from this relational standard negatively as catastrophes, monsters, etc., although such an assessment should not be mistaken for an objectively moral judgement. On the contrary, Diderot is sympathetic to these deviations, which also have 'their place' in nature.

Two ideas are important here. Nature is a continuum that extends from the simplest molecule to the most complex being, and an immanent capacity for self-ordering is ubiquitously present in nature. From the smallest molecule to the biggest whale, all entities are endowed with the basic capacity to 'sense' their place and strive towards it. Molecules are the minimal 'building-blocks' of both matter and life and entirely animated by forces; consequently, Diderot often speaks of *living molecules*. Forces and primitive forms of feeling establish a motion that takes its direction from its spatial and material context. Diderot is a pan-vitalist: matter is pervaded with life. Life emerges in relation to an ordered environment, and this external relationship determines the functional arrangement of internal parts, in a continuous organization that pervades the minimal forms of feeling that inhabit all parts of matter. Diderot writes:

> Each form has the happiness and unhappiness appropriate to it. From the elephant all the way to the aphid …, from the aphid all the way to the sensitive and living molecule, [which is] the origin of everything, there is not a point in all of nature which does suffer or feel delight.[15]

This is the basic driving force for the creation and development of natural order. Instead of the universe blindly following universal laws of nature, there is a multitude of interacting parts arranging themselves in accordance with their own 'feeling' for their appropriate position. This involves perceiving the appropriateness of arrangements, and presumably any entity can engage with the arrangement to various causally determined degrees until a feeling of harmony is established. Appropriateness is a norm, and it denotes a natural end; it conveys its normativity to our sensations. Such a normative order cannot be fully explained by universal laws alone and it guides agency and behaviour through feelings, including delight and happiness. The global emergence of order can be seen as the result of continuous actions that strive from an initial state of disorder towards a state of order. Order consists of 'arrangements in an infinite multitude of orderings which nature has *successively* taken on'.[16] In this sense, order is autopoietic.[17]

This idea of an economic universe giving rise to order incites Diderot to use expressions of purposiveness and functionality when describing nature, to a degree that has led some researchers to accuse Diderot of personifying nature.[18] However, he also indicates that the appearance of order may be grounded subjectively, not objectively, in our conflation of causes and reason. Take the following passage:

> Why does the universe seem so well-ordered to you? It is because everything is linked, in its place, and because there is not a single being that does not have a sufficient reason, unknown or known, for its position, its production, its effect. Is there an exception for the west wind? Is there an exception for grains of

sand? ... If all the forces animating each of the molecules that formed the wind which has enveloped us were known, a geometrician would prove to you that the one that inserted itself between your eye and its eyelid is exactly in its place.[19]

By stating that everything is 'in its place', Diderot ascribes purposiveness as formal directedness to nature, which seems at odds with his rejection of final causes. This apparent conflict can be explained against the backdrop of the economy of nature. Explanations need to be holistic and causal explanations will remain insufficient if they ignore the relational and reciprocal nature of causal interactions – we should be considering a broader field of contextually efficient causes (such as position, production and effect – Diderot is rather vague in this regard). Nature's economy builds on global linkage and suppositions such as order, connectivity or continuity, which serve as the external standards in accordance with which entities are 'in their place'. These global suppositions pertain first and foremost to the whole arrangement, as order and stability are relative functions and not intrinsic properties. Causal relationships are determined by these global suppositions in unique ways, as other relationships might violate higher-order global principles of order or reason. However, unlike many other natural philosophers, Diderot does not assume that these anagogical reasons or global suppositions are universal, ideal or eternal, at least not to the finite mind. They depend on context, and what counts as order in one place or time may be disorderly in another. The universe as a whole is continuously developing and transforming itself, and so is its internal order.

This is not material or goal-directed teleology, but rather a formal teleology in which events and entities must comply with external and global standards. Diderot would reject any assertion that things literally 'should' be in their place – who is telling them where to go? Nonetheless, it can be accepted that the actual course of events *ex post facto* conforms to a standard of reason which would be violated under other possible courses. Hence, events have their *reason* that cannot be associated with singular efficient *causes* as posited by mechanism, but rather with relational forces and suppositions that are of a more complex and vague nature and which determine the whole arrangement altogether. Such causal powers might not always be properly identified through empirical science, but they resonate in the living molecule.

In summary, Diderot rejects teleology in nature while embracing a type of formal teleology that allows us to understand complex and reciprocal efficient causes *as if* they were reasons for the order of the arrangement. In this way, Diderot undermines the traditional is-ought distinction, managing to reject the agent model of teleology while still holding on to an embedded normativity in nature. This has profound implications for understanding our embodied nature.

3. Humankind: Our given nature

Diderot's anthropology is organized around a few core notions such as the biological nature of the human species, our ability to reason, our perfectibility and adaptation, openness, sociability, freedom. While there is no room here for a detailed discussion,

I will reconstruct an argument that the natural but context-dependent normativity discussed above matters for humankind.

The economy of the organic body is such that its parts are functionally arranged for survival, procreation and cognition, according to what is appropriate for each species. An unconscious feeling of harmony and order pervades the entire body down to the molecular level, and it can indicate when certain parts are not in their designated places. Subjectivity emerges in accordance with different stages of organic organization: for example, consciousness comes with a sufficiently complex organization of the brain. This functional alignment of internal – external relations, which includes the feelings perceived by means of the major sensory organs, creates a reciprocal influence or 'feedback-loop' such that it makes the organism *feel* the harmonic alignment of its internal parts as well as its external relations.[20] Here again, the primacy of the whole and the relation of the parts to the whole are of importance.[21] The organization of the body determines the functions of the parts, and the innate sensitivity of matter allows for an assessment of the functionality of the body's parts that is not dependent on conscious understanding of ends. Organisms are nothing but a 'coordination of infinitely active molecules'.[22] An animal can be defined as

> a system of different organic molecules which, under the impulsion of a similar feeling and an obtuse and muted touch (*un toucher obtus et sourd*) from the creator of matter in general, combined themselves until each of them found the position best suited to its form and its comfort.[23]

Diderot acknowledges that the difference between living and dead bodies is merely a matter of arrangement.[24] We must assume that there is a continuum of forms, the so-called great chain of being that extends from the simplest molecule to the most complex organism, and everything, even the economy of nature, is in perpetual flux.[25] In this dynamic continuum, it is the persistence of innate functional traits across individuals that distinguishes one species from another. Consequently, Diderot calls a species 'the sum of a certain number of tendencies at a common term that is unique to them'.[26] The tendency that defines the species is two fold: it consists of both the statistical average of forms and the inherent striving of nature for self-organization around a common feeling or arrangement. However, it is important not to interpret the 'common term' as an unchangeable norm, but rather as that form which is appropriate for the members of the species in general, with respect to their surroundings, which ultimately is nothing but the whole of nature. The ultimate way of understanding the reciprocal purposiveness between internal arrangements and external appropriateness would be to develop an all-encompassing gaze regarding natural history.[27] As this is not possible for the finite mind, philosophically informed empirical observation is all that is available to us – and hence all our understanding of appropriateness is provisional.

Animals, including humans, are nothing but bodies. Diderot rejects explanations of human nature that invoke the mind. In the *Éléments de Physiologie* (Elements of Physiology, 1774), he argues that human nature entails human life just as much as the animal and vegetable dimension of life. It is simply organized matter defined by extension and inertia and endowed with basic forms of feeling.[28] The common assumption that the human mind is essential to our nature is a product of a rather subjective viewpoint that overtly emphasizes the social and interpersonal dimension of our life, occasionally at the expense of all other organic or material forms of existence.

Diderot's notion of humankind builds on his conception of the species as an order of arrangements and the sum of tendencies. As physical and mental capabilities stem from the organic arrangement of the body, it is problematic to speak of unique and unchangeable faculties. From a physiological perspective, more complex capabilities build on simpler ones, but the simpler forms do not entail, necessitate or strive towards the development of more complex forms. Furthermore, being staunchly anti-Platonic, Diderot rejects the idea of unchangeable and distinct types of entities in nature. Only individuals exist. However, species are not a mere heuristic either, and Diderot oscillates between emphasizing differences and continuity in organization.[29] Species are determined internally and externally. Concerning internal determination, the arrangement of individuals and their relations to each other stem from their history, and similarities of phenotype or sexual compatibility can be explained historically. Diderot adopts Buffon's idea of a 'prototype':[30] all the animals of a species originate from an ancestral being through a series of generations.[31] Bodies grow from germs or 'seminal elements', thus being shaped by past generations and by the past survival conditions of the species as a whole.[32] Common properties are transmitted by means of inheritance – 'fibers' and 'molecules' contain whatever is needed to establish affinity with the prototype and determine both individual character and similitude and compatibility with other animals. Species can thus be explained qua descent from a common ancestor and the diachronic continuity of important structural arrangements. But this should not be understood as a proto-evolutionary approach, as Diderot does not mean that one species can originate from another. Instead, the core features of the prototype are retained throughout generations. This diachronic understanding of what constitutes the nature of a species allows him to trace species-specific and observable behavioural traits ('order of their actions', as he calls it[33]) back to the origins of the species itself. The same type or 'model' informs and influences the actions of all individuals.

Regarding external determination, Diderot is inspired by ideas developed by Buffon and Maupertuis to assert that all species are shaped by their adaptation to the environment, including geography and climate, food consumption, ways of living in a community, natural lineage through migration and adaptation, as well as simple 'mutational errors' in procreation.[34] As Diderot puts it: 'we are nothing but what is appropriate (!) to the general order, to the organization, to the education, and to the chain of events'.[35] As all species are guided by their feeling of appropriateness, they are intuitively adapting their behaviour to their environment. In the *Encyclopédie* article 'Bête' (Beast), Diderot gives the examples of birds building their nests in different shapes, depending on circumstantial factors, and of beavers adapting their dams to their environment. This holds for humans as well. This view on the dependency on contextual factors and circumstantial causality is at odds with that of his more religious contemporaries: human beings are not defined by being an image of God or having a singular type of existence; they are fully integrated into nature, entirely subject to natural laws and environmental circumstances.

Regarding their physical organization, humans belong to the animal realm, but they are distinguished by means of their variability, adaptability and, above all, the perfectibility that drives the internal arrangement and external adaptation of the species towards greater appropriateness, towards the 'most suitable position'. Humans do not have a particular location or climate but are capable of adapting to all types of environments.[36] This is illustrated by the human hand that serves as a universal tool not restricted to one single purpose, as well as by the variety of languages, customs, societal institutions and the regional differences in character. Adequate forms of life can influence the development of our capabilities. Temporal development goes along with an increase in perfection, which in this context means refinement of the appropriate arrangement. For humans, perfectibility as a formal driver of adaptation and perfection is a species-wide property and hence largely culturally invariant, even though its diverse manifestations can only be understood empirically and within the different cultures.

Humans are not defined by their free will: Diderot rejects the concept of free will as an illusion – i.e. he rejects the (Cartesian) idea of an ungrounded or uncaused but causally effective volition.[37] All volitions and actions have their sufficient causes and can hence be explained empirically. The faculty of reason is the functional result of organic parts, and so is the will. As sketched above, we cognize what is good or bad in a duplicitously relational way: once with regard to ourselves and again with regard to the ends of the species within which we are situated. Humans are defined by their capacity to extend their sphere of influence and thereby improve their natural and cultural environment: they can build instruments and refine them, far beyond the grasp of their own natural organs. The human hand as a universal tool elevates humans beyond all other animals.[38] In a sense, the human being is not defined as *animal rationale* but rather as *animal faber*.

Perfectibility builds on the determination of the parts through the whole. Human beings are shaped by their environment, of which they are a part, but they can also, in contrast to animals, shape the environment in accordance with their needs and desires, by establishing a human community. Humans are always and necessarily part of a community and as such defined by the whole of their society. All living beings naturally strive towards cooperation, to a certain degree, as the natural ends of each species are aligned; as they follow a universal 'necessary order' imposed by nature, they all strive to work towards the general good of the species.[39] Any being that acted against this general good would soon cease to exist. This is where the emergence of order becomes important to anthropology. In his early Shaftesbury translation, Diderot deliberately blurs the boundaries between the natural and the social – or, to put it in more modern terms, between nature and culture. For example, Diderot translates Shaftesbury's expression 'natural affection' as 'social inclinations' ('inclinations sociales'[40]). What Shaftesbury calls natural 'moral (common) sense' thus becomes a driving factor in social integration.

Due to its functional versatility and openness, the hand can be used to form all other instruments, thereby allowing humans to develop themselves more than with any other organ that has a particular function. Furthermore, through physical labour, humans have changed their surroundings and adapted themselves cognitively to the unlimited variety of tools that are provided by the hand. While the instincts of animal species are appropriate to their organic functions, human instinct supersedes this limitation due to the unlimited physical utility of the hand. But reason is not exclusive to humans. Diderot explains in the *Réfutation d'Helvétius* (1774) that human reason is nothing but a perfectible and perfected instinct,[41] and just like other biological features, human instincts can vary quite a bit, there being no reason to assume that human reason is equally distributed. There is no need to assume a special faculty of reason because there is nothing special about reason – reason is a mere by-product of the natural metamorphosis of species. From Diderot's anti-Platonic vantage point, reason and emotions are not conceived of as opposed to each other, but as functionally aligned parts within the greater whole of human nature. Hence, there is no categorical difference between reason and other capacities.[42]

Thought is the result of sensitivity developed and exercised in the right conditions, and sensitivity is a universal property of the living molecules that compose organic bodies. Sensitivity seems dormant in an organic matter, but it can be activated when the material is incorporated into a living being. In the *Réfutation*, Diderot also claims that reason as humans' defining property is rooted in the organic structure of the human species. But such an explanation remains vague and overly general, given that there can be rather extreme individual variations. Theorizing about reason needs to take people's irrational behaviour into account. Viewing reason as the Archimedean point for philosophizing or the panacea for all daily woes is misleading – empirical observation of reason in action weakens the theoretical strength of this notion to the degree that it can hardly bear any philosophical weight.[43]

As we do not have access to the point of view from the whole to its parts, this is where science and interpretation come in, to confirm this 'lofty' philosophy. Interpretation entails the understanding of causal connections and functional tasks.[44] Being unable to provide an a priori definition of human nature, we look to experience for answers. Human nature is best determined statistically, but deviations from the statistical medium are natural and expected. This also extends into the moral realm: while human nature is good overall, evil is also expected and, to a certain degree, natural.[45] Diderot writes that the totality of the species is changing constantly and that 'man is only a common effect; a monster is only a rare effect'.[46]

There is no 'ideal' type of humans, only a common historical origin. Hence, Diderot's perspective on humankind is remarkably inclusive. He acknowledges all those usually excluded from the 'gaze' of philosophy: handicapped or physically challenged people, such as the blind and the deaf, to whom he devotes two treatises; women, whose perspective he adopts in some of his literary writings; and indigenous people, whose perspective on human issues is considered valuable. This strategy serves a dual purpose: it is used to develop a unique perspective on norms and their natural deviations, and it also highlights the systematic limits of the traditional Eurocentric ways of thinking. Diderot accuses theologians, politicians, philosophers of living in an informational 'bubble' without dissenting opinions.

But how is human nature connected to humanity? From Pufendorf to Rousseau, the original state of human nature has served as the universal standard against which society and politics must be evaluated. One of the major anthropological questions of the eighteenth century is whether humans are good or bad by virtue of their own nature and whether it is society or nature that makes human beings morally good. Diderot offers an ambivalent answer. We do not have an absolute standard to determine moral goodness. Our perspectives are developed in relation to our societal standards and our individual perspectives, and there is no transcendent 'anchor' to ground universal morality. 'There is no vice or virtue, nothing to reward or punish for.'[47] But this is not the end of it, as we have an inborn sense of what is good *for us*, at least within our respective contexts, and we also need to develop some notion of vice and virtue in order to keep society stable. While seeking to avoid the absolute claims of religious or providential morality, Diderot also steers clear of materialist nihilism, which he sees as exemplified by two of his contemporaries, Helvétius and La Mettrie. Morality may not have a transcendent, absolute foundation, but the organizational arrangement of humankind serves as a foundation for morality.[48] This will be explored in the next two sections.

4. Humanity – *what we should make of ourselves*

There is another uniquely human quality that elevates us above animality and into the moral realm: humanity. Without humanity, nobody would qualify as a proper human being, except in a semantically reduced biological sense. This is often more of a philosophical intuition than a fully fleshed-out claim or argument. Yet it can help us understand the philosophical anthropology of the enlightenment when discussing the intricate relationship between the defining qualities of humankind and humanity. This relates to the aforementioned normativity derived from the economy of nature, with the relational theory of values serving as the basis for a notion of humanity that is often merely implied. In this chapter, I will try to pinpoint some important defining features of Diderot's notion of humanity, namely our relationship with society and how we can and should shape it. Such a definition, in turn, can only be developed within a proper society.

Diderot does not use the notion of humanity very frequently. The *Encyclopedia* article 'Humanité' by Jean-François de Saint-Lambert and Edmé-François Mallet defines humanity as a 'feeling of benevolence for all men, which is hardly inflamed except in a great and sensitive soul.'[49] Diderot also emphasizes the moral significance of universal benevolence: 'The probity relative to the universe is nothing other than a feeling of benevolence which embraces the human species in general.'[50] Humanity, it seems, is dependent on a specific normative assessment of our relationship with humankind. This goes along with another related claim by Diderot. Humans develop a moral form of life which separates them from all animals:

> Animals are separated from us by invariable and eternal barriers; and we are dealing here with a system of knowledge and ideas peculiar to the human species, arising from and forming his dignity in the world.[51]

Dignity and humanity, which I take to be connected here, derive from a superior form of knowledge concerning the relationship between the individual and society that only human beings can attain. This is the topic to which I will now turn.

Humans are embedded in a community and shaped through it. All our agency will be informed and distorted by the respective traditions and communal forces, hence our nature will appear rather varied. The atomic, radically individualistic state of nature for humans is defined by chaotic, random interaction. Through time, an ordered and machine-like community arises that becomes a society when based on shared beliefs and common rules.[52] Diderot subscribes to the Hobbesian belief that society is created to protect human beings from violence and chaos by installing an artificial but functional arrangement. When a society that is based on common agreement works together, humans create their own environment in terms of an institutionalized society. This, in turn, provides the context in which human nature is deemed appropriate.

Agency is directed by the will, and hence practical normativity arises from the will. For Diderot, the will is not juxtaposed to reason. In fact, we could do without a notion of the will and should refrain from thinking of it as a distinct faculty of the mind. Just as reason and instincts derive from the biological structure of the organism, so does the will. It allows us to lean towards particular actions or values more than others, especially when its inclination or tendency is affirmed by (what we call) reason. The will relates itself to the unconscious perception of appropriateness which ranges from the 'feeling' of the living molecule to more complicated human feelings. Of these feelings, happiness and empathy stand out, along with the particular human trait of sociability. As pointed out above, each living being has a form of happiness appropriate to it, which I take to mean that happiness goes hand in hand with the appropriate arrangement of parts in a whole. Sociability or empathy do not define human nature, themselves being the result of our innate drives for self-preservation and happiness. All other drives and strivings are derived from our drive for happiness: 'There is only one passion, and that is to be happy.'[53] Self-preservation and sociability are seen as deeply intertwined: the satisfaction of our needs is felt as happiness, but it is also dependent on our interaction with others. Diderot writes, exploiting the notion of 'tendency' that he uses to define the nature of species: 'It's *me* who wants to be happy. This constant tendency (!) is the eternal, permanent source of all its duties, even the smallest. Any law to the contrary is a crime against humanity, an act of tyranny.'[54] And: 'I want society to be happy but I also want the citizens to be happy, and there are as many ways of being happy as there are individuals. Our own happiness is the foundation of all our true duties.'[55] Naturally, the will is directed at happiness, and happiness indicates appropriate relations with the context. Individual happiness is often dependent on societal factors and usually impossible to achieve without social support.[56]

Behavioural standards in society are set by authority but often conflict with the individual will. Naturally, our agency is intuitively directed at happiness, and happiness is tied to our conception of moral goodness, which has no absolute standards but relates to a societal framework requiring an artificial agreement on standards of happiness. Society can only be created by a shared belief in a common cause or higher entity, which results in a common and binding law. A group of radically independent individuals would not result in a proper society. The individual will cannot be the source of morality or legality, as it is arbitrary – as outlined above, Diderot argues against presuming a common, uniform and universal reason inherent in all human beings.

He employs this idea to criticize the claims of moral universality on multiple fronts, for example that religious authorities mistakenly assume that their contingent moral ideas are universal. As empirical evidence shows, no such universal religion exists. The cultural foundation of religion runs counter to its universalistic claims and only a pared-down version of religion, namely natural religion, can be reasonably defended. Diderot holds that we naturally strive towards a belief in God or the supernatural, but we cannot use it for moral justification or in our search for purposes in life: 'If the naturalist is asked: "Why does one suffer in this world?" he replies, "I don't have the vaguest idea". If the Christian is asked the same question, he replies with an enigma or an absurdity.'[57]

Experience shows that people are motivated predominantly by self-love, and they commit to cooperation not out of altruistic motives but because of the need to establish a reasonably safe society. Individual motivations need to be constrained by efficient and just laws which encourage certain forms of behaviour, deter people from others and create socially beneficial customs. Positive law needs to be consistent with natural law, but natural law can conflict with religious presumptions of universality. Diderot's criticism of revealed law and its universalist presumptions is most clearly presented from the perspective of the 'savage' in the *Supplément au voyage de Bougainville* (Supplement to Bougainville's Voyages, 1796), a fictionalized account of the encounter between French sailors and Tahitian natives inspired by true events. The Tahitian community is depicted as natural, gentle, equal, free and simple – it is not yet tainted by the moral corruption of modern society. Natural morality is directed at satisfying natural desires in harmony with the needs of other people. Respect for others and moral dignity naturally arise from everyday activities, independent of transcendent beliefs. Tahiti is a utopia of sexual freedom, freedom from religious authorities and social pressures. The *Supplement* contains a fictional dialogue between a European chaplain and Orou, a native of Tahiti, who shows himself to be more enlightened, unprejudiced and insightful on human issues than most of Diderot's intellectual contemporaries. Diderot uses this dialogue not only to develop his own argument but to criticize those he deems misguided by religion and authority. Many of the values and beliefs that define French culture are simply unintelligible to the natives, such as the belief in a transcendent creator or the virtues of monastic life. Tahiti is depicted as a utopian community but also as offering a glimpse of humankind as it was before the rise of organized religion. Diderot concludes by stating that once natural desires are satisfied, artificial desires arise and need to be regulated by positive or revealed law. This creates, from the perspective of the wise Tahitian, an irresolvable internal conflict between natural and artificial desires, between natural humanity and artificial social provisions. No human being can ever fully conform to their given nature, their civic duties and their religious duties at the same time. Natural and artificial desires will inevitably come into conflict with each other. In this sense, natural society is an oxymoron, as humans can either live in accordance with nature or in accordance with society but not both. Society promotes the artificial human at the expense of natural humankind.[58]

In the Tahitian community, natural humanity has not yet been distorted. As institutional society arises from such community through agreement on common and artificial beliefs, natural desires are replaced by artificial norms. Consequently, natural community is not only the source and origin of modern society but also the ideal standard to which it must be compared. Henry Vyverberg puts this concisely:

> Diderot, like most of his contemporaries, found it hard to shake off – or, more likely did not even wholly want to shake off – that corollary of nature designated as 'state of nature.' He often shared with others, moreover, a failure to distinguish this state of nature as an ideal state, as a historical phase, or as a condition found among contemporary primitive peoples. Thus again the Enlightenment view of nature wavered uncertainly between the factual, the theoretical, and the normative.
> (Vyverberg 1989, 26)

But this is not so much theoretical uncertainty as scepticism regarding claims of universality made either by observation or by theorizing. As indicated above, the notion of an economy of nature conflates the *is* and the *ought* in nature. This normativity is now juxtaposed to societal norms. What the species *is* (here and now) is intrinsically tied to what *is good for* the species (within its local and global context). Only after we have examined Diderot's relational theory of values we can discern a more nuanced notion of humanity in Diderot.

5. Humanity and the general will

Diderot does not deem it impossible to make valid normative claims. Human beings have, as members of the same species, an inherent sense of appropriateness that relates individual circumstances to the species as a whole. The normativity of any particular or individual aspects of nature can be misleading when not related to the whole. This holds for the human will as well: the individual will cannot make any universal claims. But there is a general will attributable to the species such that it serves as a standard for individual claims. The entire species is subject to this general will. In his article *Droit Naturel* (Natural Right, 1755) Diderot writes:

> But if we deny the individual the right to determine the nature of justice and injustice, before whom do decide this great question? Where? Before humankind; for only humankind may decide the issue, since the good of all is the only passion they have, particular wills are suspect; they can be good or evil, but the general will is always good: it has never deceived, it never will deceive.[59]

This mirrors the above-mentioned conception of the species as tending towards a common notion. Just as we can view variations within the biological structure of the species in terms of deviations from a prototype, we can also regard the varieties of individual or particular wills as deviations from a common will. In his anti-Platonic manner, Diderot suggests that morality can be naturalized through the concept of the general will. This means that two questions need to be answered within a naturalistic or materialistic perspective: what norms are there, and why should we follow them?

The first question is never answered in detail, but we can flesh out some implications of Diderot's writings. The general will serves as a formal standard, but it only mediately prescribes happiness as a material end, as happiness is indicating appropriateness relative to the whole. As the species is always in flux, so is the object of the general will: '[E]ven supposing that the notion of species was in perpetual flux, the nature of natural rights would not change, since they would still relate to the general will and the common desire of the whole species.'[60] The 'common desires' correspond to the 'tendency toward a common notion' introduced above and thus progress and change are possible. For example, although we can say that the species shares a common desire for happiness and an inborn need for community, this does not mean that natural deviations or profound changes in direction are impossible. Just as the common 'tendency' of the species leaves room for biological change, so the general will leaves room for social change.

The general will provides the foundation for natural right as the natural limits within which posited law can be regarded as just. Thus, it provides a normative framework for a just society towards which humans naturally strive, as only justice can provide grounds for establishing lasting security and conditions for happiness in a society. In contrast to Hobbes, Diderot's general will is not the will of the citizen but rather that of the natural human being, as it requires us to abstract from our merely individual and artificial desires. To understand the general will, we need to inquire into our common desires, which are grounded in our universal given nature. The general will should not be confused with so-called popular wisdom or common sense, which is usually distorted by artificial needs, religious beliefs or societal pressure. Given sufficient knowledge of human nature, it should be clear how the particular and the general will are aligned. The process of civilization creates an artificial human nature within us, and thus any insight into our natural needs can only be achieved by liberating ourselves from the constraints of institutionalized society and its publicly communicated framework of authority and morals. In this regard, the general will brings out the natural human being at the expense of the artificial citizen.

As society is founded on agreement, conscious reflection on common values is required. The general will makes itself *felt* directly to people living within a natural community and with their natural desires, but in an institutionalized society, where artificial desires have arisen in juxtaposition to natural desires, it needs to be reflected and made transparent. This leads astray our intuitive understanding of what is good for all of us and calls for deliberate reflection and empirical inquiries to help us understand both natural desires and the way artificial desires have veiled them. In this sense, it is a product of reason (*l'entendement*) rather than immediate volition. 'The general will is in each person a pure act of understanding.'[61] In the general will, the functional 'tendency' that determines the unity of humankind is transformed into an agreement between agents, and the merely formal determinacy of humankind is thereby attached to the material determinacy of agency through a common end. The general will should be granted legislative power so as to ensure the happiness of humankind itself because individual wills are informed and motivated by artificial desires. However, philosophical reflection is an unreliable tool for identifying the objects of the general will. What is needed is criticism of our artificial needs and the corresponding societal institutions, along with empirical observation of the commonalities of all peoples and their systems of legislation.

Humans are gifted with freedom, but that does not entail the right to command others.[62] The only relevant arrangement in which normative rights arise is the family – as long as the children are incapable of self-governance, it is the right and duty of the father to command them. Both just and unjust authorities are derived from human interaction in the form of either agreement or violence. Employing laws and executive force in the name of justice requires a special justification regarding the nature of the agreement that we need to strive for. Whereas Hobbes uses the general will to establish the authority of the sovereign out of material necessity, Diderot uses the general will to establish the *moral* equality of all human beings, who, despite all their empirical differences, are all equally subject to the general will as a common measure of rational and empirically observable decision-making. Consciousness of this moral equality under the general will is the essential factor in the constitution of humanity.

This moral equality means that the general will serves as the basis for natural right, independent of all societal particulars. It also serves as a ubiquitous normative standard by means of which the particular wills within a society can be evaluated. However, its universal claims are themselves contingent and capable of progress. As the general will is aligned with the development of the species, it too may be subject to generational change. However, this does not diminish the role of the general will in serving as the normative basis for natural rights. While the general will is usually regarded as a foundation for natural rights, I argue that there is more to it. Diderot writes:

> For an individual to know how far he ought to be a man, a citizen, a subject, a father, or a child, and when it befits him to live or die, he must address himself to the general will. It is for the general will to determine the limits of all duties. You have the most sacred *natural right* to everything that is not resisted by the whole human race. It is the general will which shall enlighten you as to the nature of your thoughts and your desires. Everything you conceive, everything you contemplate, will be good, great, elevated, sublime, if it accords with the general and common interest.[63]

The general will provides orientation within the different contexts that people need to navigate – it evaluates norms that govern the state but also the family or one's own life. Again, the chain of subsequent justifications of ends or maxims can only be set within a meaningful context by taking the whole into account, in this case humankind in its entirety. What is good for the family or the state must also, in the end, be good for humankind. The general will is a tool for progress and enlightenment in the sense that it helps us identify or even discard artificial desires and morals, thereby providing a basis for appropriate moral judgement. This is important in the realm of legislation – moral judgement and legislation are not two separate spheres of philosophy or everyday thinking. In fact, societal standards of behaviour have historically developed alongside legislation:

> I think that morally appropriate customs derive from laws. A savage people has morally appropriate customs when you see among them natural laws, humanity, gentleness, charitable acts, loyalty, good faith, etc. A civilized people has morally appropriate customs when you generally see among them natural and civil laws.[64]

The societal development of just legislation thus leads to greater progress not only in society, arts and philosophy but also in morality. This is also relevant to the development of humanity.

Diderot assumes that morality can be naturalized; i.e. observable nature can serve as both an explanation of why people act morally and as a normative foundation for all moral demands, rights and obligations that are universally valid. Ethical justification is thus tied to empirical observation and social criticism alike. Natural right entails the right to increasing moral perfection, thereby necessarily underpinning the possibility that positive law can make some progress.[65] It might even be argued that humanity's progress is also naturalized, as it can be traced back to the developmental and relational structure of humankind. 'The whole evolution of humanity is thus inscribed in the very structure of the human animal.'[66]

Diderot has been criticized of ignoring the rather formal nature of reason, which does not easily and obviously produce species-wide agreement on specific contents of thought.[67] This criticism falls short because reason takes empirical knowledge about the common nature of the species as the basis from which the contents of the general will can be derived, if only in a negative way: like the maxim that all actions that go against our common desires are wrong or the maxim that moral decision-making needs to take its own contingency into account. As indicated above, happiness becomes a *mediated* material end.

The political authority of the state issues laws that should conform to the general will, and furthermore, their decision-making should be grounded in the general will. A ruler who decrees laws that happen to coincide with the general will is still guilty of injustice: 'any prince who did good contrary to the general will would be a criminal, for the simple reason that he had exceeded his rights'.[68] Thus, the general will contradicts the colonialist attitudes of eighteenth-century France: even if a colonial empire would bring material benefits or spiritual guidance to the subjected people, as a colonizer might claim, such an empire nonetheless ignores other common needs of humankind (e.g. individual freedom and governmental autonomy), and hence it has overstepped its legitimacy.

Beyond relating to universal needs and common desires, the general will has little content on its own. It simply acknowledges (1) the universality of human nature, (2) the possibility of deviations from the norm and (3) the universal contingency that determines our human nature, especially our culturally informed self-understanding. This leads to both legislative and epistemic modesty, which acknowledges its own contingent presuppositions and, respectively, its own historical origins. The general will is therefore more of an expression of our fundamental right to re-evaluate all externally imposed duties. It reveals the need to bring our own humanity to the fore by keeping artificial desires in check, together with all the societal customs that produce and enforce these artificial desires. In so doing, it also reveals the empirical grounds on which reasonable political disagreement is possible. It does not provide any specific norm but rather the general duty to align laws with the common desires of humankind. While naturally gravitating towards individual happiness, we should collectively follow the general will, as it ensures the greatest chance of happiness relative to our status in nature. Jerome Schneewind writes: 'Seek happiness with justice in this life: if this is a moral principle, it is the one Diderot would support.'[69] The general will is not only a notion on which natural rights can be grounded, in Diderot it becomes a tool to promote happiness and humanity in accordance with reason.

By emphasizing the conceptual need to include social criticism, empirical observation, and moral motivation within ethical theory, Diderot strengthens the role that anthropologically grounded psychology plays in ethics. Ethical deliberation has only a weak impact on how ethical convictions play out in the real world; law and politics are much more important. There must be a societal impetus for citizens to transform themselves into honest citizens. It is not so much that ethics is lost in or suspended between anthropology and politics; it is rather that we need to create a society first in which ethical considerations are allowed appropriate breathing room in our agency. Such a society would require a system of widely agreed-upon beliefs that are anthropologically appropriate and politically and religiously sufficiently liberal. Such a society would be, as Élisabeth de Fontenay puts it, 'liberal, libertine, and libertarian'.[70] Just like Schneewind's statement cited above, this is rather vague, but this vagueness is due to the relational nature of appropriateness as a formal norm which by itself provides no determined material end.

One might argue that Diderot is naive in projecting the norms and duties of the state – protecting citizens and securing their liberty – onto a universal entity, namely the human species and, correspondingly, some imaginary cosmopolitan society.[71] But such a criticism mistakenly understands the general will as an applicable political program instead of a *critical* account of the emergence and limits of normativity within a materialistic world view. This normativity is, like the species itself, rooted in history, adaptable and perfectible, and as such, it can only be expressed with a significant degree of epistemic modesty. Diderot's notion of materialistic morality is based on the presumption of a functional arrangement of the species within its natural and human-made environment. Unhindered natural development and the satisfaction of common desires are the standards against which the range of human agency can be evaluated; however, it is not clear whether we can ever develop a clear conception of natural normativity that has managed to completely free itself from all societal prejudice or historical contingency. By evaluating societal morals and posited law through the lens of this natural normativity, the general will serves as both justification for and restriction on positive laws in a just society. As Diderot seems to think that appropriate morality would develop in tandem with such laws in a just society, the general will could, at least indirectly, be used to formulate a set of positive maxims and duties, through its evaluation of laws and customs. The resulting ethical system would not be a 'metaphysics of morals' but a normative anthropology. The 'ought' of the general will follows from the 'is' of the human species: it is neither desirable nor justifiable to act against human nature. The human 'ought' derives from this general concept of an economy of nature, in which 'is' and 'ought' have in fact never been fully separated.[72]

Notes

1. For an overview of different types of materialism, see Wunderlich (2016) and Wolfe (2016).
2. Kondylis (1981), 518–32.
3. In his *Réfutation de Helvétius* (Refutation of Helvétius, 1773), Diderot clearly tries to avoid the spectre of ethical relativism.
4. Diderot's *OEuvres* is methodically and conceptually heterogeneous. His texts are often literary, fragmentary, critical, aphoristic or essayistic. This diversity of perspectives and textual forms obscures the systematic relations between ideas and arguments. Diderot also displays therein a hyper-consciousness regarding the social dimension of thought and truth, and some of his texts are shaped by their social role and performative function. This should not, however, preclude us from reading Diderot as a more systematic thinker – this point has been made by Barzun (1986), Crocker (1974), Duflo (2013a) and Winter (1972). But this should come with the reservation that the systematic connection of arguments over the course of multiple texts should not be confused with the building of a fully fleshed-out system.
5. For a more detailed comparison, see Walters Jr (1971) and Clark (2008), chap. 2. For a reading that downplays Shaftesbury's influence on Diderot, see Brewer (1993), chap. 2.
6. Diderot's works are cited from Diderot, D. (1975–), *Œuvres complètes*, ed. H. Dieckmann, J. Proust, and J. Varloot, 23 vols, Paris: Hermann, whenever possible (abbreviated as DPV). All translations are my own, unless otherwise indicated.
7. *Pensées sur l'interprétation de la nature*, § XI, DPV (1981), vol. IX, 564. This idea is repeated in the *Rêve de D'Alembert* (1769): 'There is only a single great individual, the whole. In this whole, as in a machine or in any animal, there is a part that you call such and such: but if you give the name "individual" to that part of the whole, it is only a concept as false as if, in a bird, you would give the name to the wing, to a feather of the wing.' DPV (1987), vol. XVII, 139.
8. For example, Israel (2008); Israel (2013).
9. This empirical orientation of philosophy has prompted some interpreters to call Diderot's philosophy 'experimental philosophy'. Wuthenow (1994), 48.
10. *Essai sur le mérite et la vertu*, DPV (1975), vol. I, 314 fn.
11. Cf. *Pensées philosophiques* § XX, DPV (1975), vol. II, 26–7.
12. While we find a more atheist-leaning Diderot in his later writings, this is a view he still upholds in the *Encyclopedia*, for example in the article 'Bête' (Animal, 1751).
13. *Pensées philosophiques* § XVIII, DPV (1975), vol. II, 24–5.
14. See Basile (2019) for the development of this metaphor.
15. *Rêve de D'Alembert*, DPV (1987), vol. XVII, 140.
16. *Pensées philosophiques* § XXI, DPV (1975), vol. II, 29–30 (my emphasis).
17. For a slightly different interpretation of Diderot's notion of order, see Crocker (1974).
18. See Barzun (1986), 24.
19. *Salon de 1767*, DPV (1990), vol. XVI, 186–7.

20 Some modern interpreters understand such a conception as a predecessor of the notion of self-regulatory or cybernetic systems. See Rudolph (1967), for example.
21 Cf. Kaitaro (1997).
22 *Éléments de physiologie*, DPV (1987), vol. XVII, 297. Siehe Scan.
23 *Pensées sur l'interprétation de la nature*, § LI, DPV (1981), vol. IX, 84–5.
24 See especially the articles *Corruption* and *Naître* on the juxtaposition of life and death as states of material arrangement.
25 See, for example, *Rêve de D'Alembert*, DPV (1987), vol. XVII, 138–9.
26 Ibid., 139.
27 Cf. Duchet (1995), 424.
28 *Éléments de physiologie*, DPV (1987), vol. XVII, 337.
29 See Duchet (1995), 421.
30 On the relevance of the notion of a prototype, not only for our understanding of human nature but particularly for human freedom, see Stenger (1994).
31 Cf. the paper by Catherine Wilson in this volume.
32 Cf. *Pensées sur l'interprétation de la nature*, § L, DPV (1981), vol. IX, 79.
33 '[T]ous travaillent sur le même modele; l'ordre de leurs actions est tracé dans l'espece entiere …' Article 'Animal', DPV (1976), vol. V, 387.
34 See Gregory (2007), 194–5.
35 Letter to Landois, 29 June 29 1756, DPV (1981), vol. IX, 257.
36 In the *Réfutation de Helvétius*, he rebukes Helvétius for rejecting climatic influences, although he devotes little attention to this theme in the *Encyclopedia* article 'Climate'.
37 See Duflo (2013b). In the *Éléments de physiologie*, Diderot asserts that '"I want" is nothing but a word'. DPV (1987), vol. XVII, 484. Diderot conceives of the will as a function of natural needs and appetites. Cf. Warman (2020), 76.
38 Raynal/Diderot (1780), vol. VIII, 119–20.
39 See *Essai sur le mérite et la vertu*, DPV (1975), vol. I, 361. The modern liberal idea that not cooperation but competition furthers the ends of humankind is alien to Diderot.
40 See Duchet (1995), 415.
41 DPV (2004), vol. XXIV, 583. See Duchet (1995), 420–1.
42 Cf. *Réfutation de Helvétius*, DPV (2004), vol. XXIV, 540–1.
43 For a more detailed examination of how Diderot uses empirical accounts of reason and behaviour to dismantle the delusions of the philosophers, see Davidson (1986).
44 Cf. Duchet (1995, 424).
45 On the moral monster as a natural occurrence, see Hill (1973).
46 *Rêve de D'Alembert*, DPV (1987), vol. XVII, 138.
47 Letter to Landois, 29 June 1756. DPV (1981), vol. IX, 257.
48 See the *Salon de 1767*, DPV (1990), vol. XVI, 206.
49 De Saint-Lambert, J.-F., and Mallet, E.-F. (1765), 348.
50 *Réflexions sur le livre De l'Esprit*, DPV (1981), vol. IX, 302.
51 Article 'Droit naturel' (Natural Right, 1755), DPV (1976), vol. VII, 27. Translation follows Diderot (1992), 21.
52 'In the so-called pure state of nature, men were scattered across the face of the earth like an infinite number of small, isolated forces. Now and then some of these small forces would happen to meet, collide too heavily and break. The lawgivers, witnessing these accidents, sought a remedy for them, and what did they imagine? To bring the small forces together and to construct a fine machine out of them which they call society.' *Memoires pour Catherine II* (Notes to Catherine II, 1773), Diderot ([1773] 1995), 311. Translation follows Bremner (1983), 79.

53 *Éléments de Physiologie*, DPV (1987), vol. XVII, 486. Siehe Scan.
54 *Observations sur Hemsterhuis* (Notes on Hemsterhuis, 1773), cited after Strugnell (1973), 70.
55 *Observation sur le Nakaz* (Observations about the Nakaz, 1774), cited after Diderot (1992), 125.
56 Diderot's novel *Le neveu de Rameau* (Rameau's Nephew) provides a counter-example, namely a socially isolated, but profoundly happy individual that goes against all typical philosophical ideas of socially responsible humanity.
57 *De la Suffisance de la Religion naturelle* (On the Sufficiency of Natural Religion, 1747/1770), § XXII, DPV (1975), vol. II, 191.
58 The resulting feeling of unease is most clearly illustrated throughout *Rameau's Nephew*, as the tension between the intellectual and morally autonomous aspects of life and the embodied, natural tendencies. Both are represented by means of the novel's protagonists *Moi* and *Lui*.
59 DPV (1976), vol. VII, 27.
60 Ibid., DPV (1976), vol. VII, 29.
61 Ibid., DPV (1976), vol. VII, 28.
62 See Diderot's article *Autorité politique* (Political Authority, 1765).
63 Article 'Droit naturel' (Natural Right), DPV (1976), vol. VII, 28. Translation follows Diderot (1992), 20.
64 *Observation sur le Nakaz*, cited after Diderot (1992), 101.
65 See Eliane Martin-Haag: 'Mais il échappe aussi à l'historicisme, en montrant, avant Nietzsche, que la valeur immanente de la vie et du devenir reste le seul critère d'évaluation théorique, morale et politique des individus comme des peuples. … La véritable bonté consiste à préserver la possibilité du perfectionnement, et cela pour toute l'humanité, car s'il n'y a qu'un seul devoir, se rendre heureux, il n'y a 'qu'une seule vertu, la justice.' Martin-Haag (1999), 47.
66 Proust (1995), 371.
67 See Kondylis (1981), 532.
68 Raynal/Diderot (1780), vol. X, 41. Cf. Diderot (1992), 208.
69 Schneewind (2010), 468.
70 See Fontenay (1981), 73.
71 See, for example, Grünewald (2001).
72 I'd like to thank Stefanie Buchenau for helpful comments.

References

Barzun, J. (1986), 'Diderot as Philosopher', *Diderot Studies*, 22: 17–25.
Basile, G. P. (2019), 'Die Weltmaschinenmetapher von Descartes bis Kant', in M. Kisner et al. (eds), *Das Selbst und die Welt. Beiträge zu Kant und der nachkantischen Philosophie*, Würzburg: Königshausen & Neumann, 13–41.
Bremner, G. (1983), *Order and Chance: The Pattern of Diderot's Thought*, Cambridge: Cambridge University Press.
Brewer, D. (1993), *The Discourse of Enlightenment in Eighteenth-Century France: Diderot and the Art of Philosophizing*, Cambridge: Cambridge University Press.
Cassirer, E. (1968), *The Philosophy of the Enlightenment*, Princeton, NJ: Princeton University Press.

Clark, A. H. (2008), *Diderot's Part*, Farnham: Ashgate.
Crocker, L. G. (1959), *An Age of Crisis: Man and World in Eighteenth Century French Thought*, Baltimore: John Hopkins Press.
Crocker, L. G. (1974), *Diderot's Chaotic Order: Approach to Synthesis*, Princeton, NJ: Princeton University Press.
Davidson, A. (1986), 'Denis Diderot and the Limits to Reason', *Diderot Studies*, 22: 41–56.
Diderot, D. ([1773] 1995), 'Memoires pour Catherine II', in L. Versini (ed.), *Œuvres complètes*, vol. III: Politique, Paris: Bouquins, 203–410.
Diderot, D. (1975–), *Œuvres complètes*, ed. H. Dieckmann, J. Proust & J. Varloot, 23 vols, Paris: Hermann (abbr. as DPV).
Diderot, D. (1992), *Political Writings*, ed. J. H. Mason and R. Wokler, Cambridge: Cambridge University Press.
Duchet, M. (1995), *Anthropologie et histoire au siècle des Lumières*, reprint ed., Paris: Michel.
Duflo, C. (2013a), *Diderot: du matérialisme à la politique*, Paris: CNRS.
Duflo, C. (2013b), *Diderot philosophe*, Paris: Honoré Champion.
Fontenay, E. de (1981), *Diderot, ou, Le matérialisme enchanté*, Paris: B. Grasset.
Gay, P. (1996), *The Enlightenment: The Science of Freedom*, New York: Norton.
Gregory, M. E. (2007), *Diderot and the Metamorphosis of Species*, New York: Routledge.
Grünewald, B. (2001), 'Menschenrechte, praktische Vernunft und allgemeiner Wille. Zur Geschichte eines moralphilosophischen Konzepts', in P. Gregor (ed.), *Humanität, Interkulturalität und Menschenrecht*, Frankfurt a.M.: Peter Lang, 277–318.
Gumbrecht, H. U. (2021), *Prose of the World: Denis Diderot and the Periphery of Enlightenment*, Stanford: Stanford University Press.
Hill, E. (1973), 'Human Nature and the Moral "Monstre"', *Diderot Studies*, 16: 91–117.
Israel, J. (2008), *Enlightenment Contested: Philosophy, Modernity, and the Emancipation of Man, 1670–1752*, Oxford: Oxford University Press.
Israel, J. (2013), *Democratic Enlightenment: Philosophy, Revolution, and Human Rights 1750–1790*, Oxford: Oxford University Press.
Kaitaro, T. (1997), *Diderot's Holism*, Frankfurt A. M.: Peter Lang.
Kondylis, P. (1981), *Die Aufklärung im Rahmen des neuzeitlichen Rationalismus*, Stuttgart: Klett-Cotta.
Martin-Haag, E. (1999), 'Droit naturel et histoire dans la philosophie de Diderot', *Recherches sur Diderot et sur l'Encyclopédie*, 26: 37–47.
Menscing, G. (1971), *Totalität und Autonomie*, Frankfurt A. M.: Suhrkamp.
Proust, J. (1995), *Diderot et l'Éncyclopédie*, reprint ed., Paris: Michel.
Raynal, G. T. & Diderot, D. (1780), *Histoire des deux Indes*, vols. 1–10, Geneva. Pellet.
Rudolph, G. (1967), 'Diderots Elemente der Physiologie', *Gesnerus*, 24: 22–45.
de Saint-Lambert, J. F. & Mallet, E.-F. (1765), Article 'Humanité' (Humanity), *Encyclopédie*, vol. 8, 1st ed., Paris: Briasson et. al., 348.
Schneewind, J. B. (2010), *Essays on the History of Moral Philosophy*, Oxford: Oxford University Press.
Stenger, G. (1994), *Nature et liberté chez Diderot: après l'Encyclopédie*, Paris: Universitas.
Strugnell, A. (1973), *Diderot's Politics: A Study of the Evolution of Diderot's Political Thought after the Encyclopédie*, The Hague: Nijhoff.
Vyverberg, H. (1989), *Human Nature, Cultural Diversity, and the French Enlightenment*, Oxford: Oxford University Press.
Walters Jr, G. B. (1971), *The Significance of Diderot's Essai sur Mérite et la Vertu*, Chapel Hill, NC: University of North Carolina Press.

Warman, C. (2020), *The Atheist's Bible: Diderot's* Éléments de physiologie, Cambridge: Open Book Publishers.
Winter, U. (1972), *Der Materialismus bei Diderot*, Geneva, Paris: Droz.
Wolfe, C. T. (2016), *Materialism: A Historico-Philosophical Introduction*, Cham: Springer.
Wunderlich, F. (2016), 'Varieties of Early Modern Materialism', *British Journal for the History of Philosophy*, 24 (5): 797–813.
Wuthenow, R. R. (1994), *Diderot zur Einführung*, Hamburg: Junius-Verlag.

6

How do humans become human(e)?
On Rousseau's *Second Discourse* and *Emile*

Gabrielle Radica

Human nature and history

The question of the humanity of man in Rousseau is not as anachronistic as it may first appear. How man differed from other animals was indeed often discussed in Rousseau's time, and it was rather common in the mid-eighteenth century to consider two sides of the issue, the moral and the ontological. The 'Man' (*Homme*) entry in the *Encyclopedia* is thus divided into three main parts: 'Anatomical exposition of the human body', 'Natural history' and 'Morals'; while the 'Humanity' (*Humanité*) and the 'Inhumanity' (*Inhumanité*) entries, both written by Diderot, anchor man's distinct nature in his benevolence. According to Diderot, inhumanity is thus from this distinctly moral perspective the 'vice which casts us out of our species, which makes us cease to be men; the heartlessness of which nature has made us incapable'.[1]

Neither was Rousseau being very original when he would assert that man was capable of achieving both extreme goodness and extreme malice – of turning just as easily into a beast or into an angel. This Pascalian commonplace also appears in Diderot's 'Man' entry:

> Man is similar to animals in his material being; and when one proposes to understand him in the enumeration of all natural beings, one is forced to place him in the class of animals. Better and more wicked than any other of these, he deserves, on both accounts, to be at the top of the list.[2]

And it appears as well at the beginning of Rousseau's *Discours sur l'origine et les fondements de l'inégalité parmi les hommes* (Discourse on the Origin and the Foundations of the Inequality among Men, henceforth *Second Discourse*):

> It is of man that I am to speak, and the question I examine tells me that I shall be speaking to men, for one does not propose such questions if one is afraid of

---

This article has been supported by the European centre for humanities and social sciences (MESHS-Lille, France) and by the French Ministry of Higher education, research and innovation.

honoring the truth. I shall therefore confidently uphold the cause of humanity before the wise men who invite me to do so, and I shall not be dissatisfied if I prove worthy of my subject and my judges.[3]

This text features three important meanings of the word 'man': one that concerns the study of man, or anthropology: 'It is of *man* [*de l'homme*] that I am to speak'; another that concerns morals: 'the cause of *humanity* [*de l'humanité*]'; and a third that concerns man's virtue, conceived as manliness (one would use the term '*virilité*' in French): 'it is to *men* [*des hommes*] that I must address myself' means 'I'll speak to courageous men', viz. the members of the Académie de Dijon, who dared raise the problem of inequality.

It was, rather, Rousseau's method, his way of engaging with this disputed case, that made his work original. Indeed, his method was neither theological, nor was it strictly naturalistic, moral or historical. In other words, Rousseau was attempting something different from Pascal, Buffon, Diderot, Bayle and even Montesquieu. What makes man a specific kind of creature does not proceed from an original event, such as creation or original sin – a dogmatic position Rousseau rejected. Man's specificity does not lie in any eternal essence that could be achieved outside of history or observation, such as his spirituality. Philosophical speculation is of no use here. But neither is the nature of man entirely zoological. In other words, humanity does not consist only in its belonging to an animal species. It is not to be found in those human herds described by Diderot.[4] Indeed, human existence develops in so many different ways that it eludes any purely physical or anatomical perspective.

Rousseau's method allowed him to confront this variety and to explain it. If men's lives vary so much, it is because their *nature* – a term which is preferred by Rousseau over the term 'essence' – is to be understood through time. A consideration of the dimension of time will account for these variations. Man *grows* into a human being from the animal he started out as. Man becomes increasingly determined, from a state of near non-existence. In Rousseau, history thus accounts for the geographical and social diversity of man.

Rousseau's claim is not just that one and the same unique nature unfolds and varies through time and history, in the same way as a substance successively receives and holds different properties. His point is, rather, that the nature of man is to be historical. Tracing man's history thus does not only reveal how his nature has varied over time; it reveals his very nature. Rousseau's method differed from that of sceptical historians such as Pierre Bayle, for instance, who considered history as a mere chaos of facts that only needed to be enumerated.[5] The philosophical question for Rousseau was no longer: 'What is man?', but indeed: 'How do men become what they are?', 'How do men become human?' And this alone, regardless of the answer given to the question, is a philosophical project.

Rousseau discusses the constitutive relationship between human nature and time in two ways in his work. First, in the *Second Discourse,* nature and history are articulated through the notion of perfectibility; then, in *Emile,* his so-called pedagogical treatise, Rousseau tries another approach, namely an understanding of individual nature through the notion of development. Through the study of these two major works, I will explore the anthropological 'hominization' of man and his or her moral 'humanization'. I will show how the two questions remain intertwined in Rousseau, especially in the *Second Discourse*, which we will then compare with *Emile*.

Hominization, humanization and perfectibility: The *Second Discourse*

In the *Second Discourse*, Rousseau draws a classic natural law distinction between the state of nature and political or civil society – only he thoroughly subverts its meaning. Indeed, the citizen of Geneva very paradoxically offers a history of the state of nature, whereas Hobbes and Locke conceived of this state as a-historical and homogeneous. This history proceeds from the pure state of nature, which is described in the first part. Man was then nothing, or rather he was a pure animal. The second part proceeds from the starting point – or point zero – of that pure state of nature, where man is described as isolated without relations to anyone or any kind of idea or knowledge – an utter idiot. Together, these two parts of the *Discourse* form a system, in which the second develops what had remained only virtual or possible in the first.

Rousseau has 'to speak about man', and his first task is to reject what he considers inappropriate methods for doing so. Physical descriptions – of height, skin colour, body hair – are irrelevant. For sure, the human body mattered in the state of nature, but Rousseau prefers to ask what this body can do, rather than what it looks like. If the human body is specific among other animals, its specificity resides in its organization, in its relation to its environment, in its own resources, advantages and assets, not in its appearance.[6] Rousseau describes man's physical life as what makes him alive: his moving about and striving for self-preservation. Focusing on man's physical appearance, which could easily be confused with that of the ape, is ruled out as an inappropriate criterion. Rousseau does not reject natural history per se; he does reject an all too narrow natural history; that is why he is more interested in faculties and functions than in forms, shapes or physical appearance.[7]

When it comes to the metaphysical and moral dimensions of man, Rousseau also dismisses purely metaphysical arguments – that man is endowed with ideas, or that he is free – as irrelevant.

Turning now to the moral dimension, let us recall here that the French word 'moral' refers not only to the question of good and evil but also to the spiritual existence of man,[8] as well as to the relation between these last two meanings of the word.[9] Here again, classic moral notions are deemed to be of little use: neither wicked nor morally good, man will fight and protect himself whenever necessary for his survival. This does not mean, though, that he will attack his fellow creatures in a Hobbesian way, without any good reason to do so. His sense of pity keeps him from hurting feeble creatures, which shows he is endowed with pre-moral goodness. Rousseau thus rests his argument regarding man's goodness on the sole effects of his pacific behaviour, ignoring altogether the difficult issue of man's moral intentions. If his or her intentions stay beyond our reach, who will though deny that natural man acts as if he were good?

Perfectibility and teleology

Since anatomy, metaphysics and morals have all been exposed as ill-suited to the question, the argument of perfectibility remains as the only one capable of rallying the unanimous support of scholars:

> However, even if the difficulties attending all these questions should still leave room for difference in this respect between men and brutes, there is another very specific quality which distinguishes them, and which will admit of no dispute. This is the faculty of self-improvement, which, by the help of circumstances, gradually develops all the rest of our faculties, and is inherent in the species as in the individual: whereas a brute is, at the end of a few months, all he will ever be during his whole life, and his species, at the end of a thousand years, exactly what it was the first year of that thousand. Why is man alone liable to grow into a dotard? Is it not because he returns, in this, to his primitive state? and that, while the brute, which has acquired nothing and has therefore nothing to lose, still retains the force of instinct, man, who loses, by age or accident, all that his *perfectibility* had enabled him to gain, falls by this means lower than the brutes themselves? It would be melancholy, were we forced to admit that this distinctive and almost unlimited faculty is the source of all human misfortunes; that it is this which, in time, draws man out of his original state, in which he would have spent his days insensibly in peace and innocence; that it is this faculty, which, successively producing in different ages his discoveries and his errors, his vices and his virtues, makes him at length a tyrant both over himself and over nature. It would be shocking to be obliged to regard as a benefactor the man who first suggested to the Oroonoko Indians the use of the boards they apply to the temples of their children, which secure to them some part at least of their imbecility and original happiness.[10]

The notion of perfectibility is thus fundamental to Rousseau's historical definition of man, to a definition of man that lies in the description of his becoming-human. Perfectibility has been so much written about that it has become difficult to ignore the many issues raised when considering it.

As many scholars have noted, this neologism first appeared in 1755, in Grimm[11] as well as in Rousseau's works.[12] They have also suggested that this word is to be considered as both related and opposed to 'sociability' and 'perfection'. They have pointed out the pragmatic value of this notion, which is compatible with both spiritualist positions and materialist premises.[13] Although Rousseau dismisses the metaphysical debate about liberty as too vexed a question, some of his readers have wondered how distinct perfectibility is in fact from liberty and suggested that perfectibility can be considered as the empirical expression of human liberty.[14] In any case, most scholars agree that, with the notion of perfectibility, Rousseau managed to substitute history for metaphysics and, as Henri Gouhier[15] was the first to point out, to replace theology with a secular form of history. And almost all agree that perfectibility in Rousseau refers to the possibility of becoming more perfect, a possibility that does not involve any pre-defined notion of perfection. Bertrand Binoche has nonetheless shown that, however popular the term 'perfectibility' might have been early on, its popularity rested on a misunderstanding, with the term being soon understood as carrying teleological or metaphysical meanings, not unlike those of 'progress' or 'improvement'.[16] If Rousseau's efforts are often recognized, Rousseau's theoretical success is more disputed: this contradictory notion of nature, upon which perfectibility is based, is a good case in point. If nature is first void and indeterminate, if it follows no goals or ends, one may wonder what is ever to develop. Charles Bonnet, aka Philopolis, holds that nature cannot be as void as Rousseau supposes it to be and asserts: 'If the social state follows from man's faculties, it is thus natural to man.'[17]

Perfectibility and contingency

Another important discussion revolves around the question of contingency. For Louis Althusser, the notion of perfectibility is used to reveal the role of contingency in human history, to expose the contingency of humanization.[18] Conversely, French commentator Michèle Duchet argues that Rousseau's reference to the state of nature, and to man's spiritual dimension, shows that Rousseau could not break away from a metaphysical position. Indeed, in her view, Rousseau sought to argue against materialist accounts of humanization.[19] (It is worth noting here that both Louis Althusser and Michèle Duchet were Communists.)

The debate also turns around the status of causality and how perfectibility becomes active. Without external impetus, man's perfectibility would never be activated. Rousseau's rhetorical resistance to the possibility of humanity initiating its own story is quite clear: 'But who does not see, without recurring to the uncertain testimony of history, that everything seems to remove from savage man both the temptation and the means of changing his condition?'[20]

This story could very well never have begun and did so only under specific circumstances, some of which were indeed 'extraordinary'. There is, in other words, no 'humanization program' embedded in man. What are the conditions, then, that activate the meta-faculty of perfectibility, which then enables other human faculties to develop?[21] Indeed, since all men appear to have developed various faculties, those conditions must have been in place:

> Such was the condition of infant man; the life of an animal limited at first to mere sensations, and hardly profiting by the gifts nature bestowed on him, much less capable of entertaining a thought of forcing anything from her. But difficulties soon presented themselves, and it became necessary to learn how to surmount them: the height of the trees, which prevented him from gathering their fruits, the competition of other animals desirous of the same fruits, and the ferocity of those who needed them for their own preservation, all obliged him to apply himself to bodily exercises. He had to be active, swift of foot, and vigorous in fight. Natural weapons, stones and sticks, were easily found: he learnt to surmount the obstacles of nature, to contend in case of necessity with other animals, and to dispute for the means of subsistence even with other men, or to indemnify himself for what he was forced to give up to a stronger.[22]

Here Rousseau describes both ordinary and less ordinary situations whose effect is to tear man away from nature. This text obeys the methodological need to locate within the state of nature itself ways out of the state of nature. The beginnings of such a process must perforce have been very slow and imperceptible, consisting in very small steps, which is also how hominization must have proceeded.

Inadvertently and unintentionally, man evolves and improves every time he is confronted with enemies and difficulties to surmount. Behaving throughout as an animal, he nonetheless gradually becomes increasingly advantaged, increasingly distinct from animals – indeed, increasingly human. His sheer survival instinct serves to train and hone his natural abilities – he becomes more agile, speedier and stronger as he exercises and uses his natural agility, speed and strength.

We could pause here and compare this Rousseauist description with some of Condillac's accounts of the way men began using artificial signs. In his *Essai sur l'origine des connaissances humaines* (Essay on the Origin of Human Knowledge) artificial signs are not described as specific elements, specific signifiers, that are substantially distinct from natural signs. Rather, the distinction between artificial and natural signs lies first and foremost in the specific and novel use of the latter. Natural signs, becoming habitual to man, can be re-appropriated and used as artificial signs. If tears, for instance, are the natural signs and expressions of sadness, man gradually becomes aware of it, and increasingly capable of reversing this relation between signifier and signified, and of using tears as the signs of sadness. While tears would at first have followed from sadness, they now precede it, to cause it in the mind of the receiver.

In a similar way, in Rousseau's account, 'natural weapons' stand for the mediation between nature and culture, between nature and technique. While *this* weapon, *this* stone, *this* stick, was originally taken up because it lay close at hand, while it was originally used unintentionally and naturally, the sheer iteration of this use makes it less and less a natural resource and more and more a weapon. The specific property of perfectibility is that it applies to itself and thus becomes ever more effective.

Condillacian generation and Rousseauian genesis

Rousseau thus appears to lend himself to a sensualist interpretation, in that he adopts a similar epistemological approach – one that posits the fewest prerequisites possible to account for how man found his way out of these origins. This similarity has prompted some scholars like Jean Mosconi, Jacques Derrida, Michèle Duchet, Victor Goldschmidt, Jean-Louis Labussière to explore the links between Rousseau and Condillac. This intense interest raised among 1970s and 1980s French scholars who recognized the importance of anthropology, linguistics and so on. Rousseau indeed knew Condillac and even met Condillac's relatives when he worked as a preceptor for Mably family. Rousseau read this philosopher and happened here and there to discuss with him, even though he did not quote him every time.[23] If one wants to understand the process of becoming human(e) in Rousseau, it may help to assess the relations between Rousseauist genetical method on the one hand and Condillacian analytical method on the other hand.

The issues of contingency and causality are related. The more singular, the more extraordinary the causes and the occasions, the less perfection is internal to man, and the more perfectibility is dependent on man's environment. Conversely, the more comparable, the more similar you consider the causes, the more they become mere occasions for the internal development of natural faculties – and the further away perfectibility moves from contingency. In this last reading of Rousseau, only the occasions are contingent, not the developments they cause, which are generally the same, whatever the circumstances.

In Fontenelle, general and independent laws of human nature explain the course of human history.[24] Condillac's thought is different because he does not suppose any pre-existing faculty and seeks to explain the development of faculties themselves. But French scholar Jean Mosconi distinguishes Rousseau from Condillac, insofar as in Condillac a similar development of human faculties may arise from different circumstances.[25] On the contrary, Rousseau shows how very diverse or even opposite developments may arise from the same origins. In other words, there would be greater possibility and less finality in Rousseau's conjectural history than in Condillac's genesis. In Condillac, any faculty – sensation, attention, imagination, memory – may develop out of any circumstance, and any idea or sensation can give rise to attention, awareness, perception, memory, etc. Rousseau inserts between the original nature of man and the perfection of his faculties all the factual, empirical and external mediation of techniques, social relations and language that diversify the course of man's history and humanization into several configurations.

If Jean Mosconi is right about Rousseau and his commitment to real and contingent human diversity, he may have been unfair to Condillac. The latter indeed offers nominalist and culturalist accounts of the development of ideas and operations of the mind. Men acquire language and isolate new signs, but let us recall that each different language leads them to different and specific ways of thinking. Acquired faculties depend on the specificities of language, and languages are more or less well crafted, well built, depending on the culture and society by which they were formed.

Differences between Rousseau and Condillac might thus lie in other aspects of their thought than in the debate concerning the real or illusionary status of contingency. In fact, Condillac does not provide his readers with a complete genesis of man, only with the genesis of his mind, faculties and ideas. Only Rousseauian perfectibility offers a genesis of man in its entirety. Only perfectibility explains how men become human as well as humane. In Rousseau, humans develop through a comprehensive and complex process, in which their mind itself is determined by their body, temper, strength, technical skills, social relationships and sexual difference. In this regard, Rousseau gives a more nominalist account of faculties than Condillac insofar as each concrete life gives rise to various forms of mind, ideas and moral dispositions. For instance, the sense of time and duration that develops depends on whether one lives a nomadic or sedentary life; courage depends on the kind of technical, cultural and physical links one maintains with the future, with danger and with one's resources. Civilized man who has accumulated possessions is less courageous than natural man, who does not own anything and is therefore more vigorous and ready to fight.

Jean-Louis Labussière wonders whether perfectibility affects individuals in the same way it affects the human species as a whole and points out that the perfectibility of the species supposes specific individual interactions and transgenerational transmission of knowledge. It supposes various modes through which people gather together: families, societies, states, etc.[26] The perfectibility of the species is thus activated and honed by mutual relationships between individuals. As Mary Wollstonecraft had put it long ago: 'The two sexes mutually corrupt and improve each other.'[27] That is why Franck Tinland says that perfectibility is truly operative when it brings men together, and that is also why he considers the first part of the *Discourse* as describing the point zero of the history of humanity. In other words, in his view, perfectibility is not operative until men have become differentiated one from another.[28]

However, it can be argued that perfectibility intervenes much earlier and indeed that it is necessary for it to intervene earlier. Derrida remarks in *Grammatology* that once you claim that history needs to rely on some origin, you need to dig further and further back to find the point where it all really began.[29] Indeed, before anything spiritual arises in men, before perfectibility is even mentioned, Rousseau already supposes it, as we may understand from the following:

> By stripping this Being, so constituted, of all the supernatural gifts he may have received, and of all the artificial faculties he could only have acquired by prolonged progress; by considering him, in a word, such as he must have issued from the hands of Nature, I see an animal less strong than some, less agile than others, but, all things considered, the most advantageously organised of all: I see him sating his hunger beneath an oak, slaking his thirst at the first Stream, finding his bed at the foot of the same tree that supplied his meal, and with that his needs are satisfied.
>
> The Earth, abandoned to its natural fertility, and covered by immense forests which no Axe ever mutilated, at every step offers Storage and shelter to the animals of every species. Men, dispersed among them, observe, imitate their industry, and so raise themselves to the level of the Beast's instinct, with this advantage that each species has but his own instinct, while man perhaps having none that belongs to him, appropriates them all, feeds indifferently on most of the various foods which the other animals divide among themselves, and as a result finds his subsistence more easily than can any one of them.[30]

In brief, the human animal presents no specific properties and only differs from other animals in his or her ability to take on other animals' instincts and to become all of them successively, a mimetic faculty that engages him in comparisons, makes him better, stronger, etc. This faculty of man who, deprived of any instinct, appropriates all of them from other animals, is certainly here an early expression of perfectibility, in that it serves to pull man out of the state of nature. In short, locating perfectibility in the second part of the *Discourse* serves a moral conception of *humanization*, whereas identifying its effects as early on as in the first part of the *Discourse* highlights anthropological concerns and the process of *hominization*.

Becoming a human being, becoming more or less humane

Either way, perfectibility allows us to assess man's morals. Even though Wollstonecraft understood perfectibility in a teleological and even religious sense,[31] and even though she missed the point of contingency, she nevertheless agreed with Rousseau when she stated that not all enhancement and refinement led to a betterment of the human individual or of the species. As man becomes part of an increasingly complex system, the sophistication of an isolated faculty will not necessarily improve the well-being of the whole social system, and it may even on the contrary provoke distortion. Advances in human possibility that are too partial or too sectoral often have negative effects.[32] For instance, Wollstonecraft criticizes women's enhanced sense of pity, which may indeed be frivolously lavished on their dogs rather than on their children.[33] Although Fourier had not read Rousseau very thoroughly, he also drew similarly rigorous conclusions from Rousseau's thought, systematically using the word 'perfectibility' in connection with civilization: 'Civilization', he writes, 'for all its jargon of perfectibility, is very coarse in various branches of culture.'[34] Perfectibility is therefore no guarantee against misfortune or corruption. Here the lessons of both the first and the second *Discourses* are joined together by Charles Fourier: 'Our century proudly flaunts its material progress, oblivious of its political regression.'[35]

Let us not forget, however, that the object and purpose of the *Second Discourse* was to put inequality on trial. Rousseau intends to reveal the fundamental unity of the human species, to recover a common humanity beyond the social inequalities that appear to have divided humanity into several species. The political point of the book is not simply that the savage and the civilized are one and the same species, but indeed that rich and poor proceed from the same humanity, and to explain why they behave as if they did not. Thus, it may be true, as Claude Lévi-Strauss puts it, that Rousseau was the founder of social science and anthropology.[36] He indeed invites us to stop focusing on the mind and soul and to consider the body first, to turn away from ideas and to consider sentiments first, to look upon man as an acting and making being, not just as a thinking being. Man is what he makes and eats; man is how he lives. Hominization is clearly what is at stake here. But it is also true that if Rousseau can help us think through the foundation and the growing fragmentation of the human sciences, he had no intention of dissociating the prescriptive from the descriptive consequences of his *Discourse*. His purpose remained moral and evaluative. True, the conditions of moral imputation have changed, society having now become a central agent to be reckoned with in our appraisal of action from a moral standpoint. Yet the role of society, that has rendered us wicked, does not imply that morality should cease to be relevant.

Hominization and humanization are closely intertwined and mutually account for each other, even if Rousseau's arguments pertaining to each are distinct. Rousseauist perfectibility offers a single principle to explain both and to understand their mutual connections. Morals depend on techniques, cultures, commodities, symbols, social relationships, and in this respect, humanization largely depends on hominization: man is courageous when his body is trained; he becomes limp when he has accumulated too many commodities.

To become human means at once to become more individualized, to become aware of others and of oneself, and to take others into account in one's action (for instance, the deer hunter is more human than the jackrabbit hunter). Man becomes human when he stitches his clothes 'together with thorns and fish-bones', when he 'adorns' himself 'with feathers and shells', and when he 'paint[s his] body in different colors', when he 'improves and beautifies [his] bows and arrows' and when 'he makes with sharp-edged stones fishing boats or clumsy musical instruments',[37] that is, when he develops various techniques, including artistic ones. But he also becomes human when he grows fonder of his partner and when he codifies and institutionalizes his relationships with his peers. All this is inextricably both anthropological and moral. Some men hunt while others fish and still others cultivate the earth. This is an anthropological affair. But it is also a moral one, since this variety does not support a homogeneous equivalence: whereas hunters are likely to work together and cooperate, peasants are more likely to have to obey an employer and become an alienated labour force. Perfectibility explains what the *First Discourse* only asserted: men do not grow more civilized unless they become more corrupted as well. The link between morals and the civilizing process is similar to that between humanization and hominization. That is why perfectibility also helps us understand how dehumanization operates. Man may lose his humanity by exerting cruelty, like the rich, or through excessive deprivation, like the poor.[38]

The novelty and originality of Rousseau thus lies in proposing a new literary and philosophical genre. He shuns the moral history of Fontenelle and Voltaire, for whom the same human material might be indefinitely shaped by history yet its nature (ignorant, naive, etc.) will remain unchanged.[39] Rousseau does not share this perspective at all. He rather lays out the conditions of possibility for history to begin and shows that these conditions lie in the historicity of human nature itself. Human nature is transformed by and in time, not just superficially modified over time.

Nature and development: *Emile*

As Bertrand Binoche points out, Rousseau only uses the word 'perfectibility' in the *Second Discourse*.[40] What replaces it then, or stands in for it, in *Emile*? Has the notion disappeared as well as the word? The theoretical frame of *Emile* is largely different from that of the *Second Discourse*. There is no need to deal with the human species in this pedagogical and anthropological work. Yet these two works can be compared in that young Emile improves and perfects himself through the process of education. As in the *Second Discourse*, his nature unfolds and develops only through the medium of time. Although Rousseau seems to favour the notion of development over the those of perfectibility and history, and although no final point is assigned to it, nature's development is now oriented by an immanent norm, and regulated; nature has become more of a norm in this book. Rousseau's position on human nature is different here. Nature in *Emile* refers to the possibility of a harmonious development of the individual.

This specific position relies on a richer, more substantial notion of nature, which draws partially on Stoic influences. Stoic philosophers offer a notion of self-love which is more useful to achieve this goal, namely the notion of *oikeiosis*, which refers to the progressive appropriation of oneself and of all that surrounds one and matters to one. In the first pages of Book 1, Rousseau asserts:

> We are born sensitive and from our birth onwards we are affected in various ways by our environment. As soon as we become conscious of our sensations we tend to seek or shun the things that cause them, at first because they are pleasant or unpleasant, then because they suit us or not, and at last because of judgments formed by means of the ideas of happiness and goodness which reason gives us.[41]

Pleasure being presented as the primary motive for our actions, the first part of the sentence adopts an Epicurean perspective, which would have been unacceptable to the Stoics. Indeed, in letter 121, criticizing the idea that children are led by pleasure, Seneca reminds us of how the child strives to stand up even when he has fallen and suffers, thereby achieving not what he likes but what nature orders him to do.[42] However Epicurean the former argument might appear, this Senecian description can easily be linked to the passage of *Emile* in which Rousseau describes those 'little fellows' when he sees them as they

> play in the snow, stiff and blue with cold, scarcely able to stir a finger. They could go and warm themselves if they chose, but they do not choose; if you forced them to come in they would feel the harshness of constraint a hundredfold more than the sharpness of the cold.[43]

Pleasure and pain are not lasting motivations for action, and this is a Stoic point. Freedom is here more important than pleasure and this form of freedom is linked to the development of the living being. Pleasure and pain are outdone by the long-term motivation by which we search an adequacy (*convenance*) between us and objects outside us; this adequacy is again scrutinized later by rational judgement, which locates the choice of objects in the more general perspective of happiness. One can read in this movement the Ciceronian progress, from objects which are adequate to our nature to the valuation of coherence while we identify those objects – a coherence that ends up being more important than the objects themselves.[44]

This is also about the development of a *human* being, insofar as it connects the development of morals to that of culture and combines freedom to the existence of a living being. Human nature, once again, cannot be observed outside the medium of time. The main dimensions of time, in which we simultaneously become human beings and more humane persons, are duration and repetition, as well as more concrete aspects of time (growth, learning development, use). Emile and his teacher can only achieve Emile's nature by developing it over time. And it only develops through exercise, when Emile acquires the use of his limbs and of his faculties. Once again, Emile's nature has to unfold for it to exist.

Like Hobbes, and Condillac, Rousseau wants to show how culture and morals proceed from nature. But far from the naturalist perspective that conceives of nature as stable and unchanging, Rousseau's nature comprises both what man has become and how he has improved himself, as discussed in the *Second Discourse*, and resides, *Emile* tells us, in the very development of an ever freer living being. This way, whether it be as history or as development, exercise or use, time is fully included in the definition of human nature. This methodological approach precludes the possibility of separating anthropology from morals, of decoupling humanization and hominization.

Notes

1. 'Vice qui nous sort de notre espèce, qui nous fait cesser d'être homme; dureté de cœur, dont la nature sembloit nous avoir rendus incapables' (translation mine), *Encyclopédie* (1765), vol. 8, 746.
2. *The Encyclopedia of Diderot and d'Alembert* ([1765] 2019). Translation of the *Encyclopédie* entry 'Homme', vol. 8, 256: '*L'homme* ressemble aux animaux par ce qu'il a de matériel; & lorsqu'on se propose de le comprendre dans l'énumération de tous les êtres naturels, on est forcé de le mettre dans la classe des animaux. Meilleur & plus méchant qu'aucun, il mérite à ce double titre, d'être à la tête.'
3. Rousseau ([1755] 2018): 'C'est de l'homme que j'ai à parler, et la question que j'examine m'apprend que je vais parler à des hommes, car on n'en propose point de semblables quand on craint d'honorer la vérité. Je défendrai donc avec confiance la cause de l'humanité devant les sages qui m'y invitent, et je ne serai pas mécontent de moi-même si je me rends digne de mon sujet et de mes juges.'
4. Diderot ([1752] 1994), 528.
5. On historical pyrrhonism, see Binoche (1998), 76–80.
6. See *a contrario* Maupertuis ([1745] 1980); Buffon (1984) 'Variétés dans l'espèce humaine', 140 ff.: 'Tout ce que nous avons dit jusqu'ici de la génération de l'homme, de sa formation, de son développement, de son état dans les différents âges de sa vie, de ses sens et de la structure de son corps, telle qu'on la connaît par les dissections anatomiques, ne fait encore que l'histoire de l'individu, celle de l'espèce demande un détail particulier, dont les faits principaux ne peuvent se tirer que des variétés qui se trouvent entre les hommes des différents climats. La première et la plus remarquable de ces variétés est celle de la couleur, la seconde est celle de la forme et de la grandeur, et la troisième est celle du naturel des différents peuples'; 'La négresse blanche' [1777], 163; Voltaire (2020), 'Des différentes races d'hommes', 6.
7. I have to thank Stefanie Buchenau for having helped me to formulate this thought in a so accurate way.
8. As when one refers to moral beings, 'les êtres moraux'.
9. As like the soul's education to good and evil.
10. Rousseau ([1755] 2018), 60.
11. Grimm ([1755] 1867), 492: 'Le principal caractère qui le [l'homme] distingue de toutes les autres créatures de l'univers, c'est la perfectibilité ou la faculté de se rendre plus parfait. ... C'est une grande et belle question digne de l'attention des meilleurs esprits et de nos plus sublimes philosophes, savoir si cet état de perfectibilité est une prérogative et un bonheur réel pour l'homme, et si les bêtes ne sont même pas plus parfaites en ce qu'elles naissent d'abord avec le degré de perfection dont elles sont

susceptibles, et que, si elles n'ont point à devenir meilleures, elles ont d'un autre côté l'avantage de ne point dégénérer et de remplir leur vocation en obéissant à la nature'. ['The main feature that distinguishes him [man] from all other creatures in the world is perfectibility, or the faculty of becoming more perfect ... It is a grand and noble question worthy of the attention of the best minds and of our most sublime philosophers, whether this state of perfectibility is a prerogative and a real blessing for man, and whether animals are not more perfect than he, in that they are first born with the degree of perfection of which they are capable, and if they need not become better, they need not fear that they might degenerate, and they fulfill their vocation simply by obeying nature' (translation mine).] Even if Rousseau might have borrowed the term from Grimm, he alone explored its major philosophical consequences. See Binoche (2004), 13, no. 1, who quotes this text; see also his chap. 11: 'La perfectibilité indéfinie (I). Équivoques sémantiques', in Binoche (2007), 257–82.
12 Delon (1996) 712–13; Binoche (2004).
13 Goldschmidt (1983), 288–92.
14 Tinland mentions an 'empirical projection of liberty' in Tinland (2004), 69; See Passmore (1971); See also *La perfectibilité: les Lumières allemandes contre Rousseau*.
15 Gouhier ([1955] 1984), 11–47.
16 Binoche (2004), 7–12 and 13–35, 'Les équivoques de la perfectibilité'. Utopian theorists use it, either wrongly, like Fourier, or rightly, like Etienne Cabet (1840/ 1979, 35). 'As you know', he writes, 'man stands out from among all other animate beings for his reason, his perfectibility and his sociability'. Also the Germans are representative of a teleological reading of perfectibility, assimilated to perfection. For instance Moses Mendelssohn, who is the first German translator of Rousseau's *Second Discourse* in 1756, associated perfectibility, Platonic perfection and the destination or vocation of man (I also must thank here Stefanie Buchenau for having suggested me this point).
17 Bonnet (1755/1959–1995),1383 (translation mine).
18 Althusser (2013).
19 Duchet (1995).
20 Rousseau ([1755] 2018), 62.
21 Jean-Marie Beyssade points out the polysemy of the term 'faculty' in the concept of the 'faculty' that 'gradually develops the rest of all our faculties', in Beyssade (1988), 194–214. Not only is perfectibility more of a meta-faculty, but the 'faculties' that perfectibility mobilizes are many: 'reason, conscience, sociability, language, modesty, imagination, memory, to which are added pity and even I believe, self esteem' (198–9). All the faculties, both cognitive and affective, both natural and 'artificial', are thus concerned and perfectible.
22 Rousseau ([1755] 2018), 84–5.
23 See for instance the discussion about the origin of language in the *Discourse on the Origin and the Foundations of Inequality among Men*.
24 See Fontenelle (1989), 177: 'Quelqu'un qui aurait bien de l'esprit, en considérant simplement la nature humaine, devinerait toute l'histoire passée et toute l'histoire à venir, sans avoir jamais entendu parler d'aucun événement. Il dirait: la nature humaine est composée d'ignorance, de crédulité, de vanité, d'ambition, de méchanceté, d'un peu de bon sens et de probité par-dessus tout cela, mais dont la dose est fort petite en comparaison des autres ingrédients. Donc ces gens-là feront une infinité d'établissements ridicules, et un très petit nombre de sensés; ils se

battront souvent les uns avec les autres et puis feront des traités de paix, presque toujours de mauvaise foi; les plus puissants opprimeront les plus faibles et tâcheront de donner à leurs oppressions des apparences de justice, etc. Après quoi, si cet homme voulait examiner toutes les vérités que peuvent produire ces principes généraux, et les faire jouer, pour ainsi dire, de toutes les manières possibles, il imaginerait en détail une infinité de faits, ou arrivés effectivement, ou tout pareils à ceux qui sont arrivés.' ['Any sensible person, by simply observing human nature, would be able to guess all past and all future history, without prior information of any event. That man would say: human nature is comprised of ignorance, gullibility, vanity, ambition, malice, with a small dose of common sense and integrity on top, but in negligible quantity by comparison with the other components. These people will therefore pursue an enormous number of silly endeavours, and a very small number of sensible ones; they will often engage in fights with one another, and then draw up peace treaties, most often in bad faith; the more powerful will oppress the weaker, and strive to give their oppression the appearance of justice, etc. Whereupon, if this man wanted to examine all the truths that such general principles could produce, and all their possible combinations, so to speak, he would be able to picture in detail an endless series of facts that either did happen, or are very similar to facts that did happen' (translation mine).]

25 Mosconi (1966), 54 ff.
26 Labussière (2004), 91–111.
27 Wollstonecraft ([1792] 1996), 143.
28 Tinland (2004), 59–90; 70; 74–8.
29 Derrida ([1967] 1974).
30 Rousseau ([1755] 2018), 134–5.
31 She thought for instance that man had sleeping faculties that were ready to develop whenever possible; see *Vindication*, 27.
32 This is illustrated in the *Essay on the Origins of Languages*, chap. 7, where Rousseau states that sophisticated and written languages gradually lose energy as they gain clarity.
33 Wollstonecraft ([1792] 1996), 179; see also 61, 66 on perfectibility in general.
34 Fourier (1822), 48–9.
35 'C'est surtout en politique industrielle que notre siècle étale son orgueil; fier de quelques progrès en matériel, il ne s'aperçoit pas qu'il est en rétrogradation politique', Fourier (1845) 28.
36 Lévi-Strauss (1963).
37 Rousseau ([1755] 2018), 92.
38 In the same way, some passages of *Essay on the Origins of Languages* can be read as yet another application of the principle of perfectibility. Indeed, this work, which also does not feature the term itself, was written during the same period as the *Second Discourse*. The development of language is always at once cultural and moral. Every language, for instance, is characterized by the predominant type of relationship to others it supports (a 'love me' or a 'help me' relation, cf. chap. 10) and not just by its linguistic and phonetic traits.
39 See above, *Sur l'histoire*, 177.
40 Binoche (2004), 'Les équivoques de la Perfectibilité', 14. In a footnote Bertrand Binoche says he has strived to steer clear of the materialist interpretation (as opposed to Victor Goldschmidt who thinks the hypothesis is compatible with spiritualism).
41 Rousseau ([1762] 1911), 7.

42 'A baby who is set on standing up and is getting used to supporting himself, as soon as he begins to try his strength, falls down and with tears keeps getting up again until he has trained himself through pain to do what nature demands', Seneca (1987), 347.
43 *Emile*, 51.
44 Cicero (2001) III, 17, 20-2.

References

Althusser, L. (2013), *Cours sur Rousseau*, Paris: Le temps des cerises.
Beyssade, J. M. (1988), 'Rousseau et la pensée du développement. Facultés virtuelles et développement chez J. J. Rousseau', in O. Bloch et al. (eds), *Entre forme et histoire*, Paris: Klincksieck, 194-214.
Binoche, B. (1998), *Introduction à De l'esprit des lois de Montesquieu*, Paris: PUF.
Binoche, B. (2004), *L'homme perfectible*, Seyssel: Champvallon.
Binoche, B. (2007), 'La perfectibilité indéfinie (I). Équivoques sémantiques', in B. Binoche (ed.), *La raison sans l'Histoire. Échantillons pour une histoire comparée des philosophies de l'Histoire*, Paris: Presses Universitaires de France, 257-82.
Bonnet, C. ([1755] 1959-1995), 'Lettre de M. Philopolis', in J. J. Rousseau, Raymond et al. (eds), *Œuvres complètes*, 5 vols, vol. 3, 1383-6, Paris: Gallimard.
Buffon G. L. (1984), *Histoire naturelle*, ed. J. Varloot, Paris: Gallimard.
Cabet, E. ([1840] 1979), *Voyage en Icarie*, Paris-Geneva: Slatkine.
Cicero, M. T. (2001), *On Moral Ends*, Cambridge: Cambridge University Press.
Condillac, E. ([1746] 2001), *Essay on the Origin of Human Knowledge*, trans. Hans Aarsleff, New Jersey: Princeton University Press.
D'Alembert, J. & le Rond Et Diderot, D., *Encyclopédie ou Dictionnaire raisonné des Sciences, des Arts et des Métiers*, Paris: Briasson, 1765.
The Encyclopedia of Diderot and d'Alembert, collaborative translation project, University of Michigan, https://quod.lib.umich.edu/d/did, accessed 20 January 2022.
Delon, M. (1996), 'Perfectibilité', in R. Trousson and F. Eigeldinger (eds), *Dictionnaire de Jean-Jacques Rousseau*, Paris: Honoré Champion, 712-13.
Derrida, J. ([1967] 1974), *On Grammatology*, trans. G. C. Spivak, London and Baltimore: Johns Hopkins University Press.
Diderot, D. ([1752] 1994), 'Suite de l'Apologie de M. l'abbé de Prades', in *Œuvres*, 5 vols, Paris: Robert Laffont, vol. I, 509-52.
Duchet, M. (1995), *Anthropologie et histoire au siècle des Lumières. Buffon, Voltaire, Rousseau, Helvétius, Diderot*, Paris: Albin Michel.
Fontenelle, B. (1989), 'Sur l'histoire', in *Œuvres complètes*, 8 vols, vol. 3, Paris: Fayard, 169-85.
Fourier, C. (1822), *Traité de l'association domestique et agricole*, Paris London: Bossange.
Fourier, C. (1845), *Le nouveau monde industriel et sociétaire*, *Œuvres complètes*, vol. 6, Paris: Librairie Sociétaire.
Goldschmidt, V. (1983), *Anthropologie et politique. Les principes du système de Rousseau*, Paris: Vrin.
Gouhier, H. ([1955] 1984), 'Nature et histoire dans la pensée de Jean-Jacques Rousseau', in *Les méditations métaphysiques de Jean-Jacques Rousseau*, Paris: Vrin, 11-47.
Grimm, M. (1867), *Correspondance littéraire, philosophique et critique*, vol. 2, Paris: Garnier.

Hourcade, E., Morel, C. & et Yuva, A., eds (2022), *La perfectibilité: les Lumières allemandes contre Rousseau*, Paris: Garnier.
Labussière, J. L. (2004), 'Perfectibilité individuelle et perfectibilité spécifique chez Jean-Jacques Rousseau', in B. Binoche (ed.), *L'homme perfectible*, Seyssel: Champvallon, 91–111.
Lévi-Strauss, C. (1963), 'Rousseau, père de l'ethnologie', in *Courrier de l'UNESCO*, Paris, March 1963, 10–15.
Maupertuis, P. L. ([1745] 1980), *Vénus physique*, Paris: Aubier Montaigne.
Mosconi, J. (1966), 'Regards sur la théorie du devenir de l'entendement au XVIIIe siècle', *Cahiers pour l'Analyse*, 4: 47–82.
Passmore, J. (1971), *The Perfectibility of Man*, London, Duckworth.
Rousseau, J. J. ([1762] 1911), *Emile*, trans. Barbara Foxley, London: Dent.
Rousseau, J. J. ([1755] 2018), 'Discourse on the Origin and the Foundations of Inequality among Men', in V. Gourevitch (ed.), *The Discourses and Other Early Political Writings*, Cambridge: Cambridge University Press.
Seneca (1987), 'Letters', in A. Long & D. Sedley (eds), *The Hellenistic Philosophers*, vol. 1, Cambridge: Cambridge University Press, 347.
Tinland, F. (2004), 'État de nature et perfectibilité: l'effacement d'une origine', in *L'homme perfectible*, Seyssel: Champvallon, 59–90.
Voltaire, F. de Arouet (2020), *Essai sur les Mœurs et l'Esprit des Nations*, 2 vols, Paris: Garnier.
Wollstonecraft, M. ([1792] 1996), *Vindication of the Rights of Women*, Mineola, New York: Dover.

7

'In the human kind, the species has a progress as well as the individual': Adam Ferguson on the progress of 'mankind'

Eveline Hauck and Norbert Waszek

An exploration of notions of humankind[1] and humanity in the eighteenth century would be incomplete without Adam Ferguson (1723-1816): (a) his ideas are important in their own right; (b) he is a leading representative, next to David Hume and Adam Smith, of the current of thought now known as the 'Scottish Enlightenment'[2] and firmly established as a field of inquiry;[3] (c) he had a wide impact on thinkers far beyond his native Scotland and in Germany in particular: not just on Christian Garve (1742-1798; cf. Waszek 2006), Ferguson's foremost translator and an important Enlightenment figure in his own right, but also on such more eminent men as the early pre-critical Kant, on Lessing and Schiller, on Hamann, Herder and Jacobi, and up to Hegel and Marx.[4]

In the twentieth century, when Ferguson was rediscovered, he was mostly read as a forerunner of the social sciences that emerged out of an older, more normative discourse. Indeed, just like Adam Smith in Glasgow, Adam Ferguson held the chair of moral philosophy at Edinburgh University, but the subjects they treated and the way in which they elaborated them went well beyond the traditional scope of the discipline. Ferguson's marked interest in the historical development of societies from 'rude' beginnings to the modern commercial society does indeed single him out as a founding father of 'sociology' *avant la lettre*,[5] and when the early representatives of sociology as a distinct field of inquiry and an academic discipline looked back on its history or protohistory, Ferguson was often duly appreciated (e.g. Sombart 1923).

But for Ferguson himself, in spite of his sophisticated account of social development on which his lasting renown is based, 'moral philosophy' in the narrower sense does not become redundant. To sharpen the thesis: just because Ferguson saw the ambivalent character of social progress and its inherent drawbacks, individuals need moral guidance and reinforcing for their confrontation with the darker consequences of the social development. In this context, Ferguson has recourse to Roman Stoicism (in this he was not alone among the Scottish Enlightenment; cf. Waszek 1984), a current associated with Epictetus, Marcus Aurelius and certain writings of Cicero, in which the older Stoicism had synthesized with the Roman ideal of heroic action (*fortunae resistere*). How can the 'good life', an ideal inherited from antiquity, be upheld under the conditions of modern society with its alienating defects? This seems to be the ultimate question to Ferguson as a moralist.

Ferguson's *Essay on the History of Civil Society* (1767, henceforth *Essay*) is his major work and the following remarks will concentrate on it, but his two other books or textbooks (for the first was explicitly intended for his students and the second a detailed elaboration of his former lectures) – *Institutes of Moral Philosophy* (1769; the second edition, 1773, will be used – abbreviated as *IMP*) and *Principles of Moral and Political Science* (1792 – henceforth *PMPS*) – will be drawn upon for reasons of comparison or when their treatment is more elaborate. The chapter begins by a reconstruction of his *Essay* in order to spell out the exact place and significance of his reflections on humankind. In what sense is his book a 'natural history' of humankind? The question is related to the universal characteristics of human nature that Ferguson identifies and, in particular, to his account of sociability, which has to be analyzed in the contexts (a) of his reception of Montesquieu and (b) of his close cooperation with other figures of the Scottish Enlightenment. The crucial task will then be to analyze the way in which Ferguson links these reflections on human nature with his conception of the 'progress' of humankind.

Structure and contexts of Ferguson's *Essay*

A glance at the genesis of his *Essay* is not only interesting from the perspective of his intellectual development but also a privileged access to his fundamental concept of 'civil society'. His major study can be traced back to a manuscript, 'Treatise on refinement', that circulated among his friends in 1759. Although this manuscript did not survive, and its discussion must for that reason remain to some extent hypothetical, it left significant traces in the correspondence of his friends. The different reactions of David Hume, central figure of the Scottish Enlightenment, are striking: in April 1759 he wrote to their common friend, Adam Smith, in order to praise the author and his manuscript: 'Ferguson has very much polished and improved his Treatise on Refinement, and with some Amendments it will make an admirable Book, and discovers an elegant and a singular Genius' (Mossner 1977, 34). But when the final draft was ready, six years later, he disapproved of it and even advised against publishing it (Greig 1932, II, 11 f.).[6] Several explanations of Hume's change of mind have been advanced. Was it that Hume perceived Ferguson as a mere follower of Montesquieu (for the impact of Montesquieu on Ferguson, see below) and that his image of Montesquieu declined, as John Small (1864, 11) suggested? Richard Sher's explanation starts out from the tension (already hinted at) in Ferguson's *Essay* between the analytical perspective of the social scientist and the persistent normative discourse. Seen from this angle, it might well have been Hume's aversion to the 'heavily moralistic rhetoric' of the *Essay* that made him disapprove of it.[7] Duncan Forbes, in his magisterial introduction to the *Essay*, limits himself to commenting on the change of title, from 'refinement' to 'civil society' (*EHCS*, XIX f.). While the theme of 'refinement' (and indeed the term, e.g. *EHCS*, 110) remains much present in the *Essay*, Ferguson privileged 'history of civil society' when he published his study. The reason for this, according to Forbes, is that 'civil society' is a much wider concept, indeed a history of 'civilization', with all its ambiguities.

The first part of the *Essay* (out of six), which amounts to a quarter of the whole book, outlines the traits of human nature which can be observed at all stages of social development, what he calls its 'General Characteristics': beginning, conventionally enough, with (a) self-preservation (*EHCS*, 10–15); (b) a constant tendency to improve one's circumstances (6–7) but also oneself, a 'desire of perfection' (8), and (c) a 'moral sentiment' (31–40), where Ferguson comes close, but with a subtle difference,[8] to the terminologies proper to Hume and Adam Smith, e.g. 'moral apprehension', 'moral approbation', 'sympathy', etc.[9] More original is a double propensity to which Ferguson then moves on: on the one hand a 'principle of union' among humankind (16–19), but equally, and at first glance contradictorily, a 'principle of dissension' on the other (20–5). While we shall have to come back to the social disposition, and a comparison with Montesquieu, in the second part of the chapter, it is the seeming contradiction with a principle of dissension that needs to be commented upon. For Ferguson, the two dispositions are not contradictory but complementary – 'our species is disposed to opposition, as well as to concert' (*EHCS*, 21) and the very scenes of war may furnish occasions 'for the exercise of … generosity and self-denial' (23 f.). With his assertion that humans 'appear to have in their minds the seeds of animosity, and to embrace the occasions of mutual opposition, with alacrity and pleasure' (20), he is trying to go beyond an idealized picture of human nature and to take into account a fuller image of reality, for he does not want to follow 'the suggestions of fancy' (5) but rather to satisfy the requirements of empirical evidence.

A few further comments on his methodology are in place here. As opposed to speculations of an atomistic psychology/anthropology and the fanciful constructions of a 'state of nature' to the 'social contract',[10] Ferguson intends to employ observation and historical data. He is clearly inspired by Buffon's (1707–1788) multi-volume *Histoire Naturelle*, though this debt is more explicitly acknowledged in the *IMP* (e.g. 15, 20) than in the *Essay*. Buffon outlined a history of the Earth (divided into seven epochs) and examined the animal and mineral world. Ferguson also wanted to write a 'natural history' but of human beings and their 'civil society'. In order to examine the origins of society Ferguson draws on two sources, seeing parallels in their results: on the one hand, the historians of antiquity: Tacitus, Livy, Julius Caesar, etc.,[11] and the divers authors (they could be missionaries, colonial officers, explorers or simply adventurers) of a proto-ethnological literature on the other.[12] Of this rich but heterogenic literature, Ferguson refers,[13] among others, to two French Jesuits, Pierre François Xavier de Charlevoix (1682–1761) and Joseph-François Lafitau (1681–1746) – the former is often considered the first historian of 'New France' (Quebec); the latter is best known for his study of Iroquois society – but also to the German explorer and naturalist Peter Kolb (1675–1726) who provided an early account of 'several nations of the Hottentots' (subtitle of the English translation of his study of the Cape of Good Hope), including their language, lifestyle and customs. Since we find already in the texts of these authors (e.g. Lafitau 1724: I, 3 f., 18) comparisons between the 'primitive' societies they studied with the accounts of the ancient historians, it is not surprising that Ferguson uses these two sources to elaborate the 'general characteristics of human nature'. But behind the two sources he acknowledges there is a third one, though he does not announce it explicitly: his Highland background.[14] Born on the border between Highlands and

Lowlands (in Logierait/Perthshire), Ferguson was familiar with both the Lowland society and the Highland community[15] and this enabled him to think as a sociologist and a historian of society.

The second part of his *Essay* is devoted to the 'History of Rude Nations' (*EHCS*, 74–107). It is remarkable to what extent Ferguson is here enhancing the prestige and value of earlier societies, while in the eyes of many of his contemporaries they were only preliminary or even 'primitive'. Ferguson's criticizes them for their anachronistic standards:

> We are apt to exaggerate the misery of barbarous times, by an imagination of what we ourselves should suffer in a situation to which we are not accustomed. But every age hath its consolations, as well as its sufferings.[16]

He is thus anticipating Herder's argument that 'all *comparison* proves to be *problematic*' and his well-known dictum: 'Each nation has its *center* of happiness *in itself*, like every sphere its center of gravity.'[17] Ferguson distinguishes between two sorts (or two stages in the development) of 'rude nations': (a) before the introduction of private property – to which he devotes, next to the rise of personal interest, much attention – when the savage nations find their subsistence chiefly in 'hunting, fishing, or the natural produce of the soil' (*EHCS*, 81); (b) under the 'impressions of property and interest' (96 f.), when hunters become shepherds and farmers and when the 'distinction of ranks' begin (*EHCS*, 100). In certain passages (e.g. *EHCS*, 98), Ferguson refers to the former condition as 'savage' and to the latter as 'barbarous', purely technical terms for him. With the modern society to be found in 'polished and commercial nations' (188), of which he deals in later parts of his *Essay*, he thus distinguishes three stages of social development. In this manner, he shares, at least to some extent,[18] the stadial analysis of society, known as the 'four stages theory', a theorem tightly associated with the Scottish Enlightenment.[19] More fully elaborated by Adam Smith and John Millar, the four stages theory defines each stage by the predominant mode of subsistence – hunting and fishing, husbandry, agriculture, commerce – and by corresponding legal and social structures.[20]

In the third part of his *Essay*, Ferguson provides a 'history of policy and the arts' (*EHCS*, 108), and it may be significant that he changed the subtitle of the second section of this part between the first edition and the later editions of his *Essay*. What he first calls '*History of Subordination*' becomes from the 1773 edition onwards the '*History of Political Establishments*' (*EHCS*, 121 and 286), probably in order to underline that he does not want to limit his reflexion to social stratification but always take the political consequences into account. In the context of his discussion of the political establishments, Ferguson asserts one of his best-known theses – forcibly taken up in the twentieth century, but with ideological, ultraliberal intentions, by Friedrich August von Hayek (1899–1992; cf. Hayek 1967, 96–105) – which he formulates almost like a law:

> Every step and every movement of the multitude, even in what are termed enlightened ages, are made with equal blindness to the future; and nations stumble upon establishments, which are indeed the result of human action, but not the execution of any human design.
>
> (*EHCS*, 122)

While we shall have to come back to this thesis when discussing Ferguson's conception of progress in the second part of this chapter, it should be added right away that this conviction led him (more neatly than Montesquieu and David Hume) to dispense with the myth of wise legislators (Lycurgus, Solon etc.):

> Their names have long been celebrated; their supposed plans have been admired; and what were probably the consequences of an early situation, is, in every instance, considered as an effect of design. ... [W]e ascribe to a previous design, what came to be known only by experience, what no human wisdom could foresee, and what, without the concurring humour and disposition of his age, no authority could enable an individual to execute.
>
> (*EHCS*, 123)

Still in the third part of the *Essay*, as announced in its title, Ferguson is also looking at the history of arts, using the term 'arts' in its double meaning, first in the sense of applied arts or 'arts and crafts', the realm of the artisan and craftsman. The improvements in these arts will result in increased social differentiation – a topic he developed further in the later parts of the *Essay*. But he also thinks about high culture and poetry and the dangers inherent in social advances to its creation and reception (*EHCS*, 171–9): his pertinent analysis may be considered his specific contribution to the quarrel of the Ancients and the Moderns.

In the fourth part of his *Essay*, Ferguson investigates further into the consequences of social and economic improvements, notably with a brilliant analysis of the ambivalent results of the division of labour (*EHCS*, 180–8). On the one hand, it will bring greater efficiency to the production of goods which will increase in quality and in volume and render them more easily affordable by greater numbers of the population:

> By the separation of arts and professions, the sources of wealth are laid open; every species of material is wrought up to the greatest perfection, and every commodity is produced in the greatest abundance.
>
> (*EHCS*, 181)

and even personal freedom and security are furthered (*EHCS*, 191, 203). But, on the other hand, he sees and spells out bluntly important harmful consequences: beginning by the fact that uninteresting and repetitive tasks render those subjected to it ignorant and brutish:

> Many mechanical arts, indeed, require no capacity; they succeed best under a total suppression of sentiment and reason; and ignorance is the mother of industry as well as of superstition. ... Manufactures, accordingly, prosper most, where the mind is least consulted, and where the workshop may, without any great effort of imagination, be considered as an engine, the parts of which are men.
>
> (*EHCS*, 182 f.)

It is hardly surprising then that both Hegel (Waszek 1988, 205–28) and Marx found such remarks by Ferguson useful when they elaborated the theme of 'alienation'

(*Entfremdung*) – destined for a splendid career in the humanist Marxism of the twentieth century. On several occasions, Marx considered Ferguson as Adam Smith's 'teacher' or 'master'[21] and in manuscripts of the early 1860s, he explains his preference not just on the basis of priority: 'what distinguishes him [Ferguson] from Smith is that he develops more sharply and more emphatically the negative sides of the division of labour' (Marx 2013, 250). For Ferguson, the drawbacks of the division of labour do not end with the dehumanizing effects but concern the danger of losing the public and national spirit, as he shows in parts V and VI of the *Essay*.

In these last parts of his inquiry, Ferguson examines the possibilities of a 'decline of nations' which might lead to 'political slavery' (*EHCS*, 204, 236). While accepting the advances of modernity, Ferguson sees the inherent dangers of it: Ferguson thought that the prosperity and well-being produced by the division of labour might deprive the citizens of the necessary exertion of their 'active virtues' (*EHCS*, 221) and reduce them to what we may call lethargic consumers – and what Ferguson is expressing in the 'language of Cato', they 'value their houses, their villas, their statues, and their pictures, at a higher rate than they do the republic' (*EHCS*, 223). This preoccupied him with regard to the military virtues in particular. Though he knew of course that a well-trained professional army, a result of the division of labour, would be more efficient in warfare, he thought it necessary to maintain a militia in order to preserve the virtues of the citizens:

> The subdivision of arts and professions, in certain examples, tends to improve the practice of them, and to promote their ends. By having separated the arts of the clothier and the tanner, we are the better supplied with shoes and with cloth. But to separate the arts which form the citizen and the statesman, the arts of policy and war, is an attempt to dismember the human character, and to destroy those very arts we mean to improve. By this separation, we in effect deprive a free people of what is necessary to their safety.
>
> (*EHCS*, 230)

While he thus sees the dangers that threaten modern societies specifically, he is never defeatist and does not consider the decline of nations inevitable. What makes him hope is the virtue of the human beings – to which he appeals at the end of his *Essay* (*EHCS*, 280): 'Men of real fortitude, integrity, and ability, are well placed in every scene … while they are destined to live, the states they compose are likewise doomed by the fates to survive, and to prosper' – who reveal themselves exactly when they are put to the proof and have to struggle. In the end, the question which Ferguson is trying to answer in his *Essay* is how, under the specific conditions of the modern world, humanity can still realize the ideal of 'good life', of a moral and political community, inherited from antiquity.[22]

Social nature and progress of humankind

Of the 'general characteristics' that Ferguson attributed to human nature in his *Essay* (cf. the above overview), two aspects seem of particular interest in the light of the central theme of this volume and deserve to be analyzed further: the 'social dispositions'

(*EHCS*, 54) he ascribes to human nature, and his specific conception of 'progress'. To start with the social dispositions, Ferguson's Janus-faced approach needs to be recalled, standing at the crossroads of a normative and a descriptive discourse, which means that his arguments may best be dealt with under the headings of a more traditional moral philosophy and of a pioneering (proto-)sociology.

Ferguson uses many terms to designate the social inclinations[23] and opposes them, in a notable passage, to the 'selfish' ones:

> The dispositions of men, and consequently their occupations, are commonly divided into two principal classes; the selfish, and the social. The first are indulged in solitude; and if they carry a reference to mankind, it is that of emulation, competition, and enmity. The second incline us to live with our fellow-creatures, and do them good; they tend to unite the members of society together; they terminate in a mutual participation of their cares and enjoyments, and render the presence of men an occasion of joy.
>
> (*EHCS*, 51)

Even from his short section on 'moral sentiment' (*EHCS*, 31–40; cf. the somewhat richer treatment in *PMPS*, II, 116–34) it can be concluded that Ferguson shares to a large extent the emphasis on sympathy, fellow-feeling, benevolence, etc., that was characteristic of the Scottish Enlightenment, often celebrated as a school of 'moral sense'.[24] While he adds some qualifications and thus keeps a little distance,[25] Ferguson uses much of the same vocabulary and, in his later book (*PMPS*, II, 121, 122, 126) explicitly refers to Hutcheson, Hume and Adam Smith as authorities. If Hutcheson, in several ways the founding father of the Scottish Enlightenment,[26] could neither publish nor lecture without attacking Mandeville,[27] the evidence for Ferguson is less obvious (cf., for example, *EHCS*, 33), but it cannot be doubted that for him, too, the principal enemy as a moral philosopher is the 'selfish system' associated with Hobbes and Mandeville.

While all this remains relevant, Ferguson's proto-sociological perspective of humankind in society is more original and he developed this line of argument in his engagement with Montesquieu.[28] Indeed, when Ferguson expounds his conception of human nature as an essentially social being, Montesquieu is the first witness he calls upon in order to confirm his view: '"Man is born in society," says Montesquieu, "and there he remains."' (*EHCS*, 16). While his quotation is rather free – he translates himself and does not give his source – the passage seems to go back to Montesquieu's *Persian Letters*:

> I have never heard a discussion of public law which did not begin with a careful examination of the origin of societies; this seems to me ridiculous. If men did not form societies, if they sought solitude and shunned one another, one would want to discover the reason for this and find out why they lived in isolation; but they are all born connected to one another; a son is born close to his father, and remains with him: there we have a society, and also its origin.
>
> (Montesquieu 2008, 125)

That this was the passage Ferguson had in mind becomes particularly plausible with the last two lines of the quotation. The assumption of Ferguson's dependence on this passage is further reinforced by the fact that Montesquieu had spoken of 'a son is born close to his father' and Ferguson mentions the 'parental affection' as the first phenomenon that detains human beings within society (*EHCS*, 16). 'But what', as Duncan Forbes rightly observes, 'in Montesquieu is an important but brief and impatient[29] couple of sentences, is in Ferguson a clear and detailed statement of method'.[30] To argue that the cause of society is self-interest, for example, is an abstraction for which no empirical evidence can be found, whereas expressions of social faculties and propensities abound in all history. When Ferguson advances the next phenomena that underline the social nature of human beings, first 'a propensity to mix with the herd, and … to follow the crowd[31] of his species' (*EHCS*, 16 f.) and, second, a sentiment of 'attachment' (*EHCS*, 18 f., 279), he strictly applies his own method of basing himself on experience which he finds in the records of ancient history and, even more so, in the observations provided by the proto-ethnological literature (cf. above), like Charlevoix (*EHCS*, 18) and a 'Collection of Dutch voyages' (17).[32]

It is beyond doubt that Ferguson takes inspiration from Montesquieu on several important points – on the classification of governments and on the separation of powers, for example – aspects that go beyond the scope of the present chapter, and one might add that his reception of the great Frenchman was wider than that of most contemporary Brits, since Ferguson not only draws upon *The Spirit of Laws* but also the *Persian Letters* and even the 'Dialogue between Sulla and Eucrates' (*EHCS*, 84, where a passage is quoted, again somewhat freely and in Ferguson's translation). But recent research has shown that his reception of Montesquieu also includes some implicit criticism and responses (Mason 1988; Sher 1994; McDaniel 2008, 2013) and what is primordial here is that Ferguson's account of the social nature of humankind is much more elaborate than Montesquieu's.

This becomes particularly clear when Ferguson explains the third empirical element of his assertion that human beings have a social nature, the sentiment of 'attachment', an element that, at first glance, seems somewhat vague. Again in order to undermine the widespread misconception that societies are joined and are upheld for reasons of self-interest, Ferguson insists (with the martial tone typical of the Highlander – a far cry from Montesquieu, even if the latter does not condemn all wars but allows for those that avoid servitude):

> Men are so far from valuing society on account of its mere external conveniencies, that they are commonly most attached where those conveniencies are least frequent; and are there most faithful, where the tribute of their allegiance is paid in blood.
>
> (*EHCS*, 19)

To prove his point, according to his outlined method, Ferguson draws upon 'observations from the examples of men who live in the simplest condition, and who have not learned to affect what they do not actually feel' (*EHCS*, 18); in other words, he shows examples from ancient Greece, early Rome and the 'savages' he found depicted in the accounts of explorers and other travellers. The social disposition is an affection that

> operates with the greatest force, where it meets with the greatest difficulties ... In the breast of a man, its flame redoubles where the wrongs or sufferings of his friend, or his country, require his aid. It is, in short, from this principle alone that we can account for the obstinate attachment of a savage to his unsettled and defenceless tribe, when temptations on the side of ease and of safety might induce him to fly from famine and danger, to a station more affluent, and more secure.
> (*EHCS*, 19)

In contrast to this somewhat idealized image of humankind 'in the simplest condition', Ferguson clearly casts a cold eye on the 'spirit which reigns' in modern commercial society: 'It is here indeed, if ever, that man is sometimes found a detached and a solitary being: he has found an object which sets him in competition with his fellow-creatures, and he deals with them as he does with his cattle and his soil, for the sake of the profits they bring' (*EHCS*, 19).

This critical perspective shows how Ferguson's reflexions on the social dispositions are linked with his ideas on social development and thus creates a smooth transition to his complex and in parts specific conception of 'progress'. On the one hand, Ferguson clearly shares the satisfaction about the improvements made in his country – a pioneering collection of essays on the history of Scotland in the eighteenth century bears the appropriate title 'The Age of Improvement' (Mitchison 1970) – a satisfaction, even a certain enthusiasm that was often voiced by Hume and Adam Smith with relish. The improvements were not limited to economic advances and the rise of living standards but affected the political situation simultaneously:

> It has been found, that, except in a few singular cases, the commercial and political arts have advanced together. These arts have been in modern Europe so interwoven, that we cannot determine which were prior in the order of time, or derived most advantage from the mutual influences with which they act and re-act upon one another. It has been observed, that in some nations the spirit of commerce, intent on securing its profits, has led the way to political wisdom. A people, possessed of wealth, and become jealous of their properties, have formed the project of emancipation, and have proceeded, under favour of an importance recently gained, still farther to enlarge their pretensions, and to dispute the prerogatives which their sovereign had been in use to employ.[33]

Characteristically, neither Ferguson nor his friends expressed much discontent about the post-union (1707) political settlement, even less sympathy for the Jacobite rising of 1745, also called the 'Forty-five Rebellion'. Indeed as a Chaplain to the 43rd (later the 42nd) Regiment (a Highland regiment also known as the 'Black Watch'), Ferguson insisted that the soldiers should remain loyal rather than join the rebellion and should not even hesitate, if it came to such a dramatic event, to fight against their Highland 'acquaintances' and 'relations' (Ferguson [1746] 2011, 907).

But Ferguson's adherence to the social and political advances of his time is counterbalanced by his awareness of what was lost in the process. He knew better than most of his friends that a heavy price had been paid for the advantages and attractions of modern society. The dehumanizing effects of industrially divided labour have already been indicated: men become 'parts of an engine' (*EHCS*, 182) or 'cogs in the wheel' according to the popular expression. But what seems to worry him even more is the loss of the public spirit, inherent in the process:

> The separation of professions, while it seems to promise improvement of skill, and is actually the cause why the productions of every art become more perfect as commerce advances; yet in its termination, and ultimate effects, serves, in some measure, to break the bands of society ... Under the *distinction* of callings, by which the members of polished society are separated from each other, every individual is supposed to possess his species of talent, or his peculiar skill, in which the others are confessedly ignorant; and society is made up of parts, of which none is animated with the spirit of society itself.
>
> (*EHCS*, 218)

Nations can thus decline, but the decline is not inevitable; Ferguson is not advancing a kind of cyclical theory of history. The analogy he had drawn between individual development and the progression of the human species (*EHCS*, 1, 5), in order to reinforce his optimistic conclusion about social advances, has now to be qualified in order to avoid the cyclical perspective of society's decline in analogy with the old age and death of the individual:

> The human frame has ..., in every individual, a frail contexture, and a limited duration; it is worn by exercise, and exhausted by a repetition of its functions: But in a society, whose constituent members are renewed in every generation, where the race seems to enjoy perpetuated youth, and accumulating advantages, we cannot, by any parity of reason, expect to find imbecilities connected with mere age and length of days.
>
> (*EHCS*, 209)

If the decline of nations is not inevitable, progress is even less so. It certainly is not the realization of a rational plan or of a political programme. It happens rather spontaneously, by accident and needs to be interpreted *a posteriori*. It emerges out of a multitude of individual aims and ends[34] as the unlooked-for result of conflicts and compromises. In this respect, Ferguson is not so far removed from Hume, but with the latter such conclusions are somewhat hidden in several places of his *History*:

> An acquaintance with the ancient periods of their government is chiefly useful by ... instructing them in *the great mixture of accident, which commonly concurs with a small ingredient of wisdom and foresight, in erecting the complicated fabric of the most perfect government*.
>
> (Hume 1983, vol. II, 525; our own italics)

In the end, Ferguson's account of social 'progress' is a lesson of modesty to those who want to 'make history' and thus might also be discussed in the context of the debate around the 'disposability' or not (*Verfügbarkeit* and *Unverfügbarkeit*) of history, but that would be another story (cf. Koselleck 2004, 192–204; Kittsteiner 1998, 2004; Blänkner 2010).

Notes

1. Ferguson, like most of his contemporaries, does use non-inclusive language, speaking of 'mankind' and 'man' for example, rather than 'humankind' or 'human being'. The present text is striving for inclusive language but retains of course Ferguson's wording in quotations.
2. The denomination 'Scottish Enlightenment' is posterior to the phenomenon and only began to be used by historians of philosophy like W. R. Scott (1900, 261 and 265), although some nineteenth-century historians already spoke of the 'Enlightenment in Scotland'. Even in the twentieth-century, the designation 'Scottish Enlightenment' had to impose itself against competing denominations like the 'Scottish school of moral philosophy' (this goes back to Victor Cousin) or the 'Scottish Historical school' (R. Pascal, 1938 and 1939).
3. After a generation of pioneers – Gladys Bryson (1894–1952), George Elder Davie (1912–2007), Duncan Forbes (1922–1994) and Andrew Skinner (1935–2011), their publications are too numerous to be listed – the Scottish Enlightenment really established itself as a field of research in the 1980s, with such publications as R. H. Campbell and A. S. Skinner eds (1982) and I. Hont and M. Ignatieff (1983).
4. Cf. F. Oz-Salzberger (1995); Waszek (1988), 56–83; ibid. (2003), 113–19.
5. *Avant la lettre* because the term 'sociology' (*sociologie*) only came into wider use through Auguste Comte (1798–1857), but Comte had read Ferguson with benefit and included him, next to Condorcet and along with at least three other Scots, David Hume, Adam Smith and William Robertson, in his hall of fame, the *Calendrier Positiviste* (1849) on 24 November. Lehmann (1930) is the first book-length effort to establish Ferguson as a founding figure of sociology; more recently, Meek (1976) & Berry (1997) have written on the subject. For further references on Ferguson and the sociologists, see Hill (2006), 4–9.
6. This did not prevent him, loyal in his friendships as he was, from reporting the book's success in London to Ferguson and from rejoicing (Merolle 1995, I. 71–3).
7. Sher (1985), 197. Hume's disapproval stands in contrast to the clergymen among the Scottish Enlightenment, e.g. Hugh Blair (1718–1800) and William Robertson (1721–1793).
8. Ferguson limits the significance which Smith attributed to the perspective of the spectator to certain situations and in others privileges the perspective of the acting individual; cf. Kettler (1977), 443; Waszek (2003), 62.
9. Cf. EHCS, 35; *IMP*, 101–9; *PMPS*, II: 116–34.
10. Cf. Forbes in *EHCS*, xvi: 'Ferguson's break with the whole state of nature/contract apparatus is much cleaner than Hume's.'
11. Ferguson refers to them frequently, especially in Part II of his *Essay* 'Of the History of Rude Nations', e.g. *EHCS*, 93–5, 101–5 and he praises them frequently, e.g. *EHCS*, 78: 'It is from the Greek and the Roman historians ... that we have not only the

most authentic and instructive, but even the most engaging, representations of the tribes from whom we descend. Those sublime and intelligent writers understood human nature, and could collect its features, and exhibit its characters in every situation.'

12 On this literature and its impact on the Scots, see R. Meek (1976), especially chapter II: 'In the beginning all the world was America', 37–67; cf. Waszek (2003), 69f.

13 *EHCS*: 83–94 (on Charlevoix); 83–93 (on Lafitau); 22 and 102 (on Kolb, whom Ferguson mentions as 'Kolbe' or 'Kolben', as happened often in English texts).

14 Cf. Forbes in *EHCS*, xxxviii f. who insists upon the fact that Ferguson was 'unique' among the authors of the Scottish Enlightenment in being a Highlander and a Gaelic speaker and who explains how that inspiration was 'clothed' in such fashionable garbs as the admiration of Sparta and of the American Indians. In her recent thesis, Denise A. Testa (2007) has explored this field further.

15 When Ferdinand Tönnies (1855–1936) imposed this conceptual dichotomy with his masterwork (Tönnies 1887), he had studied Ferguson in detail, as is documented by his correspondence with Friedrich Paulsen (1846–1908), the Neo-Kantian philosopher and educator (Tönnies/Paulsen [1961]: 91f., 210).

16 *EHCS*, 105; cf. the corresponding passage in *PMPS*, I, 248: 'the sum of gratification or disappointment may be equal in all the different situations of men'.

17 Herder 2002, 296 f. On Herder and Ferguson, cf. Pascal (1939) & Zammito (2009), especially 67 and 85.

18 Ferguson admits only three stages: nomadic cattle breeding and sedentary agriculture form together only one stage for him. Another difference is that Ferguson – unlike Smith and others, who used the increase of population and the resulting rise in the demand of food in order to explain changes in the mode of production – does not really explain the passage from one stage to the next but contends himself with describing the different stages; cf. Forbes in *EHCS*, xxii f.

19 Cf. Meek (1976), especially chapters 1 and 4; Waszek (2003), 69–76.

20 For his fullest account of the four stages theory, see Adam Smith's *Lectures* (Smith 1978: 14ff.). John Millar (1735–1801), probably Smith's most gifted disciple, provides his version of the theory in the first chapter of his *Observations* (Millar 1771); on Millar cf. Waszek (2004a) and more recently Miller (2017).

21 Marx (2019: 139, 389) and (2013: 249). In this appreciation, Marx could only base himself on the dates of their publications and did not know about Smith's then unpublished lectures (Smith 1978).

22 Cf. Forbes in EHCS, xli: 'The clan had gone, the republics of antiquity had gone, but the good life was still possible.'

23 Among other expressions, Ferguson uses (*EHCS*, 36, 38, 53): 'amicable propensity', 'principle of affection to mankind' and 'benevolence'.

24 Cf. the brilliant survey by Raphael (1947), though he did not have the 'space' – as he put it in his 'Preface' – to include Ferguson and had to limit himself to Hutcheson, Hume, Richard Price and Reid.

25 When he praises Hume and Smith for their 'eloquence' and 'masterly tone of expression' (*PMPS*, II, 122, 126), the compliment is somewhat equivocal in Ferguson's mouth, for he clearly doubts that eloquence is the adequate test of truth.

26 The traditional view of Hutcheson as the father of the Scottish Enlightenment has been questioned by recent research: some now champion Andrew Fletcher (1655–1716) or Gershom Carmichael (1672–1729) as the founding figures.

27 As has often been said: cf. Blackstone (1965), 6; Hayek (1966), 140; Jensen (1971), 14.

28 Ferguson's *Essay* contains a number of explicit and significative references to Montesquieu (*EHCS*, 16, 65–70, 84, 151) of whom of the most striking (65) is: 'When I recollect what the President Montesquieu has written, I am at a loss to tell, why I should treat of human affairs', and he admits that he may have drawn on him on further occasions: Montesquieu was 'probably the source of many observations, which, in different places, I may, under the belief of innovation, have repeated, without quoting their author'.
29 'Ridiculous' is how Montesquieu qualifies the views of his opponents.
30 D. Forbes in *EHCS*, xvii.
31 Now obsolete spelling for 'crowd'.
32 Ferguson does not provide a precise reference, but the passage he quotes can be found in *A Collection of Voyages Undertaken by the Dutch East-India Company*, London: Freeman 1703, 57.
33 *EHCS*, 261, f. For similar views of Hume and Smith, cf. Waszek (2000).
34 What Forbes calls the principle of the 'heterogeneity of purposes', in *EHCS*, xxiii.

References

Berry, C. J. (1997), *The Social Theory of the Scottish Enlightenment*, Edinburgh: Edinburgh University Press.
Blackstone, W. T. (1965), *Francis Hutcheson and Contemporary Ethical Theory*, Athens, GA: University of Georgia Press.
Blänkner, R. (2010), 'Prozess und Ereignis. Zum Problem der Unverfügbarkeit der Geschichte', in B. Marx (ed.), *Widerfahrnis und Erkenntnis. Zur Wahrheit menschlicher Erfahrung*, Leipzig: Evangelische Verlagsanstalt, 147–76.
Bryson, G. E. (1945), *Man and society: The Scottish Inquiry of the Eighteenth Century*, Princeton, NJ: Princeton University Press.
Buffon, G. L. Leclerc de (1749–1788), *Histoire naturelle*, 36 vols, Paris: Imprimerie Royale.
Campbell, R. H. and A. S. Skinner, eds (1982), *The Origins and Nature of the Scottish Enlightenment: Essays*, Edinburgh: J. Donald.
Ferguson, A. (1746/2011), *A Sermon Preached in the Ersh Language to His Majesty's First Highland Regiment of Foot*, London: A. Millar; the text of this rare edition is reprinted (with an introduction by M.B. Arbo) in *Political Theology*, 12 (6): 900–7.
Ferguson, A. (1767/1966), *An Essay on the History of Civil Society*, ed. D. Forbes, Edinburgh: EUP [abbreviation: *EHCS*; Roman page numbers refer to Duncan Forbes' introduction].
Ferguson, A. (1773), *Institutes of Moral Philosophy: For the Use of Students in the College of Edinburgh*, first ed. 1769), The second edition, revised and corrected, Edinburgh: Kincaid, Creech, and Bell (= facsimile: New York & London: Garland, 1978) [abbreviation: *IMP*].
Ferguson, A. (1792), *Principles of Moral and Political Science: Being Chiefly a Retrospect of Lectures Delivered in the College of Edinburgh*, 2 vols, Edinburgh & London: Strahan & Cadell (= facsimile: Hildesheim & New York: Georg Olms) [abbreviation: *PMPS*].
Greig, J. Y. T., ed. (1932), *The letters of David Hume*, 2 vols, Oxford: Clarendon Press.
Hayek, F. A. (1966), 'Dr. Bernard Mandeville', *Proceedings of the British Academy*, 52: 126–41.
Hayek, F. A. (1967), *Studies in Philosophy, Politics and Economics*, London: Routledge & Kegan Paul, here chapter six: 'The results of human action but not of human design', 96–105.

Heath, E. & Merolle, V., eds (2008), *Adam Ferguson: History, Progress and Human Nature*, London: Pickering & Chatto.
Herder, J. G. (2002), *Philosophical Writings*, trans. and ed. M. N. Forster, Cambridge: Cambridge University Press.
Hill, L. (2006), *The Passionate Society: The Social, Political and Moral Thought of Adam Ferguson*, Dordrecht: Springer.
Hont, I. & Ignatieff, M., eds (1983), *Wealth and Virtue: The Shaping of Political Economy in the Scottish Enlightenment*, Cambridge: Cambridge University Press.
Hume, D. (1983), *The History of England*, ed. W. B. Todd, 6 vols, Indianapolis: Liberty Classics.
Jensen, H. (1971), *Motivation and the Moral Sense in Francis Hutcheson's Ethical Theory*, The Hague: Nijhoff.
Kettler, D. (1965), *The Social and Political Thought of Adam Ferguson*, Columbus, OH: Ohio State University Press.
Kettler, D. (1977), 'History and Theory in Ferguson's Essay on the History of Civil Society: A Reconsideration', *Political Theory*, 5 (4): 437-60.
Kittsteiner, H. D. (1998), *Listen der Vernunft. Motive geschichtsphilosophischen Denkens*, Frankfurt, Main: Fischer, 7-42.
Kittsteiner, H. D. (2004), *Out of Control: über die Unverfügbarkeit des historischen Prozesses*, Berlin: Philo.
Koselleck, R. (2004), *Futures Past: On the Semantics of Historical Time*, trans. Keith Tribe, New York: Columbia University Press.
Lafitau, J. F. (1724), *Mœurs des sauvages américains, comparées aux mœurs des premiers temps*, 4 vols, Paris: Saugrain l'aîné & Hochereau. English translation: *Customs of the American Indians compared with the customs of primitive times*, 2 vols, W. N. Fenton and Elizabeth L. Moore (eds), Toronto: Champlain Society 1974-1977.
Lehmann, W. C. (1930), *Adam Ferguson and the Beginnings of Modern Sociology: An Analysis of the Sociological Elements in His Writings with Some Suggestions as to His Place in the History of Social Theory*, New York: Columbia University Press.
Marx, K. (2013), *Zur Kritik der politischen Ökonomie (Manuskript 1861-1863)* [MEGA, II,3], Berlin: Akademie.
Marx, K. (2019), *Capital: Volume one* [1867], trans. S. Moore & E. B. Aveling, Mineola, NY: Dover.
Mason, S. (1988), 'Ferguson and Montesquieu: Tacit Reproaches?', *British Journal for Eighteenth Century Studies*, 11: 193-203.
McDaniel, I. (2008), 'Ferguson, Roman History and the Threat of Military Government in Modern Europe', in E. Heath & V. Merolle (eds), *Adam Ferguson: History, Progress and Human Nature*, London: Pickering & Chatto, 115-30 and 204-8 (notes).
McDaniel, I. (2013), *Adam Ferguson in the Scottish Enlightenment: The Roman Past and Europe's Future*, Cambridge, MA: Harvard University Press.
Meek, R. L. (1976), *Social Science and the Ignoble Savage*, Cambridge: Cambridge University Press.
Merolle, V., ed. (1995), *The Correspondence of Adam Ferguson*, 2 vols, London: Pickering.
Millar, J. (1771), *Observations Concerning the Distinction of Ranks in Society*, London: John Murray.
Miller, N. B. (2017), *John Millar and the Scottish Enlightenment: Family Life and World History*, Oxford: Voltaire Foundation.
Mitchison, R. and N. T. Philipson, eds (1970), *Scotland in the Age of Improvement: Essays in Sottish History in the Eighteenth Century*, Edinburgh: Edinburg University Press.

Montesquieu, C. L. de Secondat de (2008), *Persian Letters*, trans. M. Mauldon, introduction and notes by A. Kahn, Oxford: Oxford University Press.

Mossner, E. C. and I. S. Ross, eds (1977), *The Correspondence of Adam Smith* [The Glasgow edition of the works and correspondence of Adam Smith, vol. 6], Oxford: Clarendon Press.

Oz-Salzberger, F. (1995), *Translating the Enlightenment: Scottish Civic Discourse in Eighteenth-Century Germany*, Oxford: Clarendon Press.

Pascal, R. (1938), 'Property and Society: The Scottish Historical School of the Eighteenth Century', *The Modern Quarterly*, 1: 167-79.

Pascal, R. (1939), 'Herder and the Scottish Historical School', *Publications of the English Goethe Society*, 14 (1): 23-42.

Raphael, D. D. (1947), *The Moral Sense*, London: Oxford University Press.

Scott, W. R. (1900), *Francis Hutcheson: His Life, Teaching and Position in the History of Philosophy*, Cambridge: Cambridge University Press.

Sher, R. B. (1985), *Church and University in the Scottish Enlightenment: The Moderate Literati of Edinburgh*, Edinburgh: Edinburgh University Press.

Sher, R. B. (1994), 'From Troglodytes to Americans: Montesquieu and the Scottish Enlightenment on Liberty, Virtue, and Commerce', in D. Wootton (ed.), *Republicanism, Liberty and Commercial Society, 1649-1776*, Stanford: Stanford University Press, 368-402.

Small, J. (1864), *Biographical Sketch of Adam Ferguson, LL.D., F.R.S.E.*, Edinburgh: Neill & Co.

Smith, A. (1978), *Lectures on Jurisprudence*, ed. R. L. Meek, D. D. Raphael & P.G. Stein, Oxford: Clarendon Press.

Sombart, W. (1923), 'Die Anfänge der Soziologie', in M. Palyi (ed.), *Hauptprobleme der Soziologie. Erinnerungsgabe für Max Weber*, vol. 1, München & Leipzig: Duncker & Humblot, 5-19.

Testa, D. A. (2007), *'A Bastard Gaelic Man': Reconsidering the Highland Roots of Adam Ferguson*, PhD diss., University of Western Sydney.

Tönnies, F. (1887), *Gemeinschaft und Gesellschaft*, Leipzig: Fues. English translation: *Community and Civil Society*, ed. J. Harris, Cambridge: Cambridge University Press, 2001.

Tönnies, F. & Paulsen, F. (1961), *Briefwechsel 1876-1908*, ed. O. Klose, E. G. Jacoby and I. Fischer, Kiel: Hirt.

Waszek, N. (1984), 'Two Concepts of Morality: A Distinction of Adam Smith's Ethics and Its Stoic Origin', *Journal of the History of Ideas*, XLV: 591-606.

Waszek, N. (1988), *The Scottish Enlightenment and Hegel's Account of 'Civil Society'*, Dordrecht & Boston: Kluwer.

Waszek, N. (2000), 'History and Economy in Hume and Kant', in W. Leidhold (ed.), *Politik und Politeia. Formen und Probleme politischer Ordnung*, Würzburg: Königshausen & Neumann, 609-18.

Waszek, N. (2003), *L'Ecosse des Lumières: Hume, Smith, Ferguson*, Paris: Presses universitaires de France.

Waszek, N. (2004), 'Adam Ferguson', in H. Holzhey & V. Mudroch (eds), *Die Philosophie des 18. Jahrhunderts*, vol. 1, *Großbritannien und Nordamerika, Niederlande*, Basel: Schwabe, 603-18, 632-5.

Waszek, N. (2004a), 'John Millar', in H. Holzhey & V. Mudroch (eds), *Die Philosophie des 18. Jahrhunderts*, vol. 1, *Großbritannien und Nordamerika, Niederlande*, 596-602, 631-2.

Waszek, N. (2006), 'The Scottish Enlightenment in Germany, and Its Translator Christian Garve (1742–1798)', in T. Hubbard and R. D. S. Jack (eds), *Scotland in Europe*, Amsterdam & New York: Rodopi, 55–71.

Waszek, N. (2011), 'An Essay on the History of Civil Society d'Adam Ferguson: Contextes et lignes de Force', *Études anglaises*, 64 (3): 259–72.

Zammito, J. H. (2009), 'Herder and Historical Metanarrative: What's Philosophical about History?' in H. Adler & W. Koepke (eds), *A Companion to the Works of Johann Gottfried Herder*, Rochester, NY: Camden House, 65–92.

8

The association of science and civilization in the Enlightenment

Stephen Gaukroger

In the nineteenth century, it was the West's conception of itself as the unique possessor of a scientific mentality that marked it out as a culture that can progress to modernity. The origins of this notion can be traced to the middle of the eighteenth century, to d'Alembert's argument about how social and cultural stagnation had been overcome in the West, an argument that was, forty years later, to be reworked by Condorcet, who proposed what was to become the canonical statement of the idea of the inevitability of progress and of the idea that what drives the move towards a new, modern form of society is science.

What is civilization?

In eighteenth- and nineteenth-century explorations of human nature, the context in which questions were posed was routinely that of 'civilization': both morality and culture were measured against the template of the values of civilization, which were central to how questions on the nature of humanity were thought through. But this template, and how it was used, varied significantly. During the seventeenth and eighteenth centuries, civilization had been associated with such things as successful political institutions, a cultural and religious life, literacy levels, social cohesion, prosperity and a system of laws. There was a fascination with the Orient, with its languages and its cultures. The seventeenth-century Spanish Dominican Domingo Navarrete, for example, had even suggested that Confucianism provided a remedy for the political crisis afflicting his native Spain.[1] But by the nineteenth century, investigation of the Orient became focused on a contrast between the uncivilized East and the civilized West, a contrast in which what was considered to be the distinctive history of the Orient played a key role.

This is reflected in the nineteenth-century assessment of what the Orient had to offer. As Herren et al. note, 'nineteenth century historiography differs sharply from its predecessors. In the eighteenth century, historians, who were merely interested in the mode of unintentional discovery expressed by the concept of "serendipity", regarded Asia with curiosity and admiration. In the nineteenth century, European historians invented the Orient as underdeveloped, thus confirming Western progress'.[2] The fascination with the Orient shifted from a general interest to one focused almost exclusively on its past, enhanced by a view that the lives of its present-day occupants mirrored those of biblical times, with travellers to the Near East reporting that they were among the people spoken of by Moses and the prophets. In his *History of British India*, James Mill wrote that 'by conversing with the Hindus of the present day, we, in some measure, converse with the Chaldeans and Babylonians of the time of Cyrus; with the Persians or Egyptians of the time of Alexander'.[3]

For a number of seventeenth- and eighteenth-century writers, there was a sense that we might learn from the modern Orient, and this was a significant motivation for its study. By contrast, by the early decades of the nineteenth century, such an assessment had effectively been abandoned. It might be considered that, for late eighteenth- and nineteenth-century Europeans, it was the absence of Christianity that marked out the Orient as deficient as a civilization, given the perceived centrality of Christian values to what was distinctive about Europe, and what secured its standing as the ultimate model for all cultures. Traditionally, if there had been a foundation for civilization, it lay in Christianity. Erasmus's *Antibarbarorum* (Against the Barbarians, 1520), for example, while it called for a secular educational programme based on Greek and Latin authors, advocated this in order to instil the values of classical learning in a Christian society, and the contrast was between the demands of Christianity and barbarism, the role of classical education being to bolster the former. In Bossuet's 1681 *Discours sur l'histoire universelle* (Discourse on Universal History), which set out the model for reconciling Christian and secular history, the histories and religions of all peoples were rooted in the events described in the Old Testament. Here everything is subordinated to the history of the Church, which provides the organizing thread. There is no mention of China, India or Japan, for developments outside Christian Europe were irrelevant for Bossuet's 'universal history', which confined itself to the 'succession of empires' only insofar as they have a 'necessary connection with the history of the people of God'.[4]

But by the eighteenth century many histories incorporated China into their conception of world history, although it was simply accommodated to the Eurocentric – Christocentric model. Some writers simply identified the early Chinese emperors with the Hebrew patriarchs,[5] while others followed the biblical model in every other respect but made China the first empire after the Flood, displacing Babylon. Yet others, while rejecting China's claims to great antiquity, nevertheless included long descriptions of China. Augustine Calmet, for example, in his *Histoire universelle* (Universal History) of 1735,[6] did cover China, despite otherwise taking Bossuet as his model. By the middle of the century, China was beginning to be treated as an essential part of universal histories, and the sixty-eight-volume *Universal History* published in London between 1747 and 1768 offers a wide coverage of Chinese material.[7] Equally extensive was the treatment in Lambert's *Histoire générale* (General History), which advertised itself in its subtitle as covering virtually every aspect of social, political, scientific and artistic life in Europe, Asia, Africa and America.[8]

The association between civilization and Christianity is retained in the first appearance of the term 'civilization' in French, in 1756 in Mirabeau's *L'Ami des hommes* (The Friend of Humanity). Mirabeau writes: 'Religion is indubitably the first and most useful restraint on humanity: it is the original source of civilization; and it counsels and reminds us constantly of sociability.'[9] But from the second half of the eighteenth century, the Christian/non-Christian distinction ceased to be the operative one in understanding what civilization consisted in. A range of different models were deployed, and in considering these, a useful starting point is Osterhammel's careful treatment of the shift in conceptions of the Orient from the eighteenth to the nineteenth century. Osterhammel identifies three types of nineteenth-century historico-philosophical conceptions of the causes of the perceived backwardness of the Orient.[10] These offer different explanations of the failure of the Orient to develop.

The first of the three approaches was that of decline. Here the model, the rise and decline of empires, was one that had precedents stretching back to antiquity, and it had been a traditional concern of historians. In its nineteenth-century version the inevitability of decline (a much-used example was the decline of the early modern Mughal Empire in India) was focused on the Orient, with the British Empire for example seemingly exempt. By contrast, in the second approach, degeneration was identified as the problem. The basic idea was that nations that present themselves to us today as savage or barbarian are the descendants of high cultures that have degenerated. An example here is the early reports of America: rather than the indigenous population living in a primitive state of nature, they were the product of an early cultural flowering which had undergone a slow and gradual process of decay, and they are now long estranged from their origins. Finally, the key idea in the third approach was that of stagnation. In contrast to the other two models, a kind of evolutionary progress was taken as the norm, and this was considered to have reached its climax in Europe. As Osterhammel describes it: 'Stagnation could be diagnosed when mores and customs, knowledge and mentalities, forms of government and modes of material subsistence remained unchanged over long periods of time, when the material life and intellectual capacities of a nation or an entire civilization were stuck in neutral, so to speak.'[11]

The questions arises how adequate these models are for an understanding of the uniqueness of the West. It is far from clear where Greece and Rome fit into the schema for example. The decline model might seem to be prototypically that of the Roman Empire, yet for nineteenth-century Western thinkers there was not only a continuity with classical antiquity, but that continuity was a defining feature of the West, playing a formative role in its origins story. Nineteenth-century European commitment to the values of classical antiquity was as central as its commitment to the values of Christianity in forming its self-conception. The degeneration model also presents difficulties in this respect. As well as America, the model was also applied to Egypt, whose contemporary state of decay was contrasted with the kind of culture that must have been responsible for the pyramids in remote antiquity. But classical Greece and Rome look much the same as Egypt in this respect, and yet it is important to the nineteenth-century West's self-understanding that there is a continuity between these latter collapsed cultures and the present.

It is the stagnation model that holds the key, for this, typified in treatments of China and extended generally to the Orient, allows recognition of great cultural achievement – such as the pyramids in the case of Egypt and the Great Wall in the case of China – while relegating these achievements to the past. But more specifically, the question is not just to identify the various failings of the Orient, but at the same time to do this in a way that identifies why the contemporary West hasn't been subject to these failings. In fact, as we are about to see, there was recognition that the West, at various times in its history, had undergone the kinds of failing identified in Osterhammel's three models. So the question now is not what has allowed the modern West to *avoid* these problems, but rather what it was that eighteenth- and nineteenth-century writers believed had allowed the modern West to *recover* from these problems. And was it something different in each of the cases of decline, degeneration and stagnation that allowed this, or was it just the one thing?

Consider one possible candidate: Christianity. Why couldn't Christianity play the role of defining the success of the West, as it had earlier? It is hard to imagine what story could be told that would show Christianity to check either decline, or degeneration, or stagnation. But there is another reason why Christianity could not play this role. From the middle of the eighteenth century it starts to be argued that Christianity is actually the source of the problem, in that, in the West, it was Christianity that had induced a form of stagnation which, as it was described, was wholly on a par with that which had been considered to have held the Orient back. In this case, the question becomes that of how the West was able to overcome the degeneration that its Christian culture had engendered.

The answer was science: it is science, not Christianity, that saves us from barbarism. In 1759, for example, Linnaeus was remarking that 'only the Sciences distinguish Wild people, Barbarians and Hottentots, from us'.[12] A century later, in 1866, Thomas Huxley writes of science saving civilization from barbarism, talking of a 'new nature' created by science and manifested 'in every mechanical artifice, every chemically pure substance employed by manufacture, every abnormally fertile race of plants, or rapidly growing and fattening breed of animals'. This new nature, we are told, is

> the foundation of our wealth and the condition of our safety from submergence by another flood of barbarous hordes; it is the bond which unites into a solid political whole, regions larger than any empire of antiquity; it secures us from the recurrence of pestilences and famines of former times; it is the source of endless comforts and conveniences, which are not mere luxuries, but conduce to physical and moral well-being.[13]

At the same time, general lessons for history were being drawn from the new role given to science. In 1877, the eminent German physiologist Emil du Bois-Reymond was suggesting that the fall of the Roman Empire was due not to social, political or economic conditions but to a lack of science: Roman imperial culture rested 'on the quicksand of speculation'.[14] Historical progress was due to science alone – 'the history of natural science', he writes, 'is the actual history of mankind' – and it was science 'that made mankind mankind'.[15]

In short, from the middle of the eighteenth century, Western thinkers had begun to think that the formative feature of Western civilization was commitment to scientific enquiry.[16] It cannot be stressed sufficiently what a novel view this was, and a good example of its novelty is manifest in the changes in the perception of China. One of the earliest writers on China, Matteo Ricci, had singled out the cultivation of moral virtue, the integrity of the family and the promotion of good governance as qualities of Confucianism from which the West could learn,[17] and China clearly manifested the cultural achievements that Voltaire, for example, had identified in France since the death of Louis XIV in the areas of language, conduct and thought.[18] By contrast with the West, its scientific achievements did not match its cultural ones, but this did not diminish or disqualify the latter: quite the contrary, they showed that whether or not a society was civilized was independent of any scientific achievements. Early eighteenth-century writers such as Mairan and Hume had no doubt that China had a civilization, but that it had no science. In the 1730s, Mairan wondered how a people who had achieved such a significant level of civilization could have made so little progress in science, despite the thousands of years that they had devoted to astronomy and medicine?[19] A decade later, in 1742, David Hume drew attention to China as a well-organized state which had failed to establish the kind of successful scientific culture that he believed had contributed so much to the greatness of the West.[20]

How did the idea that what secures civilization in the West is its science arise and become established? The short answer is that, for many nineteenth-century commentators, the East has been unable to go beyond its past and emerge into modernity, and the reason for this is that it lacked the scientific culture that enables the transition to be made. This was something that comparison with the West's history, notably its success in transcending the superstition of the Middle Ages, was believed to reveal.

Science and civilization in the French Enlightenment

There are essentially two developments that launch the idea that it is science that provides the criterion of civilization. The first is a new interpretation of European history pioneered in d'Alembert and built upon in Condorcet, an interpretation that seeks an explanation for the hiatus in the development of European culture that occurred during the Middle Ages. The second is the restriction of the merits of the Orient to its past, and application of the kind of account offered by d'Alembert in the case of the Middle Ages to the Orient, which saw the solution to the stagnation of the Middle Ages as lying in the rise of science, something that failed to occur in the Orient.

It was in France that the association of science and reason came into its own and, through this, the explicit association of science and civilization. In the mid-eighteenth-century Paris, a number of accounts appeared on the causes of the differential development of civilization at different times and places, of which the most notable were Montesquieu's *De l'esprit des lois* (The Spirit of the Laws, 1748),[21] Turgot's December 1750 lecture to the Sorbonne, 'Sur les progrès successifs de l'esprit humain' (On the Successive Progress of the Human Mind),[22] the long introductory 1751 preliminary 'Discours' to Diderot and d'Alembert's *Encyclopédie*,[23] and Voltaire's *Essai sur les mœurs et l'esprit des nations* (An Essay on Universal History, the Manners, and Spirit of Nations), written between 1745 and 1751, and published in full in 1756. These accounts of civilization varied considerably. Montaigne, for example, offers a climatic account, whereas Turgot defends blind passions and ambitions as being as important as reason in the development of civilization, contrasting the West with China, where he maintains that a rational avoidance of war in China has led to a lack of interaction between different peoples and to the progress that results from such interaction. By contrast, Voltaire and d'Alembert focused on the deleterious effects of Christianity on the progress of civilization, although it is only with d'Alembert that we find the progress of civilization mapped onto the progress of reason in an explicit and systematic way. And it is here that we find the connections between science and reason being drawn in such a fashion that the progress of civilization now comes to be mapped onto the progress of science.

D'Alembert defends 'reason' – by contrast with religious teaching for example – as the sole ultimate criterion of judgement. He then makes the crucial move of associating reason with science. On d'Alembert's Lockean sensationalist programme, it is sensation alone that puts us in touch with the world and allows us to preserve our bodies and to provide them with their needs. We can achieve this either by our own observations and discoveries or by those of others which have been communicated to us.[24] The ideas generated from these sources can then be combined and connected, and his ultimate model for these connections is the algebraic procedures established in science. Once reason and our knowledge of the world have been associated with science, the main task for d'Alembert is the reconstruction of the history of the sciences, showing 'the steps by which we arrived at our present state'. What we need, he argues, is 'a historical explanation of the order in which the various parts of our knowledge succeed one another',[25] and this takes the form of a genealogy of reason showing how, in its historical forms, it converges on the project embodied in the *Encyclopédie*, which thereby represents the culmination of human cognitive endeavour and constitutes the starting point for further enquiry.

The journey to science and rationality is, on d'Alembert's account, a tortuous and circuitous one. His reconstruction of this journey begins by contrasting the order in which different forms of enquiry would be pursued if we were starting from scratch, and that in which they have been pursued since 'the revival of learning' in the Renaissance. The discrepancy is due to the fact that 'after a long interval of ignorance, preceded by ages of knowledge, the way in which ideas were reproduced was of necessity different from the way in which they originated'.[26] The ability to make progress depends not just on individual genius but on reading and conversation, and these require certain social and cultural conditions to prevail. These are necessary not only for the dissemination of results but more importantly for their production. Lack of access to the works of antiquity meant that during the Middle Ages, philosophers, 'instead of enquiring into nature, and studying man, … devoted themselves to frivolous questions about abstract and metaphysical essences; and since these often required an excess of subtlety, they became an abuse of genius'.[27] The development is, then, not a linear one: the antithesis of rationality was not to be found in antiquity but in the shift from reason to dogma in the Middle Ages.

On d'Alembert's model, the development of language and history in the wake of the revival of learning should mirror the development of the faculties in a child. But while the thinkers of antiquity had studied nature directly, in the wake of printing the new generations of thinkers had a surfeit of aids, and merely read of the discoveries of the ancients in books, revering them without being in a position to evaluate them properly, and developing a sense of the acquisition of knowledge as a painless process. The next stage was that in which this misunderstanding of what knowledge consists in was recognized for what it is, and erudition gave way to *belles lettres*, in which the 'precious metal' was separated from the dross, something which earlier indiscriminate scholars were unable to distinguish. The ancients were still admired above all others, but now with proper discrimination, so that, while they remained models to be imitated, this was no longer in a servile way.[28] Nevertheless, such scholars believed that the only way to express oneself was in a learned language (Latin), and their skill consisted in part in the adopting an elegant classical style. Finally, however, writers abandoned the idea of copying or imitating the ancients, and in this way *belles lettres* developed out of refinement and renovation of erudition, only in the end to transcend it in significant respects.

By contrast, the development of science (natural philosophy) on d'Alembert's account was a slower process, and it was obstructed by scholasticism. In the arts, poets and others had been allowed to celebrate pagan deities 'as a matter of innocent amusement', something that proved fertile ground for the imagination, and which was hardly a threat to Christianity, since no one was going to be led by this to revive the worship of Jupiter and Pluto. But things were different in science. Here, 'it was either understood, or claimed, that blind reason might wound Christianity'.[29] It was in this climate that religion, whose proper domain was restricted to faith and morals, began to take upon itself the teaching of natural philosophy, and the policing of these areas by the Spanish and Roman Inquisitions. But 'whilst ignorant or malevolent enemies thus made open war on science', it continued to be pursued in secret by some 'extraordinary men'.[30]

What d'Alembert provides in the 'Discours' is a vindication of the Enlightenment project of the *Encyclopédie* in the distinctively Baconian genre of a legitimating genealogy. Primarily at issue was the task of establishing a historical sequence in which one can follow a progression that starts with the origins of knowledge and traces a process of growth – while uncovering and analyzing various false starts – which can be shown to culminate in the present.

It was d'Alembert's protégé Condorcet, in his 1795 *Esquisse d'un tableau historique des progrès de l'esprit humain* (Sketch for a Historical Picture of the Progress of the Human Mind), who offered what was to become the canonical statement of the idea of the inevitability of progress. On Condorcet's account it is science that secures an open-endedness to historical development, going beyond d'Alembert's notion of the present as a culmination of the achievements of the past. The very idea of continuity with the past, assumed as much in d'Alembert's genealogy as in Christian historians, is put in question in the revolutionary programme of the later chapters of the *Esquisse*. What drives the move towards the new form of society that Condorcet advocates is not a development in the arts or forms of government as such, but the sciences, including the new science of political economy. As the embodiment of reason, science stands above the events that history describes, providing a prescriptive guidance that enables us to secure not just a freedom from barbarism and superstition, but something unlimited in its potential.

The 'triumph of science' scenario of d'Alembert-Condorcet adds two things to the project of establishing the uniqueness of the West. The first is an account of what the success of the West consisted in, namely its possession of a scientific culture of a kind that the Orient lacked. Here the stagnation model is clearly the appropriate one, for what they identify is the antidote to stagnation, without which stagnation would seem to be inevitable. But in their account of the significance of the Middle Ages, they raise a problem for the general stagnation account. The Middle Ages are not a hiccup in an otherwise continuous development on their account. Rather, this is a period in which Western culture began to come to an end, that is, following the degeneration route. Here, then, we have something more complex than either degeneration or stagnation taken individually. We have a development that is able to avoid permanent stagnation because it provides an antidote to degeneration. Moreover, the antidote to degeneration is not an intrinsically generated development: there is nothing in Medieval culture, on this account, that promotes the development of science. Rather, it is wholly extrinsic. This is especially important because in the nineteenth-century version of Enlightenment historiography, the West is the *only* culture that has overcome stagnation, so the way in which it has achieved this is very much a model.

The view from the East

By the later decades of the nineteenth century, the idea that it is science that enables a culture to overcome stagnation is beginning to become widely held, and not just exported outside Europe, but in crucial respects internalized in those cultures to which it has been exported. It is clear that, in late nineteenth-century China, Japan, and in the Arabic world, for example, there was no doubt that the West was at the pinnacle of social evolution for those who thought in these terms and that this was manifest in its scientific and technological achievements.[31]

The idea of stagnation is intimately connected with that of social evolution, and what the evolutionary model of social development provided was a sense of a natural process by which societies evolved. The writings of Herbert Spencer, who set out to explore how the natural process of evolution could produce a moral society, were widely translated and had an immense international following. The ranking of Western culture as the evolutionary pinnacle did not mean that everyone thought that the details of the ranking from primitive to civilized that particular stadial and evolutionary theories of civilization proposed was correct, and the ranking of some as primitive cultures was revised. Arab commentators understandably did not accept the politically convenient association of countries colonized by Western powers with primitiveness for example.[32] Moreover, for those Arabic, Chinese, Indian and Japanese literati who took up Spencer in the 1870s and 1880s, it was less a question of assimilating their own cultures to science, but rather a question of assimilating science to their own cultures. They typically traced lineages for the theory of evolution, usually in its grander 'cosmic' form. In China, Confucian notions of the perfectibility of the cosmic order were assimilated to evolutionary theory, and in India traditional Hindu cosmology was assimilated to evolution.[33]

One significant feature of the reception of Darwin in the East was that the Western notion of a conflict between science and religion was not exported. It is true that in Egypt there was some familiarity, through extracts and popularizations, with Andrew Dickson White's *History of the Warfare of Science with Theology in Christendom* (1896), but it did not always meet with the reaction that one might expect: namely, that, just as pre-Enlightenment Christianity had done, so Islam had hindered social and intellectual development. A number of senior Islamic scholars believed that the opposition to Darwin was a peculiarly Christian phenomenon, that Darwinism could easily be accommodated to Islamic teaching, and White's *History* was used as an example of the backwardness of Christianity.[34] In the case of India, where science has traditionally been seen as a secularizing force, one commentator has noted that, by the end of the nineteenth century,

> science serviced religion by effecting a wholesale transformation of practices and dispositions. Thus science became the mode of enchantment for an Indian modernity without banishing God. This was not, as orientalists had proclaimed, because India was "'spiritual'" rather than rationalist but, rather, because religion itself became disenchanted.[35]

Moreover, there are cases in which particular forms of evolutionary story were replaced by others, revealing the underlying source of interest. In Japan, for example, in the 1870s and 1880s, during the high point of the Meiji reign, there was a 'Spencer boom', with the publication of a large number of translations of his works, together with commentaries. But Spencer was replaced in the 1890s by an alternative Hegelian evolutionary narrative – based on the work of a Hegelian critic of Spencer, Thomas Hill Green – which was more religiously orientated, and so met the prevailing religious sensibilities more effectively.[36]

China is an interesting case in point. In the seventeenth- and eighteenth-century cross-cultural exchanges, the Chinese had made sense of the Western developments to which they were introduced in their own terms. Moreover, what both Western travellers and missionaries on the one hand, and the Chinese on the other, saw as the distinguishing feature of the other culture was a stable and prosperous society, and both reflected on how it had been achieved, and what they could learn from it. By the second half of the nineteenth century, such an approach has been completely overturned. With the uptake of 'evolutionary' narratives, the transition to modernity is now becoming articulated exclusively in terms of scientific and technological progress.

Anthropology and social evolution

In the Enlightenment notions with which we have been concerned, an understanding of social evolution (not to be confused with biological evolution) plays a crucial role. This could easily have been harnessed to the seventeenth- and early-eighteenth-century conceptions of the Orient, as something which paralleled developments in the West, albeit in a distinctively different way. But by the nineteenth century, the idea had emerged that social evolution, while it could theoretically have proceeded at the same rate in Western and oriental societies, was particularly prone to stagnation. There was nothing intrinsic to social evolution as such that would allow it to continue independently of any social and historical conditions. What is particularly striking about the proposed solution in the case of the West, namely that it was the triumph of science over superstition that reversed the stagnation, was the way in which it began to look like a general solution, applicable to the Orient as well as to the West, even where religion could not be identified as the source of the problem in these cases.

Notes

1 Cummins (1962), I. 6.
2 Herren et al. (2012), 12.
3 Mill (1817), I. 483.
4 Bossuet (1681), 430.
5 E.g. Pezron (1687).
6 Calmet (1735).
7 Sale et al. (1747–68).
8 Lambert (1750).
9 Mirabeau (1756–8), I, Part I, 136.
10 Osterhammel (2018), 498–517.
11 Ibid., 501–2.
12 Quoted in Koerner (1999), 94.
13 Huxley (1893–4), I. 51.
14 du Bois-Reymond (1912), I. 567–629: 584.
15 Ibid., I. 596.
16 There was the odd exception. Ernest Renan, for example, writing in the 1850s, acknowledged that China was an advanced prosperous country but lacked that crucial ingredient in European civilization, art: 'China has nothing that warrants the same of art': Renan (1859), 361–2.
17 Ricci and Trigault (1953), 337. The seventeenth-century Spanish Dominican Domingo Navarrete even suggested that Confucianism provided a remedy for the political crisis afflicting his native Spain: Cummins (1962), i. 6.
18 Voltaire (1756, 1751).
19 Mairan (1759).
20 Hume (1793), I. 123.
21 Montesquieu (1748).
22 Turgot (1844), II. 597–611.
23 'Discours préliminaire' to d'Alembert et Diderot (1777–9), I. v–lxix.
24 Ibid., I. ix.
25 Ibid., I. xxxii.
26 Ibid.
27 Ibid., I. xxxiii.
28 Ibid., I. xxxiv.
29 Ibid., I. xxxvii.
30 Ibid., I. xxxviii–xxxix.

31 On China see Haiyan (2013); on Japan, see Godart (2015); on the Arab World, see Elshakry (2013).
32 Elshakry (2015).
33 See Brown (2007).
34 Ibid., 8–9.
35 Kapila (2010), 131.
36 Godart (2015), 72.

References

Bossuet, J. B. (1681), *Discours sur l'histoire universelle a monseigneur le dauphin pour expliquer la fuite de la religion et les changemens des empires*, Paris: Mabre-Cramoisy.
Brown, M. C. (2007), 'Western Roots of Avataric Evolutionism in Colonial India', *Zygon*, 42: 423–48.
Calmet, A. (1735), *Histoire universelle sacrée et profane, depuis le commencement du monde jusqu'à nos jours*, Strasbourg: Doulssecker.
Cummins, J. S. (1962), *The Travels and Controversies of Friar Domingo Navarrete, 1616-1686*, 2 vols, Cambridge: Cambridge University Press.
D'Alembert, J. & Diderot, D. (1777–9), *Encyclopédie ou Dictionnaire raisonné des sciences, des arts et des métiers par une société des gens de Lettres, mis en ordre et publié par Diderot et quant à la Partie mathématique par d'Alembert*, 2nd ed., 40 vols, Geneva: Briasson.
Du Bois-Reymond, E. (1912), 'Kulturgeschichte und Naturwissenschaft', in idem., *Reden*, 2 vols, Leipzig: Verlag von Veit & Comp.
Elshakry, M. (2013), *Reading Darwin in Arabic*, Chicago: University of Chicago Press.
Elshakry, M. (2015), 'Spencer's Arabic Readers', in B. Lightman (ed.), *Global Spencerism: The Communication and Appropriation of a British Evolutionist*, Leiden: Brill, 35–55.
Godart, G. C. (2015), 'Spencerism in Japan: Boom and Bust of a Theory', in B. Lightman (ed.), *Global Spencerism: The Communication and Appropriation of a British Evolutionist*, Leiden: Brill, 56–77.
Haiyan, Y. (2013), 'Knowledge across Borders: The Early Communication of Evolution in China', in B. Lightman, G. McOuat & L. Stewart (eds), *The Circulation of Knowledge between Britain, India, and China*, Leiden: Brill, 179–208.
Herren, M., Rüesch, M. & Sibille, C. (2012), *Transcultural History: Theories, Methods, Sources*, Berlin: Springer.
Hume, D. (1793), *Essays and Treatises on Several Subjects*, 2 vols, Edinburgh: Tourneisen.
Huxley, T. (1893–4), *Collected Essays*, 9 vols, New York: D. Appleton & Company.
Kapila, S. (2010), 'The Enchantment of Science in India', *Isis*, 101: 120–32.
Koerner, L. (1999), *Linnaeus: Nature and Nation*, Harvard: Harvard University Press.
Lambert, C. F. (1750), *Histoire générale, civile, naturelle, politique et religieuse de tous les peuples du monde, Avec des observations sur les mœurs, les coutumes, les usages, les caracteres, les differentes langues, le gouvernement ... les arts & les sciences des différents peuples de l'Europe, de l'Asie, de l'Afrique & de l'Amérique*, 15 vols, Paris: Prault Fils.
Mairan, J. J. D. de (1759), *Lettres de M. de Mairan, au R. P. Parrenin, Missionaire de la Compagnie de Jesus, à Pekin. Contenant diverses Questions sur la Chine*, Paris: Desaint & Saillant.
Mill, J. (1817), *The History of British India*, 3 vols, London: Baldwin, Cradock & Joy.

Mirabeau, V. de R., Marquis de (1756–8), *L'Ami des hommes, ou Traité de la population*, 2 vols, Avignon: n.p.
Montesquieu, C. (1748), *De l'esprit des lois: ou Du rapport que les loix doivent avoir avec la constitution de chaque gouvernement, les mœurs, le climat, la religion, le commerce, &c.*, Geneva: Barrillot & Fils.
Osterhammel, J. (2018), *Unfabling the East: The Enlightenment's Encounter with Asia*, Princeton: Princeton University Press.
Pezron, P. Y. (1687), *L'Antiquité des tems rétablie et défenduë contre les juifs et les nouveaux chronologistes*, Paris: Martin & Boudot.
Renan, E. (1859), *Essais de morale et de critique*, Paris: Lévy Frères.
Ricci, M. & Trigault, N. (1953), *China in the Sixteenth Century: The Journals of Matthew Ricci, 1583–1610*, New York: Random House.
Sale, G. et al. (1747–68), *An Universal History, from the Earliest Account of Time*, 68 vols, London: Osborne.
Turgot, A. R. J. (1844), *Œuvres de Turgot*, ed. Eugène Daire, 2 vols, Paris: Guillaumin.
Voltaire, F. M. Arouet de (1751), *Le Siècle de Louis XIV*, Berlin: Conrad Walther.
Voltaire, F. M. Arouet de (1756), *Essai sur les mœurs, et l'esprit des nations et sur les principaux faits de l'histoire depuis Charlemagne jusqu'à Louis XIII*, Geneva: Cramer.
White, A. D. (1896), *History of the Warfare of Science with Theology in Christendom*, London: Macmillan & Company.

9

Philoctetes at the edge of humanity: The German Enlightenment debate on social exclusion and the education of feeling

Stefanie Buchenau

The eighteenth century witnessed a growing awareness of interpersonal distances and of psychological mechanisms leading individuals or groups to exclude others and deny their humanity. In a new 'global', colonial and political context, encounters with non-European peoples brought geographical distances and cultural differences into sharper focus than in earlier times.[1] The existing social, political and economic gaps within Europe also became more obvious. For the first time, certain social or humane deficits of strictly mathematical reason, its possible 'coldness' and 'indifference' were addressed.[2] And as these deficits and the psychological mechanisms of exclusion became more apparent, 'humanity' also acquired new facets of meaning. It became obvious that one's own moral value and dignity had to be linked to certain social and affective claims that could not, as earlier traditions assumed, be exhaustively expressed in duties to one's own self but also engaged one's duties towards humanity i.e. the ties binding humans to their fellow human beings.

According to a new aesthetic thought of the German Enlightenment, such an education and socialization of the human being was first to be achieved through art. What philosophers such as Schiller called an 'aesthetic education' of humanity grounded and conditioned all legal and, in a narrow sense, political institutional innovations and debates about the political citizen. Like the tradition of *humaniora* from Antiquity and the Renaissance, such an aesthetic education set itself the goal of educating people as human beings and citizens of their society; by learning to perceive humanity through the eyes of the artist, humans were thought to acquire humanity and 'participation' (*Teilnahme, Teilnehmung, Mitleid* ...) as a capacity for *Einfühlung* or identification and empathy with their world. Beauty in this particular context was principally a social and moral virtue, a form of propriety in conduct and expression; it qualified persons in the first place, and speech and figures in theatre and the arts in the second, similar to *decorum* in Latin and πρέπον in Greek. In principle, this practical perspective was already present in the very first German aesthetics i.e. Baumgarten's *Aesthetica*. But as the emphasis shifted more explicitly to interpersonal issues and mixed feelings, this trend became more manifest. In the *Philoctetes* debate, the focus was on the representations of suffering humanity and its psychological states i.e. a certain affective imagination and ability to foster human bonds.[3] To better understand how *Philoctetes* could be the birthplace of this new aesthetics and humanities programme, let us first turn our attention to the suffering Philoctetes before taking a look at his various commentators in the Enlightenment: Smith, Winckelmann, Mendelssohn, Lessing, Herder.

1. Philoctetes at the edge of humanity

Sophocles's *Philoctetes*, written in 409 BC, is not a tragedy in the ordinary sense of the word. Far from staging a tragic hero, dying a heroic death, it presents an antihero, Philoctetes, and his social death. Repudiated by the Gods and abandoned by his former Greek comrades-in-arms, Philoctetes has become a non-person, condemned to a 'living death – no friend, no home, no hope': ἄφιλον, ἔρημον, ἄπολιν, 'εν ζῶσιν νεκρόν.[4] Over the course of his nine-year stay on the grim and inhospitable island of Lemnos, he has gradually lost all those external traits that formerly characterized him as a human being: both in his appearance and in his behaviour, he resembles an animal more than a human. Dressed in rags, he dwells in a cave, drinks from a wooden bowl ('some man's crude handiwork', l. 35) and sleeps on a heap of leaves. He drags his withered foot with him and seems barely able to walk upright (l. 290, 294). For nine years the 'spotty and shaggy animals' have been his only companions. Philoctetes has also lost his language. Since he lacks any human interlocutor, he has stopped speaking (l. 232). Incredibly lonely, incredibly ill, Philoctetes has been leading a miserable existence on Lemnos, which the chorus describes and laments (l.169 ff).

This gradual dehumanization and isolation result from a double exclusion. First, Philoctetes has been expelled and repudiated by the gods. Hera sent a hydra to take revenge for the assistance Philoctetes offered Heracles. This hydra's bite disfigured Philoctetes externally, fundamentally disqualifying him as a Greek hero. But Philoctetes has also been rejected and excluded by his human fellows, namely by his companions and fellow fighters in the Trojan War. For his festering wound was so painful, foul and smelly that those around him could no longer tolerate it, nor his constant moaning and lamenting: 'his wounded foot was weeping disease' and he 'cursed the fleet with his horrendous wailing, constantly screaming and shouting' (l. 7, 10). The sight and sound of his suffering was probably far too unbearable and repulsive for them to arouse any feelings of pity and friendship. Exhausted and worn out by his howling, the crew decided to drop him off on their way to Lemnos. Rarely did travellers come to the island – but even of these, there was no one to assist him.

When Odysseus and Neoptolemus enter the island and reveal themselves as Greeks, Philoctetes can hardly believe his good fortune and – in the name of propriety – asks them to reveal their motives: 'Strangers. Who are you … ? Speak to me please, if you're friendly' (l.220, 227). His initial distrust of the visitors is totally justified. In fact, only belligerent motives have led Odysseus and his companions to visit Philoctetes. For Philoctetes still possesses bows and arrows – gifts from Heracles. Odysseus and Neoptolemus, son of Achilles, need these weapons in their fight for

Troy, and Philoctetes, despite his weakness, is still able to defend himself and shoot the murderous arrows. Odysseus there forges a perfidious plan to get his hands on Philoctetes's weapons with the help of the young Neoptolemus who was supposed to gain his trust and favour through cunning and lies. He was to pretend to Philoctetes that he too was a victim of Odysseus, who had withheld his dead father's weapons from him. Although this idea displeases the upright Neoptolemus, he allows himself to be persuaded by Odysseus for the sake of Troy's salvation: 'I'll put my shame aside and do it' (l.120), and he decides to accompany him to Lemnos. The drama begins with this visit: once in Lemnos, Neoptolemus manages to win Philoctetes's trust and make friends with him.

But when Philoctetes, again overwhelmed by pain, tries to hide his suffering, Neoptolemus is seized by pity – and by shame at his own attempts at manipulation. This change of heart makes him abandon the role assigned to him by Odysseus. He informs Philoctetes of the plot against him and restores his weapons. Neoptolemus, the young Greek, finds himself able to recognize Philoctetes, whose humanity has become unrecognizable, as his own kind – as human and Greek. Full social rehabilitation takes place after the end of the play, when Sophocles uses a *deus ex machina* to heal Philoctetes's wound. Through this healing and the restoration of his heroic outer appearance, he can be fully reintegrated into the society of the Hoplites and Greek citizens.

2. Philoctetes' aesthetic failure. Adam Smith on propriety and pain

Adam Smith devotes a short comment in his 1759 *Theory of Moral Sentiments* to Sophocles' *Philoctetes*. Its originality is best appreciated when it is compared with a famous earlier discussion of physical pain and interpretation of Sophocles's drama, dating from Roman antiquity. In Book Two of the *Tusculunae Disputationes* (Tusculan Disputations), entitled 'On bearing pain', Cicero passes severe judgement on *Philoctetes*, supporting it with both aesthetic and moral arguments. He declares Philoctetes's 'groans' (*ille clamor*) to be incompatible with duties towards oneself and notions of virtue and dignity. The fulfilment of every duty, he says, requires not only an inner effort of the soul but also the suppression of external expressions of pain.

> This is what one must pay particular attention to in pain that nothing should be done in a contemptuous, fearful, cowardly, slavish and womanish way, and above all that cry of Philoctetes must be rejected. To sigh is sometimes, though seldom, permitted to a man, not even to a woman ... The brave and wise man never sighs except to gather strength.[5]

Because the wise man's virtue forms a whole and does not allow for any deficiencies, it is incompatible with any extremely violent expression of pain: 'but if you lose a single virtue ... still if, I say, you should acknowledge that you were deficient in one, you would be stripped of all. Can you, then, call yourself a brave man, or a great soul, endued with patience and steadiness above the frowns of fortune? or Philoctetes?' (II, 33).

These statements show that Cicero, at least in this discussion, cherishes a Stoic ideal of self-control and autarchy, incompatible with the external expression of pain. Smith, for his part, condemns Philoctetes just as sharply as Cicero but from the opposite perspective. In his eyes, Philoctetes's behaviour is not incompatible with the moral duties towards himself, but rather with the social duties of propriety, which, in his view, must form the broader framework for the appreciation of his moral duties to himself. In his eyes, Philoctetes here is in line with Euripides's *Hippolytus* and Hercules from Sophocles's *Trachinians*. Because all these attempts to arouse pity in the spectator are unsuccessful and violate the rules of *decorum* or propriety, they are aesthetic failures: 'These attempts to excite compassion by the representation of bodily pain, may be regarded as among the greatest breaches of decorum of which the Greek theatre has set the example' (Smith [1759] 2002, 33). Smith nuances this critical judgement by adding that it is not his pain but other circumstances – in Philoctetes's case, his loneliness – that affect the spectator and diffuse 'over that charming tragedy that romantic wildness that is so agreeable to the imagination' (37).

His analysis of the psychological mechanism of empathy or 'sympathy' provides the deeper moral and aesthetic justification for this condemnation of *Philoctetes*. It takes its starting point from an ethical and aesthetic reflection on virtue, which Smith defines as 'propriety', the decency or appropriateness of our actions. 'Propriety is a measure for judging the actions of others, as well as our own actions. It must be our moral norm if our behavior is to meet with public praise'. In this understanding of virtue Smith is in line with Cicero's *honestas* and also with his contemporaries Shaftesbury and Hume. He argues that we never seek mere pleasure but rather recognition and love.

Empirical evidence, however, shows that there are limits to the human capacity to put oneself in the shoes of one's fellow human (or even one's former self) and imagine his or her condition. It therefore requires effort on both sides to bridge the gap and create empathic or 'sympathetic' bonds. If Smith here adopts Cicero's old distinction between amiable and respectable virtues, it is because he recognizes that empathy requires two movements (or two sets of virtue), the 'amiable' and the 'respectable' virtues: on the one hand, an effort on the part of the non-affected spectator and, on the other, an effort on the part of the afflicted person. The non-affected spectator must show willingness to lean down to the afflicted person and put himself or herself, at least to some degree, in the sufferer's place – even though he or she will never experience the same suffering to the same extent. But such a concordance of feelings is what the afflicted person most ardently desires. For this reason, the afflicted person, must, in turn, make the effort to reduce the expression of his or her suffering, to save face, and to 'straighten up' towards his or her counterpart (29).

In the case of physical pain, however, it is hard to claim such sympathy from one's fellow human being because pain does not appeal to the imagination. Using several examples of passions originating in a disposition of the body, Smith argues that there is little sympathy for strong physical sensations – hunger, sex drive and physical pain. This makes it all the more urgent, for the sake of propriety and to arouse sympathy, to contain the expression of one's own pain.

In other words, the reason why the expression of such feelings is improper is not because it is 'animal' or 'brutal' and arises from needs that we share with animals.

Against this ancient thesis, Smith objects that we share other urges with animals that do not leave the same impression of brutality and impropriety. What is improper is their inability to stir the imagination and thus cause sympathy: we cannot 'enter into' these appetites and feelings. This observation holds true even for ourselves. Once our needs are satisfied, our objects of desire cease to be pleasant. The 'respectable' virtues i.e. perseverance and dignity, are based precisely on the awareness of these limits to the human imagination.

Of course, it is possible, to some degree, to feel sympathy with someone suffering physical pain: to feel immediate danger. But the sufferer will himself or herself expect little compassion from the other person. When this expectation, however, leads him or her to withhold the expression of suffering, he or she can count on our greatest admiration. The situation is quite different in the case of sufferings or passions that originate from a particular habit of the imagination. These arouse far more sympathy than the worst physical suffering, because, embedded in a wider context where further passions such as hope or fear are stirred, such sufferings do appeal to the human imagination. It is in this context that Smith introduces the aesthetics of tragedy: we feel such deep pity for this misery that 'we weep even at the feigned representations of a tragedy' (52). These subtle observations on the psychological mechanisms of love and respect fell on fertile ground in the German-speaking eighteenth-century world.

3. His Greekness. Winckelmann on 'noble simplicity and quiet greatness'

The German Enlightenment philosophers conjointly contested Cicero's and Smith's verdict: they all acknowledged that *Philoctetes* has a genuine aesthetic value but rephrased this judgement in their own vocabulary and within the Wolffian tradition of aesthetics, asserting that Philoctetes combines 'beauty' and 'sublime grandeur'. Fundamentally, Philoctetes's 'sublime grandeur' (*Erhabenes*), not his 'propriety', is what touches and stirs the audience, leading them to perceive his beauty and form. And since they see aesthetics as a theory both of art and of human perception, since aesthetics and psychology are intrinsically linked, the experience of artistic beauty is what offers humans insights into their own soul, into their own human faculties of representation and feeling, their moral humanity and dignity.

This idea is first formulated by Winckelmann, who considers Sophocles's drama to be a Greek masterpiece. Just like Laocoon, Philoctetes is an *exemplum doloris*, and Winckelmann's commentary opens up the new comparative perspective on the two works, which Lessing will develop in further detail. In his *Gedanken über die Nachahmung der griechischen Werke in der Malerei und Bildhauerkunst* (Reflections on the Imitation of Greek Works in Painting and Sculpture) from 1755, Winckelmann writes: 'Laocoon suffers, but he suffers like Sophocles' Philoctetes: his suffering touches our soul; but we wish, like this great man, to be able to resist his pain.'[6] In this evaluation of *Philoctetes* as a masterpiece, Winckelmann at least indirectly contradicts Adam Smith's thesis that Philoctetes's suffering is both ugly and repulsive. Philoctetes is representative of the distinguishing feature of all Greek masterpieces: of their 'noble simplicity, and a quiet greatness, both in position and expression. Just as the depth of the sea remains calm at all times, no matter how raging the surface, so too the expression in the figures of the Greeks shows a great and sedate soul in all passions' (Winckelmann [1755] 1969, 20).

This does not only mean that Philoctetes exhibits moral virtue. He could be morally great and ugly at the same time. If his suffering reaches our souls, and we feel the desire to imitate him, it is because Philoctetes remains so beautiful because he keeps up a beautiful appearance even in the state of the greatest agony. For Winckelmann, this beauty is due to the fact that Philoctetes is Greek. *Our* suffering would be repulsive, just as our diseases (the pox) and signs of skin aging, 'small wrinkles separated from the flesh, lean tensions and the cavities that have collapsed' (11) are repulsive, but not *his* suffering, because Philoctetes, the Greek, cannot be anything but beautiful. We have to worry about our appearance and propriety, but not Philoctetes, for he is *all nature*, and beautiful, amiable in his nature. Whatever his present decline, Philoctetes was born under the same Greek sun as his Greek fellow citizens; it may be assumed that he was exposed to the 'same influence of a gentle and pure sky' (5), that he enjoyed the same unconstrained mental and physical education and political freedom. And it is probably for all these reasons that Philoctetes does not deviate from humanity when suffering pain. He preserves his Greek beauty.

At first glance, this thesis seems to simply testify to a bizarre philhellenism: it is well known that Winckelmann, without ever having set foot on Greek soil, was a great admirer of Greek art, whose history he traces in his *Geschichte der Kunst des Altertums* (History of Ancient Art) from 1764. At second glance, however, he appears to be initiating a fruitful line of reflection on human dignity that anticipates the central arguments of Mendelssohn, Lessing and Herder. Like them, he views Philoctetes as endowed with an aesthetic value, and artists as mediators and teachers of perception (αἴσθησῐς, in Greek) and humanity. They are able to perceive and express reality in their art so that it may help the audience to learn to see and feel. In particular, Greek artists may play this role, creating divine models and an ideal beauty that elevate and ennoble humanity as a whole. In Philoctetes's grandeur, they not only perceive the beautiful, sublime, divine form and idea of humanity, but they also express this beauty in their work, for all their fellow human beings everywhere, at all times.

The superiority of the Greek artists over all their descendants arises from their interest in both similarity and ideas. 'The sensual beauty gave the artist the beautiful nature, the ideal beauty the sublime features. ... from that one he took the human, from that one the divine' (Winckelmann [1755] 1969, 11). Winckelmann later elaborates on this idea in his *History of Ancient Art*, where he portrays Greek artists and poets as the actual founders of the religions: they 'produced the objects of sacred veneration';[7] in order to inspire reverence, they created the images that 'seemed to be taken from higher natures' and that generated those high concepts which gave wings to the imagination to 'elevate their work above itself and above the sensual realm'. And it is precisely by assembling a variety of images that these poets and artists help to form that indefinite image of beauty and perfection, 'for which humanity cannot be a suitable vessel', further approaching ever higher images of God. If the 'supreme beauty' is in God, then the more the image of human beauty resembles and conforms to the supreme being, the more perfect it becomes. In executing and creating 'that which is great in itself' 'with simplicity', 'all beauty is exalted', while our mind is 'enlarged and elevated' when representing such absolute greatness. Winckelmann understands this elevation as a gradual ascent from human to divine beauty. This idea was bound to have a tremendous influence on German aesthetics (and on the historiographical and philosophical debate). It implied that to cultivate one's own 'perception' or faculties of representation, a visit to Greece was required. A later-living non-Greek himself might not be able to perceive Philoctetes in all his beauty unless he learned to see and read nature through the Greek artist's eyes. This perspective in turn enables him to perceive Philoctetes's exemplary nature for humanity: 'The only way for us to become great, even if it is possible to become inimitable, is by imitating the ancients' (Winckelmann [1755] 1969, 4).

4. His sublimity. Mendelssohn's admiration

Mendelssohn's commentary on *Philoctetes* is quite brief, especially compared with Lessing's and Herder's. But it deserves attention for the very reason that it places Philoctetes more directly than Winckelmann's in the context of the German aesthetic tradition. From his first writings on aesthetics, Mendelssohn directly quotes Baumgarten, who had initiated a reflection on the moral character, thought and speech of the *felix aestheticus*, also introducing the old rhetorical concepts of the sublime attitude of thought, *sublime cogitandi genus*, aesthetic greatness, *gravitas* and magnanimity, *magnanimitas* into his 1750/58 *Aesthetica*.[8] But Mendelssohn is also a reader of Winckelmann and will refer his friend Lessing to Winckelmann's thoughts, and finally, Mendelssohn also establishes a connection between these concepts from the aesthetic tradition and Burke's concept of the sublime.[9] In *Rhapsodie oder Zusätze zu den Briefen über die Empfindungen* (Rhapsody or Additions to the Letters on Feelings), Mendelssohn writes:

> With Electra, who weeps over her brother's urn, we feel a compassionate grief, because she believes that the accident has happened and laments her loss. What we feel in the pain of Philoctetes is also pity, but of a slightly different nature, because the torment that this virtuous man has to endure is present and is assailing him before our eyes.[10]

In his interpretation, Philoctetes demonstrates a 'sublime disposition'. In elaborating this view, Mendelssohn draws on Burke's own observations in his *Philosophical Inquiry into the Origin of our Ideas of the Sublime and the Beautiful*.[11] Like Lessing, he emphasizes the value of Burke's writing as a collection of material: Burke is 'a great observer of nature'. He made 'observations upon observations, all of which are both profound and subtle' (401), but Mendelssohn also criticizes his insufficient philosophical and psychological justification and consideration of the higher principle of perfection: 'One can see that the doctrine of the soul of the German philosophers was unknown to him, and mere experience was not sufficient to allow him to see these profound doctrines in their systematic connection' (401). Burke's 'sublime', in Mendelssohn's eyes, amounts to the moral perfection of the represented object, which stirs the spectator's admiration and is to be distinguished from mere external honour or dignity: 'We admire in fact those who possess great riches or occupy noble positions of honor less than those who can have them and who reject them out of a noble magnanimity' (401).

For it is the presentation of such a morally sublime virtue on stage that connects us with the intrinsically great and divine and which educates us to a reasonable self-esteem of our own nature as rational beings. It enables us to acquire self-knowledge and experience our 'true dignity' and to contemplate the sublimity of our moral nature in the proper light. 'If everyone has due respect for himself, says an old philosopher, he will be inclined to obey the voice of nature'. Conversely, 'contempt for human nature … is the next path to sensual perdition'. Such disdain may be hidden 'at first under the guise of self-knowledge' and humility, but as soon as it extends 'more to the human race than to our individual', it generates 'hatred of man instead of self-knowledge, and defeats the powers of the mind too much, making us almost indifferent to good and evil' (421).

> With true humility of heart, one can be proud of the dignity of man and the place he occupies in creation. We must be of some importance in our eyes, and our actions of some importance, if we are to be seriously concerned with the good. One should learn to consider every action of man in its relation to the omnipresent lawgiver of nature, and in its relation to eternity.
>
> (421)

Philoctetes, just like Socrates in *Phaedon*, discussed in greater detail by Mendelssohn, represents a moral example and middle link to higher and unreached levels of divinity, which provides a true, 'sensual', vivid and motivating experience for the audience. Precisely because Philoctetes's suffering exceeds their (moral) cognitive capacities, because it uplifts and stirs them, it speaks to them and enables them to feel the beauty of his action.

The aesthetic pleasure that such a moral example produces is a mixed feeling, composed of love, admiration and pity, pleasure and displeasure. The audience feels love for Philoctetes's sublime perfection and endurance. It is the very sight of undeserved suffering that increases their love for a person and therefore their desire to see perfection. This aesthetic pleasure in sublime grandeur springs from the 'sensual expression of such perfection that arouses admiration'. As Mendelssohn puts it in his *Betrachtungen über das Erhabene und Naive in den schönen Wissenschaften* (Considerations on the Sublime and the Naïve in the Fine Arts), 'One has located the essence of the fine arts in the sensual expression of perfection. Now every quality of a thing is called sublime if it is capable of arousing admiration through its extraordinary degree of perfection.'[12]

More precisely, aesthetic pleasure is based on reverence or admiration as primitive passion, as the receptivity of reason, which Mendelssohn, like the Cartesian tradition, contrasts with passion. Moral perfection arouses admiration that is all the greater because the sight of undeserved suffering increases our love for the person. Tragedy draws its particular strength from this contrast. While considering admiration and pity as complementary feelings, Mendelssohn gives priority to admiration. Admiration as the first aesthetic affect is followed by pity as the second. This is the mixed emotion that this play evokes in the audience.

5. His beauty. Lessing with and against Smith

Lessing called his 1766 treatise on aesthetics and the arts 'Laocoon'. He might just as well have entitled it 'Philoctetes', for this ancient tragedy seems to be just as significant for him as the Laocoon statue. Throughout Lessing's treatise, Philoctetes serves as some sort of 'narrative' counterpart to the 'pictorial' figure of Laocoon, allowing Lessing to establish and develop his opposition between poetry and painting, or the narrative and plastic arts. The long passages devoted to *Philoctetes* in the *Laocoon* attest to the major significance of this play, to Lessing's deep engagement with artworks[13] and Sophocles's drama and with the positions of all his contemporaries: Smith, Winckelmann, Mendelssohn and even Cicero. And yet Lessing finds 'little pleasure' in Cicero's discussion of it, least of all in the philosophy he 'fishes out in the second book of his *Tusculan Disputations* on the endurance of physical pain'.[14] Cicero's philosophy seems to aim more at 'dressing a gladiator' than at educating a human being. In other words, Cicero does not realize the educational programme for forming a citizen and human being that he has himself set up. This lack of awareness also characterizes Cicero's interpretation of Philoctetes:

> He seems to see in such expressions (of bodily pain) only impatience, not considering that they are often wholly involuntary, and that true courage can be shown in none but voluntary actions. In the case of Sophocles, he hears only the cries and complaints of Philoctetes, and completely overlooks his otherwise resolute bearing.[15]

In contrast, Lessing, like his contemporaries, views Philoctetes's humanity as a necessary union of fortitude and feeling. Like his close friend Mendelssohn, with whom he has been discussing these issues for years, Lessing ascribes the aesthetic value of *Philoctetes* to a certain 'sensual' notion of perfection in the soul which also contains an affective dimension. But contrary to Mendelssohn, he grants love, or 'pity' as he writes, priority over admiration. Precisely because Philoctetes does not stir admiration, but primarily pity (*Mitleid, Teilnahme*), he is an object for the theatre according to Lessing. For admiration is, in his eyes, only 'one half of pity'[16] and 'a resting place where the spectator is to recover to new pity': 'the true poet scatters pity through all his tragedy'.[17]

If Lessing reverses Mendelssohn's order or priority between admiration and pity, it is because his focus is on a human identification and an 'identity of judgement' that Mendelssohn neglects. For too great sublimity excludes the fostering of human bonds. 'When we love a person', states Lessing, 'we share in his pleasures and displeasures;

we are happy and unhappy with him'.[18] Such love, in turn, presupposes the possibility of reciprocity, equality and 'confusion' (*Verwechslung*). In Lessing's eyes, 'equality is always the firm bond of love'.[19]

The discussion between Lessing and Mendelssohn took place long before *Laocoon* was written. It began between 1755 and 1757, with Mendelssohn's correspondence with Nicolai and Lessing on the mixed feelings of tragedy and the cathartic effect of tragedy through pity (Greek: 'ἔλεος) and fear (Greek: Φόβος), and it continued with the discussion of Burke's sublime. These reflections, however, remain present in *Laocoon*. They provide the further philosophical and aesthetic background against which Lessing can use and reverse Smith's argument. Lessing shares Smith's view of both the interpersonal mechanisms of love or 'sympathy' and the barriers that the individual's imagination places on such love. He also approves of Smith's view that physical pain is not in itself a theatrical object, since it cannot be an object of recollection and imagination. It is possible, however, to arouse compassion or pity by representing the suffering person in a wider narrative context. Lessing elaborates on the aesthetic implications of these ideas by juxtaposing Laocoon and Philoctetes, just like Winckelmann.

To arouse pity, it is necessary to establish reciprocity and to maintain a certain dignity. This is true both in the visual or plastic arts (painting, sculpture) and in the narrative arts (poetry, theatre): both Laocoon and Philoctetes need to restrain their pain. Laocoon must not open his mouth too wide; Philoctetes must not moan and scream in such a way as to break the rules of delicacy and propriety. But what matters is the overall effect and 'image'. As Lessing rightly points out, Philoctetes only begins to cry out when he finds hope of overcoming his loneliness and returning to the company of men, 'when he finds hope that he will soon leave the bleak wasteland and return to his homeland; when his whole misfortune is limited to the painful wound. Then, he weeps, he screams, he has the most horrible convulsions'.[20]

From this perspective, Lessing comes back to the key scene in which Philoctetes, unable to speak, is overwhelmed by the 'terrible, unspeakable' pain in his foot, which he tries to hide from Neoptolemus.

2nd scene (l. 730 ff)
Enter Neoptolemus and Philoctetes through the skene door.

Neoptolemus	Please, come on. Why won't you speak? You've frozen. What's wrong?
Philoctetes	A, A, A, A! (ᾰᾰ, ᾰᾰ)
Neoptolemus	What is it?
Philoctetes	Nothing to worry about. You go ahead, son.
Neoptolemus	Are you in pain? Is it your wound again?
Philoctetes	No definitely not, not that, I'm fine – O GODS!
Neoptolemus	Then why call on the gods?
Philoctetes	So they'll keep us safe and protect us … A A A A! (ᾰᾰ, ᾰᾰ)
Neoptolemus	What is wrong with you? Why won't you tell me? Stop this silence; it's obvious that something's wrong.

Philoctetes	O my son, I'm finished! I can't hide my torment
	From you ... ATATAI! It's shooting through me! Shooting
	through me! NO! Not again! NO!
	I'm finished, my boy; it's eating away at me!
	PAPAI! APAPPAPAI!PAPAPPAPAPPAPAPPAPAI!
	(παπαῖ, ἀπαππαπαῖ, παπαππαπαππαπαππαπαῖ.)

In this scene, Philoctetes expresses his pain without restraint and begs Neoptolemus to end his suffering with a sword stroke 'right at his heel'. At this point Lessing refers directly to Smith, whom he calls (erroneously, since Smith is Scottish) the 'Englishman': 'This is actually the objection of offended propriety. It is an Englishman who makes this objection; a man, therefore, not readily to be suspected of false delicacy' (43). And Lessing now elaborates on his argument in some detail, based on the psychological mechanisms described above: since 'all feelings and passions with which others can have little sympathy, become offensive if too violently expressed', nothing is more inappropriate, and more unworthy of a man, than to cry out with bodily pain (43). But this does not preclude the possibility that the audience could be led to share Philoctetes's pain. As a matter of fact, it is precisely in this empathy with the humanity of Philoctetes's character, which combines receptivity and strength, that aesthetic pleasure lies. On the basis of Smith's own assumptions, Lessing sides with Winckelmann and Mendelssohn against Smith.

> We despise a man, says the Englishman, whom we hear crying out under bodily pain. But not always; not the first time; not when we see that the sufferer does all in his power to suppress expressions of pain; not when we know him to be otherwise a man of resolution: still less when we see him giving proof of firmness in the midst of his suffering; when we see that pain, though it extort a cry, can extort nothing further; that he submits to a continuance of the anguish rather than yield a jot of his opinions or resolves, although such a concession would end his woes. All this we find in Philoctetes.
>
> (43 f.)

We feel pity when we see that a person resists this pain, showing dignity and moral grandeur. This, according to the ancient Greeks, consists 'in an equally unchanging love for his friends, as an unchanging hatred for his enemies'. Philoctetes upholds both virtues – humanity and fortitude – in all pain. He is capable both of love, expressed in the 'tears for the fate of his old friends', and of a certain pride that keeps him from forgiving his enemies.

By combining these two qualities in one person, Sophocles displays his great art of character portrayal, but such art reaches beyond the protagonist and individual character to encompass the psychological motivation and the 'interest'[21] of secondary characters. It would be implausible or unnatural for them to display great emotion, but to show indifference and be 'so cold and embarrassed as one habitually is in such cases' would neither serve dramatic purposes nor provoke pity either. In Sophocles's tragedy, however, the spectator's attention is divided between several characters and their development, including Neoptolemus and the chorus. Both, according to Lessing, are guilty of treachery and realize that this is bound to plunge Philoctetes into the greatest despair. The fact that Sophocles programs a scene in which Philoctetes becomes incapable of pretence before their eyes and gives in to his pain may not 'arouse any noticeable sympathetic feeling in them'. But this openness causes the 'noble Neoptolemus' to reflect, to develop comprehension for such intense misery, to abandon his deceitful plans and to confess the truth to Philoctetes.

> Had Philoctetes been master of his suffering, Neoptolemus would have persevered in his deceit. Philoctetes, deprived by pain of all power of dissimulation ... Philoctetes, who is all nature, recalls Neoptolemus to nature. The conversion is admirable, and all the more affecting for being brought about by unaided human nature.[22]

Tragedy affords an insight into one's own humanity. This is both elevating and a return to 'nature'. Lessing adopts Winckelmann's idea of the humanity of the Greeks and the juxtaposition of *Laocoon* and *Philoctetes*. This serves as a basis for the definition of art as such, as well as for the distinction between the genres, and the notions of 'action', 'figure' and 'beauty' serve to explore the constitutive conditions and respective perfections of 'sensual' representations. 'Action' is the principle that confers its unity on the temporal sequence of events in poetry, while 'figure' or 'body' is the spatial principle of composition in painting and the plastic arts. Although the visual and narrative arts differ in their objects ('action' and 'figure'), their mode of imitation ("Ὕλη καὶ τρόποις μιμήσεως διαφέρουσι) and respective signs, imposing different limits and specific rules, they have the same objective: beauty. Thus, they are complementary arts. Neither of them can produce its effect without the other. Only by their joint action can they achieve their purpose and represent their object in its beauty in a sensual way. As exemplified by the Laocoon statue, all painting (or the plastic arts) requires a certain moderation in the expression of feelings and contextualization: Laocoon preserves his beauty because he does not open his mouth too wide, and because surrounded by his sons, he is placed in a narrative context. And all poetry (or the narrative arts) need to contain a 'pictorial' moment within a wider narrative context through the action and staging of the characters. This is why Sophocles presents Philoctetes's suffering in one particular scene directly and without disguise. But one could even go one step further and claim that conjointly, the two arts and media, the visual and the verbal, *define* the nature of beauty as the perfection of a certain faculty of (moral) perception that, in order to be understood, needs to be experienced in art.

6. His humanity. Herder on empathy, aesthetics and anthropology

Herder showed a deep and early interest in Sophocles's *Philoctetes*. He discussed Lessing's, Smith's and Winckelmann's commentaries in detail in the 1769 *Erstes kritisches Wäldchen* (First Critical Forest) and shortly thereafter opened his treatise

Über den Ursprung der Sprache (On the Origin of Language) with a reference to Philoctetes.[23] In 1774 he also wrote an elegy entitled *Philoctetes. Scenen mit Gesang* (Philoctetes. Scenes with Singing), and he, again, mentions the play in his 1778 essay on *Plastik: Einige Wahrnehmungen über Form und Gestalt aus Pygmalions bildendem Träume* (Sculpture: Some Observations on Shape and Form from Pygmalion's Creative Dream). Manifestly, the study of *Philoctetes* and its commentators shaped both his anthropology and his aesthetics, or rather led him to explore the link between aesthetics and sensibility and to expand aesthetics into a broader educational, anthropological and moral programme for forming *Humanität*.

Herder first of all shares his contemporaries' view of the displeasure caused by the expression of physical pain. Philoctetes's cry of pain is not 'in the least pleasurable, agreeable', but 'painful' (*peinlich*, in the older sense of the German term),[24] because it inevitably reminds the audience of their own 'animality' and mortality. But Herder points out that nature has created us as beings who spontaneously express their pain and who hear the pain of other beings – like Philoctetes, who, contrary to Lessing's assertion, cries out *even before* he finds himself in human company again. As Herder explains, Philoctetes's first and lonely cry of pain, uttered after the audience has discovered his inhospitable dwelling in the first scene,[25] seems to have escaped Lessing's notice.

This observation is not directly formulated in the *First Critical Forest*. But it is the starting point for Herder's new anthropology in his treatise *On the Origin of Language*. This begins with a reference to Philoctetes, crying out in his solitude:

> Even as an animal, the human being has language. All the violent and the most violent among the violent, the painful sensations of his body, all the strong passions of his soul express themselves directly in cries, in tones, in wild inarticulate sounds. A suffering animal, as well as the hero Philoctetes, when it is attacked by pain, will whimper! will groan! and would it be immediately abandoned, on a desert island, without sight, trace and hope of a helpful creature – it is as if it breathes more freely, giving air to the burning, frightened breath. It is as if it sighed a part of its pain, and from the empty airspace at least drew new strength to suffer by filling the numb winds with groans.[26]

Philoctetes cries out even without hope that this cry will be heard by his fellow men. He cries out simply because nature did not create him as a 'separate rock' and as an 'egoistic monad' (697), but as a being whose passions, contrary to Lessing's assumption, are expressed unintentionally and directly in language and 'sounds of nature' (705) because nature, tying mutual sympathetic bonds and endowing humans with a capacity for expression and language, has ensured that they can express themselves and hear each other.[27] This is why Philoctetes's pain 'shakes my nervous system':

> Whether the shrugging, moaning man is Philoctetes is not my concern: he is an animal like me; he is a man: human pain shakes my nervous system as when I see a dying animal, a gasping dead man, a martyred being who feels like me.[28]

As Herder points out, no one is such an 'unfeeling barbarian' that 'when he sees a twitching, screaming, tormented person, a groaning, dying person, even a moaning animal, when his whole machine is suffering, this woe (*Ach*) does not reach his heart ... The sound of death can be heard – that is the bond of this natural language'. For this reason, 'Europeans everywhere, despite their education and deformity! have been stirred violently by the raw wails of the savages'.[29] These wails have a lasting effect on 'children, and people with common sense, on women, on people of tender feeling, on the sick, the lonely, the afflicted'.[30] Despite this original bond of sympathy, we only become human in the more noble and moral sense of the term when we recognize our link and similarity with the suffering person; when we are willing to bend down to him or her and recognize in his or her our own 'animality', neediness and mortality; when we are willing to regard his or her strangeness as 'sublime' and to draw 'energy' and strength from it. The actual aesthetic pleasure comes from such dynamic elevation, which begins with something displeasing (the cry). But this elevation can only take place once the audience is enabled by an *Einfühlung*, as Herder later puts it, to read Philoctetes's individual character and plunge into his world. Sophocles helps to achieve this by introducing the audience to the circumstances and world of Philoctetes in the first act: *via* the inhospitable dwelling on the one hand and the Greek heroic world of the past, in the persons of Neoptolemus and Odysseus, on the other. Through this dramatic procedure, he prepares his audience to perceive Philoctetes as the human person and Greek he is or was and is to become again.

Thus, long before the elaboration of his cultural anthropology in his *Ideen zur Philosophie der Geschichte der Menschheit* (Ideas for a Philosophy of the History of Humanity), Herder takes into account a variety of other peoples and members of the human species in his commentary on *Philoctetes* in the *First Critical Forest*. Among these, the Greeks have no special status. Not only the Homeric heroes, but also the Trojans, the Nordic peoples, the Eskimos, have the same 'human feeling', even though they do not all show it in their tears, indeed: a single tear of an Eskimo would 'dishonor the hero, his whole race, and his friend and his fatherland' (72).

But this means that the cry of pain itself cannot be the 'main tone' or the main idea of the play. On this central point, too, Herder explicitly opposes Lessing's interpretation in the *First Critical Forest*. Lessing wants 'Sophocles' Philoctetes not only to sigh anxiously and oppressively, but also to lament, to scream, to fill the desolate island with wild curses'. But actually Winckelmann had a point. Philoctetes does not cry out, or he does not always cry out. Only in the story of his enemy Odysseus does he cry out (72). On stage, in contrast, he expresses moderate suffering.

> The Philoctetes of Sophocles may decide – how does he suffer? It is strange that the impression that this piece has made on me from so long ago is precisely the one W. is looking for: that is, the impression of a hero who, in the midst of pain, fights his pain, holding it back with a hollow sigh for as long as he can, and finally, as the ah! The horrible woe! overwhelms him, still only utters single, furtive tones of wailing, and hides the rest in his great soul.
>
> (69)

According to Herder, the origin of aesthetic pleasure lies in 'the wise Sophocles' artful distribution of these various expressions of pain: 'how did he weigh the tone of fear? how carefully prepared for! how long suppressed! how often interrupted! how very consistently tempered!' Herder therefore also compares the play with a '*painting of pain* ... through all its degrees from silent to numbing pain, which kills itself, as it were, to a painting of restrained and never fully expressed pain' (72), interrupted by the chorus' song of rest, which fills the soul with 'intermediate tones of pain' and – with a song of death, an elegy.

A few years later Herder put this completely new musical interpretation into practice by writing his own elegiac *Philoctetes*. His elegy (or *Singspiel*) is composed of several 'scenes with singing'. It begins with Neoptolemus's chant. Together with his own role as dramatic figure, Neoptolemus here also takes on the role of the chorus and guides the audience's view of the miserable living conditions of the 'noble Philoctetes'.

Philoctetes. Scenes with singing. 1774

> Neoptolemus: And here in this grim desert rests
> The Noble Philoctetes
> To whom once, Hercules' arrows
> in Octa's flames, became
> Arrows of power! Look, he lies,
> and his arrows rest!
> No sooner do they devour the wretch,
> Abandoned in this desert
> His ill misery![31]

For Herder, even the Greek original seems to be basically an elegy, which he describes not as an artistic genre in the strict sense but as an area of the soul and a theme, the 'sensibility of pain and sorrow': 'Let me call Elegy, Greek, the mourning poetry ... it may be found wherever it may be, in epopee and ode, in tragedy or idyll, for each of these genres can become elegiac.'[32] Accordingly, the elegy occupies 'a separate area in the human soul, namely the sensibility of pain and sorrow'. It arises from a musical, harmonious and dynamic distribution of pain, which Herder describes in more detail in his analysis in the *First Critical Forest*. Like Lessing, he is particularly interested in the scene at the beginning of the third act.

> At the beginning of the third act he is surprised by a pain; but with a roaring scream? No: with a sudden silence, with a mute dismay, and as these finally dissolve, with a hollow warped ã ã ã ã, which Neoptolemus is barely able to express.
> (Herder [1769a] 1993, 69)

Herder calls this moment a 'scene of silent pain'; the distressed, the restless, the questioning Neoptolemus faces Philoctetes, who, far from roaring and raving, is 'groaning and sighing'. His 'bent foot, his contorted face, his chest raised by the sigh, the side hollowed by the groaning' and his unexpressed woe move the audience. And to avoid an excess of expression, Herder adds, Sophocles lets Philoctetes become furious with pain, 'swarming, groaning, pleading, angry, breathlessly regaining his senses and – falling asleep'. By refraining from screaming, Philoctetes achieves silent, concise expression 'the highest in expression that perhaps any tragic play ever staged, and only a Greek actor could achieve': 'a long, whole, complete act that fills my soul'. It is on the basis of a new expressive (musical) stance on language that Herder will reformulate Baumgarten's and Lessing's principles in the *Viertes Kritisches Wäldchen* (Fourth Critical Forest)[33] and, later, in his essay on *Sculpture*.[34] As in their aesthetics, aesthetics and psychology are intrinsically linked, and models of art serve to rethink and dissociate human reason (logos, expression) and the unity and difference between human sensory faculties. But on account of his original view of language, Herder is led to distinguish between not two, but three, complementary senses of beauty: the sense of seeing, which perceives juxtaposed parts or surfaces in space; the sense of hearing, which perceives sounds or 'subsequent parts' in time; and 'feeling', a 'material' sense which perceives 'parts on top of each other and next to each other' or bodies (force). As an object of touch, Philoctetes – his infected wound – would have 'stirred disgust' (Herder ([1778] 1994), 272). Although limping, although human and frail, he 'deserved to be seen' as a hero (274). In order to be touching and sculptural in a higher sense, such a representation needed to borrow elements from all of the fine arts, painting, sculpture, poetry and music.

Conclusion

The importance that German Enlightenment philosophers ascribe to Philoctetes refutes the common view that their aesthetic remains abstract and does not deal with the works themselves. On the contrary, *Philoctetes*, together with *Laocoon*, can be regarded as one of the major material sources of this aesthetics. From the variety of interpretations of this tragedy, a variety of aesthetic approaches emerge and will evolve further in the following years. This early aesthetics, engaged with the educational and social virtues of the arts, and with the conditions of communication and mutual understanding between human beings, laid the groundwork for a programme of 'aesthetic humanities' that today still seems worth pursuing.

Notes

1 On this issue, see already Tronto (1993).
2 For the negative connotations of 'indifference', see Baumgarten ([1739] 2013), §654.
3 A few articles discuss particular aspects and interpretations of *Philoctetes* in the German aesthetics. See in particular Weissberg (1989), Singer (2006), Vollhardt (2013), Harloe (2017).
4 Sophocles ([409 BC] 2014), l. 1018. Among the rich literature on Sophocles's play, see in particular Mauduit (1995), Segal (1999) and Vidal-Naquet (1972).

5   Cicero ([45 BC] 1927), II, 56. On Philoctetes's moaning, see also II, 19.
6   Winckelmann ([1755] 1969), 20 (translation mine).
7   See Winckelmann ([1764] 2006), II, 4, 129 (translation mine).
8   See Baumgarten ([1750/58] 2007), in particular §§281–403.
9   On the history of the sublime, between rhetorics and aesthetics, see Doran (2015).
10 Mendelssohn ([1761/ 1771] 1929), I, 396 (translation mine).
11 Burke (1757). See also Mendelssohn's review in der *Bibliothek der schönen Wissenschaften und der freien Künste* (1758).
12 Mendelssohn ([1758] 1929), 193–4.
13 Lessing ([1766] 1990), preface, xi: 'Baumgarten acknowledged that he was indebted to Gesner's dictionary for a large proportion of the examples in his "Aesthetics". If my reasoning be less close than that of Baumgarten, my examples will, at least, savor more of the fountain' (translation mine).
14 Lessing ([1766] 1990), 44.
15 Ibid.
16 Lessing, Letter to Mendelssohn, 18 December 1756. On this correspondence, see Rialland, unpublished dissertation manuscript.
17 Lessing, Letter to Mendelssohn, 18 December 1756.
18 Lessing ([1758/59] 1997), 449.
19 Lessing ([1763] 1985), 94.
20 Lessing ([1766] 1990), 42.
21 Christian Garve, in his review of Lessing's *Laocoon* and a few later essays (*Einige Gedanken über das Interessierende*), elaborates on this notion of 'interest'.
22 Lessing ([1766] 1990), 46 f.
23 For the biographical background (Herder's surgery), see also his letters from 1770, mentioned in Weissberg's article.
24 Herder ([1769a] 1993), 101.
25 Sophocles ([409 BC] 2014), l. 217.
26 Herder ([1772] 1985), 697 (translation mine).
27 For the manifold dimensions of Herder's early notions of sympathy and humanity, see also the contributions by Michael Forster and Nigel de Souza in the present volume.
28 Herder ([1769a] 1993), 101.
29 Herder ([1772] 1985), 707.
30 Ibid.
31 Herder (1877–1913), 69 (translation mine).
32 Herder ([1769a] 1993), 80.
33 Herder ([1769b] 1993), 307.
34 Herder ([1778] 1994), especially 257 ff. and 272 ff. (on Philoctetes).

References

Baumgarten, A. G. ([1739] 2013), *Metaphysics: A Critical Translation with Kant's Elucidations, Selected Notes and Related Materials*, London & New York: Bloomsbury.

Baumgarten, A. G. ([1750/58] 2007), *Ästhetik*, Lateinisch-Deutsch, trans. D. Mirbach, Hamburg: Meiner.

Burke, E. (1757), *Philosophical Inquiry into the Origin of Our Ideas of the Sublime and the Beautiful*, London: R. and J. Dodsley.

Cicero, M. T. ([45 BC] 1927), *Tusculanae Disputationes Tusculan Disputations*, Cambridge: Harvard University Press, Loeb Classical Library.
Doran, R. (2015), *The Theory of the Sublime from Longinus to Kant*, Cambridge: Cambridge University Press.
Garve, Chr. (1769), review of Lessing's *Laocoon* in *Allgemeine Deutsche Bibliothek*, vol. 9, 328–58.
Garve, Chr. (1985–86), *Gesammelte Werke*, ed. K. Wölffel, 15 vols, Hildesheim: Olms.
Harloe, K. (2017), 'Sympathy, Tragedy and the Morality of Sentiment in Lessing's Laokoon', in A. Lifschitz and M. Squire (eds), *Re-thinking Lessing's Laokoon: Classical Antiquity, the German Enlightenment and the 'Limits' of Painting and Poetry*, Oxford: Oxford University Press, 157–76.
Herder, J. G. von (1877–1913), 'Philoctetes. Scenen mit Gesang', in B. Suphan (ed.), *Sämmtliche Werke*, 33 vols, vol. 28, Berlin: Weidmann, 69–78.
Herder, J. G. von (1985–97), *Werke in 10 Bänden*, ed. G. Arnold, Frankfurt: Deutscher Klassiker Verlag.
Herder, J. G. von ([1769a] 1993), 'Erstes Kritisches Wäldchen', in *Werke*, vol. 2, Frankfurt: Deutscher Klassiker Verlag.
Herder, J. G. von ([1769b] 1993), 'Viertes Kritisches Wäldchen', in *Werke*, vol. 2, Frankfurt: Deutscher Klassiker Verlag.
Herder, J. G. von ([1772] 1985), 'Über den Ursprung der Sprache', in *Werke*, vol. 1, Frankfurt: Deutscher Klassiker Verlag.
Herder, J. G. von ([1778] 1994), 'Plastik: Einige Wahrnehmungen über Form und Gestalt aus Pygmalions bildendem Träume', in *Werke*, vol. 4, Frankfurt: Deutscher Klassiker Verlag.
Lessing, G. E. ([1758/59] 1997), 'Bemerkungen über Burke's philosophische Untersuchungen über den Ursprung unserer Begriffe vom Erhabenen und Schönen', in *Werke*, vol. 4, Frankfurt: Deutscher Klassiker Verlag, 448–52.
Lessing, G. E. ([1763] 1985), 'Minna von Barnhelm', in *Werke*, vol. 7, Frankfurt: Deutscher Klassiker Verlag.
Lessing, G. E. ([1766] 1990), *Laokoon, in: Werke und Briefe*, 12 vols, Frankfurt: Deutscher Klassiker Verlag.
Lessing, G. E. (1987), 'Briefe', in *Werke*, vol. 11/1, Frankfurt: Deutscher Klassiker Verlag.
Mauduit, Chr. (1995), 'Les morts de Philoctète', *Revue des Etudes grecques*, 108: 339–70.
Mendelssohn, M. ([1758] 1929), *Betrachtungen über das Erhabene und Naive in den schönen Wissenschaften, Jubiläumsausgabe*, ed. I. Elbogen, J. Guttmann, E. Mittwoch et al., vol. 1, Stuttgart, Bad Cannstatt: Frommann-Holzboog, 193–4.
Mendelssohn [1758/1977], review in der *Bibliothek der schönen Wissenschaften und der freien Künste*, vol. 3, 2. Stück, *Jubiläumsausgabe*, ed. I. Elbogen, J. Guttmann, E. Mittwoch et al., vol. 4, Stuttgart, Bad Cannstatt: Frommann-Holzboog, 216–36.
Mendelssohn, M. ([1761/1771] 1929), 'Rhapsodie oder Zusätze zu den Briefen über die Empfindungen', in *Jubiläumsausgabe*, ed. I. Elbogen, J. Guttmann, E. Mittwoch et al., vol. 1, Stuttgart, Bad Cannstatt: Frommann-Holzboog, 1971 ff.
Rialland, N., 'La correspondance sur la tragédie entre Lessing, Mendelssohn et Nicolai. Contribution à une genèse de l'esthétique allemande', vol. 1, unpublished dissertation manuscript.
Segal, C. (1999), *Tragedy and Civilization. An Interpretation of Sophocles*, Norman: University of Oklahoma Press.
Singer, R. (2006), 'Das Brüllen des Philoctetes. Herders kathartische Poetik der unartikulierten Töne', *Herder Yearbook*, 8: 61–82.

Smith, A. (1759/ 2002), *Theory of Moral Sentiments*, ed. K. Haakonssen, Cambridge: Cambridge University Press, 2002.
Sophocles ([409 BC] 2014), *Philoctetes*, trans. P. Meineck, Indianapolis & Cambridge: Hackett.
Tronto, J. (1993), *Moral Boundaries, a Political Argument for an Ethic of Care*, New York: Routledge.
Vidal-Naquet, P. (1972), 'Le Philoctète de Sophocle et l'éphébie', in *Mythe et tragédie en Grèce ancienne*, vol. 1, Paris: François Maspero, 159–84.
Vollhardt, F. (2013), 'Laokoon, Aias, Philoktet. Lessings Sophokles-Studien und seine Kritik an Winckelmann', in *Unordentliche* Collectanea – *Lessings* Laokoon *zwischen antiquarischer Gelehrsamkeit und ästhetischer Theoriebildung*, ed. J. Roberts and F. Vollhardt, Berlin, Boston: de Gruyter, 175–200.
Weissberg, L. (April 1989), 'Language's Wound. Herder, Philoctetes and the Origin of Speech', *Modern Language Notes*, 104.3: 548–79.
Winckelmann, J. J. ([1755] 1969), *Gedanken über die Nachahmung der griechischen Werke in der Malerei und Bildhauerkunst*, ed. L. Uhlig, Stuttgart: Reclam.
Winckelmann, J. J. ([1764] 2006), *Geschichte der Kunst des Alterthums. Katalog der antiken Denkmäler*, ed. A. H. Borbein, T. W. Gaethgens, J. Irmscher & M. Kunze (= *Schriften und Nachlass*, vol. 4, 2), Mainz: Ph. von Zabern.

10

Enlightenment moral philosophy and moral psychology: Baumgarten, Kant and Herder on moral feeling(s) and obligation

Nigel DeSouza

It is now a commonplace in our understanding of the moral philosophy of the early modern period – from Richard Tuck's interpretation of the modern natural law tradition to Alasdair MacIntyre's characterization of the 'Enlightenment project of justifying morality' – to conceive of it as centrally concerned with the foundations of morality.[1] It goes without saying that a key feature of these foundations, for the most part, was their secular and ideally universally valid nature, and while it is true that the German *Aufklärung* was distinctly less anti-religious than its fellow European counterparts, Kant and Herder nevertheless also participated in this wider pursuit. In the 1760s, the period that interests us here, while Kant would eventually (at least by the 1770 *Dissertatio inauguralis* [*Inaugural Dissertation*][2]) abandon this, both thinkers explored naturalistic explanations *and* foundations of morality, which allowed room for a more or less deistic, but still important, conception of God in the background. Another key feature of moral philosophy in the modern era, highlighted by countless scholars, is the focus not on questions of the good life but rather on questions of justice, the right, and duties and obligations to ourselves and others, to name a few relevant formulations. For Kant and Herder in the 1760s, a new concept for the German context, *moralisches Gefühl* (moral feeling), held out the prospect of serving as the linchpin in an adequate explanation and grounding of morality that reflected this focus and that was also naturalistic and secular (to the extent that it was not explicitly religious). But while they both appropriated this term, which originated from the contemporaneous German translation of the term 'moral sense' in Hutcheson,[3] they did so each in their own distinct ways. That being said, they shared the belief that moral feeling plays a key role, in general, in our sense of normativity, and more specifically, in our sense of obligation. And the importance of the notion of obligation for both is due, in turn, to the moral philosophy of Baumgarten, with whom they critically engaged and whose ethics textbooks formed the basis of Kant's lectures on moral philosophy that Herder attended and from which we have his lecture notes. The objective of this chapter, against the backdrop of a discussion of the concept of obligation in Baumgarten, Kant and Herder, is to provide an account of the rather different interpretations of moral feeling in Kant and Herder in the early 1760s and, in so doing, to provide a sense of two developing approaches to moral philosophy and to the moral nature of human beings in the German *Aufklärung*. On the one hand, the story I want to tell is one of continuity: Kant encounters the most detailed contemporaneous treatment of obligation in Baumgarten while Herder's first substantive encounter with the concepts of obligation and moral feeling are in Kant's lectures. And on the other, it is a story of breaks: Kant in this period begins to take issue with and to criticize Baumgarten's understanding of obligation while Herder's whole conceptualization of moral feeling, which he often pluralizes to moral *feelings*, fundamentally breaks with Kant's insofar as he interprets them in the context of his nascent philosophy of life.

I Baumgarten

Even if we cannot say with certainty that Herder first encountered the term 'moral feeling' in Kant's writings or lectures, he must have played a pivotal role in Herder's appropriation of it, not least because of the profound influence Kant exercised on his thought (by Herder's own admission[4]) in this formative period in Königsberg during which he attended all of Kant's lectures on a wide range of subjects and even penned his first philosophical treatise in honour of, and in engagement with, his esteemed teacher.[5] During these years that were, to be sure, equally formative for Kant's moral philosophy, we find him reading and drawing on Rousseau, Hutcheson, Shaftesbury, and Hume. The overarching framework for his developing ideas, however, was provided by Alexander Gottlieb Baumgarten. Kant based his lectures on moral philosophy on textbooks (as required by the government) and the two he used, for decades, were both by Baumgarten: the 1740 *Ethica philosophica* (Philosophical Ethics) and the more recent 1760 *Initia philosophiae practicae primae acroamatice* (Elements of First Practical Philosophy). The most important and abiding influence of Baumgarten's ethical writings on Kant was his focus on the concept of *obligationum* (obligation), which Kant in his 1763–4 ethics lectures variously translates as *Pflicht*, *Verbindlichkeit* and *Schuldigkeit* and which, aside from pointing to a 'very subtle' distinction between the latter two, he uses interchangeably.[6] And it is partly with respect to his reflections on the concept of obligation in moral philosophy that Kant found the notion of moral feeling attractive. But before examining this connection more closely, we would do well to take a look at the concept of obligation in Baumgarten's own philosophy, not least because he is also a thinker in dialogue with whom Herder develops his fundamental ideas in moral philosophy (not to mention in aesthetics and metaphysics as well).[7]

Both Kant and Herder rejected theological voluntarism – most influentially represented in the German context by Samuel Pufendorf, who was in turn influenced by Hobbes – as the foundation of our duties to ourselves, to others, and to God (in the famous tripartite division owed also to Pufendorf). Their rejection ultimately goes back to Leibniz, for whom the source of obligation lies in reason and not in divine *fiat*. As Clemens Schwaiger explains, Christian Wolff was converted to Leibniz's position following the latter's 1705 letter containing penetrating criticism of Wolff's 1703 *Philosophia practica universalis, mathematica methodo conscripta* (On Universal Practical Philosophy, Composed According to the Mathematical Method) in which Wolff defends a positivistic, voluntarist conception of obligation.[8] Wolff was also familiar with Leibniz's *Monita quaedam ad Samuelis Pufendorfii principia* (Opinion on the Principles of Pufendorf) composed in 1706 and published in 1709, in which Leibniz accuses Pufendorf of contradiction for claiming to find sufficient foundations for law in a sovereign's command alone (and not in the imperatives of reason that issue from divine reason) and yet also claiming that in the concept of a sovereign is to be found not only the power to obligate but also the *just foundation* of that power.[9] At root, for Leibniz, God does not *create* the ideas of his understanding and the ensuing possible worlds with their corresponding moral ends; rather, he chooses the best from among possible worlds. Already in the *Discourse on Metaphysics* (1686), to name but one instance, Leibniz explicitly asserts that 'the rules of goodness, justice, and perfection are [not] merely the effects of the will of God; instead, it seems to me, they are only the consequences of his understanding, which, assuredly, does not depend on his will, any more than does his essence'.[10] The just foundation of God's power, and our praise for him, is based on his infinite wisdom and goodness that we are able to recognize and that leads him to choose to create the best of all possible worlds, in which such rules obtain. Wolff professes to his change of heart in *Ratio praelectionum Wolfianarum [in] mathesin et philosophiam universam* (Reason in Wolff's Classes in Mathematics and Universal Philosophy, 1718) where he admits his failure, under Pufendorf's influence, to properly distinguish between natural and civil obligation, the former deriving, as Schwaiger summarizes, 'from the very nature of the human spirit, and remain[ing] binding upon us even if we were to concede that God does not exist'.[11] Wolff's new alternative amounts to an internalization of obligation in the form of a motive that makes us will an act as necessary, as he lays out in the *Deutsche Ethik* (*German Ethics*, 1733): 'To obligate someone to perform something, or to refrain from so doing, is simply to connect a motivating ground for willing or not willing with regard to the act'.[12] And in Wolff's perfectionist ethics, this motivating ground comes from the will's striving towards the good/perfection as furnished by the faculty of representation.

Obligation, however, is not a central feature of Wolff's moral philosophy, which centres far more on virtue, happiness, the highest good, and perfection. Rather, it is in Baumgarten that the concept of obligation takes centre stage as early as in his 1740 *Ethica philosophica*, and in the preparation of this text Baumgarten was not influenced so much by Wolff (whose important Latin writings on practical philosophy had not yet appeared) as he was by Heinrich Köhler, who was a close friend of Leibniz and who represents another line of influence of Leibniz on eighteenth-century German moral philosophy.[13] The Köhler text in question, on which Baumgarten drafted an unfinished and only posthumously published commentary, is *Exercitationes juris naturalis eiusque cumprimis cogentis, methodo systematica propositi* (Exercises in Natural Law, especially Obligatory Law Systematically Presented, 1729/1732). In short, Köhler sought to propose a foundation for natural law morality and, specifically, for the principle of obligatory norms, that was rooted neither (a) in experience nor (b) in divine revelation, but rather in reason in such a way that it escaped the problems of uncertainty and lack of universality that the first posed and, with respect to the second, that even an atheist could recognize and endorse.[14] Köhler construes human beings as part of nature whose law-like structure they are able, in actualizing their own rational capacities, to recognize and to understand, and this includes the obligatory norms according to which they are compelled, and yet also freely choose, to act in order to bring about the good, motivated both objectively by the affirmation of the universal connection of things of which they themselves are a part and subjectively by the pleasure that doing so brings.[15] Baumgarten closely studied Köhler's work, which gave his own moral philosophy a strong juridical imprint and which led him to connect practical philosophy with natural right.[16]

The centrality of obligation to Baumgarten's moral philosophy is evident in the very definitions he provides: in the *Ethica philosophica*, ethics is defined as 'the science of the internal obligations of human beings in a natural state', and in the *Initia philosophiae practicae*, practical philosophy is defined as 'the science of the obligations of a person that are to be known without faith'.[17] We see immediately that Baumgarten, like Köhler and also Wolff, is after a justification of morality that does not have direct recourse to divine revelation or *fiat*. Like them, Baumgarten will also maintain that it is through our capacity for reason that we are able to know our obligations. Whereas the *Ethica philosophica* treats of religion and duties to oneself and to others, the *Initia*, on which the former in fact depends (even though it was published two decades later), treats of the prior discipline of 'universal practical philosophy', established by Wolff in his 1703 text mentioned above and called by Baumgarten 'first practical philosophy': just as metaphysics, qua first philosophy, provides the principles to other theoretical disciplines, so is 'first (universal) practical philosophy the science containing the first principles proper and common to the rest of the practical disciplines', including ethics.[18] It should be noted that while Kant adopted the *Initia* for his lectures immediately upon its publication and that its focus on the theory of obligation was highly consequential for the development of his own moral philosophy, this focus was not in fact intentional as Baumgarten elsewhere explains that first practical philosophy is also intended to treat virtue, happiness, and even a general knowledge of human beings (even if he never lived to complete it along these lines himself).[19] Nevertheless, it *is* the case, as noted above and as his definitions make clear, that Baumgarten intended the concept of obligation to play a foundational role in practical philosophy. For this, however, the concept of nature was needed, for it is only through the right of nature that first practical philosophy generates the concept of obligation. Leibniz and Köhler palpably resonate here, but so does Wolff: in his *Philosophia practica universalis* (Universal Practical Philosophy, 1738), distinguishing universal practical philosophy from positive obligation and law, he writes: 'natural obligation arises from the essence and nature of the human being, as does the law of nature'.[20] Similarly, in speaking of the first fundamental obligation that he mentions, namely 'to commit the good and … to omit evil', Baumgarten explains that 'this obligation can be adequately known through nature, and through the natural powers of reason and its analogues, from the nature of the good and the evil that is to be committed or omitted freely, and from the nature of the human being and the human soul'.[21] He also includes here a reference to his definition of reason from the *Metaphysica* (*Metaphysics*, 1739), there defined as the capacity of the 'intellect to perceive a nexus of things perspicaciously'.[22] It is reason that allows us to grasp the laws of nature (*qua* nexus) and to derive our natural obligations from our own nature. Baumgarten echoes these ideas again later in speaking in general of our fundamental obligations:

> [T]he propositions *commit the good to the extent that you are able* including its implications, *seek perfection* to the best of your abilities, *do what is best for you to do* ... are obligatory propositions and hence laws to which nature obligates, laws which are to be sufficiently known from the very nature of the actions or agents, and are therefore natural.[23]

Like Wolff, Baumgarten also draws the contrast here with positive laws, but he does observe that these natural laws also count as divine positive laws since God, who wishes every good, divinely chooses all these natural laws, even if he does not determine what is natural.[24] The upshot of all this is Baumgarten's own contribution to the internalization, via our capacity for reason, of the moral ought. The rational grasping of our natural obligations brings with it a motive to perform them insofar as we understand, via distinct representations of good and evil, how they contribute to our or another's perfection. But whereas for Wolff the weight of a motive does not influence the presence of a duty, for Baumgarten an obligation only obtains where a *stronger* motive outweighs all others, as captured in his concept of an 'overriding impelling cause' that ultimately determines a free action (an innovation that will be echoed by Kant in his characterization of the categorical imperative).[25] Finally, in a manner clearly reminiscent of the Stoics, Baumgarten makes an explicit connection between the obligation to seek perfection and our nature: 'Whoever intends the same ends as are fixed in advance by nature ... *lives according to Nature*. Therefore, someone seeking his own perfection so much as he can lives according to nature.'[26]

II. Kant

The importance of the concept of obligation to the pre-critical Kant's reflections on moral philosophy is more than hinted at in his first published engagement on the subject, the *Untersuchung über die Deutlichkeit der Grundsätze der Theologie und der Moral* (Inquiry Concerning the Distinctness of the Principles of Natural Theology and Morality), published in 1764 but composed towards the end of 1762. In the section on morality, entitled 'The fundamental principles of morality in their present state are not capable of all the certainty necessary to produce conviction', Kant begins by stating that he will make the claim in the title clear by showing 'how little even the fundamental concept of *obligation* is yet known'.[27] He then immediately turns to a distinction that anticipates his later distinction between hypothetical and categorical imperatives and that plays a key role in his critique of Baumgarten's moral philosophy:

> The formula by means of which every obligation is expressed is this: one *ought* to do this or that and abstain from doing the other. Now, every *ought* expresses

the necessity of the action and is capable of two meanings. To be specific: either I ought to do something (as a *means*) if I want something else (as an *end*), or I *ought immediately* to do something else (as an *end*) and make it actual.[28]

Kant then observes that because the first meaning, the 'necessity of the means', in fact entails no obligation at all but rather at most recommendations, moral prescriptions for actions that also depend on a previously assumed end are similarly contingent.[29] The examples he provides of this are telling: 'I ought to advance the total greatest perfection; or: I ought to act in accordance with the will of God.'[30] The former, call it the rule of perfection (already encountered above), is of course central to the perfectionist ethics of Wolff and Baumgarten. The problem Kant is identifying here is that there must be a reason why someone ought to obey such a rule, and yet, 'if it is to be a rule and *ground* of obligation, [it must] command the action as being immediately necessary and not conditional upon some end'.[31] That is, if some reason could be given for why the rule must be followed, then that reason would become the end, and the rule or supposedly supreme principle in turn a mere means to that end. This leads Kant to conclude that 'the supreme rule of all obligation must be absolutely indemonstrable' and that the rule of perfection is 'the first *formal ground* of all obligation *to act*'.[32] Commenting on this passage, Henry Allison speculates that Kant still holds on to this principle despite what he had just demonstrated about it because he 'never completely abandoned the ethical significance of the concept of perfection [and that] rather than simply rejecting a perfectionist ethics, Kant relegated the demand to seek perfection to a merely formal status, which required supplementation by material practical principles in order to yield determinate obligations' – Allison referring here to the distinction Kant took from Crusius between formal and material grounds of cognition that plays a role in earlier parts of the treatise too.[33]

We will return to the question of how material practical principles yield determinate obligations, but first, it will be instructive to consider the same distinction between the necessity of the means and the necessity of the ends as it appears in Herder's notes from Kant's 1763–4 lectures on ethics. Here it appears that Kant puts into question the rule of perfection considered above and the nature of the obligations that follow from it by questioning what is meant by 'perfection': 'By this perfection is meant either moral perfection, and in this case the latter is already presupposed, so that this rule is not a basic one, for it presupposed a ground; or else by this perfection is meant something undetermined, e.g., health, etc., and again it is not a basic rule.'[34] In both cases any obligation to act expresses only 'the necessity of the means' in order to obtain some other end. The rule of perfection, insofar as it means 'to seek perfection as a rule … amounts to saying: Desire all perfections', which, Kant elaborates, is subjectively certain since we in fact always act according to it, but objectively, it is 'an empty proposition, since it is wholly identical'.[35] Kant is perhaps more critical of this 'proposition', calling it empty instead of merely formal, because of the distinction he has introduced here between moral and non-moral perfection. Earlier in the lectures he distinguishes between two types of goodness of 'free actions' (i.e. freely chosen actions), namely physical goodness that is measured by the consequences of the actions and moral goodness that is assessed 'not by the effect, but by the (free) intent'.[36] In the section currently under examination, he accuses Baumgarten of failing to heed a similar distinction in his *Initia*: 'though everything he says may make for great practical perfection, it does not constitute moral perfection'. Kant continues:

> The latter he omits to define, according to the taste of the philosophy of Wolf[f], which continually based perfection on the relation between cause and effect, and thus treated it as a means to ends grounded in desire and aversion. With us, both moral and physical feeling are always combined. For God, in His goodness, has for the most part laid down the same rules for practical and moral perfections. So let us set forth, not only the difference, but also the consensus between the two.[37]

Actions that bring about all kinds of practical perfections in ourselves and in others are similar to actions that bring about good consequences, and, for Wolff as well as for Baumgarten, these actions are desired by us as good because they increase perfection in ourselves or others and we feel pleasure with respect to them. That is what Kant is associating here with a physical feeling. But this is different from actions that are characterized by and contribute to one's own or another's moral perfection, where the action is deemed good because of the intention that is behind it and for which we feel a distinct pleasure that Kant here associates with 'moral feeling'. Both the rules specifying the required actions and the pleasures we feel in both kinds of perfection are combined in us. It is nonetheless essential that we grasp the distinction between them, as Kant explains: 'Free actions may be immediately good (give pleasure), not as a means to consequences, so that their value is not to be measured by the results, and they are not equivalent to the physical causes that produce the same effect.'[38] The difference between a freely chosen action and a physical cause, both of which bring about good consequences, is that only in the case of the former is there an intention to bring about those good consequences.[39]

But of course the mere existence of an intention is not enough to render the free action morally good. For this something more is needed and it is here that the notion of moral feeling comes into play, which Kant associates both in his writings and in his lectures with Hutcheson above all. In his *Inquiry into the Original of our Ideas of Beauty and Virtue* (1725), Hutcheson distinguishes in a manner similar to Kant above, between moral good and natural good.

> That the Perceptions of moral Good and Evil, are perfectly different from those of natural Good, or Advantage, every one must convince himself, by reflecting upon the different Manner in which he finds himself affected when these Objects occur to him. Had we no Sense of Good distinct from the Advantage or Interest arising from the external Senses, and the Perceptions of Beauty and Harmony; our Admiration and Love towards a fruitful Field, or commodious Habitation, would be much the same with what we have towards a generous Friend, or any noble Character; for both are, or may be advantageous to us: And we should no more admire any Action, or love any Person in a distant Country; or Age, whose Influence could not extend to us, than we love the Mountains of Peru, while we are unconcern'd in the Spanish Trade.[40]

Thus human beings are able, first, to distinguish between the goodness of human beings and their (intentional) actions, on the one hand, and the goodness of physical objects, circumstances, as well as the effects of actions that are to our advantage or serve our interest, on the other. But second, and crucially, this appreciation of the goodness of human beings and their actions relates not simply to their virtues in general but specifically to their motives. 'Every Action, which we apprehend as either morally good or evil, is always suppos'd to flow from some Affection towards rational Agents; and whatever we call Virtue or Vice, is either some such Affection, or some Action consequent upon it.'[41] This 'affection toward rational agents' is called by Hutcheson 'benevolence', defined as the 'disinterested' or unself-interested interest in the good of others; without it no virtue, not even the cardinal virtues, has any moral value.[42] And, of course, for Hutcheson it is our divinely endowed 'moral sense' that enables us to perceive these qualities and to 'feel joy' as soon as we behold unself-interested actions that 'tend to the natural Good of Mankind'.[43]

'Moral sense', as we noted in Introduction, was rendered *moralisches Gefühl* (rather than the more logical *moralischer Sinn*) in the German translation of Hutcheson which Kant owned,[44] namely the 1762 translation of the *Inquiry* by Johann Heinrich Merck. This is the translation of the term that Kant himself adopted in his writings and lectures and it is precisely to 'moral feeling' (which is the most logical translation in English of *moralisches Gefühl*) that Kant appeals in the lectures in order to capture the specific kind of perfection that he calls 'moral perfection', whose distinctness from practical perfection he accuses Baumgarten of ignoring, indeed of 'bungling', throughout the *Initia*.[45] Herder's lecture notes in fact open with a discussion of the 'disinterested feeling of concern for others' that clearly draws on Hutcheson (who is explicitly mentioned) and that captures the non-instrumental, non-means-oriented feature of the moral that Kant is after.[46]

> Pleasure in free actions directly is called moral feeling. We have a moral feeling, which is (1) universal (2) unequivocal. At neglect of another I feel displeasure, hatred; not because he has to starve, but because of the neglect, for at privation through sickness I feel pity. A great disproportion, which enhances self-interested feeling till the other feeling is outweighed, does not abolish the latter; for when we hear morally good things of another, we are touched with pleasure.[47]

Just as Hutcheson distinguishes between the motive of benevolence or disinterested interest in the welfare of others, on the one hand, and the moral sense by which we approve of, feel joy in, and admire such actions and the people who perform them, on the other, so too does Kant distinguish within moral feeling between the 'disinterested feeling of concern for others' and the feeling through which we approve of and feel pleasure in such actions, including our own. 'The moral feeling', Kant asserts, 'is unanalysable, basic, the ground of conscience'.[48]

Kant also discusses moral feeling in two works contemporaneous with the ethics lectures that Herder attended, the *Inquiry Concerning the Distinctness of the Principles of Natural Theology and Morality* (completed in 1762) that we have already discussed and the *Beobachtungen über das Gefühl des Schönen und Erhabenen* (Observations on the Feeling of the Beautiful and Sublime, completed in 1763). Returning to the *Inquiry* first, recall that Kant relegates to a purely formal status Baumgarten and Wolff's rule of perfection: 'The rule: perform the most perfect action in your power, is the first *formal ground* of all obligation *to act.*'[49] Immediately following this discussion Kant turns to the bases of equally 'indemonstrable *material* principles of practical cognition' that are necessary to generate actual, determinate obligations.[50] Kant adduces what he calls the recent realization that 'the faculty of representing the *true* is *cognition*, while the faculty of experiencing the *good* is *feeling*' and explains that just as there are unanalysable concepts relating to objects of cognition, 'so too there is an unanalysable feeling of the good (which is never encountered in a thing absolutely but only relatively to a being endowed with sensibility)'.[51] It is this feeling of the good – that 'Hutcheson and others [refer to by] the name of moral feeling' – that is the material ground of otherwise indemonstrable practical principles and determinate obligations such as, to take the example Kant gives here, 'love him who loves you'.[52] The feeling itself is the basis of our endorsement of the obligation, our motive to act in accordance with it, *and* our approval of actions that fulfil it. We do also subsume this kind of practical principle or obligation under the supreme formal rule of obligation (to perform the most perfect action in one's power), but that subsumption is immediate, Kant says, as we can offer no further ground for it that would explain 'why a special perfection is to be found in mutual love', and thus the principle remains unproven practically. While Kant's argument is somewhat less than satisfying here, its structure fits with the spirit of the *Inquiry*, which is oriented towards showing that philosophy must begin from given, confused concepts that it then seeks to analyse, and not from definitions. In the case of the feeling of the good, if it is in fact simple and *un*analysable, then, insofar as we know it 'by means of certain inner experience', this feeling can serve as the given basis of material practical principles.[53]

Returning to the lectures on ethics, and pursuing our discussion of Kant's critique of Baumgarten, Kant in fact revisits the rule of perfection (i.e. the obligation to seek one's own perfection) as enunciated by Baumgarten in the *Initia*, and which Baumgarten also glosses there (as we saw above) as 'living according to nature'.

> Hence the supreme law of morality is: act according to your moral nature. My reason can err; my moral feeling, only when I uphold custom before natural feeling; but in that case it is merely implicit reason; and my final yardstick still remains moral feeling, not true and false; just as the capacity for true and false is the final yardstick of the understanding, and both are universal.
>
> The sole moral rule, therefore, is this: Act according to *your moral feeling!*[54]

What is immediately striking here is that Kant revises, even replaces, Baumgarten's obligation to seek perfection in order to align it with his own conception of the moral, as captured by the concept of moral feeling. The albeit purely formal rule of perfection qua 'supreme rule of all obligation' that we encountered in Kant's *Inquiry* is now transformed into a rule of *moral* perfection that is centred on moral feeling. The repetition of the same distinction familiar from the *Inquiry* between the two faculties of cognition and feeling adds weight to the claim that we should read this passage with the relevant section of Kant's *Inquiry* in mind. Finally, the second quote above is taken from the section of Herder's notes that we discussed earlier in which Kant is precisely discussing Baumgarten's rule 'to seek perfection' and which repeats his (for us) astonishing revision to this rule.

In a similar vein, Kant also touches on the question of theological voluntarism in the lectures and insists that our concept of the morally good cannot derive from divine command or *fiat*: 'even in God, morality must exist, and every conception of the divine *arbitrium* [will] itself vanishes, if morality is not presupposed'.[55] Affirming and in turn praising the goodness of God's choosing to create this world, as well as being able to recognize the moral obligations it contains as good, become impossible on the voluntaristic theory. And, again, our particular mode of access to this morality, qua 'being endowed with sensibility' (to recall the formulation from Kant's *Inquiry*), is moral feeling. 'In education, we have first to awaken the moral feeling, and then must apply it to God's *arbitrium*', for otherwise moral obligations are only obeyed for external reasons, such as the fear of God's punishment and we are back to the necessity of the supposedly moral action as in fact merely a means to another end. 'He who has a notion of the external obligation, without the inner, sees the motivating grounds as tasks, which do not make him moral at all, but merely politically crafty ... Thus the cultivation of moral feeling takes precedence over the cultivation of obedience.'[56] Nevertheless, although Kant insists on the primacy of moral feeling here too, he does maintain that 'our moral perfection becomes incomplete, if it arises solely from inner morality' and leaves out the divine will as a supplementary 'ground of external obligation for our morality' – not as a will that punishes but as a will that is both 'immediately good' and the 'supreme basis of moral actions' – which, when added to the primary moral ground, makes our moral actions also pious ('religious acts').[57]

It is of course well known that Kant would eventually abandon this project of basing moral obligation in moral feeling. Both in the *Observations on the Feeling of the Beautiful and the Sublime* and in the ethics lectures (which reflect the content of the former) Kant tries to align acting from moral feeling with acting from moral principles, as we see in the following passages from these works, respectively:

> Thus true virtue can only be grafted upon principles, and it will become the more sublime and noble the more general they are. These principles are not speculative rules, but the consciousness of a feeling that lives in every human breast and that extends much further than to the special grounds of sympathy and complaisance. I believe that I can bring all this together if I say that it is the feeling of the beauty and the dignity of human nature.[58]
>
> For only he performs a morally good action, who does it from principles, not as a means, but as an end.[59]

How a feeling can be the basis of necessary and universal moral principles – a feeling that, even if it does 'live in every human breast', is nonetheless a contingent matter of fact – is a problem that Kant would soon grapple with before eventually, in the critical philosophy, distinguishing between the moral law qua objective, rational principle and ground of morality, on the one hand, and the moral feeling of respect for the moral law, on the other.[60] We see this in Kant's *Remarks* on the *Observations*,[61] written immediately following the latter's publication as well as in his *Announcement* for his 1765–6 lectures where, although he mentions how the distinction between good and evil in human actions can be known through sentiment and indeed praises Shaftesbury, Hutcheson, and Hume for having 'penetrated furthest in the search for the fundamental principles of morality', he nonetheless characterizes their attempts as 'incomplete and defective'.[62] He will on several occasions in the future direct his criticisms at Hutcheson specifically, as in *Reflection* 6634 from 1769/70: 'Hutcheson's principle is unphilosophical, because it introduces a new feeling as a ground of explanation, [and] second sees objective grounds in the laws of sensuousness'.[63] This brief discussion of the turn Kant will take is sufficient for our purposes here. For one of the key objectives of this chapter is to show how Kant's adoption – even if only ultimately temporarily – of the concept of moral feeling as the ground of morality in the early 1760s influenced Herder's appropriation of it, and it is to this final objective that we now turn.

III. Herder

Soon after his departure from Königsberg for Riga in 1764 (and thus soon after his attendance at Kant's complete 1763–4 ethics lectures and possible his further attendance at the beginning of the next set held in the 1764 Winter semester) Herder turned his attention to an essay competition announced in 1763 by the Bern Patriotic Society. The final, though still unfinished, version from 1765 bears the title: *Wie die Philosophie zum Besten des Volks allgemeiner und nützlicher werden kann* (How Philosophy Can Become More Universal and Useful for the Benefit of the People). In a manner similar to Kant in this period, Herder critically reflects on philosophical methodology in areas such as metaphysics, logic and, important for our purposes, moral philosophy (Haym 1880, 49) The section on the latter opens as follows:

> Our moral theory [*Moral*] is a science of our obligations [*Verbindlichkeiten*]. It shows us our duties [*Pflichten*] in a new light. Since it depicts for us reasons in clear colors, it destroys, though, prejudices and bad principles. It educates the philosophically virtuous man, the sublime wise man, who is not clothed in false illusion, who raises himself above the crowd. – Oh, too many praises for even one perhaps to be true.[64]

Although one might also hear an echo of the opening of Rousseau's *First discourse*, the reference in this passage to Baumgarten's definitions of ethics and first practical philosophy as the science of our obligations is undeniable. The task Herder sets himself in this section, as its title reveals, is to ask: 'are there philosophical truths which should be made universal in order to destroy principles which are practical prejudices and to make people morally good?'[65] His answer is not a simple 'no'; rather, he calls upon philosophy to rethink its approach to this question and to abandon the misguided approaches that it has hitherto adopted, one such approach clearly being that of

Baumgarten. In this Herder is reflecting a point he makes repeatedly in the 1760s in his critical engagement with the thought of Baumgarten, Wolff, and even Mendelssohn, and that is indeed a leitmotif running throughout the current essay: in a word, their kind of approach to philosophy reifies and hypostasizes products and processes of human thought that are always historically, culturally, and spatio-temporally specific into supposedly universal concepts and rules.[66] Although the general point applies to other areas of philosophy too, what this approach to moral philosophy fails to pay sufficient attention to is the roots of any ostensibly valid moral concept or moral rule in the lower regions of the soul, which are the true foundation of human morality: 'Everything that the principles and maxims of moral theory [*Moral*] say, each person knows, implicitly and obscurely.'[67] And it is *this* knowing that *is* in fact universal:

> Has the people real practical bad principles contrary to morality [*Moralité*]? I think not. For the majority of them does not in fact act in accordance with any principles in the strict sense. In accordance with what? The bridle that guides him. Thanks to nature, which created us, it is not cognitions but *sensations*, and these are all good. They are voices of conscience, our leader, sent by God. They can be made weaker, but not obscured.[68]

Moral philosophy, Herder claims, is nothing but 'a collection of rules which are mostly too general to be applied to individual cases'. As such they are powerless against prejudices because these are not 'real practical bad *principles*' that are products of the upper, rational regions of the soul; rather such prejudices are products of the lower, sensuous regions, where they 'have lodged themselves in the finest nerves, ... molded themselves together with the strings of our hearts'.[69] Herder asks: 'can our moral philosophy [eliminate them]?' The answer comes swiftly: 'Oh, on the contrary, it [i.e. moral philosophy] is a new impediment. As soon as sensation turns into principle it ceases to be sensation. I think, I consider, I grasp moral duty – my viewpoint is quite different, I unlearn its opposite: to act, to apply the principle.'[70] Instead, most people already know, albeit 'implicitly and obscurely', what these principles are commanding. Herder explains:

> But obscurely? Yes to be sure, obscurely. But this obscurity is a shadow of the rule's dignity, it is inseparable from what is moving. All the light that the philosopher gives the rule makes a thing distinct that was already certain for me beforehand. He teaches it to my understanding. And my heart, not the understanding, must feel it. If rules make people virtuous, then clothes make men, then the philosophers are gods, they are creators.[71]

Herder's whole project of *Bildung*, laid out most famously in his *Journal meiner Reise im Jahr 1769* (Diary of My Voyage in the Year 1769), which involves the shaping of peoples in their culture from the bottom-up, starting from the 'obscure', as it were, in part through the arts such as poetry, literature, etc., points to the more effective path for eliminating prejudices and 'making people morally good'. In this he should in fact have seen how fundamental aspects of Baumgarten's philosophy were very much sympathetic to his project, for Baumgarten maintained, against an overly rationalistic moral philosophy, that, for human beings with their rational *and* sensuous capacities, only a moral truth or obligation that is also *intuitively* grasped can be truly motivating morally, and poetry, for example, is able to express such a moral truth in intuitive form. As Stefanie Buchenau explains, while Wolff's *Philosophia practica universalis* (1703) 'was the first sketch of a lifelong project to use practical ethics as an affective science for directing his fellow man's inclinations', it is Baumgarten who 'challenges the philosopher's ambition to carry out this project without the assistance of art and aesthetics'.⁷² Nevertheless, philosophy, or rather a reformed philosophy, does still have a role to play here. His criticisms of moral philosophy that we have considered notwithstanding, Herder comes to the following conclusion:

> Moral theory, in order to remain philosophy, must remain nothing more than a metaphysics of the will which scouts out my sensations, my strength, my moral feelings [*moralischen Gefühlen*], and my basic drives – the animal, the spirit, great depths of divinity, and infinite elucidations, etc. Then it must erect our obligations from these drives, up to the highest first concept of morality [*Moralität*], of a law. It must bring this to the sharpness of metaphysical demonstration. It must not only cite the vices but explain them etc.⁷³

Just as Herder at the end of his essay calls for the 'Copernican'⁷⁴ transformation of philosophy into anthropology, he here calls for what we might call the integration of moral philosophy with moral psychology, specifically for the constitutive connection between the sensations, drives and *moral feelings* of the actual human being and the obligations of moral theory.⁷⁵

Herder, it will be recalled, had just heard Kant lecture on moral feeling, but the manner and context in which he uses the term here, and in the plural, points to a rather different framework from that of Kant for his own conceptualization of it. For in speaking also of sensations, strength, drives, and even the animal, Herder is adducing features of the human being qua natural, living organism. And here one encounters the deep influence of Shaftesbury, whom Herder was enthusiastically reading during this period, whom he praised to Kant in a 1768 letter, and whom he also explicitly mentions in this essay. While Shaftesbury, like Hutcheson who drew on him, was a theorist of moral sense, he fundamentally differs from the latter insofar as he conceptualizes the moral sense within the context of a rich philosophy of nature. In both the *Inquiry Concerning Virtue, or Merit* and *The Moralists: A Philosophical Rhapsody* (1711), much more frequently than moral sense, Shaftesbury speaks of natural or social affections and explains how such affections, both in animals and in human beings, are fitted both to the good of their individual 'system' qua organisms and species and to the 'SYSTEM *of all Things, and a Universal Nature*' that is, in turn, evidence of divine providence.⁷⁶ In human beings, in addition, 'arises another kind of Affection towards those very Affections themselves' through which they affirm the natural affections as 'worthy' by grasping how they contribute to the public interest.⁷⁷ What this amounts to, as I discuss elsewhere, is a modern appropriation of ancient Stoic dispositional innatism, according to which moral notions are taken to be *emphutoi* or innate, not because any concepts are innately fully known, but rather because individuals possess a disposition or inclination (*prolepsis*, which Shaftesbury also renders as 'pre-conception' and 'pre-sensation') towards virtuous behaviour that in turn implies a disposition to form the (ethical) belief that that behaviour is right; it is in this sense that certain ethical ideas and beliefs can be taken to be innate.[78] Shaftesbury's connection of these affections to providential nature is likewise an echo of the Stoics, for whom nature, too, is providential: in the words of Dominic Scott, 'for the Stoics Nature and God are equivalent'.[79] For them it is not only a fact that human beings are innately disposed to develop certain moral behaviours and notions, but it is further the case that these notions can be taken to be trustworthy in virtue of the fact that since human beings themselves are parts of nature, their innate tendencies are equally natural and will more likely than not promote rather than detract from nature as a whole.[80]

In this connection of morality to nature, and to our nature as human beings, Shaftesbury was not the only major influence on Herder. Of the trio of thinkers Herder more than once mentions as having most shaped his thought – namely Leibniz, Shaftesbury, and Spinoza – we must also note here the influence of Leibniz, who, like Shaftesbury invokes Stoic notions such as prolepsis in his defence of dispositional innatism, against Locke, in the *Nouveaux Essais sur l'Entendement Humain* (New Essays on Human Understanding, 1765), from which Herder made extensive, and sometimes reformulated, excerpts. Most relevant for our purposes here is Leibniz's rejection of Locke's claim that the desire for happiness and aversion to misery, qua *inclinations*, are not products of reason and thus not practical truths. Rather, Leibniz responds, 'an inclination which is expressed by the understanding becomes a *precept* or practical truth; and if the inclination is innate then so also is the truth – there being nothing in the soul which is not expressed in the understanding'. And that inclination, in turn, is first experienced inwardly as an 'instinct' that is initially sensed, not rationally known, as confused knowledge.[81] These practical instincts also extend to more clearly moral ones. Indeed, because of the sheer importance of morality, Leibniz maintains, God has given human beings instincts to lead them directly to right action without the aid of reasoning, as expressed in natural instincts such as a 'general social instinct' and love between the sexes and for offspring (extending even to affection and gentleness between animals), even if reasoning is nevertheless ultimately required for morality to be made completely certain.[82] In his own briefer account of a passage in which Leibniz summarizes these complementary roles of instinct/feeling as the confused perception of an innate truth and of the distinct knowledge of reason, Herder writes: 'Without reason indeed of course not convincing; but still a sensation, an obscure feeling [*dunkles Gefühl*] of an innate truth that must be illuminated [*aufgeklärt*].'[83] Herder ostensibly deliberately *mis*translates Leibniz's French *confus* with the German word for 'obscure', whose importance for Herder we have already seen in the 1765 essay, where he employs it in a similar manner.

It is against this backdrop, therefore, that Herder's concept of moral feelings, which makes its first appearance in the 1765 essay, should be understood. Herder combines these Leibnizian and Shaftesburian elements to yield a conception of moral feelings that is naturalistic, psycho-physiological, and rooted in a divine providence that also operates *through* nature. And it is this conception that will continue to be elaborated in Herder's future writings in the context of his evolving and multifaceted philosophy of life that he will build upon his anti-dualist and interactionist conception of the soul – body relationship.[84]

Leibniz bequeathed to the Enlightenment a robust anti-voluntarism in moral philosophy that included both rationalistic and naturalistic dimensions. As we have seen, while Kant initially endorsed both of these dimensions, he ultimately came to abandon the latter as inconsistent with the former. A natural moral feeling could never be the source and ground of a rational moral principle. Herder, however, continued to see these two dimensions as inextricably intertwined, holding the rational to be inconceivable without the natural, from which it necessarily derived. But Kant and Herder also differed in their conceptions of the 'natural'. Whereas for Kant, even when he did accept it, moral feeling was really only conceived of in perceptual and normative terms, for Herder it was also grounded in the sensuous that was itself part of a natural, providential order. What we have then in Kant and Herder's reflections on morality in the 1760s are two nascent approaches to the relationship between the natural and the normative that would continue to diverge, the reconciliation of which, to this day, remains an unfinished project.

Notes

1 See e.g. Tuck (1983) (but see Straumann [2015] for a challenge to Tuck's interpretation of Grotius) and MacIntyre (1981).
2 See e.g. Reich ([1935] 1939), 341, but see also Henrich ([1963] 2012), 27 for a much earlier dating of Kant's abandonment of this project.
3 Wolfgang Leidhold, the recent editor and translator of a modern German edition of Hutcheson's *Inquiry into the Original of Our Ideas of Beauty and Virtue*, bemoans the choice by German translators in the eighteenth century of *moralisches Gefühl* for 'moral sense' instead of *moralischer Sinn* and claims that this led to no small amount of confusion in the reception of Hutcheson in Germany at the time. See Hutcheson (1986), LXII. As I argue below (and in DeSouza 2014), it was indeed of great philosophical significance, rather than a source of confusion, for Herder.
4 See Herder's tribute to Kant as a teacher in the *Briefe zur Beförderung der Humanität*, Herder (1883), 324–5.
5 Namely, the *Versuch über das Sein* (*Essay on Being*) from 1763. For a critical translation, see Noyes (2018).
6 Kant AA 27.1, 13. At the same time, Kant does also assert here that *jus naturae* demands *Schuldigkeiten*, whereas ethics demands *Verbindlichkeiten*. The former can be translated as 'liabilities' and the latter as 'obligations'.
7 In what follows I am drawing on the recent work of Clemens Schwaiger (2000, 2008, 2009, 2011) and Alexander Aichele (2004) who both maintain (following Schmucker [1961], 59 and *pace* Henrich ([2012]1963, 22ff.) that Baumgarten, and not Crusius or even Wolff, was the primary source for Kant's focus on obligation both in his lectures on ethics and in his moral philosophical writings. Most recently, Henry Allison (2020, 86) has expressed his agreement with this point.
8 Schwaiger (2009), 63–5.
9 Leibniz (1988), 73–4; Leibniz (1768), 281.
10 Leibniz (1989), 36; G IV, 428.

11 Schwaiger (2009), 64.
12 Wolff (1733), §8, quoted in Schwaiger (2009), 67.
13 Schwaiger (2000), 248–9; Aichele (2004), 116.
14 Aichele (2004), 115.
15 Ibid., 121–3, 131.
16 Schwaiger (2000), 249.
17 Baumgarten (1740), §1, 5; Baumgarten (2020 [1760]), §1, 37.
18 Baumgarten ([1760] 2020), §7, §6, 38; cf. Schwaiger 2011, 131.
19 Schwaiger (2011), 131; Fugate & Hymers (2020), 1–2.
20 §290, quoted in Baumgarten ([1760] 2020), 48.
21 Baumgarten ([1760] 2020), §39, 53.
22 Baumgarten 2013 (1739), §640, 232.
23 Baumgarten ([1760] 2020), §70, 67.
24 Baumgarten ([1760] 2020), §69, 67.
25 Baumgarten ([1760] 2020), §§12ff, 41–2; Schwaiger (2000), 252.
26 Baumgarten ([1760] 2020), §45, 55.
27 Kant (1992), 272; AA 2, 298.
28 Ibid.
29 Ibid.
30 Ibid.
31 Kant (1992), 272; AA 2, 298–9, my emphasis.
32 Kant (1992), 273; AA 2, 299.
33 Allison (2020), 87.
34 Kant (1997), 10; AA 27, 16.
35 Ibid.
36 Kant (1997), 4; AA 27, 4.
37 Kant (1997), 10; AA 27, 16.
38 Kant (1997), 4; AA 27, 4.
39 Kant of course makes the same point in the *Groundwork of the Metaphysics of Morals* (Kant 2012, 16; AA 4, 401): 'Thus the moral worth of the action does not lie in the effect that is expected from it, nor therefore in any principle of action that needs to borrow its motivating ground from this expected effect. For all these effects (agreeableness of one's condition, indeed even advancement of the happiness of others) could also have been brought about by other causes, and thus there was, for this, no need of the will of a rational being; even so, in it alone can the highest and unconditional good be found.'
40 Hutcheson ([1725] 2004), 89.
41 Ibid., 101.
42 Ibid., 103, 101–2. Note the clear echoes (and not just etymologically) of Hutcheson's concept of benevolence in Kant's concept of the 'good will' in the *Groundwork*.
43 Ibid., 91.
44 Warda (1922), 50. My thanks to Ansgar Lyssy for directing me to this source of evidence.
45 Kant (1997), 10; AA 27, 16.
46 Kant (1997), 3; AA 27, 3.
47 Kant (1997), 4; AA 27, 4–5.
48 Kant (1997), 5; AA 27, 5.
49 Kant (1992), 273; AA 2, 299.
50 Ibid., my emphasis.

51 Ibid.
52 Kant (1992), 273–4; AA 2, 299–300.
53 Kant (1992), 258; AA 2, 286.
54 Kant (1997), 5, 10; AA 27, 6, 16.
55 Kant (1997), 6; AA 27, 10.
56 Kant (1997), 6–7; AA 27, 10–11.
57 AA 27, 10, 17–18; Kant (1997), 6, 10–11. This inclusion of the divine will as a supplementary motivating ground is similar to the claim in Baumgarten ([1760] 2020), §69, 66–7. For discussion see Frierson 2015. Henrich 2012 (1963) shows how, in engaging with Leibniz's *Theodicy*, Kant came to the insight already in the early 1750s that 'in the will of God there is a principle of relation to goodness that cannot be derived from the idea of a possible order in the world [in turn determined by the necessity of eternal natures]. As the best of all things, God thus surmounts the necessity of eternal natures through the grounding of will and satisfaction entirely unique to himself, and which only pursues the boundlessly good' leading to the conclusion that '[t]he will is not perfect that wants some good, but the object of a good will is the perfect' (19, 20).
58 Kant (2011), 24; AA 2, 217.
59 Kant (1997), 9; AA 27, 15.
60 Cf. Clewis (2012), 128–32. See also Henrich ([1957/58] 2009), 34 ff. and Walschots (2017), 41 ff., 46 ff.
61 In the *Remarks*, Kant begins to speak of the moral feeling and moral perfection in terms of freedom, e.g. 'The will is perfect insofar as it is, in accordance with the laws of freedom, the greatest ground of the good in general; the moral feeling is the feeling of the perfection of the will' (Kant [2011], 158; AA 20, 136–7) quoted in Clewis (2012), 131.
62 Kant (1992), 297, 298; AA 2, 311.
63 AA 19, 120; my translation.
64 Herder (2002), 12; Herder (1985), 115.
65 Ibid.
66 To give only one example, from a 1769 letter to Mendelssohn: 'Nothing in the world, I believe, has generated more opinions and perhaps also more errors than that one has realized abstract concepts and then taken them for individual existences. Thus do we realize the word nature, virtue, reality, perfection. Originally these concepts were nothing more than abstractions, relations of this to that, shadows and colours of things, as it were; we make them into things themselves and fancy for ourselves skills, which the soul collects like pieces of money, realities that originally were only relations and that we think of as positions, perfections that we individualize and thus give to the soul.' Herder (1977), 179–180, my translation.
67 Herder (2002), 13; Herder (1985), 115.
68 Ibid., translation modified, emphasis added.
69 Herder (2002), 14; Herder (1985), 116.
70 Herder (2002), 13; Herder (1985), 116.
71 Herder (2002), 13; Herder (1985), 115–16.
72 Buchenau (2013), 189.
73 Herder (2002), 15; Herder (1985), 117–18.
74 Herder most likely heard Kant use this metaphor in his lectures, although not necessarily employed as it is here.
75 Herder (2002), 29; Herder (1985), 134.

76 Shaftesbury (2001), vol. II, 9, 12.
77 Ibid., 16, 18.
78 Scott (1988), 144–5; cf. DeSouza (2022); Shaftesbury (2001), vol. II, 230; vol. III, 130–1.
79 Scott (1988), 147.
80 Ibid.
81 Herder (1987), 42–3; Leibniz (1996), 89–90 (G V, 81–2).
82 Herder (1987), 43; Leibniz (1996), 92–3 (G V, 84–5).
83 Herder (1987), 44.
84 For further discussion, see DeSouza (2014), which examines Herder's psycho-physiological elaboration of the moral feelings of 'self-feeling' (*Selbstgefühl*) and sympathy (*Mitgefühl*), and DeSouza (2017), which gives an overview of Herder's conception of the soul-body relationship.

References

Aichele, A. (2004), 'Sive vox naturae sive vox rationis sive vox Dei? Die metaphysische Begründung des Naturrechtsprinzips bei Heinrich Köhler, mit einer abschließenden Bemerkung zu Alexander Gottlieb Baumgarten', *Jahrbuch für Recht und Ethik/Annual Review of Law and Ethics*, 12: 115–35.

Allison, H. (2020), *Kant's Conception of Freedom: A Developmental and Critical Analysis*, Cambridge: Cambridge University Press.

Baumgarten, A. G. (1740), *Ethica philosophica*, Halle: Carl H. Hemmerde.

Baumgarten, A. G. (1760), *Initia philosophiae practicae primae acroamatice*, Halle: Carl H. Hemmerde.

Baumgarten, A. G. (2020), *Elements of First Practical Philosophy*, ed. C. Fugate & J. Hymers, London: Bloomsbury Academic.

Buchenau, S. (2013), *The Founding of Aesthetics in the German Enlightenment: The Art of Invention and the Invention of Art*, Cambridge: Cambridge University Press.

Clewis, R. (2012), 'Kant's Distinction between True and False Sublimity', in S. Shell & R. Velkley (eds), *Kant's Observations and Remarks: A Critical Guide*, 116–43, Cambridge: Cambridge University Press.

DeSouza, N. (2014), 'The Soul-Body Relationship and the Foundations of Morality: Herder contra Mendelssohn', *Herder Yearbook*, 12: 145–61.

DeSouza, N. (2017), 'The Metaphysical and Epistemological Foundations of Herder's Philosophical Anthropology', in A. Waldow & N. DeSouza (eds), *Herder: Philosophy and Anthropology*, 52–71, Oxford: Oxford University Press.

DeSouza, N. (2022), 'Stoic Dispositional Innatism and Herder's Concept of Force', in Manja Kisner & Jörg Noller (eds), *The Concept of Drive in Classical German Philosophy: Between Biology, Anthropology, and Metaphysics*, 61–82, London: Palgrave MacMillan.

Frierson, P. (2015), 'Herder: Religion and Moral Motivation', in L. Denis & O. Sensen (eds), *Kant's Lectures on Ethics: A Critical Guide*, Cambridge: Cambridge University Press, 34–50.

Fugate, C. & Hymers, J. (2020), 'Translators' Introduction', in Baumgarten (2020), 1–32.

Henrich, D. (2009), 'Hutcheson and Kant', in K. Ameriks, O. Höffe, N. Walker (eds), *Kant's Moral and Legal Philosophy*, 29–57, 58–73, Cambridge: Cambridge University Press.

Haym, R. (1880), *Herder nach seinem Leben und seinen Werken dargestellt*. Vol. I, Berlin: R. Gaertners Verlagsbuchhandlung.

Henrich, D. (2012), 'Concerning Kant's Earliest Ethics: An Attempt at a Reconstruction', in S. Shell & R. Velkley (eds), *Kant's Observations and Remarks: A Critical Guide*, 13-37, Cambridge: Cambridge University Press.
Herder, J. G. (1883), *Herders sämtliche Werke*, ed. B. Suphan, vol. 18, Berlin: Weidmannsche Buchhandlung.
Herder, J. G. (1977), *Briefe*, vol. I, ed. W. Dobbek & G. Arnold, Weimar: Böhlaus Nachfolger.
Herder, J. G. (1985), *Frühe Schriften 1764-1772*, ed. U. Gaier, Frankfurt am Main: Deutscher Klassiker Verlag.
Hutcheson, F. (1986), *Über den Ursprung unserer Ideen von Schönheit und Tugend*, Hamburg: Felix Meiner Verlag.
Herder, J. G. (1987), *Herder und die Anthropologie der Aufklärung*, ed. W. Pross, München: Carl Hanser Verlag.
Herder, J. G. (2002), *Philosophical Writings*, trans. and ed. M. Forster, Cambridge: Cambridge University Press.
Hutcheson, F. (2004), *An Inquiry into the Original of Our Ideas of Beauty and Virtue: In Two Treatises*, ed. W. Leidhold, Indianapolis: Liberty Fund.
Kant, I. (1992), *Theoretical Philosophy, 1755-1770*, ed. D. Walford & R. Meerbote, Cambridge: Cambridge University Press.
Kant, I. (1997), *Lectures on Ethics*, ed. P. Heath & J. B. Schneewind, Cambridge: Cambridge University Press.
Kant, I. (2011), *Observations on the Feeling of the Beautiful and Sublime and Other Writings*, ed. P. Frierson & P. Guyer, Cambridge: Cambridge University Press.
Kant, I. (2012), *Groundwork of the Metaphysics of Morals*, ed. M. Gregor & J. Timmerman, Cambridge: Cambridge University Press.
Leibniz, G. W. (1768), *Opera Omnia*, vol. 4, pt. III, ed. L. Dutense, Geneva: Apud Fratres de Tournes.
Leibniz, G. W. (1988), *Political Writings*, ed. P. Riley, Cambridge: Cambridge University Press.
Leibniz, G. W. (1989), *Philosophical Essays*, ed. R. Ariew & D. Garber, Indianapolis: Hackett Publishing Company.
Leibniz, G. W. (1996), *New Essays on Human Understanding*, ed. P. Remnant & J. Bennett, Cambridge: Cambridge University Press.
MacIntyre, A. (1981), *After Virtue*, Notre Dame, IN: University of Notre Dame Press.
Noyes, J. (2018), *Herder's Essay on Being: A Translation and Critical Approaches*, Rochester: Camden House.
Reich, K. (1939), 'Kant and Greek Ethics', *Mind*, 48 (191): 338-54.
Schmucker, J. (1961), *Die Ursprünge der Ethik Kants in Seinen Vorkritischen Schriften und Reflektionen*, Mesenheim am Glan: A. Hain.
Schwaiger, C. (2000), 'Ein "missing link" auf dem Weg der Ethik von Wolff zu Kant. Zur Quellen- und Wirkungsgeschichte der praktischen Philosophie von Alexander Gottlieb Baumgarten', *Jahrbuch für Recht und Ethik/Annual Review of Law and Ethics*, 8: 247-61.
Schwaiger, C. (2008), 'Baumgartens Ansatz einer philosophischen Ethiksbegründung', *Aufklärung*, 20: 219-37.
Schwaiger, C. (2009), 'The Theory of Obligation in Wolff, Baumgarten, and the Early Kant', in K. Ameriks, O. Höffe & N. Walker (eds), *Kant's Moral and Legal Philosophy*, 58-73, Cambridge: Cambridge University Press.

Schwaiger, C. (2011), *Alexander Gottlieb Baumgarten – ein intellektuelles Porträt Studien zur Metaphysik und Ethik von Kants Leitautor*, Stuttgart-Bad Cannstatt: frommann-holzboog.

Scott, D. (1988), 'Innatism and the Stoa', *The Cambridge Classical Journal*, 34: 123–53.

Shaftesbury, A. A. C. (2001), *Characteristicks of Men, Manners, Opinions, Times*, ed. D. Den Uyl, Indianapolis: Liberty Fund.

Straumann, B. (2015), *Roman Law in the State of Nature: The Classical Foundations of Hugo Grotius' Natural Law*, Cambridge: Cambridge University Press.

Tuck, R. (1983), 'Grotius, Carneades and Hobbes', *Grotiana*, 4 (1): 43–62.

Walschots, M. (2017), 'Hutcheson and Kant: Moral Sense and Moral Feeling', in E. Robinson & C. Suprenant (eds), *Kant and the Scottish Enlightenment*, 36–54, London: Routledge.

Warda, A. (1922), *Immanuel Kants Bücher*, Berlin: Martin Breslauer.

11

Herder on humanity

Michael N. Forster

Humanity is a central concept in Herder's philosophy, both early and late.[1] However, he tends to use two different words for it in those two periods: during the 1760s and 1770s preferring the word *Menschheit*, during the 1780s and 1790s the word *Humanität*.[2] This change in terminology is of some interest in its own right.[3] More importantly, it goes hand in hand with some significant changes of doctrine between the two phases. The present article will try to explain Herder's conceptions of humanity during both phases and the main differences between them. It will also offer some pointers towards their evaluation, especially in comparison with each other. Herder once wrote that 'the first, uninhibited work of an author is ... usually his best; his bloom is unfolding, his soul still dawn'.[4] Whether or not that is *generally* true, it does, I think, turn out that Herder's own earlier conception of humanity as *Menschheit* is in important ways both more original and more philosophically defensible than his later conception of it as *Humanität*.

The 1760s and 1770s: *Menschheit*

The concept of humanity already appears frequently and saliently in Herder's writings from the 1760s and 1770s, usually under the name *Menschheit*. The two most important texts in this connection are the *Abhandlung über den Ursprung der Sprache* (Treatise on the Origin of Language [henceforth: *Treatise*]), 1772, and *Auch eine Philosophie der Geschichte zur Bildung der Menschheit* (This Too a Philosophy of History for the Formation of Humanity [henceforth: *This Too*]), 1774. The following are some of the main doctrines that constitute this early version of the concept.

A first and fundamental such doctrine is a descriptive thesis to the effect that – contrary to the views of polygeneticists such as Voltaire, with their conception that there are deep biological differences between different races of human beings rooted in their having had distinct genetic origins – humankind constitutes a single species with a single origin, so that whatever differences in race may occur are merely superficial. This thesis is already salient in the *Treatise* of 1772 (where Herder champions it against Voltaire, albeit without naming him explicitly in this specific connection).[5] Herder cites various sorts of evidence in support of this thesis in the *Treatise*, including similarities in behaviour among all human beings, their shared possession of culture, not only their shared possession of language but also the similarity of their languages, the absence of any convincing evidence of deep biological differences between them, and a (today more quaint-sounding) argument to the effect that contrary to first appearances divine providence would not have been foolish to risk everything on a single origin instead of multiple origins.[6]

A second fundamental doctrine is again a descriptive thesis that Herder already develops in the *Treatise*, this time one concerning the difference between human beings and (other) animals – a sort of philosophical anthropology. The thesis is complex and goes roughly as follows: human beings are distinguished from (other) animals by their possession of language, reason and culture. For example, Herder writes that 'language is the real differentia of our species from without, as reason is from within'.[7] Moreover, this difference has the following explanation: the size of an animal's sphere of activity (i.e. the range of environments in which it lives and the variety of activities in which it engages) is inversely proportional to the extent to which its behaviour is steered by instincts. Non-human animals, such as bees and spiders, have very limited spheres of activity and are enabled to cope with them by very fixed instincts, whereas human beings have a much wider sphere of activity and are much freer of fixed instincts.[8] What picks up the slack in the case of human beings, enabling them to cope with the wide variety of environments and tasks that they confront, is a certain capacity for abstracting features of experience from their own affective responses to them and then re-identifying those features, a capacity that Herder calls 'awareness' (*Besonnenheit*). For this capacity supplies the basic building blocks – the 'characteristic marks' (*Merkmale*) – for general concepts, which in turn constitute the basic building blocks for judgement and reasoning.[9] This capacity of *Besonnenheit* is already linguistic in character.[10] And language is ultimately social,[11] taking the form of deeply different national languages that are suited to different environments and ways of life.[12] Language – and therefore also the thinking that it enables – develops over time, and it does so by preserving and accumulating the experience of its many individual users, so that its resources grow to far outstrip anything that any individual would ever have been able to achieve alone.[13] (A recent theorist, Michael Tomasello, has aptly called this the 'ratchet effect'.) This Herderian philosophical anthropology is both highly original and in many respects extremely plausible.

A third fundamental doctrine is again a descriptive thesis, this time one to the effect that it belongs to the nature of human beings to be kind towards other human beings, albeit that they also have impulses to be hostile towards them in certain situations. Thus near the start of the *Treatise* Herder develops an account according to which the cries of sensation of animals in general resonate in a way that induces sympathy among conspecifics and this is true of humankind in particular.[14] But the same work and other early writings also qualify this doctrine by noting that human beings have hostile, aggressive tendencies as well, especially towards other groups of human beings. For example, in the *Treatise* Herder explains the linguistic and cultural differences that occur between geographically proximate peoples in the following terms: 'the basis of this difference between such near little peoples in language, manner of thought, and manner of life is – *reciprocal familial and national hatred*'.¹⁵ And in *This Too* he similarly emphasizes that different cultures have usually regarded each other with hatred.¹⁶

A fourth doctrine is again descriptive in character: a highly original meta-ethics that can be described as a form of sentimentalism, but a distinctive form of it that also accords an important role to cognition in the moral sentiments involved, is pluralistic and is in addition relativistic (in a sense of this term to be specified). More precisely, this doctrine holds that moral values lie more fundamentally in sentiments than in cognitions, albeit that they essentially involve the latter as well, for example requiring general concepts for the conceptual structuring of the sentiments in question; that these sentiments vary deeply from period to period, culture to culture and even to some extent individual to individual; and that they moreover generally do so in ways that are *functional* relative to the specific forms of society and modes of life in which they occur. Thus, Herder already commits himself to a form of moral sentimentalism in *Wie die Philosophie zum Besten des Volkes allgemeiner und nützlicher werden kann* (How Philosophy Can Become More Universal and Useful for the Benefit of the People, 1765), then going on in *This Too* (1774) to call the moral sentiments in question *Neigungen* (inclinations). His position here is ultimately indebted to Hume's sentimentalism, via his own teacher the pre-critical Kant, who was also sympathetic to it.¹⁷ However, in contrast to, and in significant improvement on, Hume's version of sentimentalism, Herder's version also makes a case – especially clearly in the *Kritische Wälder* (Critical Forests, 1769) – that moral sentiments, and indeed all sentiments of adult human beings (e.g. their perceptual sensations), are essentially infused with cognition: concepts, beliefs and even inferences.¹⁸ In *This Too* Herder hints at two important arguments in support of his moral sentimentalism: first, he echoes a famous and powerful argument that Hume had already developed: moral judgements are intrinsically motivating (one cannot really believe that it is right to do X or wrong to do Y without having at least some motivation to do X or not to do Y), but cognition is motivationally inert, only sentiments possess the power to motivate ('reason is and ought only to be the slave of the passions', as Hume famously wrote in *A Treatise of Human Nature*); therefore the basis of moral judgements must consist in sentiments rather than in cognitions. Thus Herder himself writes in *This Too*:

> The philosophy of our century is supposed to cultivate [*bilden*] – what else would that mean than awakening or strengthening the inclinations [*Neigungen*] through which humankind is made happy – and what a gulf for this to happen! Ideas actually only produce ideas.¹⁹

Second, Herder also hints at an argument that draws on his pluralism and relativism. Concerning these pluralism and relativism themselves, first of all, again in contrast with, and in significant improvement on, Hume's position (Hume had argued rather implausibly in *An Enquiry Concerning the Principles of Morals* [1751] and *Of the Standard of Taste* [1757] that the seemingly deep differences in moral values that are found are in reality only superficial), Herder espouses the pluralist position that many profoundly different forms of moral sentiment – many profoundly different moralities – occur. He already develops this proto-Nietzschean insight (Nietzsche would famously later write that there are 'many moralities'), on the basis of considerable empirical knowledge of different historical periods and societies, in early texts such as *Von der Veränderung des Geschmacks* (On the Change of Taste, 1766),[20] *Versuch einer Geschichte der lyrischen Dichtkunst* (Attempt at a History of Lyric Poetry, 1766) (especially concerning the differences between Homeric values and our own)[21] and the loose notes related to his *Reisejournal* (1769) (especially concerning the various distinctive moralities of peoples in America, Africa and Asia, as known from travellers' reports),[22] indeed even to the extent of pointing out in the first of these works (as Nietzsche more famously later would) that in some cases moral values have not only changed from period to period or culture to culture but have actually become *inverted*.[23] Then in *This Too* Herder develops this insight further into an account according to which the deeply different moralities that have occurred historically have moreover in each case been functionally suited to the specific social contexts and forms of life in which they have occurred (a sort of relativism): the ancient Egyptians' value of diligence suited their urban, industrial and agricultural society; the Phoenicians' and Greeks' value of freedom suited their seafaring, trading, worldly societies; the Romans' values of courage and endurance suited their warlike, imperialistic societies; and so on. In addition to being important in their own right, this pluralism and relativism also implicitly support his sentimentalism because they promise to provide a perfectly sufficient explanation of the various specific forms of morality that have occurred historically in terms of their functional roles in the societies to which they have belonged *without any need for recourse to moral facts in addition*. This whole early meta-ethics is again a highly original contribution of Herder's. Moreover, I would argue that it is essentially correct.

A fifth important feature of Herder's early concept of *Menschheit* is that it combines such descriptive doctrines as the above with others that are instead *normative* in character: certain first-order moral ideals. Herder's combination of purely descriptive with normative components in the concept is a striking aspect of his use of it in *This Too a Philosophy of History for the [zur] Formation of Humanity [Menschheit]*[24] – evident, for example, in the work's very title and in its ideal of a 'Socrates of humanity [*Menschheit*]'.[25]

Sixth, more specifically, the term *Menschheit* implies the moral ideal of *cosmopolitanism*, i.e. the ideal that *all* human beings should be accorded moral respect regardless of their nationality, race, class, gender, religion or whatever. However, the term also implies a highly original *version* of this ideal. The sort of cosmopolitanism that the Stoics, the Christian tradition and the Enlightenment had championed had been predicated on an assumption that people at all times and places fundamentally share the same moral values (call this 'homogenizing cosmopolitanism'). However, Herder, in the light of his pluralistic and relativistic meta-ethics, sees that this assumption is factually mistaken. Moreover, he sees that any attempt to *make* it true so that it can serve as the basis for cosmopolitanism would involve unacceptable coercion. He therefore instead develops a new form of cosmopolitanism that accords moral respect to all peoples and individuals despite (or even in part because of) the deep differences in their moral outlooks that occur (call this 'pluralistic cosmopolitanism'). The following passage from his notes for the *Reisejournal* of 1769 affords an early example of this pluralistic cosmopolitanism (an example in which he especially appeals to the fact of deep differences in moral outlooks in order to warrant preferring such a form of cosmopolitanism over traditional homogenizing cosmopolitanism):

> A great article ... It presupposes that each nation has its riches and distinctive features of spirit, or character, as of country. These must be sought out, and cultivated. No human being, no land, no people, no history of a people, no state is like the other, and consequently the true, the beautiful, and the good is not alike in them. If this is not sought, if another nation is blindly taken as a model, then everything suffocates.[26]

The following passage from *This Too* (1774) likewise implies pluralistic cosmopolitanism (but this time emphasizing the consideration that any attempt to overcome the deep differences in moral outlooks that exist in order thereby to establish a basis for homogenizing cosmopolitanism will be unacceptably coercive):

> The universal dress of philosophy and love of humankind [*Menschenliebe*] can conceal oppressions, violations of the true, personal freedom of human beings, citizens, and peoples, just as Cesare Borgia would have liked it. All that in accordance with the accepted first principles of the century [i.e. the eighteenth], with a decent appearance of virtue, wisdom, love of humankind, and care for peoples.[27]

The fact that Herder champions this highly original version of cosmopolitanism explains how he can in *This Too*, without falling into inconsistency, on the one hand, express deep scepticism about the usual cosmopolitanism of the Enlightenment (for example, writing deprecatingly of 'universal love of humankind [*allgemeiner Menschenliebe*]' and being 'friends of humankind [*Menschenfreunde*] and citizens of the world' now that 'all national characters have been extinguished')[28] but then, on the other hand, go on to commit *himself* emphatically to a form of cosmopolitanism:

> Socrates of our age! ... *Citizen of the earth*, and no longer citizen of *Athens*, you naturally also lack the *perception* of what you should do in Athens ... Teach virtue in such a light and clarity as Socrates in his age was not able to!; encourage to a love of humankind [*Menschenliebe*] which, if it could exist, would be *truly more than love of fatherland and fellow citizens*! ... Socrates of humanity [*Menschheit*]![29]

Herder's pluralistic cosmopolitanism is indeed so original and so different from the homogenizing cosmopolitanism of the tradition that it may initially strike some readers as self-contradictory. However, it is not, and the source of that impression will be such readers' own confusion, not Herder's.

Seventh, as can already be seen from the passage on a 'Socrates of humanity' just quoted, as well as from other passages in *This Too* and in other early works, Herder, less originally but still importantly, also integrates into his concept of *Menschheit* a set of more specific virtues from the pagan Greek, Christian and Enlightenment traditions. In particular, he invokes the figure of Socrates in the quoted passage in order to convey such virtues as truthfulness (recall Socrates in the *Apology*) and not harming others (recall Socrates in the *Crito*).

An eighth doctrine that the early Herder intimately associates with his concept of *Menschheit*, understood now as this whole set of both descriptive and moral features, is a thesis that history is progressively developing *Menschheit* and can be better understood in this light – hence the full title of *This Too a Philosophy of History for the Formation of Humanity* [*Menschheit*] and hence also the work's attempt to demonstrate that the historical development of humankind has been cumulative in character, generating a sequence of deeply different cultures that nonetheless build on each other and thereby ultimately advancing the cause of the specific moral values that have been discussed above.[30] In *This Too* Herder infers from this character of history that there is a purposiveness at work in history, but he cautiously refrains from claiming to know the specific nature of the purpose(s) involved.

Ninth and finally, in his earlier works Herder also tends to use the word *Menschheit* in a way that implies a *contradistinction* to God and religion (not their involvement). Thus it is the central thesis of the *Treatise* that the language that belongs to human nature has a natural, human origin, not a divine one (as Herder's contemporary Johann Peter Süßmilch had recently argued). And accordingly, we find such passages in the work as the following:

> If an angel or heavenly spirit had invented language, how could it be otherwise than that language's whole structure would have to be an offprint of this spirit's manner of thought? ... But where does that happen in the case of our language? Structure and layout, yes, even the first foundation stone of this palace, betrays humanity [*Menschheit*]![31]

The 1780s and 1790s: *Humanität*

Let us now turn to Herder's later philosophy.[32] While it never displaces the word/concept *Menschheit* entirely, the word/concept *Humanität* comes to play an increasingly central role in his works during the 1780s and 1790s, functioning as one of the main words/concepts in *Ideen zur Philosophie der Geschichte der Menschheit* (*Ideas for the Philosophy of History of Humanity* [henceforth: *Ideas*]), 1784–91 and appearing in the title, as well as constituting the main theme, of the *Briefe zu Beförderung der Humanität* (*Letters for the Advancement of Humanity* [henceforth: *Letters*], 1793–7).

As Hans Dietrich Irmscher notes in his commentary on the latter of these works, the concept is notoriously difficult to pin down exactly.[33] Irmscher helpfully quotes Herder's own vague and expansive remark about it in the *Ideas*:

> I wish I could encapsulate in the word *humanity* everything that I have so far said about the human being's noble formation to reason and freedom, to finer senses and drives, to the most delicate and the strongest health, to filling and ruling the earth.[34]

And Irmscher proposes that the concept should be seen as an 'undefinable ... idea, suitable – like Kant's regulative principles – for ordering manifold phenomena under a single perspective'.[35] This seems to me roughly correct. Indeed, I would point out that it is a fairly *common* feature of Herder's central philosophical terms/concepts to combine a considerable number of related but disparate meanings in such a way. (We have already seen this in the case of the term/concept *Menschheit*. Further good examples of it are *Bildung* and *Einfühlung* [strictly: *sich hineinfühlen*].[36])

Irmscher consequently goes on to try to identify the various elements of Herder's concept of *Humanität*. The ones that he mentions are the following: (a) an idea, based on the sort of lack of fixed instincts and compensating potential for self-formation that Herder had already posited as distinctive of humankind in the *Treatise* (1772), that humankind is self-producing;[37] (b) an idea that this self-production is open-ended in and as culture;[38] (c) a certain ideal of (psychic) wholeness that Herder finds reflected in Greek sculpture;[39] (d) an idea that humankind is in a sense the centre of the cosmos and its coming to self-awareness;[40] (e) an idea that humankind's self-production takes a historical form and involves self-limitation;[41] (f) an idea that it also combines individuality with a striving for the (re)establishment of unity;[42] (g) an idea that humanity includes both cognitive and ethical aspects, both *Vernunft* and *Billigkeit*;[43] (h) an idea that there is a contradiction or tension in humankind's self-production between individuality and linear progression;[44] (i) an idea that literature is a prime means for forming the sense of humanity;[45] (j) an idea of appropriating the past interpretively by continuing and developing it;[46] and (k) an idea that humanity goes beyond mere *Bildung* to include politics as well.[47]

With the possible exception of component (j), Irmscher's ascription to Herder of an idea of appropriating the past interpretively by continuing and developing it (which probably reflects Irmscher's well-known but dubious reading of Herder's hermeneutics as proto-Gadamerian in character),[48] all of these ideas can indeed be found in Herder's works as parts of, or at least in close connection with, his concept of *Humanität*. Moreover, several of them really are *central* aspects of the concept, especially (a) humankind's self-production, (b) this self-production as occurring in and as culture and as open-ended, (c) humankind as the centre of the cosmos, (d) humankind's self-production as historical and (e) humanity's inclusion of both cognitive and ethical aspects, both *Vernunft* and *Billigkeit*.

Nonetheless, Irmscher's account remains inadequate. This is in part because most of the other ideas that he lists are more ideas *about* humanity than components of the very concept itself (or, at best, marginal components of the concept). It is in part because his list omits many of the most central components of the concept. And it is in part because his list fails to show some important connections between the various components of the concept that Herder really has in mind.

So let me now attempt to give a more satisfactory account of what Herder means by *Humanität* (in the process gratefully taking over from Irmscher's list the points that seem genuinely helpful).

(1) A first and fundamental component of the concept is a continuation of the earlier Herder's descriptive thesis from the *Treatise* that (contrary to the views of polygeneticists such as Voltaire) humankind constitutes a single species with a single

origin and that racial differences are only superficial. Thus the *Ideas* includes a section titled 'Despite appearing on earth in such diverse forms, the human species [*Geschlecht*] is one and the same kind [*Gattung*]',[49] in the course of which Herder in particular argues that the conception of some previous thinkers (such as his former teacher Kant, who had in the meantime published his influential essay *Von den verschiedenen Rassen der Menschen* [On the Different Races of Humans], 1775) according to which there are a small number of deeply different races of human beings is mistaken because whatever racial differences occur are endless in number, continuous in their transitions into each other and merely superficial.[50] The *Letters* then articulates the same position (incorporating a slightly more explicit and fuller critique of Kant's racial theory).[51] In these two later works Herder's position remains basically the same as it had already been in the *Treatise*, the only significant difference being that the intervening publication of Kant's racial theory now prompts Herder to focus more heavily on refuting such theories than before.

(2) A second component of Herder's concept of *Humanität* is a continuation of the complex philosophical anthropology of the *Treatise*. As for the earlier Herder, for the later Herder of the *Ideas* and the *Letters* human beings are distinguished from the (other) animals by their possession of language, reason, culture and (he now sometimes adds) religion. However, he now concedes that the division is somewhat less sharp than he had earlier thought, for example observing in the *Ideas* that some apes attain a certain passive understanding of language through being taught by humans and that they border on reason.[52] The later Herder also seems to retain the rest of his complex philosophical anthropology from the *Treatise*, albeit much more vaguely than before. For, although he nowhere re-states it even nearly as clearly or fully in later works such as the *Ideas* (where he instead tends to concentrate on humankind's upright posture as a differentia between humankind and animals), some passing remarks in that work nonetheless suggest that he remains essentially faithful to it.[53] And the following passage from an unpublished draft of the work reinforces that impression:

> If the human being had an instinct like the bee, the ant, the beaver, etc., if he had such a uniform nature and such a determinate activity as these and almost every species of animal, then one could look among human beings for an unchangeable ants', bees', and beavers' republic. But since not even a shadow of this is to be found in or about us and human nature with its needs, drives, and works of art takes a quite different course, I do not know how so many worthy men have come up with the idea of trying to construct from the history of the humankind of all parts of the world and nations bee-hives and anthills in accordance with unchangeable rules of nature.[54]

(3) A third fundamental component of Herder's later concept of *Humanität* is a descriptive thesis to the effect that it is part of the basic nature of human beings to be kind towards other human beings (rather than indifferent, aggressive or cruel towards them). This thesis is a continuation of his position from the start of the *Treatise* but differs from it in tending to drop the important qualification that he makes in the *Treatise* and in *This Too* concerning the existence of a more hostile, aggressive side

of human nature as well. Hence in the *Letters* he sharply criticizes Kant's doctrine (in *Über das radikal Böse in der menschlichen Natur* [On Radical Evil], 1792 and *Die Religion innerhalb der Grenzen der bloßen Vernunft* [Religion within the Limits of Reason Alone], 1793) that there is an element of radical evil in human nature.[55]

(4) As in the case of his early concept of *Menschheit*, a fourth fundamental component of Herder's late concept of *Humanität* is not descriptive but instead *normative* in character: a certain *moral ideal*. Herder makes it clear that the concept includes such a component in the following passage from the *Letters*, where he traces the moral ideal in question back to Greece and Rome and sharply contrasts it with the normativity of mere law:

> Among the Romans, to whom the word humanity [*Humanität*] actually belongs, the concept had reason enough to develop itself more definitely. Rome had hard laws against serfs, children, foreigners, enemies; the upper classes had rights [*Rechte*] against the people, etc. Whoever pursued these rights with great strictness could be righteous [*gerecht*], but he was not thereby humane [*menschlich*]. The noble who voluntarily waived these rights when they were unjust, who acted towards children, slaves, underlings, foreigners, enemies not as a Roman citizen or patrician but as a human being was humanus, humanissimus ... Since, therefore, humanity [*Humanität*] first won its name as a tamer of hard civic laws and rights ..., let us honor this word and the thing itself ... We need it as much as the Romans. For if you now look ahead in history you will see that there came a time when the word human being [*Mensch*] (homo) received a quite different meaning, coming to mean a bearer of duties, a subject, a vassal, a servant. Whoever was not that had no right ... Let us then adopt the Greeks' and Romans' concept of humanity [*Humanität*], for this barbaric human right [*Menschenrecht*] makes us shudder.[56]

(5) Again in (at least partial) continuity with his earlier concept of *Menschheit*, a fifth fundamental component of Herder's later concept of *Humanität* is a more specific moral ideal that Herder includes within the broader moral ideal of *Humanität*: *cosmopolitanism*, or the ideal that *all* human beings should be treated with moral respect regardless of nationality, race, class, gender, religion and so forth. Herder emphasizes this as a component of his concept of humanity strongly in both the *Ideas* and the *Letters*, for example in the latter work quoting with warm approval Fénelon's remark, 'I love my family more than myself; more than my family my fatherland; more than my fatherland, humankind.'[57] Herder sometimes in his later writings also seems to retain the highly original and deeply motivated *pluralist* version of cosmopolitanism that he had championed in his earlier works. For example, he writes at one point in the *Letters*:

> The nature-investigator presupposes no *order of rank* among the creatures that he observes; all are equally dear and valuable to him. Likewise the nature-investigator of humanity ... In that period when everything was taking form, nature developed the form of the *human type* as manifoldly as her workshop required and allowed.

> She developed ... various *forces* in various proportions, as many of them as lay in her type and as the various climes of the earth could develop in form. The negro, the [native] American, the Mongol has gifts, talents, preformed dispositions that the European does not have. Perhaps the sum is equal – only in different proportions and compensations. We can be certain that what in the *human type* was able to develop on our round earth has developed or will develop ... The original form, the *prototype of humanity* hence lies not in a single nation of a single region of the earth; it is the abstracted concept from all exemplars of human nature in both hemispheres. The *Cherokee* and the *Huswana*, the *Mongol* and the *Gonaqua*, are as much letters in the great word of our species as the most civilized Englishman or Frenchman.[58]

However, for the most part the *Ideas* and the *Letters* rather tend to revert to the more traditional *homogenizing* sort of cosmopolitanism that Herder had earlier critiqued and rejected. (We shall see why shortly.)

(6) Again in continuity with his earlier position, a sixth component of Herder's late concept of *Humanität* is likewise a more specific moral ideal that he includes within the broader moral ideal of humanity: a specification that the moral respect that one owes to all people includes such specific duties as not deceiving them, not harming them, exercising moderation in one's relations with them and actively helping them. In the *Letters* Herder champions these four virtues as four forms of what he calls 'national honor [*Nationalruhm*]'.[59]

(7) A seventh component stands in much sharper contrast with his earlier position: a certain strategy that he now develops of arguing *from* the aforementioned descriptive theses *to* the aforementioned moral ideals. According to the Herder of the *Ideas* and the *Letters*, it is somehow *because* all human beings belong to a single species whose racial differences are only superficial (descriptive thesis (1)) and it belongs to their nature to be kind to other human beings (descriptive thesis (3)) that all human beings deserve respectful treatment (normative thesis (5)) and that this respectful treatment should include such specific performances as not deceiving or harming them, but instead exercising moderation in relations with them and helping them (normative thesis (6)).[60] A representative passage for this line of argument (among many that could be cited) is the following one from the *Ideas*:

> Neither the pongo nor the longimanus [i.e. species of animals] is your brother, but the [native] American, the negro is. So you should not oppress, murder, rob him; for he is a human being, as you are.[61]

(8) Again in sharp contrast to his earlier position, an eighth component of Herder's later concept of *Humanität*, largely based on the line of argument just mentioned, is a certain meta-ethical position: *moral universalism*. According to the later Herder, cosmopolitanism and its closer specification in terms of not deceiving or harming people but instead exercising moderation in relations with them and helping them are moral values to which all human beings are committed (at least implicitly). Thus, in addition to developing the abstract argument just sketched in support of such

a position, he also goes to considerable trouble in the *Letters* to try to vindicate it empirically by showing that Homer was already committed to the moral values in question,[62] that the visual art of classical Greece was so too,[63] and that they are also clearly championed by Christianity.[64]

(9) A ninth component is again a certain meta-ethical position. The highly original meta-ethics of Herder's earlier writings – a moral sentimentalism incorporating cognition, pluralism and relativism – is sometimes still echoed in his later writings as well. For example, just as *This Too* had implied moral sentimentalism by referring to moral attitudes as *Neigungen* [inclinations], so the *Letters* still does so by calling them *Gesinnungen* [attitudes]. And the long passage that I recently quoted from the *Letters* concerning 'the nature-investigator of humanity' still strongly suggests Herder's earlier moral pluralism and relativism as well. However, in his later writings Herder tends more strongly to *retreat* from his earlier highly original meta-ethics towards a much less original one: As the introduction of component (7) (Herder's abstract argument) would lead one to expect, his sentimentalism-incorporating-cognition now often tips over into being an outright cognitivism – as, for example, when in the *Ideas* and the *Letters* he conceives humanity as combining *Billigkeit* [justice] with *Vernunft* [reason].[65] Moreover, as the introduction of component (8) (Herder's moral universalism) would lead one to expect, he now tends to retreat from his earlier conception that moral outlooks are profoundly plural and relative to specific social contexts and forms of life in favour of moral universalism.

(10) A tenth component is again new: a certain contradistinction of *Humanität* as a normative ideal from, and preference of it over, the ideal of *human rights* (*Menschenrechte, the rights of man, les droits de l'homme*) that had become a prominent feature of political discourse during the 1780s and 1790s in the context of the American and French Revolutions.[66] This position can be seen clearly in the long passage from the *Letters* that I quoted earlier ('Let us ... adopt the Greeks' and Romans' concept of humanity [*Humanität*], for this barbaric human right [*Menschenrecht*] makes us shudder'). A large part of Herder's motivation here was obviously to retain the same substantive moral-political goals as the American and French Revolutionaries had championed using the discourse of *human rights* (he was a great sympathizer with both revolutions), but at the same time avoid any endorsement of the aggression, violence and class warfare that the actions of the Revolutionaries (especially in France, in the form of the execution of Louis XVI and the *Terreur* of 1793) had associated with that terminology. However, Herder also has additional reasons for preferring his ideal of *Humanität* over that of *human rights*. For example, as can be seen from the same passage in the *Letters*, he is also motivated by the consideration that whereas the ideal of human rights is a *legalistic* one, that of humanity is a *moral* one – which he thinks is the more fundamental and the more appropriate level at which to locate the values in question. And, although he says little explicitly on the subject, it seems likely that he has further reasons as well, including the following: Whereas the ideal of human rights implies a *possession* of the rights in question and is hence modelled on the institution and value of property-ownership, the ideal of humanity does not in this way unduly privilege what the left-wing Christian Herder would consider to be the (at best) only rather secondary institution/value of property. Whereas the ideal of human rights

is mainly focused on protecting individuals from their own governments but leaves them less protected against abuses inflicted on them from outside their countries, such as war and imperialism – indeed sometimes even functioning as an ideological rationalization for such abuses (recall here Herder's concern that '[t]he universal dress of philosophy and love of humankind can conceal oppressions, violations of the true, personal freedom of human beings, citizens, and peoples, just as Cesare Borgia would have liked it') – the ideal of humanity is not limited or ideologically pernicious in these ways. Whereas the ideal of human rights, due to its legalistic background, implies that there are certain preconditions for possessing them, such as having and living up to corresponding duties and being able to lay claim to the rights in question, which would exclude many people from possessing them (e.g. infants, the mentally disabled and whole peoples who have no commitment to human rights), the ideal of humanity is free of this disadvantage. And finally (a consideration that is rooted in Herder's – especially for his time – unusually high degree of moral concern for animals), whereas the (victim-focused) ideal of human rights leaves the rest of the animal kingdom entirely unprotected, the (agent-focused) ideal of humanity can in principle include animals under the aegis of its protection.[67]

(11) An eleventh component of Herder's concept of *Humanität* is a thesis that humanity, in the descriptive and normative senses already explained, is both the centre of the cosmos (as Irmscher notes) and the purpose of history, which is developing it ever more fully. This thesis is prominent in both the *Ideas* and the *Letters*.[68] It is basically a much less cautious, more ambitious revision of Herder's earlier position in *This Too* that the observable cumulative development of *Menschheit* over the course of history is evidence *that* there is a purpose to history but does not tell us *what* that purpose is.

(12) Finally, in contrast to Herder's earlier position with its tendency to conceive *Menschheit* in *contradistinction* to the divine and religion, a twelfth component of Herder's later concept of *Humanität* lies in precisely these. Thus in the *Ideas* he writes that 'religion is the highest humanity of the human being'.[69] And he adds that God is the ultimate source of our humanity:

> No, kind divinity, you did not abandon your creature to murderous hazard. You gave the animals instinct, you implanted your own image, religion and humanity, into the soul of the human being.[70]

Menschheit or *Humanität*?

Now, when one divides up Herder's concepts of *Menschheit* and *Humanität* into their respective constitutive multiplicities of distinct doctrines in this way, it becomes clear, I think, that it is quite possible, and perhaps even likely, that some of the doctrines in question will turn out to be more defensible than others. I take this in fact to be the case, especially where the concept of *Humanität* is concerned. In other words, I suggest that this concept turns out to be a mixture of defensible and problematic doctrines. By contrast, I believe that the multiplicity of doctrines that Herder earlier championed under the heading of *Menschheit* was as a rule not only more original but also more defensible. So let me now run through the various doctrines that make up his conception of *Humanität* again in order to try to show these things, beginning with those that seem strongest, then proceeding to those that seem more problematic.

Doctrine (1), Herder's descriptive thesis, common to both his earlier conception of *Menschheit* and his later conception of *Humanität* (aside from some refinements concerning race in the latter), that humankind constitutes a single species with a single origin and that racial differences are merely superficial, has essentially been confirmed by scientific research conducted since his time and hence seems to be more or less straightforwardly true. Important scientific contributions towards showing this were already made early in the twentieth century by a great admirer of Herder who had a background in the natural sciences and became the founder of American cultural anthropology: Franz Boas. Subsequently, the development of the disciplines of palaeoarchaeology and genetics has virtually settled the matter. For, although the simple scientific story told until recently to the effect that the whole of humankind stems from a single source of *homo sapiens* in Africa that got dispersed to other parts of the world in a single event of migration no longer seems scientifically tenable, having now given way to the more complicated picture that multiple waves of migration of *homo sapiens* out of Africa occurred and that in addition they then interbred with Neanderthals (and probably also Denisovans) to a significant extent,[71] the level of genetic homogeneity among all modern humans is nonetheless extremely high, so that we really do constitute a single species whose seeming racial differences are little more than skin-deep.

Doctrine (2) – the descriptive thesis that Herder develops most clearly and fully in the *Treatise* and then implicitly retains in his later period according to which human beings are distinguished from (other) animals by their possession of language, reason, culture (and religion), the deeper explanation of this difference lying in the fact that unlike (other) animals, which have fixed instincts that enable them to cope with limited environments and tasks, human beings are relatively free of fixed instincts in a way that enables them to cope with many different environments and tasks, the role of fixed instincts being taken over in their case by linguistic-cognitive abilities that are deeply social and flexible in character, and which exploit the ratchet effect of accumulating the experience of many individuals over many generations – seems highly plausible as well. Indeed, one of the most convincing contemporary theories of the nature of the difference between human beings and (other) animals, that developed by the psychologist and linguist Michael Tomasello, argues along strikingly similar lines.[72] Herder's later version of this thesis has both disadvantages and advantages compared to his earlier version of it. The main disadvantage is that his articulation of it becomes much less clear. The main advantage is that he now softens the dividing line between human beings and (other) animals in the way that I mentioned above.[73]

Doctrine (4), Herder's *normative* commitment – common to his earlier *Menschheit* and his later *Humanität* phases – to humanity as a moral ideal seems very attractive as well.

In particular, doctrine (5), his more specific commitment to a moral ideal of *cosmopolitanism* as part of his ideal of humanity, is very attractive. It is, indeed, a striking fact about modernity (in sharp contrast to earlier periods of history) that nowadays virtually all nations and religions are committed to some sort of cosmopolitanism or at least pay lip service to it. On the other hand, I would argue that the more specific version of cosmopolitanism that Herder preferred during his earlier period – pluralistic cosmopolitanism – was not only much more original but also much more defensible than the traditional homogenizing version of cosmopolitanism to which he tends to revert in his later period. (For a little more on this subject, see below.)

Likewise, doctrine (6), Herder's more specific commitment – again essentially common to his earlier *Menschheit* period and his later *Humanität* period – to such particular moral values as not deceiving or harming people, but instead exercising moderation in relations with them and helping them, seems very attractive and is accepted by most nations and religions today.

Finally, thesis (10), Herder's preference for his ideal of *Humanität* over the competing ideal of human rights, also seems attractive, namely for the several reasons that he gives or at least hints at in support of it, and which I sketched above: that unlike the ideal of human rights, the ideal of humanity correctly locates the values in question at the deeper level of morality rather than the more superficial level of law; that unlike the ideal of human rights, which focuses mainly on abuses of victims by their own governments to the neglect of those, such as war and imperialism, that are inflicted from outside their countries, and which sometimes even provides ideological rationalizations for the latter abuses, the ideal of humanity protects equally against both sorts of abuse; that unlike the ideal of human rights, which protects only human beings but leaves other animals completely without protection, the ideal of humanity can protect both; and so on. (Whether it would therefore be a good idea to attempt to switch from the *terminology* of 'human rights' to Herder's preferred terminology of 'humanity' today, in a world where the former terminology rather than the latter has already become so deeply, and in many ways beneficially, rooted, is another question. An attractive alternative might be the compromise of retaining that terminology but re-configuring it at a *conceptual* level, by for example coming to treat its implication of legal normativity as merely a metaphorical way of expressing moral normativity, and in addition binding it tightly to equally valorized further ideals that proscribe international abuses and the abuse of animals, in order to enable it to conform more closely to the spirit of Herder's ideal of 'humanity'.[74])

These seem to me the *positive* components of Herder's late concept of *Humanität*, the ones that are defensible and valuable. However, it should be noted that for the most part these components were anticipated and are shared by his earlier concept of *Menschheit*.[75] And it should also be observed that in some of these cases Herder's earlier conception of *Menschheit* not only articulated them first but also did so more clearly (as in the case of (2), his philosophical anthropology) or in a more original and defensible specific form (as in the case of (5), his cosmopolitanism).

Moreover, the remaining components of his later concept of *Humanität* – doctrines (3), (7), (8), (9), (11) and (12) – are all much more problematic, especially in so far as they deviate from corresponding positions held during his earlier period. So let me now turn to discuss these further doctrines in a more critical vein.

Doctrine (3), Herder's later *unqualified* claim that it belongs to human nature to be kind towards other human beings rather than indifferent, aggressive or cruel towards them is unfortunately very questionable indeed. Certainly, kindness is a widespread human trait, especially kindness towards particular sorts of people in particular sorts of circumstances. But the pervasiveness in human history of warfare, genocide, torture, rape, enslavement, oppression, exploitation and so on – of which, like the earlier Herder, the later Herder was certainly not unaware –[76] suggests that selfishness and cruelty are at least as much a part of human nature as kindness is. As we have seen, the early Herder had paid greater theoretical heed to this fact, drawing the lesson that there is also a dark side to human nature. Subsequently, in the middle of the nineteenth century, such historically knowledgeable and clear-eyed thinkers as Jacob Burkhardt and Friedrich Nietzsche drew a similar lesson from their own review of history, in opposition to positions like the later Herder's. Moreover, since they wrote, the horrors of the twentieth century (seventy million slaughtered in two world wars, six million of them helpless Jewish victims of the Holocaust, similarly horrific numbers killed under Communism in the Soviet Union's Gulags, China's Cultural Revolution, and the Killing Fields of Cambodia, and so on) have underscored the lesson in red. Furthermore, recent research on our closest – and extremely close – relative in the animal kingdom, the chimpanzee, has revealed an uncannily similar combination of kindness and cruelty to that which we see in the history of our own species: much kindness, certainly, especially towards members of an individual's own group, but also much intra-group competitiveness and cruelty (as has been richly documented by Frans de Waal in his book *Chimpanzee Politics*)[77] as well as much hostility and cruelty towards outside groups, even including the periodic waging of a sort of warfare against them (such as the warfare that broke out among rival groups of chimpanzees in the Gombe Stream National Park in Tanzania in 1974–8 and that was observed with horror by a shocked Jane Goodall).[78] Put together with the similar evidence provided by our own history, this evidence from ethology strongly suggests that both sides of our behaviour – both our kindness towards certain conspecifics in certain contexts and our competitiveness and cruelty towards other conspecifics in other contexts – are deeply rooted in our nature. Kant's idea of an element of radical evil in human nature was therefore in all probability much closer to the truth than Herder was prepared to allow during his later period.

Doctrine (7), it will be recalled, is the thesis – absent from the earlier Herder but developed by the later Herder – that it is somehow *because* all human beings belong to a single species with only superficial racial differences (descriptive thesis (1)) and it belongs to their nature to be kind to other human beings (descriptive thesis (3)) that all human beings deserve moral respect (normative thesis (5)) and that this respect should include such performances as not deceiving or harming them, but instead exercising moderation in relations with them and helping them (normative thesis (6)). However, there are serious problems with this line of argument. One prima facie problem with it is that it seems to try to derive an *ought* from an *is* (or rather several *oughts* from several *ises*), a project that, as Hume famously pointed out, seems logically doomed to failure. But perhaps Herder's aspiration is a little more modest and less clearly illegitimate than that: roughly, an attempt to at least limit the range of viable *oughts* by showing that many competing *oughts* would have to rest on *ises* that turn out to be false. Unfortunately, though, even when read in this charitable way, his argument still runs into serious problems. Concerning the inference from his first descriptive thesis – the facts of the unity of the species and of the superficiality of racial differences – to the ideal of cosmopolitanism, while the facts in question may indeed rule out *some* ways of espousing an anti-cosmopolitanism as based on factual errors, in particular ways of doing so that appeal to differences of species or race between certain groups of human beings, it would still leave open the possibility of doing so on the basis of national or cultural differences (which for Herder are far from superficial). And concerning the inference from the same descriptive thesis together with the further descriptive thesis of the basic kindness of human nature to the appropriateness, more specifically, of such kindly moral principles as not deceiving or harming others, but instead exercising moderation in relations with them and helping them, this faces severe problems as well. For one thing, as I have just pointed out, there is every reason to think that human nature is as much cruel as kind. For another thing, to the extent that it *is* kind, might not a morality regard such kindness as a temptation, a weakness, rather than as something to be encouraged? Nietzsche's argument in his early work *Homer's Wettkampf* (*Homer's Contest*) to the effect that Homeric society valorized cruelty, strife and agonality rather than humanity implies both of these points (as does his later argument that the morality of sympathy or pity is only *one*, historically rather local, form of morality and that it could and should be rejected in favour of another, more egoistic form of morality that rather *proscribes* sympathy and pity). To forestall any misunderstanding here: My point is not that there is anything wrong with Herder's moral ideals, but just that his strategy of argument in support of them does not work.[79]

Doctrine (8) – the later Herder's moral universalism, and in particular his conception that cosmopolitanism and the elaboration of it in terms of not deceiving or harming people, but instead exercising moderation in relations with them and helping them (for short, 'humanity'), are values that all human beings are (at least implicitly) committed to – is highly problematic as well. This is in part because the abstract argument that he gives in support of it (the one we just considered) does not work, as we just saw. But it is also in part because, contrary to the later Herder's view, such moral universalism is empirically implausible. So let us now consider this further problem.

As I mentioned earlier, Herder attempts in the *Letters* to demonstrate the empirical plausibility of his moral universalism by considering a series of cultures in the Western tradition, especially Homeric culture,[80] the culture of classical Greece as reflected in its sculpture[81] and Christianity,[82] in order to show that these all imply cosmopolitanism and such kindly values as not deceiving or harming others, but instead exercising moderation in relations with them and helping them ('humanity').

Homer constitutes an especially important and interesting part of Herder's case. Herder interprets Homer as a champion of 'humanity' (the first section of the *Letters* that deals with this subject bears the title 'On Homer's Humanity in His *Iliad*').[83] Nietzsche would later take issue with this Herderian interpretation of Homer in *Homer's Contest*, objecting that so far from championing humanity, Homer and his culture rather valorized cruelty, strife and agonality. I suggest that the truth lies somewhere in between these two interpretations. On the one hand, as Edith Hall has argued in her excellent book *Inventing the Barbarian*,[84] unlike much of the literature from the *classical* period, especially tragedy (and, one should add, the philosophy of Plato in *Republic*, book 5 and Aristotle in the *Politics*), Homer does seem to have a sort of proto-cosmopolitan sensibility. This can be seen, for example, from the facts that in the *Iliad* he gives sympathetic portrayals not only of Achaean figures such as Achilles but also of figures on the Trojan side such as Hector and Priam and that he tries to be similarly even-handed when characterizing the two sides in the Catalogue of Ships. It can also be seen from the fact that in the *Odyssey* he gives a sympathetic depiction of the Phaiacians. So to this extent Herder's reading can be defended against Nietzsche. However, on the other hand, when one realizes that the seemingly compassionate passages in Homer on which Herder and readers like him tend to focus, such as Hector saying farewell to his son on the battlements or Priam visiting Achilles to plead for, and receiving, the return of his son Hector's corpse, are rather few in number and that they are massively outweighed by such features of the texts as the fundamental predication of the plot structures of both the *Iliad* and the *Odyssey* on the assumed moral necessity of taking bloody revenge for a slight (respectively, Menelaos's moral need to do so for Paris's theft of his wife, and Odysseus's moral need to do so for the suitors' consumption of his substance, wooing of his wife, and demeaning of his son during his absence from home), the endless lurid descriptions of killings on the battlefield in the *Iliad*, the sympathetic depiction of Odysseus's skills at lying and deceiving both in the Dolon-episode of the *Iliad* and throughout the *Odyssey*, and so on, it seems that Herder's association of Homer with such kindly values as an aversion to deceiving or doing harm and a commitment to moderation and helping is much further from the truth than Nietzsche's association of him with a valorization of cruelty, strife and agonality. Nor does the admitted proto-cosmopolitanism in Homer do much to support Herder's *overall* case in the end. For, as I mentioned in passing, authors from the classical period (both literary and philosophical) are often, instead, emphatically anti-cosmopolitan. Moreover, it would be easy to find even more extreme examples of anti-cosmopolitanism in other historical cases (e.g. the Aztecs).

Herder's appeal to the striking anthropocentrism and anthropomorphism of classical Greek sculpture does not convincingly support his attribution of an ideal of 'humanity' to the *classical* period either. For *how much* of humankind was being celebrated in this sculpture (all of it or just (certain) Greeks?)? And *for which traits* (honesty, kindness, harmlessness and so on or cunning, martial courage, mastery and so forth)? These questions can in fact be answered with considerable confidence, at least at a generic level, though not by restricting oneself to the evidence provided by sculpture as Herder restricts himself, but by also taking the period's literature and philosophy into account. Aside from Homer and a few other forerunners (e.g. the Sophist Hippias and the Cynics), cosmopolitanism only really began to enter the moral picture in the West late in the fourth century BC (especially with the appearance of the Stoic Zeno's *Republic* at the end of it). Also, while the classical period's literature and philosophy show that such specific virtues as not deceiving or harming people *did* in fact begin to emerge by the fifth century BC (think, for example, of Sophocles's *Philoctetes* and *Ajax*, respectively, or Plato's *Apology* and *Crito*, respectively), it also shows that they only did so alongside the persistence of their more traditional Homeric opposites (recall, for instance, Plato's many anti-heroes – obviously modelled on real contemporaries – such as Euthydemus and Dionysodorus in the *Euthydemus*, Thrasymachus in the *Republic* and Callicles in the *Gorgias*). So not only does Herder's attempt to read his ideal of 'humanity' out of classical sculpture prove to be an unnecessarily indirect and blunt means of assessing the moral outlook of the period, since literature and philosophy provide much better evidence about it, but in addition, contrary to Herder's perception that the sculpture of the period provides clear evidence of the hegemony of his moral ideal of 'humanity' at the time, literature and philosophy both show the moral outlook of the period to have been deeply ambiguous in the ways just sketched and thereby strongly suggest that the same is probably true of the meaning of its sculpture as well.

Finally, Christianity is a more promising candidate for the role of a cultural tradition that champions 'humanity'. For not only have many Christians embraced this very ideal explicitly (e.g. Thomas Aquinas), but in addition Christianity from an early period included an ideal of cosmopolitanism (originally borrowed by Saint Paul from the Stoics), and the specific virtues that Christianity exalted from the start centrally included such virtues as not deceiving or harming people, but instead exercising moderation in relations with them and helping them. But, of course, Christianity, as merely one small tessera in the great mosaic of human history and cultures, is far too historically and geographically restricted to do much to support Herder's moral universalism.

In fairness to the later Herder, one further observation is worth making here, though. Although Herder generally holds a rather negative and even prejudiced view of Chinese culture in the *Ideas*, at one point in the work he includes Confucius in a list of earlier representatives of humanity.[85] Had he pursued this line of thought further, it would have allowed him to strengthen his empirical case significantly. For Confucius did strongly champion an ideal that is quite reasonably translated as 'humanity', namely *ren*; he did conceive it in a cosmopolitan spirit (for example, insisting that the good man will behave in his usual manner even when he is among barbarians); and he did also include within it such specific virtues as not deceiving or harming people, but instead exercising moderation in relations with them and helping them. Nonetheless, finding that a certain morality is approximately shared by two great cultural traditions, namely (a strand of the later Greek and Roman pagan tradition and) the Christian tradition plus the Chinese tradition, still falls far short of showing it to be *universal*.

Indeed, as we have seen, there is a diametrically opposed line of argument in Herder's own earlier thought, which in the end seems much more plausible. Recall that Herder in the *Treatise* develops a very attractive philosophical anthropology that emphasizes the extreme *plasticity* of human nature and that, in keeping with this, he often in his early thought emphasizes that profound *variations* occur in moral values from period to period, culture to culture and even individual to individual, indeed going as far as to observe that moral values not only change or vary in deep ways but in certain cases actually become inverted. This position seems much more convincing than the later Herder's moral universalism – not only thanks to the support that it receives from his very plausible philosophical anthropology, but also, and especially, thanks to the support that it receives from the sort of careful empirical survey of the moral values of different historical periods, cultures and individuals that he himself undertook or at least began. Subsequent research has deepened and extended this survey considerably, reinforcing the early Herder's conclusion – for example, Nietzsche's work on the moral values of Greek antiquity versus modernity in *Homer's Wettkampf* (Homer's Contest), *Zur Genealogie der Moral* (On the Genealogy of Morals), and other texts, the similar but more philologically scrupulous work on the same subject by Arthur Adkins in his book *Merit and Responsibility*,[86] and – with a much broader historical and cultural focus – Edward Westermarck's *The Origin and Development of the Moral Ideas*.[87]

Nor does Herder's superior earlier position conflict with his strong commitment to cosmopolitanism, as it might initially seem to. For, as we have seen, it instead motivates him to develop a new, original and much more defensible form of cosmopolitanism: in place of the traditional *homogenizing* form of it that was predicated on a false assumption of moral universalism (or on a coercive aspiration to impose such universalism), a *pluralistic* form of it that holds that all people should be treated respectfully despite, or even in part because of, the diversity of their moral outlooks. Recall in this connection the following passage from Herder's notes related to his *Reisejournal* of 1769 (already cited earlier):

> A great article ... It presupposes that each nation has its riches and distinctive features of spirit, or character, as of country. These must be sought out, and cultivated. No human being, no land, no people, no history of a people, no state is like the other, and consequently the true, the beautiful, and the good is not alike in them. If this is not sought, if another nation is blindly taken as a model, then everything suffocates.

This pluralist cosmopolitanism was subsequently taken over and developed further by the leading Romantics, especially Schleiermacher in his *Monologen* (*Soliloquies*), 1800 and Friedrich Schlegel in his *Vorlesungen über Transzendentalphilosophie* (Lectures on Transcendental Philosophy, 1800–1). In my view, it constitutes the single most important contribution to philosophical reflection on cosmopolitanism from the eighteenth century (though it has been strangely overlooked in the relevant literature, for example most recently by Pauline Kleingeld in her otherwise excellent book on that subject, *Kant and Cosmopolitanism*).[88]

Doctrine (9) – Herder's later tendency to renounce his highly original early meta-ethics according to which moral outlooks are more fundamentally matters of sentiment than of cognition (though also essentially involving the latter), plural, and relative to the forms of society and modes of life within which they occur, in favour of a meta-ethics that is cognitivist, universalist, and renounces relativism – is largely based on his new development of positions (7) and (8) (his abstract argument and his moral universalism). Besides being much less original than his earlier meta-ethics, it therefore also collapses philosophically together with those two positions.

Doctrine (11), Herder's doctrine that the realization of *Humanität* is the centre of the cosmos and the purpose of history was already rather implausible at the time when he advanced it – in part because the very application of the concept of a purpose to the cosmos or history is dubious (as he indeed himself acknowledges at points in the *Ideas* when his sympathies with Spinozism are uppermost), in part because the moral ideal of humanity is much more historically local than he allows (as has already been discussed), and in part because the horrors of past history were far from disappearing at the time when he wrote but were instead continuing in such forms as warfare, imperialism and slavery (as he indeed himself often lamented). But in the wake of the quantitatively and qualitatively even more appalling atrocities of the twentieth century – again, 70 million killed in two world wars, 6 million of them innocent victims of the Holocaust, similar numbers under Communism, and so on – the doctrine now looks implausible to the point of being tragically absurd. Although Herder's earlier position during his *Menschheit* period shared some dubious common ground with this later position – especially a teleological conception of the cosmos and of history – its agnosticism about the specific nature of the purpose that the cosmos or history is realizing seems, in this light, a significant advantage.

Finally, doctrine (12), the doctrine that religion is the highest expression, and God the source, of the ideal of *Humanität*, would likewise be extremely difficult to defend today. For, thanks to the Scientific Revolution, the Enlightenment, and atheistic theorists of the nineteenth century such as Marx and Nietzsche, the arguments against religion in general and Christianity in particular have advanced from strength to strength (Herder indeed himself involuntarily contributing to this advance in certain ways).[89] Viewed in this light, Herder's earlier ideal of *Menschheit*, with its strong tendency to *bracket out* religion and God, again looks distinctly superior to his later ideal of *Humanität*.

Conclusion

In sum, Herder has two distinguishable models of humanity: an earlier one for which he usually employs the term *Menschheit* and a later one for which he often prefers the term *Humanität*. His earlier model was not only stunningly original in a number of important respects but also deeply insightful. His later model also has certain virtues, but these are mostly ones that it inherited from and shares with the earlier model. Beyond that inheritance, it generally lapses into positions that are both less original and less plausible. In the end, then, this does indeed turn out to be a case where, as we saw Herder himself putting it, 'the first, uninhibited work of an author is ... his best; his bloom is unfolding, his soul still dawn'.

Notes

1   Two German editions of Herder's writings are cited in this article: *Johann Gottfried Herder Werke*, ed. U. Gaier et al. (Frankfurt am Main: Deutscher Klassiker Verlag, 1985–) [abbreviation: FHA] and *Johann Gottfried Herder Sämtliche Werke*, ed. B. Suphan et al. (Berlin: Weidmann, 1877–) [abbreviation: S]. In addition, wherever possible, references are given to the English translations in *Herder: Philosophical Writings* (2002) [abbreviation: HPW].
2   Cf. Bödeker ([1990] 2004), 1090.

3   Cf. ibid., which explains Herder's earlier avoidance of the word *Humanität* in terms of certain aristocratic and rationalistic connotations that it had already acquired. However, I would suggest that two further important reasons for his earlier preference for the term *Menschheit* over the term *Humanität* but later shift from the former towards the latter were the following closely connected ones: (1) Voltaire (and other French Enlighteners) had already made *humanité* a central ideal; the early Herder, especially in *Auch eine Philosophie der Geschichte zur Bildung der Menschheit* (*This Too a Philosophy of History for the Formation of Humanity* [henceforth: *This Too*], 1774), was strongly concerned to attack Voltaire philosophically and therefore avoided the equivalent German term *Humanität*, but the later Herder, especially in the *Briefe zu Beförderung der Humanität* (*Letters for the Advancement of Humanity* [henceforth: *Letters*], 1793–7), softened considerably in his opposition to Voltaire and therefore became less averse to using it. (2) Voltaire (and other French Enlighteners) had conceived such moral values as *humanité* as *universal* (see e.g. Voltaire's *Le Philosophe ignorant* [*The Ignorant Philosopher*], 1766, ch. 38 'Morale universelle'); the early Herder of *This Too* strongly opposed that conception, but later on, in the *Ideen zur Philosophie der Geschichte der Menschheit* (*Ideas for the Philosophy of History of Humanity*, 1784–91) and in the *Letters*, he instead came to sympathize with it. In accordance with this twofold explanation, note that, having written *This Too* largely as a polemical work against Voltaire (beginning with its very title, which was directed against Voltaire's *La Philosophie de l'histoire* [*The Philosophy of History*], 1765), later on, in the *Letters*, Herder wrote the following conciliatory footnote about him: '[Voltaire's] praise [of Montesquieu] is well known: *l'humanité avoit perdu ses titres; Montesquieu les a retrouvés*. Whatever people may say to the contrary, humanity [*die Menschheit*] owes much to Voltaire himself. A series of essays on history, philosophy, and legislation, concerned with the enlightenment of the understanding, and so on, sometimes in a mocking and sometimes in a didactic tone, are written to serve just that. His *Alzire*, *Zaïre*, and so on similarly' (FHA 7:696).
4   *Vom Erkennen und Empfinden der menschlichen Seele* (*On the Cognition and Sensation of the Human Soul*), 1778, FHA 4:367 = HPW, 219.
5   FHA 1:795, 801-4 = HPW, 150, 156-9. Cf. *This Too*, FHA 4:11 = HPW, 272-3.
6   FHA 1:795, 801-4 = HPW, 150, 156-9.
7   FHA 1:732-3 = HPW, 96.
8   FHA 1:711-12 = HPW, 77-8.
9   FHA 1:711-24 = HPW, 78-89.
10 FHA 1:769-75 = HPW, 127-32.
11 FHA 1:783 6 = HPW, 139 41.
12 FHA 1:791-5 = HPW, 147-50.
13 FHA 1:800-1, 805-6 = HPW, 155-6, 159-62.
14 FHA 1:697-702 = HPW, 65-9.
15 FHA 1:796 = HPW, 151, emphasis original. Cf. FHA 1:796-8 = HPW, 151-3.
16 FHA 4:21, 39 = HPW, 281, 297.
17 Herder attended Kant's lectures on ethics in Königsberg during the early 1760s, a period when Kant himself espoused a version of Hume's sentimentalism, and Herder is indeed the main source of the transcriptions of those lectures that have survived.
18 See *Kritische Wälder* (*Critical Forests*, 1769), esp. S 4:5, 13-15, 35-6. Cf. *On the Cognition and Sensation of the Human Soul*.
19 FHA 4:65 = HPW, 320.
20 FHA 1:149-60 = HPW, 247-56.

21 S 32:125-6.
22 S 4:462-78.
23 FHA 1:160 = HPW, 256. Herder repeats this point in several other places, sometimes even in his later period (see e.g. an essay from 1783 at S 15:138).
24 Note that 'for [zur]' here means both *concerning* and *in the service of*.
25 FHA 4:91 = HPW, 343. Usually in the eighteenth century, as still today, the term *Menschheit* has only descriptive senses, not normative ones (as e.g. *Menschlichkeit* and *Humanität* do): roughly, it means either humankind as a whole or the quality of being human. So Herder's inclusion of normative implications in its very meaning here is unusual. Indeed, the textual evidence that he does so, while I find it persuasive, is somewhat equivocal (e.g. 'Socrates of humanity [*Menschheit*]' could *just* mean: Socrates who makes all of humankind the object of his concern), so that it might with at least some plausibility be denied that he does so. The issue at stake here is of some philological interest and (along with several additional questions of a similar nature) would be worth pursuing further here if my purpose in this article were more philological than it is. However, the issue is not very philosophically important, in effect merely amounting to a choice between saying that Herder expresses the normative ideals in question by using the word *in a way that builds them into its very meaning* versus saying that he does so *but without building them into its very meaning, so that they are only closely associated with it*.
26 S 4:472.
27 FHA 4:99 = HPW, 351.
28 FHA 4:64, 75 = HPW, 319, 329.
29 FHA 4:90-1 = HPW, 342-3. Incidentally, Herder's assumption in this passage that the historical Socrates (unlike his own imagined 'Socrates of humanity') was no cosmopolitan is almost certainly correct (despite a long tradition of interpretation stretching from Cicero up to the present day that says the contrary). Plato's *Republic*, book 5 is the most startling evidence for this but not the only evidence.
30 Herder already adumbrates a similar account in the *Treatise*, at FHA 1:799-801, 806-7 = HPW, 154-6, 160-1.
31 FHA 1:736 = HPW, 99.
32 Cf. for this part of the account Forster (2018), 224ff.
33 Irmscher (1991), 817 = FHA 7:817.
34 FHA 7:817. Quoted by Irmscher from S 13:154 = FHA 6:154.
35 FHA 7:817.
36 Cf. Forster (2012, 2019).
37 FHA 7:818.
38 FHA 7:819-20.
39 FHA 7:820-4.
40 FHA 7:824-6.
41 FHA 7:826-9.
42 FHA 7:829.
43 FHA 7:830-1.
44 FHA 7:832-3.
45 FHA 7:833-4, cf. 836.
46 FHA 7:834-5.
47 FHA 7:836-7. In an essay published just a few years after Irmscher published this account, Hans Adler presented a similar picture, especially focusing on aspects (a) and (b): Adler (1994).

48 For a discussion and critique of this reading, see Forster (2018), ch. 2.
49 FHA 6:251-6.
50 See esp. FHA 6:255-6.
51 FHA 7:698-702 = HPW, 393-7.
52 FHA 6, bk. 1, esp. 116-18, 141.
53 See e.g. FHA 6:142-9.
54 S 13:448-9.
55 FHA 7:746-50 = HPW, 420-4.
56 FHA 7:151-3. Hans Adler is therefore mistaken when he argues that Herder's concept of humanity is purely descriptive rather than moral (Adler [1994], 65). Adler's deeper mistake here is to have misread the criticism that Herder develops of certain moral ideals closely related to that of humanity, such as *Menschlichkeit* and *Menschenliebe*, in favour of his own ideal of humanity (see FHA 7:147-8), as a rejection of the former ideals *because of their moral character*, whereas Herder in fact only rejects them because they have *specific* moral connotations or implications that he does not like, in particular in the case of *Menschlichkeit* that of a sort of soppy sympathy and in the case of *Menschenliebe* that of a sort of commitment to the species at the expense of any commitment to individuals.
57 FHA 7:692 = HPW, 389.
58 FHA 7:698-702 = HPW, 394-5.
59 FHA 7:660-4. Cf. the similar seven moral 'attitudes [*Gesinnungen*]' that he goes on to advocate in the work (FHA 7:720-6 = HPW, 404-9).
60 In this connection, Robert Clark has perceptively noted a certain affinity between Herder's position and Aristotle's: '"Humanity" is both an ideal condition and a definable real quality … This notion of "humanity" is clearly patterned on Aristotle's philosophy of becoming … transferred to the field of eighteenth-century humanitarian thought' (Clark [1955], 314).
61 FHA 6:255.
62 FHA 7:173-83.
63 FHA 7:363-84.
64 FHA 7:318-19, 752, 805.
65 FHA 6:647-64, esp. 651, 655; FHA 7:739ff. = HPW, 417ff.
66 Concerning this component, cf. Forster (2017); also, Forster (2018), ch. 9.
67 For a more detailed discussion of all these reasons, see the two works cited in the preceding footnote.
68 See e.g. FHA 6:154, 187, 630-5.
69 FHA 6:160.
70 FHA 6:378. Accordingly, Wilhelm Dobbek (1949) argues convincingly that for the later Herder religion is the ultimate foundation of the ideal of *Humanität* (18, 44, 49-50, 98-118, 140-1, 159 ff.). Whether Dobbek's enthusiasm for this position is warranted is quite another question.
71 For an excellent, concise, and up-to-date treatment of these issues, see Condemi & Savatier (2019).
72 See Tomasello (1999).
73 This move anticipates the work of Charles Darwin in the nineteenth century, as well as that of a whole series of cognitive ethologists from the late twentieth century, such as Sue Savage-Rumbaugh, Dorothy Cheney and Robert Seyfarth, Donald Griffin and Irene Pepperberg.
74 For more on these issues, see Forster (2017) and (2018), ch. 9.

75 Note also that the two most significant exceptions – the component of (1) that argues in detail against theories of race and (10), the contradistinction of *Humanität* to human rights – are both ones whose absence from the earlier concept of *Menschheit* is mainly just due to the fact that the issues involved had not yet become salient at that time as they had by the later period, namely after Kant had published his theory of race in 1775 and the American and French Revolutions of 1787 and 1789 had brought the ideal of human rights to prominence.

76 For example, Herder writes in the *Ideas*: 'What form of inhumanity is there that has not become habitual for some human being, some nation, indeed often a whole series of nations … ? What foolish idea could one think of that has not in reality been enshrined in inherited tradition here or there? Lower than the human being can no rational creature stand … Depending on the hands he falls into he is molded accordingly, and I do not believe that any form of human moral life is possible that has not been lived in by a people or by an individual from a people. All vices and atrocities are played out in history before eventually here and there a more noble form of human thoughts and virtues appears' (FHA 6:342-3).

77 de Waal (2007).

78 It is true that bonobos are at least as closely related to us as chimpanzees and behave much less aggressively. But which of the two species do we most closely resemble in our behaviour?

79 It would be interesting to compare the failure of Herder's argument with that of generically similar arguments that have been developed by other philosophers, for example Martha Nussbaum's neo-Aristotelian argument for the universality of certain moral values.

80 FHA 7:173-83, 188-96.

81 FHA 7:363-84.

82 FHA 7:318-19, 752, 805.

83 FHA 7:173.

84 Hall (1989).

85 FHA 6:652: 'What pure understanding and just morality is, about this Socrates and Confucius, Zoroaster, Plato and Cicero are in agreement.'

86 Adkins (1960).

87 Westermarck (1912).

88 Kleingeld (2011).

89 Concerning Herder's involuntary contributions to it, see Forster (2018), ch. 10.

References

Adkins, A. W. H. (1960), *Merit and Responsibility: A Study in Greek Values*, Oxford: Clarendon Press.

Adler, H. (1994), 'Johann Gottfried Herder's Concept of Humanity', *Studies in Eighteenth-Century Culture*, 23: 55–74.

Bödeker, H. E. ([1990] 2004), 'Menschheit, Humanität, Humanismus', in O. Brunner, W. Conzer & R. Koselleck (eds), *Geschichtliche Grundbegriffe*, vol. 3, Stuttgart: Klett-Cotta, 1063–128.

Clark, R. T. (1955), *Herder: His Life and Thought*, Berkeley: University of California Press.

Condemi, S. & Savatier, F. (2019), *A Pocket History of Human Evolution: How We Became Sapiens*, New York: The Experiment.

Dobbek, W. (1949), *J.G. Herders Humanitätsidee als Ausdruck seines Weltbildes und seiner Persönlichkeit*, Braunschweig: Georg Westermann.
Forster, M. N. (2012), 'Bildung bei Herder und seinen Nachfolgern: drei Begriffe', in K. Vieweg & M. Winkler (eds), *Bildung und Freiheit. Ein vergessener Zusammenhang*, Paderborn: Schöningh, 75–90.
Forster, M. N. (2017), 'Herder and Human Rights', in A. Waldow & N. DeSouza (eds), *Herder: Philosophy and Anthropology*, Oxford: Oxford University Press, 224–39.
Forster, M. N. (2018), *Herder's Philosophy*, Oxford: Oxford University Press, 2018.
Forster, M. N. (2019), 'Interpretation and Imagination: Herder's Concept of Einfühlung', in G. Gentry and K. Pollok (eds), *The Imagination in German Idealism and Romanticism*, Cambridge: Cambridge University Press, 175–89.
Hall, E. (1989), *Inventing the Barbarian: Greek Self-Definition through Tragedy*, Oxford: Oxford University Press.
Herder, J. G. (1877–), *Johann Gottfried Herder Sämtliche Werke*, ed. B. Suphan et al., Berlin: Weidmann [abbreviation: S].
Herder, J. G. (1985–), *Johann Gottfried Herder Werke*, ed. U. Gaier et al., Frankfurt am Main: Deutscher Klassiker Verlag [abbreviation: FHA].
Herder J. G. (2002), *Herder: Philosophical Writings*, ed. and trans. M. N. Forster, Cambridge: Cambridge University Press [abbreviation: HPW].
Irmscher H. D. (1991), 'Herders Humanitätsbriefe', in H. D. Irmscher (ed.), *Johann Gottfried Herder Werke*, vol. 7, Frankfurt am Main: Deutscher Klassiker Verlag, 809–40.
Kleingeld, P. (2011), *Kant and Cosmopolitanism: The Philosophical Ideal of World Citizenship*, Cambridge: Cambridge University Press.
Tomasello, M. (1999), *The Cultural Origins of Human Cognition*, Cambridge, MA: Harvard University Press.
de Waal, F. ([1982] 2007), *Chimpanzee Politics: Power and Sex among Apes*, Baltimore: Johns Hopkins University Press.
Westermarck, E. (1912), *The Origin and Development of the Moral Ideas*, London: Macmillan and Co.

12

Blumenbach on the varieties of the human species

François Duchesneau

Johann Friedrich Blumenbach (1752-1840) was probably the principal German biological theorist on the human race issue at the end of the eighteenth century. Simplifying to a maximum, one might say that he addressed two questions related to that issue. On the one hand, how, that is by which mechanisms, similar or dissimilar to those involved in animal species variations, did heritable anatomical and physiological differences come about among representatives of the human species? On the other hand, did these differences flow from a single stem species or, alternatively, did the present varieties or races originate from different stock species? Even if they had ideological and moral underpinnings, it was, at least for Blumenbach, essential to pursue the investigation on these issues as a matter of natural history, with the methods of experimental philosophy being strictly applied to them. This is not to say that speculative considerations were absent from his arguments and conclusions. On the contrary, such philosophical views would be constantly present because he always considered that the empirical data he started from and worked on, including his pioneering observations of skulls, were to accord with a systematic conception of the living organism, animal as well as human.

The series of Blumenbach's publications on the race issue started with his doctoral dissertation, *De generis humani varietate nativa* (On the Natural Varieties of Mankind), defended in Göttingen in 1775, and published in 1776. A second edition of that work came out of the press in 1781 and a third one, which formed an almost entirely original piece, in 1795. In parallel, Blumenbach resumed elements of the theory he had thus exposed, in the several editions of his *Handbuch der Naturgeschichte* (A Manual of the Elements of Natural History, first German edition in 1779; first English edition in 1825), *Institutiones physiologicæ* (Elements of Physiology, first Latin edition in 1787; first English edition in 1795) and *Handbuch der vergleichenden Anatomie* (A Short System of Comparative Anatomy, first German edition in 1805; first English edition in 1807). Of special interest are also his *Beyträge zur Naturgeschichte* (Contributions to Natural History), the first part of which was published in 1790 and republished in 1806 with additions, which provided useful complements about his theory of human varieties. *The Anthropological Treatises of Johann Friedrich Blumenbach* were edited as a complete set by Thomas Bendyshe and published by Longman and Green in London in 1865.[1] These include English translations of the first and third editions of *De generis humani varietate nativa* and of the additions to the first of the *Beyträge*.[2]

1. The initial hypothesis

When writing the first edition of his doctoral dissertation *De generis humani varietate nativa*, Blumenbach was not yet in possession of his physiological concept of the formative drive (*Bildungstrieb*) and had not yet adhered to a specific form of epigenesis in order to account for generation. On generation, at the time, he endorsed Albrecht von Haller's and Charles Bonnet's late preformation theory, which involved the pre-existence of germs in eggs, along with the potential structuring influence of spermatozoa.[3] The question he wished to address in his dissertation was that of the causes of deviation affecting the pre-set course of generation for any given species, and responsible for natural differences in the constitution of the reproduced individuals. That these differences should be natural was of foremost importance. Blumenbach would exclude from his standard concept of variety monstrosities and pathologies, the former including infertile hybrids and the latter including congenital morbid conditions, such as albinism, for one could identify them as non-adaptive anatomic or physiological traits. His critical analysis of the causes of variation involved two presuppositions. On the one hand, in normal conditions, the generative process is species-specific and has been programmed according to an appropriately designed organic pattern. On the other hand, physical or human causes may influence the unfolding of the specified generative process and make the organic constitution of individuals of a given type de-generate, that is, deviate from the original, species-specific form. The effects of such causal actions can fall into two different categories: either they enhance the viability and reproductive capacity of the individuals affected, and the alterations thus produced induce functional variations that may endure; or they fall short of providing any adaptation and are thus unable to yield a typical variety of the involved species. Indeed, in such a case, the term 'adaptation' is not to be understood in a Darwinian sense, but rather in that of a teleological adjustment in structures and functions for a type of living being in a given natural setting. The principal causes of variation are the climate and the modes of life and of upbringing.[4]

Should hybridization be added to these causes? Although Blumenbach would not exclude the possibility that there could be rare cases of fertile hybrids among kindred species, he was sceptical about the possibility of raising a theory of specific variations therefrom and applying it in particular to hybrids of joint human and animal origin. He would in fact disqualify all empirical evidence to that effect. As a consequence, it could be inferred that, in principle, pending attested facts to the contrary, all varieties of a given species flow from alterations of the primeval generative stock for that species and that such alterations do not prevent different variants of that type from interbreeding and producing fertile offspring. Interestingly enough, Blumenbach did not simply rely on Georges-Louis Leclerc de Buffon's notion of species based on interbreeding and reproduction in order to exclude hybridization from his pattern of variety production;[5]

he would also refer to a set of taxonomic criteria to segregate between humans and the higher primates they could be compared with.

These discriminating criteria related both to mental capacities and bodily structures, without there being strict structure – function correlations between these two sets of characters. Concerning the former, the mental ones, Blumenbach insisted on a predominance of rational capacity in humans compared to animals, and inversely in the case of instincts. Concerning bodily structures, he specified anatomic and physiological differences that discriminately characterized the types of human organisms beyond any possible variation: for instance erect posture, bi-mane condition, skull and brain dispositions, etc. The comparison in terms of mental aptitudes is particularly telling, since Blumenbach, referring to Hermann Samuel Reimarus's classification of instincts in his *Betrachtungen über die Triebe der Thiere* (Considerations on the Drives of Animals, 1760),[6] is keen on extending to human beings the possession of some mostly 'artificial instincts' (*Kunsttriebe*), while endowing them with emotional capacities, speech and reason. Human reason is to be conceived of as 'a developing germ, which in the process of time, and by the accession to a social life and other external circumstances, is as it were developed, formed, and cultivated'.[7] In a long passage devoted to comparative anatomy, Blumenbach raises doubts about all positively sustained analogies between humans and the higher primates. His objective is that the question of the relationship between the varieties of mankind be addressed in reference to what can be considered the set of stock properties from which all human natural effects may have derived. This means that close kinship is expected between the various organic and mental constitutions that result from those properties. It is with this requirement in mind, but without having developed his own epigenetic theory yet, that Blumenbach first addressed the question: 'Are men, and have the men of all times and of every race been of one and the same, or clearly of more than one species?'[8]

Blumenbach takes the latter alternative to be based on ideological prejudices and rushed conclusions. A better course necessarily implies

> to inquire into the structure of the human body, to consult the numerous anatomical authors and travellers, and carefully to weigh their good faith or carelessness, to compare parallel examples from the universal circuit of natural history, and then at last to come to an opinion, and investigate the causes of variety.[9]

Blumenbach's typology of varieties is essentially based on a systematic survey of the general bodily constitution, stature and colour, complemented by observations on the structure and proportion of individual organs, with a presumed common stock of mental dispositions. Such sets of features must clearly differ from one variety to another. But overall these sets of discriminative features, considered as average characteristics, need to be significantly representative of geographically located populations and to have been regularly transmitted to their offspring. On this basis, Blumenbach initially identified four varieties or races of men, but, as early as the second edition of his main treatise, in 1781, he changed to five varieties and kept to that taxonomy from then on. In accordance with the terminology he then adopted, these are the Caucasian, Mongolian, Ethiopian, American and Malay varieties, with this additional specification, that the

Mongolian might be reckoned as a middle term between the Caucasian and Ethiopian, and the Malay between the Caucasian and American.[10]

According to a scheme of progressive degeneration, the first variety apparently represents the closest approximation to the original type. As mentioned in the 1781 note, 'all these [Caucasian] nations regarded as a whole are white in colour, and, if compared with the rest, beautiful in form'.[11] But it would be too simple to state that this merely shows ideological bias on behalf of Blumenbach, for three reasons. First, in other circumstances, he acknowledges that such an appraisal reflects a Eurocentric system of aesthetic values bred into our own mental constitution. Thus, other viewpoints are indeed possible and appear to flow from different, but equivalent mental constitutions. Such an argument may be particularly inferred from his evaluation of the intellectual and affective potential of the so-called negroes, in section XIII, *Of the Negro in particular* of the later *Beyträge zur Naturgeschichte*.[12] In the case at hand, the conclusion of this section can be rightly referred to as follows:

> Finally, I am of the opinion that after all these numerous instances I have brought together of negroes of capacity, it would not be difficult to mention entire well-known provinces of Europe, from out of which you would not easily expect to obtain off-hand such good authors, poets, philosophers, and correspondents of the Paris Academy; and on the other hand, there is no so-called savage nation known under the sun which has so much distinguished itself by such examples of perfectibility and original capacity for scientific culture, and thereby attached itself so closely to the most civilised nations of the earth, *as the Negro*.[13]

Second, Blumenbach considers that all the other colours have originated from white due to physiological processes that affected the mucous tissue under specific climatic conditions. Third, variations in skull shape in particular seem to have followed patterns that can be traced back to the Caucasian template as being the most regular, or at least the most balanced between potential extremes, although it appears that significant harmony might be found in the other templates as well. However, those alternative harmonies would need to be analysed through comparisons with the Caucasian system of morphological and physiological features. Thus, in 1795, Blumenbach points to this latter system as forming the 'medial variety of Mankind'.[14]

At the same time, Blumenbach appeals to a twofold principle of relativity that he applies to the morphological and physiological traits on which his typology of varieties is grounded. Let me quote from section 82 of the 1795 treatise, entitled 'Characters and limits of these varieties':

> To this enumeration, however, I must prefix a double warning; first, that on account of the multifarious diversity of the characters, according to their degrees, one or two alone are not sufficient, but we must take several joined together; and then that this union of characters is not so constant but that it is liable to innumerable exceptions in all and singular of these varieties. Still this enumeration is so conceived as to give a sufficiently plain and perspicuous notion of them in general.[15]

This means that the typology can only be grounded on a highly complex matrix of characters, which can only provide a relative representation of the organic and integrative systems of the human variants accounted for. Furthermore, it is quite evident that infinitely different hybrids between those variants are not only possible but are actually to be found.

Two further arguments underpin Blumenbach's principle of relativity. One has to do with the rejection of any great chain of beings, with clearly graded boundaries between life forms, especially in terms of distinct degrees of a given simple morphological pattern. For Blumenbach, this scheme, inherited from physico-theology, falls short of having any true foundation in the order of nature and cannot serve to establish any Linnean classification of natural kinds. These reservations are found clearly expressed in the introductory letter to John Banks that prefaces the 1795 treatise. Blumenbach indeed notes that Carl von Linné was the first to introduce a division of mankind into species, when he attempted, in the first edition (1735) of his *Systema naturæ* (*System of Nature*), to classify mammalians according to their mode of dentition, a rather obvious feature that related to their external conformation.

Contrary to Linnæus, the Göttingen physiologist intends 'to substitute for that artificial system one more natural, deduced from the universal characteristics of the mammalia'.[16] He correlatively questions the idea that all natural productions might fit the scheme of a continuously graded scale or chain in terms of their morphological configuration. It is not that he denies some epistemic credentials to the principle of continuity. But, on the one hand, the choice of a single morphological criterion creates an illusion of continuity where significant gaps can easily be evidenced. On the other hand, there may be a positive use for the continuity principle if it is paired with a ranking of life forms according to their 'universal condition', that is according to a correlation of the 'greatest number of external qualities in which they coincide with each other'.[17] In Appendix I of the *Beyträge*, entitled *Über die Stufenfolge der Natur* (On the Gradation of Nature), Blumenbach refers to an essay by Jean-André De Luc which had been submitted in 1791 for a prize of the Academy of Haarlem.[18] De Luc had argued on metaphysical grounds that imperceptible gradation would not characterize the relationship between types of natural entities, but that 'the harmony of the creation is rather supported by marked differences, having defined boundaries between them'.[19] This can be understood as meaning that continuity acts as a regulative principle for theorizing the relationship between the various qualities composing the integrative natural systems that each and every life form represents. Thus Blumenbach asserts: 'the very greatest use may be made of this very metaphorical image [of continuity] not only towards the exercise of observation, but also with the greatest advantage towards the regular use of a natural system in the description of nature, and also for the most advantageous arrangement of natural collections'.[20] Infinite possible variations among the individuals characterized by those natural types support this notion of their forming definite natural systems. While distinct and therefore discontinuous patterns correspond to the various life forms, a deep analogy may govern the comparison of one with another and indeed Blumenbach does not exclude the possibility that new patterns may arise in the course of natural history as variants of former ones, and that these fit the shifting economy of the various systems of nature as the latter undergo successions of catastrophes.

I shall not expand much on this point, but Blumenbach's conception of taxonomic classifications and their relation with the notion of a presumed great chain of being resembles Leibniz's formerly expressed views, which were to be found for instance in the letter to August Christian Gackenholtz of 23 April 1701[21] and passages of the *Nouveaux Essais sur l'Entendement humain* (New Essays on Human Understanding).[22] In the former, Leibniz resumed the idea that one should not base the taxonomy of plants and animals on a single feature, but on several characteristics whose combination represents in adequate fashion the integrative unity of a machine of nature that reproduces itself and yields sets of functions according to a developmental plan of its own. On the other hand, when dealing with the notion of a great chain of beings, Leibniz disqualified the idea that species might differ by the tiniest variant feature. Gaps need to occur between the various sets of anatomical and physiological features that characterize the actual cohabiting species in any specific geographical environment. Continuity may be found in the degree of variation of the typical features for individuals of a given species. Continuity can also be found in the overall pattern of the system formed by coexisting species: this system changes gradually, though continually, while constantly maintaining the same distribution of primitive forces, underpinning the formation of organic bodies. I am not arguing that Blumenbach adopts this strict Leibnizian stance but that an analogous epistemic pattern underlies his conception of the varying economy of morphological and functional traits for any given species within the order of nature.

And this conception is the grounding piece for the conclusion Blumenbach formulates on the issue of the monogenic versus polygenic origin of the human varieties. He states that he has empirically demonstrated that these varieties based on sets of distinctive traits, such as shape of skull, colour, texture of hair, stature, figure and proportion of parts, etc., run into one another 'by insensible transition' and that the absence of true discontinuity in this case can be accounted for by reference to the 'causes and ways of degeneration' and the analogy with 'generation in the other domestic animals'.[23]

> [This] brings us to that conclusion, which seems to flow spontaneously from physiological principles applied by the aid of critical zoology to the natural history of mankind, which is *that no doubt can any longer remain but that we are with great probability right in referring all and singular as many varieties of man as are at present known to one and the same species.*[24]

As mentioned, the key to the inference from this conclusion resides in a set of considerations jointly drawn from the principles of physiology and critical zoology, which means that the categories of the natural history of life forms are in this case re-evaluated from a theoretical viewpoint, that of Blumenbach's theory of vital forces.

2. The remodelled hypothesis

Blumenbach, who had started his anthropological investigations as a direct follower of Haller, shifted course between the second and third editions of the *De humani generis varietate nativa* and in the last one rearranged all the empirical comparative data collected so as to fit with the premises of what may be termed the 'formative drive' (*Bildungstrieb*) theory. Initiated in the essay *Über den Bildungstrieb und das Zeugungsgeschäfte* (On the Formative Drive and Generative Process, 1781), this reform of the generation theory and its extension to the explanation of all physiological functions really came to fruition in the *Institutiones physiologicæ* (Elements of Physiology, 1787).[25] And this move to vital forces is precisely referred to in the section on *Causes of degeneration* of the 1795 anthropological treatise as follows:

> Animal life supposes two faculties, depending upon the vital forces as primary conditions and principles of all and singular its functions; the one, namely, of so receiving the force of the stimuli which act upon the body that the parts are affected by it; the other of so reacting from this affection that the living motions of the body are in this way set in action and perfected. These are the hinges on which all the physiology of the animal economy turns. And these are the fountains from which, just as the business itself of generation, so also the *causes of degeneration* flow.[26]

The way the argument is structured is peculiar to the anthropological context. Once the classical refutation of the preformation theory has been spelled out, Blumenbach evokes the necessity of admitting that organisms come about by epigenetic formation from the amorphous stage of the organic fluids involved, which themselves consist in purely inorganic components. The *Bildungstrieb* or *nisus formativus* is a specific power whose vitalizing effect shapes the various structures of an organism. This organism develops according to the type of the parent bodies that contributed the genetic matters wherein the formative drive arises and acts. This formative drive holds in itself the teleological project without which the formation and operations of organisms could be neither achieved nor conceived. And it intervenes in guiding the causal efficient processes that are also necessarily involved towards this achievement. Interesting enough, Blumenbach uses a Kantian-inspired formula to present this twofold explanatory frame for accounting for generative processes:

> By properly joining together the two principles which explain the nature of organic bodies, that is the physico-mechanical with the teleological, we are conducted both by the phenomena of generation, and by sound reasoning, to lay down this proposition: That the genital liquid is only the shapeless material of organic bodies, composed of the innate matter of the inorganic kingdom, but differing in the force it shows, according to the phenomena: by which its first business is under certain circumstances of maturation, mixture, place, &c. to put on the form destined and determined by them; and afterwards through the perpetual function of nutrition to preserve it, and if by chance it should be mutilated, as far as it lies in its power to restore it by reproduction.[27]

Now, I shall not directly enter the still ongoing discussion about the constitutive (in Blumenbach) versus the purely heuristic and regulative conception (in Kant) of the teleological principles invoked to account for organic processes and thus attempt to dissociate Blumenbach's position from Kant's.[28] For me, there is no question that

Kant agreed with the methodological implications of the hypotheses that Blumenbach was framing up in his physiological enquiry about the laws of generation and organic development. The other way around, Blumenbach would have been admitting that resorting to teleological judgements implied a theoretical divide between the presumed principle of vital organization and the analytic representation of the mechanisms involved.[29] With this conception in mind, I wish to address the question of how the *Bildungstrieb* concept provided theoretical grounding for Blumenbach's hypotheses about human varieties.

Let me premise here a result from previous analyses of mine about Blumenbach's typology of vital forces. The more specialized vital forces, such as contractility, irritability, sensibility and the individual life of special organs, operate in structures that have been produced by the formative drive: thus they may be considered as outcomes of the latter. They are triggered by specific stimuli and implement their function through specific motions. But, at the same time, they can retroact on the formative drive itself and contribute to some transformation of its reproductive power. It is worth noting that the *Bildungstrieb* is to be identified not with a *sui generis* causal entity but with a system of phenomenal effects that imply the interaction of various types of stimuli, some due to environmental conditions, others due to inner transformations of the genital and generative materials, and still others fostered by the interrelation of parts and processes in the constituted organism. It can easily be concluded from these arguments that the formative drive of an actual organism comprises a primeval organogenetic determination: whereas this determination originally corresponded to the archetypal system of characters of its true species, it would have undergone successive alterations and adjustments under the impact of changing sets of external and internal stimuli.

What is fascinating with this conception is that the original specific archetypes or, more exactly, their respective formative drives stand as postulated entities that cannot be demonstrated from the empirical data presently available. But these archetypal drives, if we could perchance gain access to them, would provide the only true ground for assessing the transformational potential the individuals belonging to the historical species are endowed with, and the limits of plasticity in development following therefrom. It is quite evident that, contrary to Kant, who thought that the degenerative scheme was entirely programmed in, and unfolded from, the seeds (*Keime*) and predetermined dispositions (*Anlagen*) of the various species,[30] Blumenbach did not set any a priori limits on the potential for metamorphosis within species but noted some empirical ones based on our a posteriori experience of actual degenerative transformations.

There are three ways in which the formative drive can be deviated from its determined course of action. The first is the production of monsters, through some disturbance of this force, which may be endogenously or exogenously caused. In principle, the morphological or physiological deformations thus produced are *scherzi della natura*, fantasies of nature; they do not induce hereditary effects and thus do not fall within the scope of naturalists attempting to identify what may count as significant causes of degeneration. The second way is the production of hybrids from different species. This process, even when breeding true occurs, is normally impeded by the infertility of offspring. Blumenbach would not completely exclude such an option; however, he merely seems to have phrased a speculative suggestion that repeated mating of this kind might, in the long term, 'impart to [the formative drive] a singular and anomalous direction'.³¹ A third way of variation is what is properly called degeneration, which can also refer to the hybridization process between varieties of the same species.

> And so it happens that the continuous action, carried on for several series of generations of some peculiar stimuli in organic bodies, again has great influence in sensibly diverting the formative force from its accustomed path, which deflection is the most bountiful source of degeneration, and the mother of the varieties properly so called.³²

As already noted, these varieties cannot be discriminated on tight-bound sets of morphological, physiological or ethological criteria, since exceptions will always be found of individuals lacking some trait or other. And it can be further remarked that there are infinite degrees among individuals nominally belonging to the same variety for any of these definitional characters. Above all, the boundaries between varieties of the same species cannot be strictly assigned, since the grounding for this discrimination would have to be the existence of incompatible formative drives, unable to trigger successful reproduction, which is clearly not the case between individuals belonging to different so-called human races.

So what do those human varieties boil down to? Their formation and establishment have depended upon geographic isolation of populations, upon constantly intervening climatic and feeding conditions, upon interbreeding among representatives of the same population and lack of intercourse between heterogeneous populations, upon cultural effects due to different uses and applications of a common stock of intellectual faculties. Blumenbach expected that most, if not all, of the different characters among varieties arising therefrom might be considered revertible or at least changeable for individuals transposed in another variety's setting.

As a consequence, in the *Beyträge* (1790, 1806), Blumenbach stressed even more neatly the reasons why he should reject the polygenic origin hypothesis on the one hand and support a relativized typology of the human varieties on the other hand. In section X, he jointly questioned the incompatible opinions that white humans (Caucasians) do not belong to the same species as dark-skinned Africans (Ethiopians) and that humans do not form a species distinct from that of one sort of the higher primates. He insisted that the question should be treated by applying methods proper to the 'natural history of mankind',³³ in which the elements of doctrine should be exactly patterned after relevant sets of facts, duly collected and analysed. For him, an important principle to apply consisted in taking into account the 'physiology of organised bodies' as a general basis for comparisons and tracing degenerative processes across various animal species so as to relativize the presumed manifest disparities between sets of representatives of the human species. It was also deemed important to search for and investigate the intermediate varieties and transition forms that would link together the apparently extreme kinds of humans. This pronouncement is very telling:

> We must never forget that there is not a single one of the bodily differences in any one variety of man, which does not run into some of the others by such endless

shades of all sorts, that the naturalist or physiologist has yet to be born, who can with any grounds of certainty attempt to lay down any fixed bounds between these shades, and consequently between their two extremes.[34]

What is strongly stressed all along in the *Beyträge* is that the present five varieties of the human species have resulted from a long evolutionary history. The plan of the first part of the work had been conceived on purpose to highlight this assumption and grant particular meaning to the concept of degeneration as applied to mankind. Let me list the titles of the sections that lead to the core thesis:

1. On Mutability in the Creation.
2. A Glance into the Primitive World.
3. A Preadamite Primitive World Has Already Lived out Its Existence.
4. Remodelling of the Primitive World.
5. Changes in the Present Creation.
6. Degeneration of Organised Bodies.
7. Especially in the Domestic Animals.
8. Degeneration of the Most Perfect of All Domestic Animals – *Man*.[35]

It is obvious that transformist visions of the natural world were in the mood of the day, when Blumenbach was writing this piece, but, for him, these evolutionary ideas were to be somehow annexed and adjusted to the *Bildungstrieb* theory, which would thus acquire additional connotations as the key interpretative concept concerning the genesis of human varieties.

Let me now trace back the main demonstrative steps to this end. Blumenbach posited as highly probable that there had been extinctions of previous species and creations of new ones in the course of natural history, but without implying that developmental processes could have fallen short of abiding by fairly constant teleological and causal principles. Extinction is a demonstrated fact, since a great part of the preserved fossils do not correspond to present-day species. It is impossible to explain facts of that nature without admitting that successive revolutions have remodelled the conditions that allow new living species to appear. There must be a common sharing of principles between earlier life forms and later ones, and this sharing has to do with the 'general powers of nature to bring forth the new organic kingdom, similar to those which had fulfilled that object in the primitive world'.[36] Such principles boil down to relevant species-specific formative drives acting on and reacting to the physical and chemical conditions prevailing in the changing constitution of organic fluids. 'Only the formative force having to deal with materials, which must of course have been much changed by such a general revolution, was compelled to take a direction differing more or less from the old one in the production of new species.'[37] It meant that in revolutionary phases there occurred or came about original wild types that could not be identified as being either monsters or degenerative forms of a previously existing type. Such original wild types may be presumed to originate from significant mutations in the organization of structures and functions that the formative drives determined. But, as we know, those structuring organic agents may only be identified from a survey of the effects they are supposed to cause, preserve and regulate. It is the mutated conditions as observed through their particular and distinct characters that specify that original forms of *Bildungstrieb* have thus intervened. An instance of this origination of new organisms requiring previously non-existing formative drives is provided by the discovery of parasites in domestic races that were not found to be present in the original wild type. But we are essentially left to evaluate a posteriori the power of mutability in nature and the specific nature of the agents involved from the degenerative effects that produce sufficiently resilient varieties. Now, if the causal mechanical origin of degeneration is principally to be sought in the 'influence of climate, aliment, and mode of life',[38] this influence yields true variations of the archetypal form, if, and only if, the formative drive is affected and modified in its generative operations to the point of replicating such alterations through breeding and reproduction: this process is qualified as degenerative since it would implement divergences from the initial wild type, which divergences in most cases can only be hypothesized, short of any empirical evidence available about the traits of the original stock.

To study degeneration and the way it operates, the best data and analogies can be gathered from recording the natural and artificial processes of differential variation that affect species of domesticated animals more strongly than their wild equivalents. Mutability in the former is much greater than in the latter. But the highest degree of mutability should be predicated of humankind considered as a natural species. The reason for this resides in humans' capacity for domesticating themselves as if it were their presumed natural condition, that is, for reacting to manifold stimuli that can be considered the causes of degeneration, for adjusting their organization and behaviour to manifold conditions and modes of life, and for thereby inducing by so doing further and further adaptations through diverse adjustments of their formative drive. Hence this provocative inference:

> The difference between [man] and other domestic animals is only this, that they are not so completely born to domestication as he is, having been created by nature immediately a domestic animal. The exact original wild condition of most of the domestic animals is known. But no one knows the exact wild condition of man. There is none, for nature has limited him in no wise, but has created him for every mode of life, for every climate, and every sort of aliment, and has set before him the whole world as his own and given him both organic kingdoms for his aliment. But the consequence of this is that there is no second animal besides him in the creation upon whose *solidum vivum* so endless a quantity of various *stimuli*, and therefore so endless a quantity of concurring causes of degeneration, must needs operate.[39]

Under these conditions, the reference to an original archetype, as the major determinant of all the traits to be attributed to the natural kind, and as the norm for evaluating the morphological, physiological and mental effects of degeneration, fades from sight. What comes to the fore instead is the notion of a polymorphic and multifunctional formative drive from which countless varieties of resulting effects, physiological, mental and ethological flow. As the various bodily structures and vital forces elicit the potential contained in the formative drive, the physiological study of the human varieties should focus on the peculiar features that condition the exercise of these forces as derived from the quite versatile human formative drive. An instance of such a peculiarity consists in the fine and dense mucous membrane that underpins live contractility and, as a major component of the organic body, displays multiple sites for degenerative modifications, in particular those affecting skin colour. Contractility embodies the formative capacity that produces the manifold variations of that quality among human types, but there are numerous indications that these acquired qualities have never been entirely stabilized and that further transformations and even reversions could take place under changing external circumstances.

As live contractility is the least of the vital forces deriving from the formative drive, we can easily presume that, ascending to the consideration of the higher ones, we would be able to highlight a considerably larger capacity for variation and adjustment of individuals and subsequently of populations in the case of mankind, compared with the other animal kinds. Because all vital forces come about as effects of the structuring activity of the *Bildungstrieb*, the constitutive and adaptive formative drive can indeed be viewed as the essential foundational piece that grounds Blumenbach's anthropology. In turn, allegiance to this theoretical principle warranted the physiologist's belief in the monogenetic origin of the five human varieties he identified. It also supported his argument that these varieties run into one another by the infinite shades affecting their typological properties.

3. An approach different from Kant's

Now, for the sake of a conclusion, it seems appropriate to point to differences between Blumenbach's theory on human varieties and that of Kant. Both were indeed grounded on some common principles. Kant and Blumenbach postulated that the formation of organisms proceeds from formative drives or forces that convey the species type from parents to offspring. And this formative drive triggers varying effects in the structures of the organic beings in development according to the physical and chemical conditions governing these beings' interactions with their environment. On the other hand, both theorists believed that, in interbreeding, the individual patterns of the parent organisms tend to yield blends of both forms. The causal and teleological activity of the formative force is thus constantly adjusting organic processes so as to maximally maintain the replication of the specific form in line with its general structural and functional traits, while permitting contingent variations in the particular features that characterize individual offspring.

For Kant, races within a given species come about as predetermined effects of dispositions comprised in the original species-specific germs, dispositions that we may consider as pre-ordained to allow adjustments to the various geographic and climatic settings to which the human species migrated. The essential trait that differentiates those races within humankind is skin colour. This trait remains stable through interbreeding, and observations of its transmission in cases of racial hybridization are presumed to confirm how it can be disseminated according to blending ratios among the hybrids produced. Kant is clearly a monogenist theorist but one who grounds the discrimination of the four races he posits on predetermined genetic dispositions that get expressed through a typology of morphological – physiological dispositions, paradigmatically signified by skin-colour differences.

Blumenbach's theory works out differently since he does without predetermined dispositions underpinning the formation of varieties. Indeed, all varieties flow from adjustments of the formative drive to the external conditions under which this force creates the building up of the individuals of the species whose form it embodies. Some of these adjustments can be sufficiently stable to generate genetically transmissible patterns that yield the complex sets of morphological and physiological traits featured by the five main varieties of the humankind. But these sets of characteristics only represent abstract averages, and this means that the properties of those varieties comprise manifold degrees. There are no determinate borderlines separating the several varieties because of the common endowment in biological and cognitive powers that characterizes the species they belong to. Although Blumenbach posits that the humankind possesses a species-specific nature significantly different from that to be found among the higher animal forms, especially in terms of cognitive powers, he does not exclude the possibility that natural-historical processes may have entailed mutations of the stock formative drives. Thus there might have occurred, in some former epoch of nature, a prehistory of the formative drives that we currently identify by and through their current species-specific effects. But, since we do not have any access to the set of features that originally embodied the species-specific properties of the humankind, previous to their current variations, we can leave aside all speculations on our relationship with the pre-Adamite world. Doubtlessly, Blumenbach's appraisal of the human condition remains confined within the limits of a natural-historical approach whose most significant theoretical premise consists in admitting formative drives that provide sufficient reasons for the observable features that make us differentiate human populations from one another. Such an empirical discrimination of varieties is doubly relative. On the one hand, it is to be considered as historically contingent since it depends upon special adaptations of the original human formative drive to changing biogeographical circumstances. On the other hand, the core species-specific properties that the formative drive yields, notwithstanding those variations, cannot be derived from a metaphysical view of what the human nature might consist of. The sets which these properties form can only be empirically assessed from the consequent behaviour of humans in their diverse vital surroundings. And it might not even be absurd to presume that the formative drive that yields those emergent phenomena has itself resulted from previous mutations of organic forces in nature. A divine plan for the creation might still be predicated that would make sense of a normative concept of human nature. But Blumenbach, the naturalist, remains reluctant to admit metaphysical presuppositions that would imply extrapolating from natural-historical data to a transcendent system of final causes. He prefers to pragmatically endorse a limited and essentially heuristic teleological interpretation of the specific harmony of traits and actions that seems to be required to account for the historical development of humans as similarly endowed organic beings throughout their variations.

Notes

1. Blumenbach, *Anthropological Treatises*. This is the edition that is referred to in the present chapter.
2. Blumenbach (1776, 1795 and 1806) translated into English, are to be found respectively in *Anthropological Treatises*, 65–143; 145–324; 325–42.
3. On Haller's theory of generation, see Monti (1990), Duchesneau (2012), 403–44. On Bonnet's theory of organic bodies, see Duchesneau (2006).
4. Blumenbach, *Anthropological Treatises* (1776), 71–2.
5. See Sloan (1979).
6. See Bolduc (2013).
7. Blumenbach, *Anthropological Treatises* [1776], 82.
8. Ibid. (1776), 97–8.
9. Ibid. (1776), 98.
10. Ibid. (1795), §80–1, 264.
11. Ibid. (1781), 100.
12. Ibid. (1806), 305–12.
13. Ibid. (1806), 312.
14. Ibid. (1795), §89, 275. The non-hierarchical and non-essentialist nature of Blumenbach's typology of human varieties has been well analysed by Junker (2019).
15. Ibid. (1795), §82, 265.
16. Ibid. (1795), 150.
17. Ibid. (1795), 151.
18. See *Discours préliminaire*, in De Luc (1798), XXVII–CXXVIII.
19. Blumenbach, *Anthropological Treatises* (1806), 315.
20. Ibid. [1806], 317.
21. Letter to G. G. Gackenholtz, in Leibniz (1768), II-2, 169–74.
22. *Nouveaux Essais sur l'entendement humain*, 3.6.12 and 4.16.12, in Leibniz (1962), VI, 6: 307 and 473. For interpretations, see Duchesneau (2010), 107–17; Smith (2011), 243–50, 303–10.
23. Blumenbach, *Anthropological Treatises* (1795), §90, 275–6.
24. Ibid. (1795), §90, 276.
25. On Blumenbach's physiology and theory of generation, see Duchesneau (2014), 113–35; Duchesneau (2018), 379–415; Zammito (2018), 186–214.
26. Blumenbach, *Anthropological Treatises* (1795), §32, 193–4.
27. Ibid. [1795], §33, 194. The beginning of that quotation evokes a formulation to be found in Kant's *Critique of Judgement*, §81, Kant (1968), AA V, 424, with reference to Blumenbach's doctrine of the *Bildungstrieb*.
28. That debate started with Richards (2000). Richards's critique was essentially addressed to Timothy Lenoir's unduly assimilative interpretations in Lenoir (1982).
29. See Duchesneau (2018), 410–12.
30. Kant's theory of generation and race formation developed stepwise in his essays: *Von den verschiedenen Racen der Menschen* (1775); *Bestimmung des Begriffs einer Menschenrace* (1785); *Über den Gebrauch teleologischer Principien in der Philosophie* (1788). For interpretations, see Sloan (2002); Huneman (2008); Duchesneau (2018), 425–39.
31. Blumenbach, *Anthropological Treatises* (1795), §33, 196.
32. Ibid. [1795], §33, 196.

33 Ibid. (1806), 298.
34 Ibid. (1806), 297–8.
35 J. H. Zammito provides a remarkable analysis of Blumenbach's paleontological views, in Zammito (2018), 215–44, and Zammito (2019).
36 Blumenbach, *Anthropological Treatises* (1806), 287.
37 Ibid. (1806), 287.
38 Ibid. (1806), 291.
39 Ibid. (1806), 294.

References

Blumenbach, J. F. (1776), *De humani generis varietate nativa liber*, Göttingen: Vandenhoeck.
Blumenbach, J. F. (1779), *Handbuch der Naturgeschichte*, Göttingen: Dieterich.
Blumenbach, J. F. (1781), *Über den Bildungstrieb und das Zeugungsgeschäfte*, Göttingen: Dieterich.
Blumenbach, J. F. (1787), *Institutiones physiologicae*, Göttingen: Dieterich.
Blumenbach, J. F. (1795), *De humani generis varietate nativa*, 3rd ed., Göttingen: Vandenhoek and Ruprecht.
Blumenbach, J. F. (1805), *Handbuch der vergleichenden Anatomie*, Göttingen: Dieterich.
Blumenbach, J. F. (1806), *Beyträge zur Naturgeschichte*, 2nd ed., Göttingen: Dieterich.
Blumenbach, J. F. (1865), *The Anthropological Treatises*, trans. and ed. Thomas Bendyshe, London: Longman, Roberts, & Green.
Bolduc, J. S. (2013), 'La théorie des instincts d'Hermann Samuel Reimarus', *Dix-Huitième Siècle*, 45: 585–603.
De Luc, J. A. (1798), *Lettres sur l'histoire physique de la Terre, adressées à M. le Professeur Blumenbach*, Paris: Nyon.
Duchesneau, F. (2010), *Leibniz: Le vivant et l'organisme*, Paris: Vrin.
Duchesneau, F. (2012), *La Physiologie des Lumières: Empirisme, modèles et théories*, Paris: Classiques Garnier.
Duchesneau, F. (2014), 'Blumenbach on Teleology and the Laws of Vital Organization', *Verifiche*, 43 (1–3): 113–35.
Duchesneau, F. (2018), *Organisme et corps organique de Leibniz à Kant*, Paris: Vrin.
Huneman, P. (2008), *Métaphysique et biologie: Kant et la constitution du concept d'organisme*, Paris: Kimé.
Junker, T. (2019), 'Blumenbach's Theory of Human Races and the Natural Unity of Humankind', in Rupke and Lauer (2019), 96–112.
Kant, I. ([1775] 1968), *Von den verschiedenen Racen der Menschen*, in Berlin-Brandenburgische Akademie der Wissenschaften (ed.), *Kants Gesammelte Werke*, Berlin: Walter de Gruyter (henceforth AA), I. 2, 427–43.
Kant, I. ([1785] 1968), *Bestimmung des Begriffs einer Menschenrace*, in Kant, AA I. 8, 89–106.
Kant, I. ([1788] 1968), *Über den Gebrauch teleologischer Principien in der Philosophie*, Kant, AA I. 8, 157–84.
Kant, I. ([1790] 1968), *Kritik der Urteilskraft*, in Kant AA V, 165–485.
Leibniz, G. W. (1768), *Opera omnia*, ed. L. Dutens, Geneva: Fratres De Tournes.
Leibniz, G. W. (1962), *Sämtliche Schriften und Briefe*, VI-6, Berlin: Akademie-Verlag.

Lenoir, T. (1982), *The Strategy of Life: Teleology and Mechanism in Nineteenth Century German Biology*, Dordrecht: Reidel.

Monti, M. T. (1990), *Congettura ed esperienza nella fisiologia di Haller: La riforma dell'anatomia animata e il sistema della generazione*, Florence: Olschki.

Richards, R. J. (2000), 'Kant and Blumenbach on the Bildungstrieb: A Historical Misunderstanding', *Studies in History and Philosophy of Biological and Biomedical Sciences*, 31: 11–32.

Rupke, N. & Lauer, G., eds (2019), *Johann Friedrich Blumenbach: Races and Natural History, 1750–1850*, London: Routledge.

Sloan, P. R. (1979), 'Buffon, German Biology, and the Historical Interpretation of Biological Species', *British Journal for the History of Science*, 12: 109–53.

Sloan, P. R. (2002), 'Preforming the Categories: Eighteenth-Century Theory and the Biological Roots of Kant's a priori', *Journal of the History of Philosophy*, 40: 229–53.

Smith, J. E. H. (2011), *Divine Machines: Leibniz and the Sciences of Life*, Princeton: Princeton University Press.

Zammito, J. H. (2018), *The Gestation of German Biology: Physiology from Stahl to Schelling*, Chicago: University of Chicago Press.

Zammito, J. H. (2019), 'The Rise of Paleontology and the Hybridicization of Nature: Blumenbach and Deluc', in Rupke and Lauer (2019), 197–232.

13

Can Kant's man be a woman?

Charlotte Morel

This volume being in English gives me the opportunity to make a play on words. It would not have been possible in German, since Kant's native language does make the distinction between the two terms in play here, *Mensch* and *Mann*.[1] But my facetious title reminds us that, although Kant of course makes use of the proper German universalizing term for mankind, i.e. *Mensch* as an individual *specimen* of *Menschheit*, we are still justified in entertaining doubts about a gendered bias in his consideration of humanity. Moreover, such a bias becomes even more problematic when we consider that his thought on this question goes so far as to shape, philosophically speaking, the humanity concept as an *ideal of Enlightenment*.

As is now very well known, many of Kant's assertions about women, which we cannot fail nowadays to view as crude misogyny, suggest that he did not necessarily include women in the enlightening goal. This goal he assigned to the development of humankind and to human beings, insofar as they are morally in charge of attaining *majority of reason* and of using *principles* to reach the status of an active moral subject.[2] This indeed is an issue which feminist thought has been very eager to explore since what is now known as the Gilligan – Kohlberg controversy and its repercussions.[3] Actually, I do not intend to pronounce a new verdict convicting or acquitting Kant of misogyny, with or without mitigating factors. It is not my intent to convict or acquit the German Enlightenment, with Kant as its spokesperson, of a discourse that is ideologically oppressive, even unconsciously, and directed against the female part of mankind.[4] But we shall reflect on what Kant writes regarding the conflict between humanity (as universal) and empirical differences – here, gendered differences (as particularities) – which may enable us to determine what remains of undoubtable interest, whatever Kant's strong ambiguities on this subject. Our theme thus appears to evoke a daunting issue introduced by Kant: how are the ideal and the empirical structurally connected in the human being?[5] We should recall here how Michel Foucault showed that the very connection between Kant's anthropology and 'critical enterprise' had to be the focal point of the debate.[6]

Another question is whether the very way in which Kant factually, or textually, deals with such concrete human particularities reveals to us an insufficient, since merely formal, conception of universality. After Hegel, that is the claim made against

Kant once again by many contemporary authors, and not only feminist ones.[7] Jumping ahead to what I think comes out of this inquiry: Kant's 'anthropological' statements make explicit a perspective that happens to be crucial because it is indeed causative here – that is, the issue of desire (between the sexes). From this perspective, is it in all respects true to say that Kant's conception of the subject is a disembodied one, as feminist thinkers have argued in the wake of Gilligan's book?[8]

1. How does the particular connect to the universal? The universal and the female

1.1. General issue

Formulating the general problem as above has the advantage of showing why feminist thought actually found in Kant very much more than a (misogynistic) opponent. Indeed, the two sides can be said to *share* the problem of connecting humanity considered as an ideal with the concrete particularities of the empirical human individual.[9]

The problem here reveals itself as twofold. First, it arises for every empirical difference we can think of; that is, for every human particularity that could place an individual in a dominated minority within a social or political group of a dominant and different nature.

Second, there is the gendered empirical difference between men and women – particularly in the light of Kant's view of women – which implies a further assumption regarding the relationship of the particular to the universal. It has been one of the great achievements of feminist thought to reveal this and to show how the universal is at risk of being identified with the masculine (which, by definition, is the particular). Moreover, feminist thought has pointed out the consequence of such identification: that women have been *denied* the legitimacy or even ability to understand and orientate their subjective acts relative to a universal level sufficient to determine their meaning (as governed by an ideal). This also holds for Kant's view of women.

As critical philosophers, we know that we must tread carefully when dealing with the concept of the universal. On the one hand, talking about 'human' and 'humanity' means considering all empirical differences (ethnical, cultural, sociological and so on) as governed by a universal level that transcends them. In this respect, the Enlightenment with its universalist perspective provides a real chance of emancipation. On the other hand, this emancipatory perspective would entirely vanish in the following case: if the universal were not what it is claimed to be. This would mean that it could unconsciously represent an empirical difference, *while* claiming to be universal. In this way, the universal reach of subjectivity is, so to speak, appropriated by the male part of the human species. Feminist scholars have given different names to this conceptual shift. For example, Seyla Benhabib calls it a 'substitutionalist universality'. Here, the part is substituting for the whole (e.g. when only men have legitimate access to the universality of the *public sphere*[10]). Etienne Balibar calls this a 'synecdoche of the universal'.[11]

1.2. An internal contradiction in Kant

Regarding Kant and the issue of women, let us consider the relationship of each sex to *morality* as one side of this more general problem.

(a) First, we need to consider how the concept of humanity is linked to the concept of morality and to the structure of an ideal: Kant explicitly characterizes humanity as an *idea* (in his technical sense of the term). What makes this humanity an ideal is thus purely *derived from* moral nature: the 'human being' (*der Mensch*) is in itself an 'end', and even a 'final end for creation' insofar as he is the subject of moral law (*Critique of Judgment*).[12] As such, he takes his guidance from 'the idea of humanity, which he … carries in his soul as the archetype of his actions', though on the empirical level he is unable to fulfil this 'idea of what is most perfect in its kind' (*Critique of Pure Reason*).[13] Therefore, it is 'the moral disposition in us' that stands for the dimension of humanity in us, turning out to be 'indissociable' from this dimension and *acting as* the 'true ideal' (*Conflict of Faculties*).[14]

Moreover, considering the critical phase of Kant's moral philosophy, morality itself is now structurally linked to the perspective of universality regarding the maxims of our actions (see the first and second formulas of the categorical imperative in the *Groundwork of the Metaphysics of Morals*).[15] Therefore, acting morally should mean acting not only as an individual with his/her particular motives but as *human* as well: i.e. from the universal point of view of *any* representative of humankind. It should also mean *considering everyone*, from this universal point of view, as such a representative (see the last wording of the categorical imperative).[16]

(b) But if we also consider Kant's pre-critical texts from 1764, we are now faced with a difference between men and women with regard to the way morality is conceived. Actually, this contrast between two opposite gendered understandings of virtue appears as a consequence, in the ethical field, of the paradigmatic distinction between the sublime and the beautiful, which gives the whole text of the *Observations on the Feeling of the Beautiful and Sublime* its consistency. Such a distinction applied on an ethical level requires distinguishing between a sublime-oriented and a beautiful-oriented virtue so that, in Kant's text, the *conceptual* distinction between the sublime and the beautiful is in harmony with the difference between the sexes.

> The virtue of the woman is a *beautiful virtue*. That of the male ought to be a *noble virtue*. Women will avoid evil not because it is unjust but because it is ugly, and for them virtuous actions mean those that are ethically beautiful. Nothing of ought, nothing of must, nothing of obligation. To a woman anything by way of orders and sullen compulsion is insufferable. They do something only because they love to, and the art lies in making sure that they love only what is good. It is difficult for me to believe that the fair sex is capable of principles, and I hope not to give offense by this, for these are also extremely rare among the male sex.[17]

And indeed, only the 'noble' male virtue will correspond to the later characterization of morality as obeying moral *law*. Conversely, women's virtue, referred to as beautiful, will no longer fit this later conception of morality and has to be excluded from the realm of morality, being assigned instead to the field of *pathological* motives.[18]

Regarding both (a) and (b), when considering the whole of Kant's philosophy (while *not* trying to consider the issue of distinguishing in this work between *two* lines of thought, the anthropological and the critical),[19] we come up against real difficulties. Two contradictions appear.

The first is the most obvious and has already been mentioned: how could Kant consistently locate the 'categorical imperative of the Enlightenment' in the attempt to gain majority of reason and yet exclude women from this ideal?[20] The second concerns the moral ideal defining humanity, which coincides with one of the poles of an empirical difference (i.e. with masculine, not feminine, virtue), such that we can (or even *must*) object, from a purely internal or philosophical perspective, that the empirical element has intruded into 'pure reason'. Thus Kant himself puts us in a position to invalidate either (1) his empirical typology of the difference between the sexes[21] or (2) the whole conception of morality as a pure relation to law: when we assume (1), paradoxically, this relation can no longer be pure.

Of these two aporias, the second should be more difficult to deal with as well as posing a greater threat to Kant, since what it threatens is the consistency of the system itself.[22] In fact, the first contradiction could be said to be located on the anthropological level, whereas the second concerns the critical level. In the first case, the question is that of empirical differences which are at risk of conflicting both with purity in reason and its correlate regarding the orientation of the subject towards universality. In the second case, the issue we face is how individuals pragmatically deal with normative demands such as the categorical imperatives, while somehow failing to connect properly with a more accurate interpretation of the empirical-social world.[23]

Confronted with this distance in time between these 'critical' and 'pre-critical' conceptions of an undivided human morality, *or* a twofold gendered morality, it might be tempting to consider the possibility of Kant having simply *moved* from one position to the other. Then, this could be seen as an expression of a critical shift in the field of the practical, since it now means that no empirical difference between humans can be regarded as legitimate cause for relegating them to any different position with regard to the now common ideal of humanity. But as we know, this way out does *not* seem feasible: indeed, there is evidence that this gendered idea persists, strictly speaking, in the anthropological writings based on Kant's lectures on this topic delivered from 1772 until the end of his professorship in 1797, and the final publication of a fully revised version of this course in 1798. So that these later considerations related to our gender issue are now explicitly assigned to *anthropology*, which Kant himself introduced as an academic discipline: that is, as can be inferred from the *Architectonic* in the *Critique of Pure Reason*, a discipline which should not really be part of the *system* of philosophy[24] but which Kant still saw as part of the training or education of the philosopher.

It is true that these considerations are no longer as significant as they were in the *Observations*; the very explicitly construed parallel of a male 'noble virtue' and a female 'beautiful virtue' has disappeared.[25] Nevertheless, it is still stated that 'feminine virtue or lack of virtue is very different from masculine virtue or lack of virtue, not only in kind but as regards incentive'.[26] The moral quality of a woman should then be 'patience',[27] but above, we find the following definition of patience as opposed to courage.

> *Courage* ... rests on principles and is a virtue ... Accordingly, *patience* is not courage. Patience is a feminine virtue; for it does not muster the force for resistance but hopes to make suffering (enduring) imperceptible through habit.[28]

And again, in the *Collegentwürfe* from the 1780s: 'Patience is not courage. The latter [is] male, the former female (to get accustomed is virtue for donkeys).'[29] The statements about female minority are to be found in the published text from 1798. There are remarks from 1776 to 1778 on that point as well,[30] and finally, still in the published version, we only find one remark about exceptional women showing true *character*.[31]

Obviously, Kant does not manage to align pragmatic expectations concerning the female sex and ideal prescriptions for '*Menschen*', i.e. representatives of humankind in general. But this is exactly why I assume that, although Kant's statements about women amount to misogyny, his work as a whole does not really conflict with feminist approaches. Rather, it faces, as a *system*, the very same problem these latter strive to raise and to discuss,[32] namely how *can* empirical differences between humans (objects of a philosophical *anthropology*) ever conflict with the ideal determination of humanity (as a corollary to the *critical* dimension of practical reason)?

1.3. Kant and feminist thought: (Quite) a complex confrontation

I am perfectly aware that 'feminist thought' cannot legitimately be evoked as if it were a homogeneous whole with a single voice. Indeed, the *Different Voice* which Carol Gilligan manifested in her controversial debate with Lawrence Kohlberg about a gendered bias in the representations of 'what is good' has actually given way to further different voices in the field of feminist approaches confronting Kantian thought. Robin Schott, as an editor of the collective work *Feminist Interpretations of Immanuel Kant*, reminds us in particular how the wider question of *Enlightenment* and of an *enlightened reason* has divided feminist thinkers.[33] In the current state of affairs, automatically viewing 'Kantian thought' and 'feminist thought' as incompatible is no longer an option.[34]

Of course, starting from the Kohlberg – Gilligan discussion, we can identify a large stream of positions objecting to Kant as the spokesperson of ethical formalism, assuming that such a formalism in principle opposes or even excludes the 'concrete ethics' or 'connectedness' which feminist approaches seek to promote. Nevertheless, some less common positions take a conciliatory, synthesis-seeking view: 'universalism' should not end in 'disembedded ethics', nor should 'concrete' ethics ever abandon what remains the essential strength of universalism: a perspective on how to reverse alienation. Actually, concreteness implies two directions here, i.e. the need to consider one or both of the following factors in the ethical field: (1) bodily matters or (2) concrete ways of connecting with other people, including using every possible means of feeling, empathizing, caring.[35]

Here we also encounter what rapidly became a major disjunction of perspective between feminist approaches, i.e. between a *universalist* and a *differentialist* approach. As for the way Kant's corpus tackles the issue of women's recognition, what is at stake clearly appears to be how to maintain a universalist perspective while also recognizing the difference between the two genders. Thus, Kant's moral and 'formal' ethics cannot really be rejected *in favour of* a feminist differentialism (promoting care and feeling).[36] Even though such an ethical claim is diametrically opposed to Kant's, the treatment of women's feelings under feminist differentialism does not seem – to me – very different from Kant's theorizing on female virtue in the pre-critical *Observations*.[37]

In what comes next, I will discuss Kant's enlightened demand for universalism with regard to humanity while also questioning his assumptions about women in the 'anthropological' part of his work, wherein I also include the texts from 1764. Our guideline will then be the internal problem we have just stated: if an empirically gendered element (i.e. the masculine) intrudes into 'pure reason', the very structure of the critical system seems to be disrupted. Nevertheless, this does not imply any refutation of the critical enterprise in itself, whose aim is to elucidate, on the theoretical side, the transcendental, and on the practical side, the ideal, positing them as valid philosophical foundations for human life or action. Rather, I am interested in exploring a different understanding of their genesis, which may involve something other than 'pure' reason and question the notion that ideality can primarily be anchored in the way subjects have to deal with desire, even when guided by reason. I will show how the Kantian perspective on women is situated within a larger issue that can be found in his anthropological writings. This issue could be referred to as an attempt to anatomize the relationships between (gendered) individuals as desire relationships. We are actually dealing here with a possible re-connection of the anthropological and the critical thought of Kant, although extended, so to speak, beyond Kant himself.

2. Can universality in reason be pure?[38]

2. 1. Kant's *observations* as an anatomy of desire

Let us take a closer look at the *Observations on the Feeling of the Beautiful and Sublime*. Its third part is dedicated to '*the distinction of the beautiful and sublime in the interrelations of the two sexes*'. Clearly, and as is widely acknowledged, Kant himself begins by distancing his text from a philosophical perspective by adopting the role of an *observer*.[39] We can only concur with Kant scholar Ursula Pia Jauch when she notes that Kant's perspective in this text, especially in the third section, is subjective, as he himself admits. That is, it presents us *explicitly* with the perspective of a male observer, insofar as men are clearly referred to as 'we'.[40]

So that when, in one of the next sentences, Kant uses the indefinite to express what 'one expects' ('*erwartet man*') from each sex, it is clear that these expectations can be understood as *men*'s expectations. At the end of this first paragraph, we would also be justified in concluding that using the adjective 'charming' to qualify the difference between the sexes itself is nothing but a male appreciation of Kant's own criteria: first, the feeling of beauty itself has been associated with 'charm', and second, the very intent of section three is to link men to the sublime and women to beauty.

But what is 'charm'? The original German term is '*Reiz*': 'Das Erhabene *rührt*, das Schöne *reizt*' ('The sublime *touches*, the beautiful *charms*.'[41]). In German it is quite obvious that this term applied to women, among other 'objects of the feeling of beauty' (title of section one), takes on a specific meaning. I assume that the overall perspective of this male observer in section three is governed by this gendered meaning – which would then also explain why it is so important here that 'it is here not enough to represent that one has human beings before one: one must also not forget that these human beings are not all of the same sort'.[42] Later on in the text, Kant is, as a matter of fact, very clear on that point: 'However, since no matter how far one might try to go around this secret, the sexual inclination is still in the end the ground of all other charms (*Reizen*).'[43]

Indeed, terms like '*Reiz*', '*reizend*' and '*reizen*' are used so frequently throughout the text that there is really no doubt that this attraction shapes the main perspective from which the fuller subject is considered here[44]: 'the ends of nature are aimed more at *ennobling* the man and *beautifying* the woman by means of the sexual inclination.'[45]

Consequently, the attraction between the sexes explains why the conceptual gendered opposition between beautiful and sublime finally turns into a mirroring process:

> The woman has a preeminent feeling for the *beautiful*, so far as it pertains to *herself*, but for the *noble* in so far as it is found in the *male sex*. The man, on the contrary, has a decided feeling for the *noble* that belongs to *his* qualities, but for the *beautiful* in so far as it is to be found in the *woman*. From this it must follow that ….[46]

In the end, the attraction between the sexes appears to be both

(1) the cause of men/women *being assigned to* their respective side of the sublime/beautiful distinction (as is *expected of* them); 'being assigned' meaning here possessing 'particular characteristics' ('*eigentümliche Züge*', '*Eigenschaften*');[47] as well as, within these characteristics, a particular '*sense*' of the quality each sex has been allotted ('Women have a stronger innate feeling for everything that is beautiful, decorative, and adorned'[48]).
(2) the cause of either sex developing the *opposite sense* to some extent, that is, a sensitivity to what *it expects from* the other (see the previous quotation)!

At this stage, let us merely consider that, in this work, the until then very serious philosopher Kant purposely stops being purely a philosopher in order to adopt a 'situated' perspective which enables him to both evoke and analyse a social fact: the difference between the sexes is accompanied by sexual attraction. As a consequence, I entirely share Jauch's unwillingness to address such 'observations' as if they were crudely contradicting the later critical ethical system.[49] And indeed Kant himself attempts to be clear about this: 'but as far as strict moral judgment is concerned, it does not belong here, since in the sentiment of the beautiful I have to observe and explain only the appearances'.[50]

This of course does not prevent Kant's perspective in these *Observations* from proving to be misogynistic. What we have here is 'standard' sexism concerning the expectations of men with regard to women (as well as the expectations of women with regard to men, *as our male observer can report them*).[51] But we can at least take comfort in the thought that we are *not* dealing with any philosophical claim that such expectations as they actually manifest themselves correspond to what *ought to be*.

Nevertheless, I am aware that this interpretation remains, to a certain extent, incomplete and am prepared to explain my reading of Kant's intentions further. Insofar as our observer actually remains at the level of *observation* so as to *analyse* things, I would tend to praise his accuracy and to be grateful for it. As a reader, similar to other readers, I can make sense of the apparent dichotomy of Kant's universalism and his misogyny in the following way. This text actually *unveils* for us how the gendered interaction based on sexual attraction is able to shape the very perception of what the other sex *is*, as well as wishes, expectations and prescriptions about what the other sex *should* be. The latter is here understood as a *hypothetical* imperative: what it *should be in order to tally best with the empirical desire* connected to the gender difference itself.[52]

But this is precisely the point at which an *analytic* conception of anthropology should not turn into a *pragmatic* one. As we know, Kant defines anthropology in its pragmatic dimension as the 'knowledge of the human being [which] concerns ... what he as a free-acting being makes of himself, or can and should make of himself'.[53] This is the reason why the great issue of pragmatic anthropology is *education*. As a consequence, this kind of anthropology cannot avoid normativity.

Do the remarks of our observer also come under such pragmatism? The answer is yes. Indeed, the essay also contains corresponding remarks about an appropriate female education – that is, appropriate to the perception of women as 'charming' and to the further expectation of them *remaining* charming above all other characteristics.

> Deep reflection and a long drawn out consideration are noble, but are grave and not well suited for a person *in whom the unconstrained charms should indicate nothing other than a beautiful nature*. Laborious learning or painful grubbing, even if a woman could get very far with them, destroy the merits that are proper to her sex, and on account of their rarity may well make her into an object of a cold admiration, but at the same time *they will weaken the charms by means of which she exercises her great power over the opposite sex*. ... The beauties can leave Descartes' vortices rotating forever without worrying about them, even if the suave Fontenelle wanted to join them under the planets, and the attraction of their charms loses nothing of its power even if they know nothing of what Algarotti has taken the trouble to lay out for their advantage about the attractive powers of crude matter according to Newton.[54]

Writing this essay, which is *not* an academic treatise, Kant knows there will be many women in his readership. Is this why he proves that he knows how to be even more

Machiavellian than the men he is speaking of in the next argument, against encouraging women to cultivate scholarliness and knowledge?

> It seems to be malicious cunning on the part of men that they have wanted to mislead the fair sex into this perverted taste. For well aware of *their weakness with respect to the natural charms of the latter, and that a single sly glance can throw them into more confusion than the most difficult question in school*, as soon as the woman has given way to this taste they see themselves in a decided superiority and are at an advantage, which it would otherwise be difficult for them to have, of helping the vanity of the weak with generous indulgence.[55]

This means that the argument developed here is always based on the premise that men are, literally, in thrall to their sexual attraction towards women.[56]

In the *Observations*, virtue in turn is related to its effect on men's attraction to women: the 'pretty woman' ('*hübsch*') with nothing more than 'external charms' ('*äußere Reize*') will not appeal in the same way as the one whose face expresses moral virtue. But *what* moral virtue, since male and female are assumed to oppose each other according to the overall disjunction of the sublime and the beautiful? We should be surprised to see Kant applying here the very distinction between beautiful and sublime *within* the feminine pole:

> As for the expression of the features, the eyes and the mien that are moral, this **pertains either to the feeling of the sublime or of the beautiful.** A woman in whom the agreeable qualities that become her sex are salient, especially **the moral expression of the sublime**, is called *beautiful* in the proper sense; one whose moral design ... announces the qualities of the beautiful, is *agreeable,* and if she is that to a higher degree, **charming** (*reizend*).[57]

It becomes obvious here that when Kant assumes the disjunction of the beautiful and the sublime to be parallel to the difference between the sexes, he is actually proposing what we would call *ideal types* much more than inferring a pattern on the basis of empirical observation (though claiming to do so).[58] And Kant assumes that the expression of the sublime by a woman appeals more strongly to certain men (or at least, as he almost confesses, to him).[59] According to Kant, the reason for this is the stronger 'feeling of the sublime' in men.[60]

All this could be taken as internal limitations of Kant's overall conception in this text. As we have seen, there is an essential ambiguity in the ethical qualities Kant is pointing out, such as the 'feeling of the sublime': does possessing this quality mean tending to have a certain kind of feeling *oneself,* in one's own *ethos*? Or does it mean having a 'sense' for a quality *in others*? But having this '*feeling of*' in the second meaning seems, in turn, to depend on the first, i.e. having the ability to feel this way. In other words, men who are endowed with 'a feeling for the sublime' enjoy in women the expression of the same moral quality. Although the reader might not automatically take issue with this, characterizing one sex by only *one* of the paradigmatic 'senses of' 'beautiful' or 'sublime' does not fit the book's overarching thesis. If, due to his sense of the sublime in both meanings of the term, a man A is attracted by a woman B, this implies that this woman B possesses and expresses the 'sense of the sublime' in its first meaning. In short, the very way in which Kant accounts for men's desires here conflicts with the general premise of a strictly gendered virtue.

In the end, this kind of 'inconsequence' is all that prevents Kant from making a far worse pronouncement than he actually does on women's moral education. If he were to take this to the bitter end, he would probably wind up with the same conclusions as when he objected to women engaging in erudition and knowledge. Indeed, in order to prevent men from suffering too badly from their 'weakness towards [the] natural charm' of women, would it not be better to have nothing but pretty and *not* charming or even beautiful women, insofar as the former, just like ' a bunch of flowers', can arouse nothing more than 'a cold approbation'?[61]

That this is *not* the case proves to me that the crucial factor in the analysis here is not primarily the distinction between the sublime and the beautiful but rather the very *fact* of attraction: the latter being indeed both an *object* of analysis *and*, once analysed (taking the opposite paradigmatic qualities, beautiful and sublime, as *possible directions of attraction*), the real *means* of performing the correlated analysis of the difference between the sexes. But since the observation is 'situated', the very distinction between sublime and beautiful (as a result of the first analysis) could well prove to be distorted when no longer treated as an *analysed fact* but used in addition as an *analysing perspective*: male desire for women targets them in fact from *both* directions of attraction, so what is the purpose of labelling the sexes with these opposing directions?

Up to this point in my analysis of this text, I think that there is no other way out than to underline the instrumentalizing perspective regarding the female part of the 'equation', which derives from the situated perspective of the observer. If women are also given a sense of morality and noble qualities, then once more it is only *because of men*. We need to account for two different expectations from men.

(1) First, they *expect to be desired* as 'noble souls': here we need to refer to the previous quotation again.
(2) Second, they expect to benefit from women desiring them as 'noble souls'. The benefit lies in their being incited towards moral perfection – as demonstrated by the following part of the previous quotation:

> From this one can judge what powerful influences the sexual inclination could have in ennobling especially the masculine sex if, in place of many dry lessons, the moral feeling of woman were developed in good time.[62]

To conclude this textual analysis, I will consider a last remark by Kant, made about women in an analysis of the moral value of sexual modesty. Here, however, I would like to suggest that we can apply it to Kant's men as well: 'a supplement to principles [is accordingly most necessary] … ; for there is no case in which inclination so readily becomes a sophist cooking up complaisant principles as here'.[63]

When it comes to this 'supplement to principles', offered here to women in place of the propensity to act morally in the later Kantian meaning of this term (i.e. based on moral *principle*s), we would advise the male observer not to dismiss it too fast for his own sake. Otherwise, he strongly risks showing *himself to be the sophist* here, with his gendered pretensions to 'sublimity' in the approach to morality.[64]

Actually, what does this 'supplement' consist of? I assume it is to be found in the 'way we desire'. Applied to men, this remark would then mean that the assumption of 'pure' moral principles without this 'desire supplement' could well be deceptive. And if, on the contrary, we recognize the effectiveness of desire *in bringing the subject to principles* and in helping to *sustain the meaning of principles* within moral agency, the result might be very different. Far from promoting a 'pathological' instance instead of morality, that is abolishing morality and principles, desire here can be considered as a generative factor which can also inform a *critical positive* perspective on the ideal effectiveness of moral principles.

If feminist thought is what it takes to remind us of this very point, then I'd go along with it. That would enable me to answer my title's question in the affirmative: women reflecting on their distorted image (or men reflecting on women's distorted image of men) using Kant's conceptual tools can, in so doing, still be Kantians. Kant's 'supplement to principles' (i.e. taking into account the empirical desire issue) no longer prevents us from addressing ideal universality – and thus proving to be *human* beings. Indeed, this is a lesson to be learnt from Kant's anthropology – when we challenge it to its limits.

Notes

1 See the comment by Étienne Balibar on a text from Mary Wollstonecraft: there is only one word in English to mean both what German distinguishes as '*Mann*' and '*Mensch*', i.e. the male human being and the human being generically speaking, as a representative of his kind ('*Gattungswesen*'); as a consequence there can be 'a great difference between man and man'; Balibar (2011), 479–80.
2 Insofar as knowledge is the goal (*sapere aude* ....), the first issue is the gendered characterization of the intellect. On this matter see for instance Jauch (1989), 71–81. The second issue is a gendered characterization of virtue, mainly in the 1764 text which we will be discussing in this chapter.
3 See Gilligan (1982), Kohlberg (1981), Benhabib (1987) and Schott (1997b).
4 I would point out that the mention of the 'entire fair sex' in the beginning of *What Is Enlightenment* does not prejudge what *could be* done by women to engage, in addition to 'the overwhelming majority of mankind', in a process of freeing themselves from minority or non-age under the guidance of their (male) 'guardians' (Kant ([1784] 1996), 16–17; ([1784] 1969); AA VIII, 35). Unlike other remarks by Kant (for instance, where women are compared to children), here women are included in this whole of a humankind whose enlightened status has just been pronounced. That in their case the problem is a more specific one, though, is clear from the very mention of the female part of humankind as a collective ('the entire fair sex'). Only *other* texts from Kant reveal that his overall conception of women within society – through his theory on marriage, where husbands are in fact recognized in their role as guardians of their wives (*Anthropologie*, §48: Kant ([1798], 1973); AA 7, 209; *Observations*: Kant ([1764] 1969); AA 2, 240) – barely

goes beyond a *theoretical* recognition that women are just potential minors *among others if it were not* for the empirical fact of a state of society and civil law. In that sense, I would agree that *as a whole*, Kant's statements about women do show the 'failure of his attempts to match the ethical postulates of Enlightenment to the features of the woman ideal in a developing bourgeois society', as stated by Bennent (1985), quoted by Jauch (1989), 36. However, the *effect* of *this* text itself about Enlightenment should not be minimized. To this extent, the universality implied by the Kantian concept of humankind does correspond to 'intensive', 'symbolic' or 'ideal' universality, which Balibar defined among other kinds of 'universalities'; Balibar (1997), 441, 444.

5   I fully agree with Patrick Frierson's account of the problem here when he says that the 'divided response to Kant's thought highlights ... the problem that arises within Kant's own anthropology' or a 'tension internal to Kant'; Frierson (2013), 99.
6   See Foucault (2002), for instance 12–13, 20. Foucault's position on this problem is well known: 'De la *Critique* à l'*Anthropologie*, il y aurait comme un rapport de finalité obscure et obstinée'; Foucault (2002), 13.
7   For a summary of this debate see Sedwick (1997), 78, and Benhabib (1987), 92.
8   See Schott (1997b), 9–10; Benhabib (1987), 81 for instance.
9   Cf. Frierson (2013), 99–100, quoted below.
10 See on the one hand Kant's characterization of a 'public use of reason' in *What Is Enlightenment?*; Kant ([1784] 1996), 17; ([1784] 1969); AA VIII, 37); and on the other hand §48 of the *Anthropology* (see above, footnote 4).
11 Benhabib (1987), 81; Balibar (2011), 480, when commenting on Mary Wollstonecraft's text (see footnote 1): 'C'est là exactement ce que j'appelle la synecdoque de l'universel, conformément à la définition classique de ce trope: prendre la partie pour le tout. D'un côté l'homme c'est tout l'homme, de l'autre l'homme c'est la moitié de l'homme'.
12 Kant ([1790] 2000), §86; ([1790] 2000); AA V, 442, 444, 445.
13 Kant ([1787] 1998), 397; ([1787] 1973); AA III, 248: '... Zwar kein einzelnes Geschöpf unter den einzelnen Bedingungen seines Daseins mit der Idee des Vollkommensten seiner Art congruire (so wenig wie der Mensch mit der Idee der Menschheit, die er sogar selbst als das Urbild seiner Handlungen in seiner Seele trägt) ...'.
14 Kant ([1798] 1996), 280; Kant ([1798] 1973), AA VII, 58: 'diese moralische, von der Menschheit unzertrennliche Anlage'. i.e. 'dieses wahre (nicht erdachte) Ideal'.
15 Kant ([1785] 1996), 73; Kant ([1785] 1973); AA IV, 421.
16 Ibid., 80; AA IV, 429.
17 Kant ([1764] 2011), 39; Kant ([1764] 1969); AA II, 231–2; Kant's emphasis.
18 *Cf.* in the *Groundwork of the Metaphysics of Morals* the opposition between 'practical and pathological love'; Kant ([1785] 1996), 55; ([1785] 1973), AA IV, 399.
19 On this subject, see the following contribution from G. Zöller.
20 See Jauch (1989), 88–9, 98: there appears to be a threat in how 'women develop to humanity' ('*Menschenwerdung der Frau*').
21 *Cf.* Frierson (2013), 99: according to him, the 'dominant response among those sympathetic to Kant'.
22 Compare to Zöller's statement in this volume.
23 In his contribution, Zöller points out that we should not contrast Kant's anthropology against his moral philosophy. I agree on this last point because of course the human being is peculiar in being at the same time '*Naturmensch*' and '*Vernunftmensch*'. What human beings are, were and will be (anthropology) 'does not prejudice' what reason

commands them to be ('anthroponomy': see *Metaphysics of Morals*, Kant ([1785] 1973), AA VI, 406). But I am addressing a different difficulty in this chapter.

24 The 'Architectonic' in the *Critique of Pure Reason* indicates that a fully developed anthropology should stand in parallel to empirical physics (being the empirical study of liberty in man, whereas physics is the study of nature and its determinism).

25 *Cf.* Frierson (2013), 96: these claims regarding female virtue in the *Anthropology* are seen as 'a mere remnant of an earlier view'.

26 *Anthropology,* Kant ([1798] 2006), 209; AA VII, 307.

27 Ibid.

28 *Anthropology,* Kant ([1798] 2006), §77, 154; AA VII, 256–7.

29 Kant (1969); AA XV, 848 [1515]. And also: 'Standhaftigkeit *ohne Hofnung und Furcht ist Männlichkeit*' (AA XV, 846).

30 Kant (1969), AA XV, 229–30, [528]; AA XV, 558 [1263] (certainly from 1772 to 1775): '*[Frauen] jederzeit große Kinder; aber sie machen Kindereyen, und wir haben daran Wohlgefallen*'; AA XV, 558 [1265].

31 Kant ([1798] 1973), AA VII, 308. Recall here the previous definition of 'character' in the *Anthropology*: 'But simply to have a character signifies that property of the will by which the subject binds himself to definite practical principles that he has prescribed to himself irrevocably by his own reason', *Anthropology,* Kant ([1798] 2006), 192; AA VII, 292. See also Zöller's contribution in this volume: one has or shows 'character' 'as a rational being' (*als Vernunftwesen*). An unavoidable difficulty then arises from the fact that the *Anthropology* also contains remarks denying some human groups the ability to *develop* 'character' in that sense.

32 *Cf.* Frierson (2013), 99–100: 'What seemed to be a tension internal to Kant, one that he lamely resolved by simply settling into misogyny and ignoring the problems this raised for his transcendental anthropology, appears as a real problem for anyone who finds plausible both Kant's arguments for universal norms governing thought, choice, and feeling and the importance of empirical sensitivity to human differences in thinking about how those norms play out in the world.'

33 Schott (1997b), 8: 'Some feminists argue that the Enlightenment tradition of individual reason, progress, and freedom, is a precondition for the discourse of women's liberation ... On the other hand, theorists like Jane Flax argue that the Enlightenment conception of a universal, rational subject is antithetical to feminist notions that the self is embedded in social relations, that the self is embodied, and is thus historically specific and partial.' See also Schott's own contribution in Schott (1997a, chap. 'The Gender of Enlightenment'), 329–36.

34 As Schott underlines: 'Some contributors appropriate Kant's philosophy to address feminist concerns positively ... Other contributors explore the internal contradictions of Kant's philosophy, the way in which it fails to meet its own standards ... Still others use the tools of Kant's philosophy to go beyond itself' (Schott 1997b), 1, 5.

35 Benhabib (1987), p. 81 in particular.

36 In Schott's anthology (Schott 1997a), this 'feminist anti-Kantian' claim is represented by Jean Rumsey: Rumsey (1997), 125–44. Schott summarizes these feminist debates about an ethics of care in Schott (1997b), 10. Alternatively, some thinkers argue that 'Kant himself contributes to the development of an ethics of care', such as Paley (2002), Miller (2005), Nagl-Docekal (1997).

37 Kant ([1764] 2011), 36: 'Women ... have many sympathetic sentiments, good-heartedness and compassion. ... They are very sensitive to the least offense and are

exceedingly quick to notice the least lack of attention and respect toward themselves. In short, they contain the chief ground for the contrast between the beautiful and the noble qualities in human nature, and even refine the male sex'; Kant ([1764] 1969), AA II, 229; Kant ([1764] 2011), 38; AA II, 230: 'The content of the great science of woman is rather the human being, and, among human beings, the man ... One will seek to broaden her entire moral feeling and not her memory, and not, to be sure, through universal rules.'

38 For a more general consideration of this problem, see also David-Ménard (1997), in particular chap. 1: '"*Aussi souvent qu'on voudra ...*" – Les structures de désir et le concept d'universel'. Schott (1994) concentrates on purity, not morality, which will be my focus here.

39 First section, end of first paragraph: 'more with the eye of an observer than of the philosopher' (Kant ([1764] 2011), 13, AA II, 207).

40 '[T]here lies in the character of the mind of this sex features peculiar to it which clearly distinguish it from ours and which are chiefly responsible for her being characterized by the mark of the *beautiful*. On the other hand, we could lay claim to the designation of the *noble sex*' (Kant ([1764] 2011), 35; AA II, 228). Jauch (1989, 66–7) qualifies this formula as a '*pluralis androcentricus*'. Later on in the *Observations*, Kant himself (rhetorically) admits that his analysis of the charming woman risks assuming a still more personal form of subjectivity: 'for in such cases the author always seems to portray his own inclination', Kant ([1764] 2011, 44); Kant ([1764] 1969, AA II, 236).

41 Kant ([1764] 2011, 16); Kant ([1764] 1969, AA II, 209); Kant's emphasis.

42 Ibid., 35; 228.

43 Ibid., 41–2; AA II, 234.

44 I counted twenty-nine occurrences on seventeen pages.

45 Kant ([1764] 2011, 47); Kant ([1764] 1969, AA II, 240); Kant's emphasis.

46 Ibid., Kant's emphasis.

47 Kant ([1764] 1969, AA II, 228); *passim*.

48 Kant ([1764] 2011, 36); Kant ([1764] 1969, AA II, 229).

49 Jauch (1989, 67).

50 Kant ([1764] 2011, 42, AA II, 234).

51 See quotation in footnote 46 and the following sentences in Kant's text: 'A woman is little embarrassed by the fact that she does not possess certain lofty insights ... By contrast, she demands all of these qualities in the man, and the sublimity of her soul is revealed only by the fact that she knows how to treasure these noble qualities in so far as they are to be found in him.' Ibid., 47–8, AA II, 240.

52 In this perspective, I am aiming at something different from Robin May Schott's commitment to 'uncover [Kant's] implicit theory of power with regard to both economic and sexual relations', insofar as this would amount to putting him on trail. In the end, Schott's emphasis on Kant's 'hostility toward sensuality' and 'asceticism' also conveys a different point. Schott (1994, 128, 130).

53 *Anthropology*, preface. Kant ([1798] 2006, 3; AA VII, 119).

54 Kant ([1764] 2011, 36–7, AA II, 229–30), my emphasis.

55 Ibid., 37–8, AA II, 230, my emphasis.

56 Indeed, Kant tends to describe the empirical interaction between the sexes as determined by a desire for domination; he underlines the female strategy of *using their charm towards men*. In the *Observations* he writes: 'If things come to the extreme, the man, confident of his merits, can say: *Even if you do not love me I will*

force you to esteem me, and the woman, secure in the power of her charms, will answer: *Even if you do not inwardly esteem us, we will still force you to love us*' (AA II, 242). See also in the Anthropology: Kant ([1798] 1973), AA VII, 273 (§ 85b), AA VII, 305, 309–10 ('Pragmatische Folgerungen'). Both these last passages concern the relationships between husbandand wife in marriage, from a pragmatic viewpoint.

57   Kant ([1764] 2011, 43, AA II, 236). Kant's italics, my emphasis.
58   See also the very clear formulation at the beginning of section three (Ibid., 35; AA II, 228; Kant's emphasis): 'Here it is not to be understood that woman is lacking noble qualities or that the male sex must entirely forego beauties; rather one expects that each sex will unite both, but in such a way that in a woman all other merits should only be united so as to emphasize the character of the *beautiful*, which is the proper point of reference, while by contrast among the male qualities the *sublime* should clearly stand out as the criterion of his kind'; and later in the text (Ibid., 42; AA II, 235): 'The noble qualities of this sex, which nevertheless, as we have already noted, must never make the feeling of the beautiful unrecognizable.'
59   See above, footnote 40.
60   Ibid., 48, AA II, 241: 'it is apparent that their enchantment is often effective only on nobler souls, while the others are not fine enough to be sensitive to them'.
61   Ibid., 43, AA II, 236.
62   Ibid., 48, AA II, 241.
63   Ibid., 41, AA II, 234.
64   See Frierson (2013, 101): 'infatuation with the "charming difference …" made him blind.'

References

Balibar, É. (1997), 'Les universels', in *La crainte des masses*, Paris: Galilée, 421–54.
Balibar, É. (2011), *Citoyen Sujet et autres essais d'anthropologie philosophique*, Paris: PUF.
Balibar, É. (2016), *Citizen Subject. Foundations for Philosophical Anthropology*, trans. S. Miller, New York: Fordham University Press.
Benhabib, S. (1987), 'The Generalized and the Concrete Other: The Kohlberg-Gilligan Controversy and the Feminist Theory', in S. Benhabib and D. Cornell (eds), *Feminism as Critique. Essays on the Politics of Gender in Late-Capitalist Societies*, Cambridge: Polity Press, 77–95.
Bennent, H. (1985), *Galanterie und Verachtung. Eine philosophiegeschichtliche Untersuchung zur Stellung der Frau in Gesellschaft und Kultur*, Frankfurt am Main & New York: Campus Verlag, 96–108 ('Kontroverse Weiblichkeitsbilder Kants').
Miller, C. S. (2005), 'A Kantian Ethic of Care?', in B. S. Andrew, J. Keller & L. H. Schwartzman (eds), *Feminist Interventions in Ethics and Politics: Feminist Ethics and Social Theory*, Lanham: Rowman and Littlefield, 111–27.
David-Ménard, M. (1997), *Les constructions de l'universel. Psychanalyse, philosophie*, Paris: PUF.
Foucault, M. (2002), 'Introduction à l'Anthropologie de Kant', in E. Kant, [1798], *Anthropologie du point de vue pragmatique*, Paris: Vrin, 11–79.
Frierson, P. R. (2013), *What Is the Human Being?*, London & New York: Routledge.
Gilligan, C. (1982), *In a Different Voice*, Cambridge: Harvard University Press.
Jauch, U. P. (1989), *Immanuel Kant zur Geschlechtsdifferenz. Aufklärerische Vorurteilskritik und bürgerliche Geschlechtsvormundschaft*, Vienna: Passagen.

Kant, I. ([1764] 1969), *Kants Gesammelte Schriften* [Akademie-Textausgabe], ed. Preußische Akademie der Wissenschaften; vol. 2: *Vorkritische Schriften II. 1757–1777*, ed. P. Gedan, K. Lasswitz, P. Menzer, M. Frischeisen-Köhler & E. Adickes, 1905, 1912², reprint 1969, Berlin: De Gruyter.

Kant, I. ([1764] 2011), *Observations on the Feeling of the Beautiful and Sublime and Other Writings*, ed. P. Frierson & P. Guyer, Cambridge & New York: Cambridge University Press.

Kant, I. ([1784] 1969), *Kants Gesammelte Schriften* [Akademie-Textausgabe], ed. Preußische Akademie der Wissenschaften; vol. 8: *Abhandlungen nach 1781*, ed. P. Menzer, H. Maier & M. Frischeisen-Köhler, 1912, 1923², reprint 1969, Berlin: De Gruyter.

Kant, I. ([1784] 1996), *Practical Philosophy*, ed. and trans. M. J. Gregor (*The Cambridge Edition of the Works of Immanuel Kant*), Cambridge: Cambridge University Press.

Kant, I. ([1785] 1973), *Kants Gesammelte Schriften* [Akademie-Textausgabe], ed. Preußische Akademie der Wissenschaften; vol. 4: *Kritik der reinen Vernunft* (1781¹); *Prolegomena; Grundlegung zur Metaphysik der Sitten; Metaphysische Anfangsgründe der Naturwissenschaft*, ed. B. Erdmann, P. Menzer, A. Höfler, 1903, 1911², reprint 1973, Berlin: De Gruyter.

Kant, I. ([1787] 1973), *Kants Gesammelte Schriften* [Akademie-Textausgabe], ed. Preußische Akademie der Wissenschaften; vol. 3: *Kritik der reinen Vernunft*, (1787²), ed. B. Erdmann, 1904, 1911², reprint 1962 and 1973, Berlin: De Gruyter.

Kant, I. ([1787] 1998), *Critique of Pure Reason*, ed. and trans. P. Guyer & A. Wood (*The Cambridge Edition of the Works of Immanuel Kant*), Cambridge: Cambridge University Press.

Kant, I. ([1790] 1974), *Kants Gesammelte Schriften* [Akademie-Textausgabe], ed. Preußische Akademie der Wissenschaften; vol. 5: *Kritik der praktischen Vernunft; Kritik der Urtheilskraft*, ed. P. Natorp & W. Windelband, 1908, 1913², reprint 1962 and 1974, Berlin: De Gruyter.

Kant, I. ([1790] 2000), *Critique of the Power of Judgment*, ed. P. Guyer, trans. P. E. Matthews (*The Cambridge Edition of the Works of Immanuel Kant*), Cambridge: Cambridge University Press.

Kant, I. ([1798] 1973), *Kants Gesammelte Schriften* [Akademie-Textausgabe], ed. Preußische Akademie der Wissenschaften; vol. 7: *Der Streit der Facultäten; Anthropologie in pragmatischer Hinsicht*, ed. K. Vorländer & O. Külpe, 1907, 1917², reprint 1973, Berlin: De Gruyter.

Kant, I. ([1798] 1996), *Religion and Rational Theology*, ed. and trans. A. Wood & G. Di Giovanni (*The Cambridge Edition of the Works of Immanuel Kant*), Cambridge: Cambridge University Press.

Kant, I. (1969), *Kants Gesammelte Schriften* [Akademie-Textausgabe], ed. Preußische Akademie der Wissenschaften; Abteilung III. 'Handlscgriftlicher Nachlass', vol. 15: *Anthropologie*, ed. E. Adickes, 1913, 1923,² reprint 1961 and 1969, Berlin: De Gruyter.

Kant, I. (2006), *Anthropology from a Pragmatic Point of View*, ed. and trans. R. Louden, Cambridge: Cambridge University Press.

Kohlberg, L. (1981), *Essays on Moral Development*. Vol. 1. *The Philosophy of Moral Development: Moral Stages and the Idea of Justice*, New York: Harper & Row.

Nagl-Docekal, H. (1997), 'Feminist Ethics: How It Could Benefit from Kant's Moral Philosophy', in R. M. Schott (ed.), *Feminist Interpretations of Immanuel Kant*, University Park: The Pennsylvania State University Press, 101–24.

Paley, J. (2002), 'Virtues of Autonomy: The Kantian Ethics of Care', *Nursing Philosophy*, 3 (2): 133–43.
Rumsey, J. (1997), 'Re-visions of Agency in Kant's Moral Theory', in R. M. Schott (ed.), *Feminist Interpretations of Immanuel Kant*, University Park: The Pennsylvania State University Press, 125–44.
Schott, R. M. (1994), 'Rereading the Canon: Kantian Purity and the Suppression of Eros', in Bat-Ami Bat On (ed.), *Modern Engendering*, New York: State University of New York Press, 127–40.
Schott, R. M., ed. (1997a), *Feminist Interpretations of Immanuel Kant*, University Park: The Pennsylvania State University Press.
Schott, R. M., ed. (1997b), 'Introduction', in R. M. Schott (ed), *Feminist Interpretations of Immanuel Kant*, University Park: The Pennsylvania State University Press, 1–20.
Sedwick, S. (1997), 'Can Kant's Ethics Survive the Feminist Critique?', in R. M. Schott (ed.), *Feminist Interpretations of Immanuel Kant*, University Park: The Pennsylvania State University Press, 77–100.

14

'Anthroponomy'. Kant on the natural and the rational human being

Günter Zöller

Vor dem wildesten Thiere dürfte man sich nicht so fürchten,
als vor einem Gesetzlosen Menschen.

—I. Kant, *Naturrecht Feyerabend*[1]

This chapter aims at assessing the alleged anthropological dimension of Kant's practical philosophy and proceeds in four sections on the recent anthropological turn in work on Kant, on the manifestly marginal status of anthropology in Kant's overall *œuvre*, on the special split status of the human being in Kant, and on the normative nature of Kant's practical philosophy. The focus is on the historic and systematic relation between Kant's various works in physical and cultural anthropology ('human nature') and his entirely differently based and alternatively oriented work in moral philosophy, comprising juridical law and ethics, which draws on an account of reason-ruled freedom ('rational nature'). Particular attention is paid to the intricate interplay between the natural and the normative in Kant's assessment of the forms and norms of human individual and social existence. The chapter argues for the primacy of principles over facts and of obligation over inclination in Kant's praeter-anthropological account of rationally free willing and doing.[2]

1. One or many?

The past few decades have seen a substantial increase in the quality and quantity of scholarly and philosophical work devoted to Kant worldwide. First, the Anglophone world emerged out of its narrow and monoglot focus on the first half of the first *Critique* and on the first two sections of the *Foundation for the Metaphysics of Morals*, discovering and exploring the wider scope and deeper grasp of Kant's foundational theoretical and practical philosophy. This extension and expansion soon was followed by similar forays into Kant's critical aesthetics and his mature moral philosophy, including ethics and the philosophy of right. Further fields of emerging Kant studies have included the philosophy of history and political philosophy.

The material basis for much of this renaissance or rather *naissance* of philosophical work on Kant in the Anglophone world, which has its counterpart in similar changes in scholarship on Kant throughout Continental Europe, South America and East Asia, has been the comprehensive editorial project of the Cambridge Edition of the Works of Immanuel Kant, under the general editorship of Paul Guyer and Allen Wood.[3] The voluminous volumes of the Cambridge Edition published so far, with a few more in planning and preparation, have made available to the English-language reader virtually the entire Kantian *corpus* in modern translations that supply introductions, factual and linguistic notes as well as bibliographical information. The Kant so prepared and propagated comprises the extensive pre-critical writings as well as the critical works, the printed works as well as the correspondence, and the literary remains (*Nachlass*) as well as the lecture transcripts (*Vorlesungsnachschriften*), the latter sorts of texts in substantial selections – not to mention the *Opus postumum* in an edition that surpasses the work's current presentation in the Academy Edition, with the latter itself in the process of being revised, redone and rearranged under the auspices of the Berlin-Brandenburg Academy of Sciences.

To be sure, the worldwide editorial work on Kant undertaken over the past couple of decades is as much a reflection of the widened view and the wider work on the Kantian *corpus*, as it itself has played a causal role in shaping and directing that global development. Moreover, the spread of the new English-language editions (many of them also issued as separate study texts, outside the Cambridge Kant Edition format) and of the recent work based on them, which has gone well beyond their more narrow home bases – chiefly Germany and the United States – is as much due to the global connectedness of philosophical work, as it has strengthened the connections and collaborations between Europe and North America, between Europe and South America (especially Brazil and Argentina) and between Europe together with North America and East Asia (especially China).

But the editorial expansion of Kant's works and the associated extension in scholarship on Kant, to be found worldwide, has not only increased and enlarged the general acquaintance with Kant's work. The featured texts by Kant, previously either completely unknown, hardly studied or little appreciated, have brought into view aspects, sides and dimensions of Kant's philosophical work hitherto invisible and therefore effectively inexistent. For one, Kant's canonical texts, chiefly the three *Critiques*, have been placed into the wider context of the publications and the unpublished materials surrounding them by way of earlier preparation and further articulation. Moreover, the acquaintance with published and unpublished works by Kant that are contemporaneous with the critical canon has introduced a broadened view of Kant's *œuvre*, which has come to be seen as not limited to its critical core but encompassing Kant's wider role and larger effect as a public intellectual and an academic teacher of considerable renown and substantial reputation.

Most importantly, though, the sheer scope and the intellectual import of the further texts by Kant that have come to the fore and have received academic attention and scholarly scrutiny worldwide in recent years have managed to modify and revise the received image of Kant. Behind, next to or ahead of Kant the critical philosopher, the transcendental idealist, the moral rigorist and the aesthetic formalist, there has emerged another, differently oriented and alternatively ambitioned Kant, whose primary concern is not with principles and prescriptions, with norms and rules, with pure reason and a priori conditions, but with the factual circumstances of human existence in the natural and cultural world – in a word, with Kant the natural and cultural human historian, or Kant the anthropologist. In fact, the very term for the disciplinary treatment of human beings as such, 'anthropology' (*Anthropologie*), owes its introduction into modern academia largely to Kant and his innovative treatment of this subject matter, which he developed over decades in a popular public lecture course eventually published under the title *Anthropologie in pragmatischer Hinsicht* (Anthropology in a Pragmatic Regard).

To be sure, the existence of an entire anthropological *œuvre* in Kant had long been known and even appreciated. The published textbook of his long-standing lecture course on the subject, which first appeared in 1798, had been included among his main works, and scholars had taken note of Kant's scattered contributions to contemporary debates in physical and cultural anthropology, such as the pathology of bipedality and the taxonomy of stable human subspecies ('races'). Still the anthropological works largely had been considered marginal rather than major, accidental rather than essential and circumstantial rather than central in the context of Kant's overall philosophical project, with its well-established focus on synthetic cognitions a priori of various kinds and in distinct domains. The very designation given by Kant to his published anthropology ('in a pragmatic regard') seemed to indicate the decisive disciplinary difference between the prudential aims and strategic orientation of worldly anthropology and the genuinely practical, moral focus of the specifically critical treatment of juridical law and ethics in Kant's practical philosophy qua moral philosophy.

Still there have been, more recently, readers and interpreters of Kant who have sought to mine the other, specifically anthropological Kant not for purposes of supplementation and completion only, but with the intent of confronting the critical Kant with an altogether alternative and radically revised Kant – one perceived to be more compatible with contemporary as well as current sensibilities and standards of a naturalist, realist or common-sensical persuasion, from which the official, critical Kant is perceived to have diverged to his own disadvantage and at his own detriment, as that view would have it.[4] Such a reassessment of the critical Kant in the light of the anthropological Kant – of the critic of reason in the light of the natural historian, of the supranaturalist in the light of the naturalist – has been most prominent but also rather controversial in moral matters. To certain scholars it has seemed that Kant's anthropological *œuvre* effectuates a metacritical correction of the seeming severity and the sustained single-mindedness of Kant's critical scrutiny of human life under the norms and forms of pure reason, in particular in the latter's guise as pure practical reason or pure will.

Anthropologically geared rereadings of Kant in general and of Kantian moral philosophy in particular typically portray themselves as correctives or counterweights to the perceived one-sidedness and alleged imbalance of Kant's core positions in philosophy. Against the latter's focus on form and function, they tend to maintain the indispensable import of material and matter; against its apriorism, they stress empirical factors and features; against its necessitarianism and universalism, they insist on contingent conditions; and against its orientation towards the normative, they stress the natural. On those readings, Kant appears less as a solitary revolutionary who completely changed the course of (Western) philosophy, and more as a congenial contemporary, akin to the likes of Tetens and Lambert in the German Enlightenment and to Smith and Hume in the Scottish Enlightenment. The Kant so created is less monumental and more human but also less radical and more moderate – perhaps a reflection of a current age and a contemporary culture such as ours that seeks the ordinary and praises the average.

In a larger perspective that takes into view the extended history of the reception and effective history of Kant's philosophy and the spread and development of scholarship on Kant, the anthropological Kant of recent vintage comes to stand in a long line of adaptations and assimilations that, again and again, have sought to integrate Kant's work into current concerns – from the anti-Hegelianism and scientism of the neo-Kantians in the second half of the nineteenth century through the traditionalism of the ontological or metaphysical Kant interpretation of the early twentieth century to the analytic reconstructionism of the 1960s and the claims on Kant made in the name of more recent philosophical fashions such as the philosophy of mind and neurophilosophy. In each case, the Kant so retrieved and reconstructed was made to match a prevailing philosophical culture and its specific standards. To be sure, in all these cases the attempted appropriations and actualizations could claim evidence and support for their readings and rewritings in Kant himself. Yet the plurality of positions so developed out of Kant over the course of time also indicates that none of them were quite able to capture Kant completely and comprehensively.

The same seems to hold for the anthropological Kant and for Kant the natural historian of current concern. By focusing on the natural at the expense of the normative and on the factual at the expense of the principled, the naturalists and culturalists among Kant's recent readers risk losing sight of the normative core and the critical centre of Kant's enterprise. In particular, reading Kant primarily as an anthropologist and a natural historian detracts and deflects from the non-empirical dimension of the critical philosophy, which – while not transcendent in the deficient sense exposed and eliminated by Kant himself – maintains the non-empirical basis of experience and, most importantly, the non-empirical character of the freedom involved in radically rational volition.

Moreover, the recent readings that feature Kant the anthropologist and natural historian tend to disturb, if not distort, the overall structure and the precise proportions of Kant's philosophy in its entirety, as designed and developed by Kant in response to reason's own purposive structure, as he conceived of it. The dimension of application so stressed by the anthropological apologists of Kant risks reducing Kant's non-empirical double theory of nature and freedom ('pure philosophy') to mere preliminaries for an empirically enriched account of situated and socialized subjectivity. In the process, the practical tends to collapse into the pragmatic and the categorical into the conditional. Most importantly, though, the narrow focus on actual application and empirical instantiation obscures the intended import of Kant's critical account of nature and freedom, which is not the field of the empirically or culturally given, but the domain of principles governing nature and freedom under the guise of the a priori forms of nature and the a priori norms of freedom – what Kant termed, in both cases, their 'metaphysical first principles' (*metaphysische Anfangsgründe*).

The applied dimension of Kant's philosophical project that emerges from its critical core therefore is not an anthropology, however practically portioned, but a 'metaphysics of morals' (*Metaphysik der Sitten*) that operates under a general – and to that extent anthropological – premise, viz. human social coexistence on a finite earth surface, and that proceeds to subject human freedom, in its two manifestations as the outer freedom of choice and the inner freedom of conviction, to rational rules of juridical law and ethics. In a remarkable development in recent research, concurrent with – but also contrary to – the naturalizing notions governing a good deal of wider work on Kant, there has been an upsurge of interest precisely in Kant's critical theory of law and right, including the latter's development out of natural law (*ius naturale, ius naturae*), as documented in a fascinating understudied text from 1784, the transcript of Kant's lecture course on natural law (*Naturrecht Feyerabend*), which recently has been re-edited twice in its German original, one of which in the context of a translation into Italian,[5] and has been translated into three further languages (English, Spanish and Portuguese), in addition to having become the object of scholarly scrutiny and philosophical analysis worldwide.[6]

The Kant to come out of that body of work (and the related recent research initiatives on Kant's lectures in moral philosophy and on his published philosophy of juridical law and ethics in the late *Metaphysics of Morals*) is neither the austere assessor of pure reason nor the empirically embedded historian of human nature but the astute analyst of the juridical and ethical principles governing human society in general and civil society in particular with special regard to its purposive as well as principled development.

2. The unasked question

Prominent proponents of an assertively anthropological reading of Kant do not stop at supplementing the critical philosophy with facts and features pertaining to the human condition. They also tend to take Kant's sustained concern with things human to form the very core and centre of his philosophical thinking. To that effect, anthropological readers of Kant – readers of the entire Kant in an anthropological vein – resort to Kant's own occasional explicit identification of philosophy with anthropology. In particular, the anthropological Kantians like to cite Kant's cosmopolitical conception of philosophy in the introduction to the printed version of his long-term lecture course on logic, the so-called *Jäsche Logic* (1800), so named after its editor-compiler, Kant's former student, Gottlob Benjamin Jäsche.

Considering philosophy not in terms of its scholastic conception (*Schulbegriff*) but with regard to its cosmic concept (*Weltbegriff*), which aims not at knowledge for its own sake but is concerned with the reference of all cognition to morality as the 'final end' (*Endzweck*) of 'human reason' (*menschliche Vernunft*), Kant, in the *Jäsche Logic*, lists four questions to which the entire area ('field', *Feld*) of philosophy under its cosmic conception can be brought:

1) What can I know?
2) What ought I to do?
3) What may I hope for?
4) What is the human being?[7]

More specifically, Kant assigns the first question, concerning possible knowledge, to metaphysics; the second one, concerning obligated action, to morals; the third one, concerning permissible (or requisite) hope, to religion; and the fourth one, concerning the human being as such, to anthropology. In addition, though, he declares in the same context that 'all of this' – meaning all four questions and their correlated areas – could be considered 'anthropology'. In support of this *revirement*, which involves as much a reduction *to* anthropology as an expansion *of* anthropology, Kant specifies that the first three questions refer to (*sich beziehen*) the fourth and final one, concerning the human being.

Straightforward as Kant's statement regarding the universal scope of anthropology in the introduction to the *Jäsche Logic* might seem, it turns out to be a sole, one-time pronouncement on the matter to that effect – a *hapax legomenon*, as the Greeks would have it. None of the preserved and published transcripts of Kant's logic lectures from three decades, on which the published handbook of 1800 is supposed to be based, contains a corresponding passage. Nor is there a matching mention of anthropology's virtual identity with philosophy cosmically conceived anywhere else in the Kantian *corpus*. Moreover, there is reason to doubt the authenticity of the *Jäsche Logic* on the matter, given the work's character as a handbook compiled by Jäsche at the very end of Kant's academic life and philosophical activity.

To be sure, there are two other, earlier instances of Kant listing and labelling the questions posed by philosophy in the cosmic understanding. In one of those, a letter to Carl Friedrich Stäudlin from 4 May 1793,[8] written to accompany the sending of his recently published *Religion in den Grenzen der bloßen Vernunft* (Religion within the Limits of Reason Alone), Kant also enumerates the four questions – explicitly assigning the third one ('What may I hope for?') to his new work in moral religion. But unlike in the later instance from the *Jäsche Logic*, Kant does not additionally assign all of philosophy (in the cosmic sense of the term) to anthropology taken in the widest meaning. Instead he refers the fourth question ('what is the human being?') solely to his long-standing academic practice of the lectures on anthropology.

The other instance involving the questions posed by philosophy in the cosmic sense to be found in Kant does not even involve the question constitutive of anthropology ('What is the human being?') but is limited to the first three questions in the counting of the *Jäsche Logic*. The question catalogue *sans* anthropology is to be found in the *Critique of Pure Reason*, more specifically in the Canon of Pure Reason (in the Transcendental Doctrine of Method at the very end of the work), which details the possible practical uses of reason with regard to its final purpose and was taken over unchanged from the first into the second edition of the work (1781 and 1787, respectively). The common core of Kant's canonic questions in the first *Critique* is the motivational set-up of reason in its possible pursuits ('interest', *Interesse*). According to the *Critique of Pure Reason*, the first question – 'What can I know?' – reflects the theoretical and specifically the purely theoretical or 'speculative' interest of reason. The second question – 'What ought I to do?' – conveys the practical and specifically the ethico-practical or moral interest of reason. The third question – 'What may I hope for?' – combines reason's theoretical interest and reason's practical interest by inquiring into objects not to be grasped or begotten on their own, solely by theoretical means, as investigated by the first question ('What can I know?'), but introduced as the hoped-for consequences of a prior moral conduct that is in accord with the answer to the second question ('What ought I to do?').[9]

The Canon of Pure Reason of the first *Critique* recognizes no further basic question of philosophy cosmically conceived, beyond the three questions allocated to the merely theoretical, merely practical and theoretico-practically mixed modes of 'pure philosophy' (*reine Philosophie*). In fact, the Canon of Pure Reason makes no mention of anthropology at all, whether as a philosophical sub-discipline with its own question – as in the later letter to Stäudlin – or as a covering term for worldly philosophy in its entirely – as in the *Jäsche Logic* later yet. To be sure, anthropology is mentioned in another part of the first *Critique*'s Transcendental Doctrine of Method, viz. the Architectonic of Pure Reason. But Kant's point in introducing the title there is rather to exclude the discipline so designated from all of non-empirical or 'pure' philosophy – *vulgo* 'metaphysics' – given anthropology's status as an 'applied philosophy' (*angewandte Philosophie*)[10] analogous to physics qua 'empirical doctrine of nature' (*emprirische Naturlehre*).[11]

The principled exclusion of anthropology from the core of philosophy critically conceived attests to the strictly limited status and function of the discipline called 'anthropology' in Kant's overall system. Anthropology in Kant is applicative rather than basic and is practical, or rather 'pragmatic', in its intent. More specifically, as '*moral* anthropology' the sustained study of the human being is to address the factual conditions for the effective realization of normative morality. Moreover, as '*pragmatic* anthropology', it is to instruct human beings about themselves with an eye towards their effective dealings with each other. In neither of those capacities is anthropology in Kant central to the critical core of his thinking. It serves an adjuvating purpose and a mediating function in the systematic transition from pure reason to the actual human life to be led under the principles of reason (*Vernunft*) and with the guidance of judgement (*Urteilskraft*).

But not only is anthropology essentially marginal, while also being marginally essential, in Kant's overall scheme of things philosophical. The very question posed by anthropology – 'What is the human being?' – is non-standard and even ill-formed by the criteria of Kant's critical thinking. To begin with, the anthropological question deviates grammatically as well as semantically from the three proper questions of interested reason. The latter are all phrased in the first person singular ('I') and involve verbal predicates expressive of interested reason's range ('to know', 'to do', 'to hope'; *wissen, tun, hoffen*). Moreover, each of those three basic forms of reason's egologically articulated range is further qualified by a different matching modal verb ('can', 'ought', 'may'; *kann, soll, darf*), thus indicating the specific attitudinal approach involved in each of the three questions: with knowing assessed as to the condition of its possibility, doing with regard to the conditions of its obligatedness (*obligatio, Verbindlichkeit*) and hoping with respect to the conditions of its permissibility (*dürfen*), or rather requisiteness (*bedürfen*).[12]

By contrast, the anthropological base question, 'What is the human being?', abandons the first-person perspective in favour of a third-person neutral formulation and replaces the twofold verbal predicate structure (main verb in the infinitive, auxiliary verb in the first-person indicative) with the generic verb of predication ('is'). Semantically speaking, the question characteristic of anthropology substitutes the novel, critically cast question type involving the grounds and limitations of interested reason with the old-style 'metaphysical' question type that implies there being an essence to a thing, which then is to be ascertained and stated as such. Yet for the critical Kant, essential definitions, if they are possible at all, only can occur at the very end of philosophical investigations, as their final and formal result. Definitional questions therefore can never serve in an opening move made for purposes of a preliminary definition that is to head further inquiry, which had been the method and practice in the Wolffian school philosophy whose manuals consisted – to a large extent – in an extended, or rather overextended, string of (stipulative) essential definitions of philosophical concepts, as evident in A. G. Baumgarten's hugely influential metaphysics handbook (*Metaphysica*).

But not only is the essentialist form of the anthropology's question, 'What is the human being?', epistemically problematic, on Kant's considered view about definitions in philosophy. The very entity whose essential identity is targeted in the anthropological question eludes definitional fixation. For Kant and his contemporaries, the human being as such had become an object of inquiry and investigation, informed by novel discoveries about the physical attributes and the cultural practices of people in distant lands and remote times. The emerging discipline of anthropology – a combination of physical and cultural anthropology or of *Anthropologie* and *Ethnologie*, as the German terms would have it – a development of which Kant can count as a cofounder, was based on recent new evidence in that regard and developed in rapid response to current discoveries and to the systematic challenges they posed to received views of the human being. What previously had been identified and entified, so to speak, as a stable and reliable 'human nature', proved an area of variation and deviation from alleged norms and presumed standards. Under those circumstances, the question to be posed by anthropology might rather have been 'What is the human being not?', suggesting a rhetorical question in the face of all the things that human beings were proving to be capable of and liable to do to themselves, to others and to each other.

3. The animal without character

Its problematic epistemic status and open future as a science of sorts notwithstanding, anthropology was to become an important aspect and area of Kant's mature philosophical thinking. In the process, the inappropriate essentialist concern with the assumed substance of the human being came to be replaced with a functionalist focus on the possible unitary force and agency behind the plural and divergent manifestation of human existence. The key concept in Kant's own functionalist reformation of emerging anthropology was the notion of 'character' (*Charakter*), more specifically that of the species character of the human being or of the generic character of the 'human species' (*Menschengattung*).

The Kantian concept of character has its origin in his critical account of causation in general and his account of human causal action in particular. In its originally cosmological and subsequently psychological meaning, 'character' in Kant serves to designate the modal base for manifest causal actions considered prior to and independent of particular antecedent causes. Moreover, the critical Kant distinguishes between the transtemporal, generic or 'transcendental' character of a given action and its cis-temporal, particular or 'empirical' character. Specifically with regard to human causal action, Kant also calls the former the 'manner of thinking' (*Denkungsart*) and labels the latter the 'mode of sensing' (*Sinnesart*).[13]

In applying the action-theoretical term 'character' in his developing anthropology, half of which eventually consisted in an 'anthropological characteristic' (*anthropologische Charakteristik*), Kant resorts to a concept suited for rendering the unity underlying the multiple manifestations of some set of forces or powers. Moreover, Kant avails himself of the term 'character' for the differential designation of various characteristic sets of forces or powers in human beings. In particular, Kant's anthropology applies the concept of character to distinct populations of human beings singled out, chiefly, in terms of gender, ethnicity or nationality. In addition, Kant uses the term and concept with regard to the human species in general, thus attributing to the human being considered collectively and comprehensively a character of its own.[14]

Yet rather than simply extending the previous attribution of a particular fixed character, based on gender and the like, to the human being as such and in general, Kant's attribution of a human species character involves the very denial of such a fixed and firm character. To begin with, Kant considers the human species character elusive on epistemic grounds. As he points out, defining the character of a given species of beings requires comprehending those beings under a covering concept which they share with other beings constituting a common *genus*, before distinguishing the subset in question qua species from its other constituent members. Yet in the extraordinary case of human beings, considered as earthly rational beings (*irdische vernünftige Wesen*), this logical requirement would involve the prior cognition of 'rational non-earthly beings' (*vernünftige, nicht-irdische Wesen*) – a cognition not available though by any possible experience.[15]

Faced with the definitional dilemma of a species without a genus or a genus with one species only, Kant resorts to a strictly empirically based characteristic of the human being as such ('earthly'), placing the latter squarely among other living beings to be found in nature ('system of living nature', *System der lebenden Natur*).[16] But even among living natural beings, human beings cannot be singled out through a naturally occurring specific character or a species character. Instead Kant declares the very lack of a character in the ordinary, fixed sense to be the character (of sorts) of the living beings that human beings are – with the further proviso that the human being, who as such is considered to be devoid of a fixed, materially specific character, is to acquire one on his (or her) own. On Kant's account, the proto-character of the human being – its quasi-character of lacking one for the purpose of getting one – is based on the human being's general ability to self-perfection according to self-set purposes (*vermögend ... sich nach seinen von ihm selbst genommenen Zwecken zu perfectioniren*).[17]

Kant describes the trajectory of human generic self-perfection as the self-induced stadial development from an animal endowed with the capacity for reason (*mit Vernunftfähigkeit begabtes Thier, animal rationabile*) to an animal that is rational by itself (*aus sich selbst vernünftiges Thier, animal rationale*).[18] More specifically, Kant details three successive staging areas for the human process of rational self-perfection: human self-preservation at the individual and species level, human training and education for family life and human rule of social life according to 'principles of reason' (*Vernunftprincipien*).

Kant further details the human condition by comparison with possible other rational beings on earth, who would be differently organized from human beings. The point of this fictitious contrast is to draw attention to a human trait that might be missing in beings otherwise not unlike us (or might even be found in human beings, if they happened to be somewhat differently constituted). The characteristic human trait in question is the propensity for 'discord' (*Zwietracht*) rather than 'concord' (*Eintracht*) in and among human beings. Kant portrays the basic fact about human social existence – their 'unsocial sociability' (*ungesellige Gesellligkeit*),[19] to use the phrase from Kant's *Idee zur einer allgemeinen Geschichte in weltbürgerlicher Absicht* (Idea for a Universal History with a Cosmopolitan Intent,1784) – as part of an embedded teleology of nature. By introducing the 'germ of discord' (*Kern der Zwietracht*) into the human being generically considered, nature or rather Nature (with a capital 'n') has, so to speak, intended the human being to obtain concord only by 'one's own reason' (*eigene Vernunft*) and through purposively induced self-perfection.

Kant calls the sum total of the human efforts at rational self-perfection 'progressive culture' (*fortschreitende Cultur*). He also explicitly concedes that the overall gradual advancement of human rationalization or rational humanization involves 'many a sacrifice of the pleasures of life' (*manche Aufopferung der Lebensfreuden*).[20] More specifically, Kant distinguishes a threefold generic 'disposition' (*Anlage*) that distinguishes the human being from 'all other natural beings' (*alle übrigen Naturwesen*). Kant conceives of the three exclusively human dispositions as arranged in an ascending sequence. First there is the 'technical' predisposition for the essentially mechanical handling of things. Second comes the 'pragmatic' disposition for the essentially social strategic use of other human beings. Third is the 'moral' disposition for the essentially lawful and constitutively free acting towards oneself and others.

While the open human species character, as assessed by Kant, distinctly diverges from the fixed species character of other living beings, both kinds of character share the combination of causation and teleology in the exercise of animal agency. On Kant's understanding, character as such – whether naturally given or culturally acquired – co-conditions an animal's actions, which ensue under occasioning ambient circumstances on the basis of the underlying character. While the occurrence of an actual action is an instance of efficient causality (*Wirkursache*), the manifest match between a general character and a particular action is teleological, if not in intention then at least in effect. In Kant's preferred parlance, informed by the contemporary discourse about matters of fit and functionality, the generic character of an animal reflects the latter's 'destination', 'vocation' or 'calling' (*Bestimmung*). In particular, for Kant, character and vocation stand in an epistemic relation, with observable character – character to be observed in action – providing the cognitive grounds for ascertaining a given animal's specific vocation: 'The character of a living animal is that from which its vocation can be ascertained in advance' (*Der Charakter eines lebenden Wesens ist das, woraus sich seine Bestimmung zum voraus erkennen läßt*).[21]

On Kant's account, the vocation of a non-rational, 'mere' animal (*animal brutum*) is such that it is achieved, normally or typically, in each individual of the species to which the animal in question belongs. Generally speaking, non-rational animals are 'destined' (*bestimmt*) to develop their inherent dispositions in each and every exemplar of their species. By contrast, human beings have a twofold destination or vocation, one stemming from their status as mere animals, the other from their status as rational animals. Moreover, the two kinds of vocation involve different modes of development and forms of attainment. In particular, on Kant's construal, the 'natural vocation' (*Naturbestimmung*)[22] of the human being is achieved, like that of all other animals, in each and every individual – at least normally or typically so. By contrast, the 'rational vocation' (*Vernunftbestimmung*)[23] of the human being can only be attained 'in the species' (*in der Gattung*), effectively involving numerous individual human beings over many generations, none of whom is to achieve the human vocation but each of whom is to contribute to its infinite approximation.[24]

Historically speaking, Kant's distinction between the human being's natural and rational vocation, along with his outright denial of a fixed specifically human character, breaks with a strong teleological tradition going back to Aristotelian natural philosophy that treats the human being as part and parcel of a nature broadly conceived and governing human and non-human animals alike. In addition, Kant's differential treatment of developmental achievement at the human individual and species level breaks with the prevailing contemporary tradition, as epitomized by Johann Joachim Spalding and Moses Mendelssohn, which has the 'vocation of the human being' (*Bestimmung des Menschen*) involve each individual as such and for itself in the protracted pursuit and eventual achievement of its entire vocation. By contrast, for Kant, the rational vocation of the human being, in addition to being based on generic dispositions, involves history – human history, to be precise – as the spatio-temporal arena for the intergenerational development of natural dispositions into cultural achievements. Accordingly, Kant's species anthropology issues in a philosophy of universal history – a history written in a philosophical vein and with a cosmopolitan intent.

4. *Nomos* and *anthropos*

Kant's critical distinction between the human being qua natural human being or 'human being of nature' (*Naturmensch*) and the human being qua rational human being or 'human being of reason' (*Vernunftmensch*)[25] combines extensional identity with intensional difference. One and the same being – individually and generically considered – can be, indeed must be, regarded from two mutually exclusive perspectives. In one regard, the human being presents itself as an animal among other such 'living beings' (*Lebewesen*), differently abled through his capacity for reason but essentially identical in its ultimate adherence to laws of its 'inner nature' (*innere Natur*). In the other aspect, that same being – as type as well as token – emerges as praeter-naturally positioned under a supranatural law ('moral law', *Sittengesetz*) and as a co-legislative member of a non-natural, 'moral order' or 'moral world'.

In addition to juxtaposing the two modes of human being Kant considers the two as developmentally related and normatively ordered: the human being is to advance beyond a merely natural manner of existence – initially so by natural means, chiefly the cunning device of inner-species competition ('unsocial sociability'), and eventually so on the basis of specifically moral and, for that matter, 'free' deliberation and decision. To be sure, the natural preparation for cultural development in general and for the culture of morality in particular can only reach so far. Put in terms of the third *Critique*'s account of the power of teleological judgement, the 'last purpose' (*letzter Zweck*)[26] of nature in the latter's overall order does not yet encompass the 'final end' (*Endzweck*)[27] of the world as to its very existence and meaning. The latter includes freedom, involves the will and implies the moral law.

The disciplinary manifestation of Kant's dual, animal-rational or zoo-logical account of the human being is the strict, systematic separation between anthropology and 'moral philosophy' (*Moralphilosophie*), with the former falling entirely within the sphere of nature and the latter residing exclusively in the domain of freedom. On Kant's mature account, moral philosophy coincides completely with 'practical philosophy' (*praktische Philosophie*), at the explicit exclusion of technical cognition involving skills and pragmatic considerations involving prudence. Moreover, moral-practical philosophy in Kant is subject to a twofold complete disjunction between juridical law (*Recht*) and ethics (*Ethik*). For Kant, the wider sense of the moral – in its basic opposition to the natural – encompasses the moral ordering of outward action through juridical law as well as that of inward motivation through ethics, with the former involving the grounds and bounds of 'outer freedom' (*äußere Freiheit*) and the latter those of 'inner freedom' (*innere Freiheit*).[28]

But the scope and intent of Kant's moral, juridical as well as ethical philosophy is not limited to the human being in the manner of a 'practical anthropology' (*praktische Anthropologie*).[29] According to Kant, the addressee of purely practical philosophy and the target of its moral law is not the human being only, not even the human being qua rational being, but any and all beings relevantly like this human being, viz. all beings endowed with a 'rational nature' (*vernünftige Natur*) in addition to possessing, or rather being possessed by, a 'sensory nature' (*Sinnennatur*). The wider scope of practical philosophy beyond the specifically human may not amount to much in extensional terms, given that experience provides no evidence of such creatures. But in intensional terms, the difference makes a difference in that the moral law, along with its dual articulation in juridical law and ethics, is neither based on exclusively human features nor is it valid for human beings only.

More yet, the generic character of the moral law underlying juridical law and ethical law – and as such conceptually distinct from either of the latter – is not even limited in its range and application to beings relevantly similar to 'us' humans. On Kant's construal, the moral law, in addition to holding for sensuously affected rational beings like us, also pertains to perfect beings (if there are such beings), including perfect finite beings that are not affected by a sensory nature, such as the angels of religious mythology, and even God as the most perfect being (*ens perfectissimum*), who, for Kant, is not the arbitrary author of the moral law but its rationally bound lawgiver. To be sure, for Kant, the wider, praeter- and even superhuman scope of the moral law is a matter of conceptual clarification and fictional contrast only. In effect, in Kant's practical philosophy, the moral law, along with its specifications as plural juridical and ethical laws, takes on the form of an unconditional command ('categorical imperative'), specifically addressed to beings that are sufficiently 'unholy' (*unheilig*)[30] to tend to transgress the moral law, in spite of cognizing its claim and content full well. Under those conditions, factually confirmed for human beings only and conceptually to be extended, not to all finite beings as such, but to those only that are susceptible to pathological affection ('unholy') – beings rationally ruled yet sensuously inclined – the moral law takes on the imperative guise of 'obligatedness' (*Verbindlichkeit*), 'obligation' (*Verpflichtung*), 'duty' (*Pflicht*), 'constraint' and 'coercion' (*Zwang*).

Kant conveys the strictly normative dimension of the moral law with respect to its obvious addressees ('us') by contrasting the factual focus of anthropology with the counterfactual claims of 'anthroponomy' (*Anthroponomie*),[31] a term meant to suggest not the extensional limitation of the moral *nomos* to human beings but their subjection to a law that is practical in character and addresses their rational core. In addition, the pairing of '*nomos*' and '*anthropos*' in Kant's coinage 'anthroponomy' – a *hapax legomenon* in the Kantian *corpus* – conveys the legislative process behind the rule of the moral law as involving 'unconditionally lawgiving reason' (*unbedingt gesetzgebende Vernunft*).[32]

On Kant's considered view, the principal grounds and the absolute claims of the moral law firmly fall outside the sphere and the scope of specifically anthropological considerations and eminently exceed the limited circle of the human species. If there is to be a 'moral anthropology', it will be concerned solely with the actual application of previously and independently established and warranted moral (juridical as well as ethical) rules and regulations in a supplementary enterprise that draws on facts and features of human psychology and sociology in order to lend empirical efficacy to originally non-empirical principles. Still even the formation of the non-empirical, a priori principles of morals involves, prior to their subsequent application, in addition to foremost formal features, chiefly the supreme form of 'universal legislation' (*allgemeine Gesetzgebung*),[33] certain elements of content not be taken from reason alone.

Previously in Kant's critical *œuvre*, the 'metaphysical first principles' (*metaphysische Anfangsgründe*) of extended nature that constitute the systematic transition from the *Critique of Pure Reason*'s account of nature 'in general' (*überhaupt*) to a metaphysics of material nature ('pure physics') had required recourse to a generic proto-empirical content-object or object-content, viz. matter as the movable in space. Now, in establishing a 'metaphysics of morals' (*Metaphysik der Sitten*) as the sum total of a priori moral principles, Kant takes recourse to a set of extrarational factors that inform not only the later application but already the first formation of the moral principles.

To begin with, there is the generic feature already mentioned that beings like us, not only finite but also 'unholy' as they are – as 'we' are – follow the moral law only 'reluctantly' (*ungern*).[34] From this basic circumstance arises the need for matching the appeal of the inclinations with a countervailing force that exercises constraint and even 'coercion' (*Zwang*). Moreover, the element of constraint so introduced into moral matters comes in two varieties, in strict correlation with the twofold divisions of morals into juridical law and ethics. In the sphere of juridical law and its institutionalization as 'public', publicly sanctioned law, the constraint operates externally in grounding as well as bounding 'external freedom' by means of the judiciary (and penitentiary) system. In the domain of ethics, the constraint occurs internally in enabling and limiting 'inner freedom' by means of self-control with regard to one's affects and self-mastery with respect to one's passions.[35]

In particular, Kant argues that the 'self-coercion' (*Selbstzwang*) involved in ethical action is 'free' and 'mutual' (*gegenseitig*) – free in that the moral law requires freely exercised assent and mutual in that the self-constraint involved works both way. On Kant's portrayal of the human condition, or rather of the 'unholy' condition in general, sensuously affected rational agents not only follow the moral law reluctantly, if they do follow it, against the opposition of countervailing inclinations. They also disobey the moral law reluctantly, if they do disobey it, by giving in to their countervailing inclinations. Their disobedience to the moral law is as reluctant as their obedience to it. Moreover, for Kant, the ambivalent condition of 'mutually opposed self-coercion' (*wechselseitig entgegengesetzte[r] Selbstzwang*)[36] is marked by an inexplicable as well as incontestable factual preponderance of reluctant disobedience of the moral law over reluctant obedience to the moral law. In this situation, ethics aims at habitually readying the rationally compromised moral agent for the struggle with oneself that is ethical life.

According to Kant, the acquired disposition for ethical action – acquired through sustained and never really ending moral self-cultivation – is 'virtue' (*Tugend*), understood as 'moral strength of the will' (*moralische Stärke des Willens*)[37] in the ancient, Roman republican understanding of the term and concept. Drawing on the juridico-political analogy that informs much of his thinking about moral matters in general and ethical affairs in particular, Kant casts the form and function of (ethical) virtue as adding to the *legislative* role of reason in authoring the law ('autonomy', *Autonomie*) the *executive* authority of strength of moral willing in aiding its implementation ('autocracy', *Autokratie*).[38]

Kant's moral philosophy may not be grounded in anthropology, much less coincide with anthropology however defined and refined. But in terms of its foundation and articulation Kant's twin practical philosophy of juridical law and ethics is inspired and shaped by the classical, essentially republican conception of self-rule within and without, domestic and foreign – rendered as the rule of law in juridical matters and as the rule of one's reason over one's passions in ethical matters.[39] The secret of Kant's moral metaphysics is not anthropology but politics or rather political art and science.[40]

Notes

1 AA 27.2/2:1320.
2 This chapter is part of a larger research project on freedom and law in Kant's republicanly inspired practical philosophy to whose earlier instalments will be referred throughout.

3   Kant (1995ff.)
4   See e.g. Louden (2000).
5   Kant (2016).
6   Zöller (2015a), (2017a) and (2017b).
7   AA 9:25.
8   AA 11:429–30.
9   A 805/B 833.
10 A 848/B 876.
11 A 849/B 877.
12 See Zöller (2013).
13 AA 6:479.
14 Zöller (2022).
15 AA 7:321f.; also AA 15:602.
16 AA 7:321.
17 AA 7:321.
18 AA 7:321.
19 AA 8:20.
20 AA 7:322.
21 AA 7:329.
22 AA 7:324.
23 AA 5:257.
24 See Zöller (2001) and (2015b).
25 AA 6:435.
26 AA 5:431.
27 AA 5:477.
28 AA 6:406.
29 AA 4:338.
30 AA 6:379.
31 AA 6:406.
32 AA 6:406.
33 AA 4:403.
34 AA 6:279 note.
35 See Zöller (2015b).
36 AA 6:279 note.
37 AA 6:405.
38 AA 6:383. See Zöller (2010).
39 See Zöller (2018), and (2021).
40 See Zöller (2011).

References

Kant, I. (1995 ff.), *The Cambridge Edition of the Works of Immanuel Kant*, ed. P. Guyer & A. Wood, Cambridge: Cambridge University Press.

Kant, I. (2016), *Lezioni sul Diritto Naturale (Naturrecht Feyerabend)*, ed. N. Hinske & G. Sadun Bordoni, Milano: Bompiani.

Louden, R. (2000), *Kant's Impure Ethics. From Rational Beings to Human Beings*, New York: Oxford University Press.

Zöller, G. (2001), 'Die Bestimmung der Bestimmung des Menschen bei Mendelssohn und Kant', in V. Gerhardt, R. P. Horstmann & R. Schumacher (eds), *Kant und die Berliner Aufklärung. Akten des 9. Internationalen Kant-Kongresses (26. bis 31. März 2000 in Berlin)*, vol. 4, Berlin & New York: Walter de Gruyter, 476–89.

Zöller, G. (2010), 'Autocracy. The Psycho-Politics of Self-Rule in Plato and Kant', in E. Balsamão Pires, B. Nonnenmacher & S. Büttner-von Stülpnagel (eds), *Relations of the Self*, Coimbra: Coimbra University Press, 385–404.

Zöller, G. (2011), 'Kant's Political Anthropology', *Kant Yearbook*, 3: 131–61.

Zöller, G. (2013), 'Hoffen-Dürfen. Kants kritische Begründung des moralischen Glaubens', in D. H. Heidemann & R. Weicker (eds), *Glaube und Vernunft in der Philosophie der Neuzeit/ Foi et raison dans la philosophie moderne*, Hildesheim & New York: Olms, 245–57.

Zöller, G. (2015a), '"Without Hope and Fear". Kant's Naturrecht Feyerabend on Bindingnesss and Obligation', in Robert Clewis (ed.), *Reading Kant's Lectures*, Berlin & Boston: De Gruyter, 346–61.

Zöller, G. (2015b), 'Die Bestimmung des Menschen. Ein Diskurs in der deutschen Spätaufklärung', in O. Müller & G. Maio (eds), *Orientierung am Menschen. Anthropologische Konzeptionen und normative Perspektiven*, Göttingen: Wallstein 80–91.

Zöller, G. (2017a), 'Allgemeine Freiheit. Kants Naturrecht Feyerabend über Wille, Recht und Gesetz', in B. Dörflinger, D. Hüning & G. Kruck (eds), *Zum Verhältnis von Recht und Ethik in Kants praktischer Philosophie*, Hildesheim: Olms, 71–88.

Zöller, G. (2017b), '"Lois de la liberté". Autonomie et conformité à la loi dans le cours Naturrecht Feyerabend de Kant', in S. Grapotte, M. Lequan & M. Ruffing (eds), *Kant. L'Année 1784. Droit et philosophie de l'histoire*, Paris: Vrin, 351–9.

Zöller, G. (2018), '"Inborn Freedom". Kant's Republicanism and Its Historico-Systematic Context', in V. L. Waibel, M. Ruffing & D. Wagner (eds), *Nature and Freedom. Proceedings of the 12th International Kant Congress*, vol. 1, Berlin, Boston: De Gruyter, 693–709.

Zöller, G. (2021), '"[W]ahre Republik." Kants legalistischer Republikanismus im historischen und systematischen Kontext', in J. Chr. Merle & C. Freiin von Villiez (eds), *Kants Metaphysik der Sitten Zwischen Rechten und Pflichten*, Berlin, Boston: De Gruyter, 201–222.

Zöller, G. (2022), 'Kultur und Charakter. Kant über die Bestimmung des Menschen', in T. Morawski (ed.), *Kant and Culture*. Rome: Sapienzia University Press, 167–185.

Zöller, G. (forthcoming), '"(D)ieser wechselseitig entgegengesetzte Selbstzwang." Kant über ethische Freiheit', in D. Hüning & G. Kruck (eds), *Kant und die Tugendethik* Hildesheim, New York: Olms.

Index

Action 34–6, 45–8, 61–3, 66–71, 80, 85, 107–9, 115, 150, 154, 216, 251–6
   free 167, 168, 170
   human 173, 230, 251
   moral 169–72, 227, 256
Aesthetic 143–51, 154, 158, 212, 243–44
   German 143, 149
   pleasure 150, 153, 156–7
   value 147–8, 151
Agency 36, 46–7, 64, 78–80, 87–93, 235, 251–2
Anatomy 29, 43–8, 100–2, 209–11, 214
Animal 21–3, 32, 43–52, 82–6, 99–101, 144, 190, 194–6, 209–11, 217, 252–3
   domestic 214, 218–19
   human 45, 92, 106
   non-human 21, 45
   rational 21–5, 252
   realm 29, 44, 84
Animality 33–4, 86, 155–6
Anthropology 81–85, 214–5, 220, 228–32, 235, 243–56
   cultural 29, 35–8, 156, 195, 200, 243, 245, 250
   moral 249, 255
   philosophical 184, 190, 200
   social 29
Anthroponomy 243, 255
Antiquity 115, 117, 120, 132–3
   Egypt 132–3, 139, 186
   Greece 34, 122, 132–3, 144–9, 153–8, 186–93, 198–201
   Persia 132
   Phoenicia 186
   Rome 34, 122, 133–4, 145, 186, 191–3, 200
Appearance 50, 53, 101, 144–45
   beautiful 148
   of human beings 20
   physical 20, 101

Beauty 143, 147–50, 154, 227–8, 231–4
Behaviour 45, 83, 87–8, 144–6, 200, 219–21
   Irrational 85
Benevolence 60–7, 70–1, 86, 99, 121, 170
Bildung 174, 189
Body 18–21, 29–30, 45–47, 82–3, 101, 108, 146, 154, 215, 218, 220
   Embodiment 19, 24–5, 36, 72, 81, 173
   and mind 18, 21, 29, 37
Brutality 49, 51, 146–7

Capacity 64–8, 84, 143, 155, 184, 219–20
   capability 21, 32, 84
   for reason 166–7, 252, 254
Categorical imperative 167, 227–8, 255
Causality 35–7, 61, 81–3, 105, 169, 251–2
   causal explanations 81
   efficient causes 81, 215, 252
   final causes 77, 81
Character 61, 68–73, 153, 229, 251, 253
   Characteristics 211, 214, 221, 231–2, 252
   individual 83, 156
   moral 149
   of the human species 251–2
   universal 115, 116, 213
Civilization 32, 49–53, 90, 105–7, 107–8, 116, 131–40
Colonization 30, 49–50, 92
Common sense 90, 156
Conduct 63–6, 71, 73, 135, 249
Cosmopolitanism 73, 93, 186–7, 191–2, 195–201, 252–3
Creation 52, 79–80, 100, 165, 218, 221
Culture 31, 54, 84, 104–5, 109–10, 131–9, 174, 184–90, 195, 198
   high 119, 133, 254
   scientific 135, 138

Degeneration 32, 36, 133–4, 138, 214, 216–20
Desire 32–5, 67, 88–93, 146–7, 230, 234–5
   common 90, 92, 93

of perfection 117, 150
Development 29, 45–8, 80–4, 91–3, 105, 108–9, 138–9, 214–6, 220–1
　of character 153–4
　social 115, 117, 118, 123, 138–9
Dignity 54, 86, 88, 143–53
Disposition 63, 117, 146, 211, 216, 220, 221, 252–6
　moral 227, 252
　social 121–3
Drive 32, 87, 175, 211, 216
　formative drive 210, 215, 216–21
　sexual 36, 146
Duty 15, 32, 87, 90–3, 143–5, 163–7, 192, 255
　civic 88
　externally imposed 93
　moral 145, 174
　religious 88
　social 145
　to one's own self 143

Economy of nature 78, 81–2, 85–9, 94
Education 66, 83, 108, 143, 150, 232, 252
　classical 132
　educational programme 132, 151, 155
　mental and physical 148
　moral 234
Einfühlung 143, 156, 189
Empathy 87, 143–6, 153, 229
Empirical 81, 84, 193, 215–6, 221, 225
　evidence 88, 117, 122, 146, 210, 219
　knowledge 38, 92, 186
　observation 82, 85, 90–3, 233
Enlightenment 59, 144, 177, 186–7, 225–6, 228–9
　German 143, 147, 158, 225, 246
　moderate 54
　project 137, 163
　radical 53
　Scottish 30, 36, 115–16, 121, 246
Enthusiasm 24, 25, 43, 48, 50, 123
Epicureanism 25, 54, 109
Epigenetic 211, 215
Ethics / ethical 77–78, 93, 164–8, 170–3, 229–30, 243–7, 254–6
　meta- 185–6, 192–3, 201
Evil 32, 34, 50, 67, 85, 166–7
　Radical 191, 197

Exclusion 143, 144
Extinction 53, 54, 218

Faculty 19, 21, 24, 84–5, 101, 105, 109
　of cognition 171
　of comparing ideas 47
　of feeling 36, 171
　human 103, 105
　human understanding 15, 17
　of knowledge 24, 33, 217
　of moral perception 154
　of perfectibility 103
　of reason 84–5
　of representation 147, 149, 165
　of reproduction 48
　of self-improvement 102
Feeling 80, 82, 86–7, 144–7, 151, 158, 171, 176, 229, 233
　faculty of 36
　of harmony 80, 82
　human 156
　of humanity 69
　mixed 150, 152;
　moral 163–4, 169, 170–3, 175–7
　of the beautiful 172, 231
Fibers 36, 83
Final causes 77, 81, 221
Force 34–6, 60–1, 72–3, 216, 221, 256
　driving 80
　formative 217–18
　of nature 53, 54
　primitive 214
　vital 214–16, 220
Formation 20, 217, 255
　of organic bodies 214–15, 220
　of the earth 44, 53
　of varieties 221
Fossil 218
Freedom 35, 88, 109, 137, 186, 243–7, 254–6
　as liberty 77, 93, 102
　personal 119
　political 148
Functions, functionality 80–5, 93, 210–11, 215–16, 249, 256

Gender 186, 191, 225–35, 251
Generation 48–54, 216, 253
Genius 37, 116, 136

Index

Geography 35, 83, 100, 143, 184, 200
  physical geography 54
God 18, 31, 52, 163–5, 176, 188, 194, 202, 255
The good 62, 66–7, 165–6, 170–5
Great chain of being 82, 213–14
Growth 83, 100, 107–9, 137, 143, 184

Happiness 60, 66–8, 71–2, 87, 90–3, 109, 165–6, 176
History 29–30, 34–36, 71, 99–110, 115–25, 132–7, 188–9, 194, 199–202, 221, 253
  Conjectural 36, 49–51, 105
  human 34, 103, 105, 196
  natural 37, 82, 101, 116–17, 209–18
Holism 79–81
Hominization /Humanization 101–10, 252
Human rights 193–6
Humanity 50–4, 59–61, 66–8, 71–4, 77, 86–92, 100, 120, 143–9, 153–4, 189–202, 225–9
  idea of 18–25, 148
  ideal of 194–202, 208, 228
  nature of 131
  principle of 59–61, 67–73
  sense of 60
  sentiment of 70, 72
Humankind 24–5, 71–3, 77–8, 83–93, 116–17, 121–2, 183–90, 195, 199, 219, 221, 227, 229
  party of 59, 73–4
Hybrid / Hybridization 210, 217, 220–1

Idea 60, 78–80, 83, 88, 101, 105, 109, 116, 189–90
  abstract 15–18
  innate 23, 33
  of progress 131, 137

Ideal 81, 115, 186, 193, 196–8, 202, 227, 235
  beauty 148
  of enlightenment 225
  of humanity 194–202, 208, 228
  of human rights 193, 196
  moral 120, 191–3, 195, 200–2, 228
Inclination 87, 176, 185, 193, 243, 256
  sexual 231
  social 84, 121

Individuum 15–25, 30–8, 52–4, 73, 82–93, 102, 106–8, 115–24, 174–6, 184–9, 194–5, 197, 200, 210, 216–17, 225–30, 253
  human 15–16, 22, 107, 243, 253
Instinct 32, 44, 84–7, 176, 189

Justice 54, 63–6, 71, 90–1

Language 24, 49, 68–73, 104–5, 155, 158, 183–90, 195, 244
Law (juridical) 16, 31–2, 88, 90–3, 165, 243, 245, 247, 254–6
Law (moral) 17, 29, 30–5, 91–2, 227, 254–6
Life 49, 64, 80, 84, 177
  common 66, 70, 71, 72
  forms of 186, 193, 213
  human 82, 230, 245, 249
  modes of 185, 201, 210
  purpose of 53, 88
  social 211, 252
  the good 163
Literacy / Reading 74, 105, 131, 136–7, 244–7
Loneliness / Solitude 144, 146, 152, 155–6
Love 72–3, 146–7, 150–3, 176, 187
  self-love 60–1, 65–8, 71–3, 88, 109

Marriage 48
Materialism 25, 46, 53, 77–9, 86, 93
Matter 45–6, 53–4, 77–82, 85, 181
Mechanism 45–6, 81, 143, 146–7, 152–3, 215, 219
Metaphysics 77–9, 102, 166, 173, 213, 243, 246–50, 255, 256
Mind 16, 18, 29, 31, 36, 80–2, 105
  embodied 79
  human 36, 79, 83
Monogenesis 214, 220–1
Morals 34, 71, 93, 102, 107–10, 137, 185, 201, 243, 248
Moral judgement 71, 80, 91, 185, 231
Morality 16–7, 25, 54, 71–3, 78, 85–93, 131–3, 165–7, 172–3, 176–7, 198, 200, 227–8, 234–5, 247–54
  foundation of 60–1
  principles of 24, 173

Nation 30–6, 38, 50, 118, 120–4, 133
Natural history 37, 82, 101, 209, 213, 214, 217–18, 221
Natural right 15, 33, 89–93, 166
Nature 29–35, 54, 60, 66–7, 73, 77–86, 100–4, 108–10, 116–21, 136, 149, 155, 176, 188–90, 197–8, 246–7, 251–5
   human 33–7, 59–68, 71–4, 82–94, 100, 108–10, 131, 150, 200, 221, 247, 250
   of humanity 131
   laws of 37, 45, 167
   moral 150, 164, 171, 227
   notion of 103, 109, 166
   return to 153
   state of 31–33, 87, 101–6
Natural law 30–32, 38, 83, 88, 101, 163, 165, 247
Naturalism 16, 59, 79, 88–9, 163, 176–7, 221
Normativity 71–2, 77–82, 86–93, 115–16, 186, 191–6, 232, 243, 254–5

Obligation 163–8, 171, 175, 243, 248, 250, 255
   moral 32, 92
   natural 167
Order 22, 33, 69, 79–84, 136–8, 213–14
Organism/organic 48, 82–5, 175, 209–11, 215–20
   molecules 45, 53
Organization 80, 82–3, 210, 216, 218–19

Pain 34, 47, 67, 109, 144–7, 152–8
Perfection 84, 92, 105, 108, 149–51, 154, 165–8, 171
Perfectibility 33, 81, 84, 100–8, 138
Perspective 23, 61, 85–6, 88, 99, 149, 189, 230–1
   comparative 147
   first-person 23, 250
   holistic 80
   physiological 83, 100
   practical 143
   universal 226
Physico-theology 213
Physiology 36–7, 45, 214, 217
Pity 101, 107, 144–7, 150–3, 198
Platonism 16–9, 25
   anti- 83, 85, 89

Pluralism 185–7, 193, 196, 201
Politics, political 33–6, 53, 78, 85, 92–3, 116–24, 189, 256
Polygenesis 183, 189
Practical philosophy 166, 173, 243, 245, 254–6
Predetermination 216, 220, 221
Preformation 192, 210, 215
Principle of continuity 213
Progress 50–4, 90–2, 115, 118, 124–5, 133–39
   evolutionary 133
   historical 134
   of reason 136
   scientific 135, 139
   social 115, 125
Prototype 83, 89, 133
Prudence 245, 254
Public 34, 65–7, 120–4, 175, 226, 244–5, 256
   public good 69, 70
purposiveness 80–2, 188

Rationality 19–22, 24–5, 91, 136, 175, 251–6
Rationalization 194, 196
Reason 20–5, 30, 32, 44–8, 59, 60–5, 70–2, 84–7, 92, 135–7, 164–8, 184, 190–3, 195, 211, 215, 228, 233, 246, 249, 254–5
   pure 228, 230, 245–9
Reductionism 77
Relativism 23, 78, 185–6, 193, 201
Religion 35, 77, 86–93, 137–40, 166, 186–91, 194–6, 202, 248, 255
Reproduction 46–50, 210, 214–17, 219

Savages / Barbarians 32, 36, 48–53, 88, 103, 107, 118, 122, 132–4, 156, 199–200
Science 30, 46, 81, 85, 131–40, 166, 173–5, 250, 256
Sensation 29, 45–7, 80, 105, 136, 174–6, 184–5
Sentiment 59–62, 107, 173, 185–6, 201
   of humanity 70, 72
   moral 59–62, 67–73, 117, 121, 185, 193
Skin 50, 101, 195, 217 220–1

Slavery 30, 36, 49, 51, 53, 120, 197, 202
Social conditions 134, 136, 140
Socialization 33, 143
Society 30–5, 63–7, 73–4, 85–93, 105–7, 121–4, 143
   modern 88–9, 116, 118, 120, 124
Species 21–4, 49–54, 78–89, 90–4, 175, 192, 195, 214–21, 251–5
   human 15, 18, 21, 81–6, 106–8, 117, 124, 156, 183–4, 189–90, 209–223, 226, 245, 251
   animal 100, 209, 217
State 33–4, 91–3, 106, 120
State of nature 31–3, 87, 101–6, 117, 133
Stimulus 47, 216, 219
Stoicism 31, 146, 167, 175–6, 186, 199–200
Subjective 80–3, 166–8, 226, 230
Sublime 70, 147–52, 156, 171–2, 227, 230–5
Sympathy 59–61, 66–73, 117, 121–3, 175, 184–5, 198–9

Taxonomy 211, 214, 245
Teleology 10, 81, 102, 252–4
Teleological judgments 216, 254

Typology 211–13, 216–17, 220, 221, 228
Transformism 218
Transformation 33, 54, 90–3, 108, 171, 175, 212, 216, 220
Type/Archetype 20–5, 81–5, 133, 210–21, 254

Universality 88–9, 198, 228–35
Utility 44, 60–6, 69

Variation 50–2, 85, 89, 100, 200, 209–14, 250
Variety 100, 108, 156, 158, 209–14, 217–19, 221
   human 29, 38, 50, 85, 210–20, 221
   racial 183, 190, 195, 198, 211, 217–21, 245
Vice 67, 68, 70, 73, 86
Violence 53, 47, 86, 91, 193
Virtue 34, 49, 61, 66–70, 73, 86, 145–6, 153, 165–6, 176, 188, 227–34, 256
   female 229–30
   social 62, 63, 65, 68–70, 143, 158
Vocation 253